SORROW'S PROFILES

SORROW'S PROFILES
Death, Grief, and Crisis in the Family

Richard J. Alapack

KARNAC

First published in 2010 by
Karnac Books Ltd
118 Finchley Road
London NW3 5HT

British Library Cataloguing in Publication Data

A C.I.P. for this book is available from the British Library

ISBN-13: 978-1-85575-621-2

Typeset by Vikatan Publishing Solutions (P) Ltd., Chennai, India

Printed in Great Britain

www.karnacbooks.com

CONTENTS

ABOUT THE AUTHOR

Richard J. Alapack, Ph.D., an Associate Professor of Psychology at the Norwegian University of Science and Technology, researches Love-Death from existential, phenomenological, and hermeneutic standpoints. His two recent books showcase the fruits of his career-long labor. This current work on the various faces of sorrow treats death related themes including mother's death, sibling bereavement, talk with your child, about death, suicide, murder, divorce, revenge and mercy, regret, and longing. Love's Pivotal Relationships: The Chum, First Love, Outlaw and the Intimate Partner (2007) takes up the phenomena of love and its derangement: sensuality, sexually, passion and tenderness, jealousy, heartbreak, the lovesick "blues," and betrayal. However, power fades, money vanishes, fame is fickle, ambition is foolish, and only love endures. What matters most, therefore, are Richard's love-bonds with his beloved Chili, with his three splendid, creative children, Nicole, Richard and Orion, and with his three bright and beautiful granddaughters, Sophie, Olivia and Natalie Grace.

INTRODUCTION

"Be absolute for death ... ."

Shakespeare, *Measure for Measure*

Death is life's basic imperative. "Each of us has this to do: to die" (Lingis, 2007, p. 130). For us earthlings, finite and mortal, dying occurs with 100% certainty. *That* we die is *definite*, but *when* and *how* are *indefinite* (Heidegger, 1927/1962).

Furthermore, our being-unto-death is uniquely human. Nothing dies as we do. Animal behaviour betrays no evidence that our four-legged friends are aware of their impending end. We death-bound subjects, on the other hand, live with the realization of our inevitable demise, imagine its coming, and even sense when it looms. Death is our constant companion, always on the horizon of life, and a pervasive variable in all that we do or refrain from doing. It is peculiarly mine, my "own most" act, the one for which I can never designate a pinch-hitter. Beyond any distinguishing fingerprints, my death individualizes me. I must die on my own.

How do we live these meanings? We experience our death during our ordinary comings and goings, in our beginnings and endings, in our choices, failures, disappointments, and losses, in the changes we both actively orchestrate and passively endure. In a simple dictum, the Tsonga-Shangana people capture the lived reality of dying daily: "Death is in the leg; we walk with it" (Vutlhari bya Vatsonga [Machangana], 1936/1981, p. 289). Our actual biological or medico-legal death just halts our dying. It is the death of death. When we die physically, the world goes out of play. We leave the picture. We stop walking. The pronouncement that I am dead is, in fact, my death as experienced by observing others, those who survive me, still living on the earth that I have exited.

All of us dwell, at one time or another, on the other side of this description. We have survived the death of a near and dear one, or have been rejected, abandoned, jilted, spurned, or betrayed. We know what it's like to have been left behind, but still lingering in the picture. An ending by death or break up devastates me, breaks my heart, and saddles me with memories. I ache and long for the deceased or living corpse who is not coming back. My opening sentence, therefore, requires modification. Another constituent of life's over-arching imperative is suffering loss. We all must sorrow. Grief is a 100% sure bet. We all take our turn at misery.

Sorrow's profiles are part of this imperative: regret, revenge, longing, and the various crises and catastrophes of daily life—both natural disasters to which we must respond and over which we have little control, and man-made disasters such as divorce, suicide, murder, oil catastrophes, and racism which we can influence with wise choices and courage.

Orientating comments

Death and grief are 100% certain. Seminal and decisive thinkers such as Kierkegaard, Nietzsche, and Heidegger have criticized mainstream Western thinkers for failing to give them their due. They are right. My narratives and reflections serve understanding. I do not write to explain, conquer, or defeat grief; I orchestrate no quick-fix that would overcome regret, or liquidate longing. Instead I seek personal and in-depth knowledge of sorrow's profiles.

Is learning to live with loss the best that we can do? No, it is not. We can find a place for suffering, disappointment, and death exactly where they belong: at the centre of everyday life. Even while our heart is bleeding and a-breaking, vitality percolates within raw life. How must we think, research, and communicate so that we might unleash that vitality?

I include the human heart. I give a blood transfusion to the narrow rationalism and positivism that dominates research in the psycho-medical sciences. The heart is the mind ... warmed. Logic alone can no more generate knowledge that is relevant, useful, earnest, and concerned than can a bleeding heart which is not mentally focused. Into the cognitive behavioural medical disciplines I truck psyche and spirit.

Two hundred years is a long time. Within the span of history, however, it is a twinkle of the eye. The scientific ideology which dominates nowadays, born in the Glory Days of the 19th century, is only a tiny comma within the long paragraph of humankind's seeking to know. What is the scoop on modern rational-empirical science? It rules the roost, that's for sure. It sets the standard for what the culture recognizes as knowledge. It dictates both what counts as an observation and what is deemed as being a valid argument. One must bow to its conventions in order to publish research findings that would be regarded as valuable. Conformity is mandated because the rational community swears by its processes and procedures, by its forms and formats. The rational community decrees that its positivistic paradigm harbours "known standards". So a straight-jacket of standardization laces all that pertains to the social order, from health issues to politics. Since this homogenized ideology privileges prediction, control, repetition, and verification, it outlaws whatever is unfamiliar and maverick. It drapes a noose around the neck of alternative ways of searching and presenting knowledge. It pre-empts discovery and chokes creativity, spontaneity, and passion.

There are many ways, however, for science to be science. There are many ways to generate knowledge-claims. Over the span of a half century, Amedeo Giorgi (1970; 2009) has demonstrated the pervasive and mutually implicative relationship between approach (paradigm or vision), method, and content in psychology. My scientific vision draws inspiration from existential phenomenological thinking which "converges" with psychoanalysis according to Maurice Merleau-Ponty (1960) or "merges" with it according to Jacques Lacan (1966/1977, p. 35). And to generate lifeworld findings,

I use the qualitative methods that such thinking spawns, including hermeneutics.

"Anthropologists today recognize that no society that survived over time could have done so unless its knowledge of its environment was fundamentally sound" (Lingis, 2007, p. 87). Throughout history, marvellous civilizations have blossomed without access to natural scientific models and methods. Likewise, no seeker of knowledge about Death and Sorrow needs to be hamstrung by that limited standpoint. I use the phenomenological tool of bracketing that suspends credence in the theories and methods of modern science. I put them out of play.

Sharing findings: The communicative act

Humankind over the millennia has made knowledge claims about the person–world relationship and has come to terms with Death and Sorrow through a broad spectrum of dramaturgical forms. Since time immemorial, humans have used rituals, myths, music, dance, parables, legends and stories to share knowledge. During modernity, novels, portraits, and stories have done the trick. In terms of phenomena that fall under the purview of psychology and psychiatry, Sigmund Freud creates a new genre, the case history that gives us Hans, Dora, the Wolf Man, and the Rat Man that James Hillman calls 'soul stories'. Erik Erikson evolves the form of psychohistory to showcase the identity developing stories of Luther, and Gandhi. C.S. Lewis employs autobiography to offer us precious gems concerning the process of grieving. Using masks and pseudonyms, Nietzsche and Kierkegaard share the results of their individual self-reflective searches and in the process give us an inspirited human psychology.

There is no compelling scholarly reason for contemporary social scientific and medical researchers to ape the staid formats employed by academic journals. To showcase Love-Death-Sorrow, the American Psychological Association manual is a minimally enlightening style. Why do the gatekeepers demand its use? Is it not merely the political action of club members obeying arbitrary rules? More cynically, one asks, "Why is Power and Money supporting something so unremarkable?" Although the genuine answer might elude me, I take liberty to hold in abeyance such modes of writing. In attempting to capture a wide range of sorrow's profiles, I do not just stretch the envelope with a variety of narrative forms—I burst it.

I tell the tale of watching my mother slowly die; I narrate the talks I had, flying by the seat of my pants, when my little daughter's Nana died. I present a parable about a "Divorced House"; I employ an existential therapeutic dialogue to deal with murder. I use stories to theme racism and suicide; I interpret novels, songs, poems, and films to comprehend revenge, regret, and longing. My writing is deliberately and consciously outside the academic norm. In the context of knowledge expressed over the millennia, it is retro, a throwback. I am either one step ahead or behind. You will judge.

Am I only exercising an obstinate personal preference? No. Following Heidegger, I invoke the original meaning of "thinking". The Old English word *"thanc"* meshes thinking and the heart. *Thanc* bespeaks life's fundamental unity, prior to any dualistic breakdown into cognition and emotion, head and heart, inner and outer, and self-world. The following sentence will be a chant throughout this book: The heart is the mind ... warmed.

> *"thanc"* ... means man's inmost mind, the heart, the heart's core, that innermost essence of man which reaches outward most fully and to the outermost limits, and so decisively that, rightly considered, the idea of an inner and an outer world does not arise ... The *thanc*, the heart's core, is the gathering of all that concerns us, all that we care for, all that touches us insofar as we are, as human beings (Heidegger, 1954a/1968, p. 144).

Thanc captures the human touch. It is the language of genuine caring. For me, it is the leaven to help me to help both ordinary individuals and workers in the caring professions to access vitality about sorrow's profiles. Within these phenomena, I dwell and *thanc* extremely personally. I invite you, too, to crawl into your library of life in order to dwell upon your emotions, your memories, and your pain. This book is not about "them" but about "us", about you and me. May my words both pluck your heart strings and challenge your brain. "Everything that rises must converge" (De Chardin, 1961, p. 265).

PART I

CHAPTER ONE

Grief: The algebra of loss

eath has paid a visit. Devastating deprivation assaults my entire existence. I am in agony. Grief is swallowing me up. Since time immemorial, humankind knows it is sorrow's season, the time to mourn. Our haste to forget, documented in the academic debate about continuing bonds, merely reflects ignorance about the a-temporal and indestructible dimensions of experience. It shows a poverty of wisdom about the human predicament. We ordinary humans must learn how to live with loss and with the persistent presence of our deceased beloved in memory and in our actions (Lingis, 2007) The deceased is not gone like a piece of equipment or any ready-to-hand item. I will remain with her continually, in a mode of respectful solicitude (Heidegger, 1927/1962).

The loss of the loss

Grief is the natural spontaneous psychological response to *the loss of the loss*. What do I mean? If I do not know that I have lost my wallet, I have no emotions to express about the pickpocket who, at this very moment and at my expense, is eating a salmon fillet with rice, green beans, and a bottle of French white wine in the city's most chic restaurant. As soon as I realize it is missing, look for it where I think I probably placed it, search frantically because it is not there, realize that my driver's license, my credit cards, my passport are in it, and remember that foolishly I was carrying with me too much cash ... then comes the reaction to the loss. When the loss is more serious than my measly wallet with a few thousand dollars in it, it transforms my world. The loss or death of a loved one, which leaves a gaping hole in my world, is of that ilk. Part of my self is missing, whatever meaning that dead person took with her. A truly significant loss carves a Hole in the Whole.

A Hole in the Whole! No small potatoes, eh! Grief is not just a simple or a single feeling. It is a cluster of passion of the soul: hurt, anger, bitterness, rage, fury, loneliness, regret, relief. Which emotions will surface, and the valence of the passion, depends on the nature of the loss or upon "who" is gone. It is always singular. While we look for patterns, themes, and general structures, we must never lose sight of the fact that grief is as unique as one's fingerprints. Even though we all go to school on the west's love of discrete stages and phases, we must also honour the maverick dimensions of grief which gushes with no limits and no boundaries.

In these chapters, "lost object" will refer mostly to a physical death. But minor deaths must be mourned too: a broken romance, loss of one's job, moving to another country, moving out of your house, getting promoted at work. Other chapters will treat in detail a few of these myriad death experiences: divorce, longing, regret, suicide, and murder.

Such losses trigger grief. Grieving is a long, elaborate and passionate process which starts, ebbs and flows, bogs down, dead-ends, and begins again before it optimally reaches a resolution. Freud (1917e [1915]) calls the process a labour or a work of hyper-investing our attachment to the lost object ... in service of detaching ... so that we might re-bond. The purpose of the next three chapters is to elaborate that sentence.

Phase I: Consciousness of the bond to the lost object: Meanings and emotions

Death drives home the reality of the bond between the lost object and me. It is a cliché that sometimes I do not know what I have ... until

I lose it. More precisely, that expression signifies the psychological insight that I do not appreciate the *meaning-to-me* of the object until it is gone, or until I throw it away. With the 'moment' of knowing comes grief, my gut level response to the loss of the loss. The first phase of grief-work is thus to drive home the significance of the loss and to drum up the heartfelt emotions associated with it.

A Hole blown into the Whole! This shattering creates existential, psychological, and spiritual disruption. In the face of the missing part, disequilibrium reigns. In the face of mounting chaos, I become disoriented. The floundering and discombobulating quality of grief stems from a triple whammy. What is that? I must come to terms with a significant loss while at the same time that loss adumbrates my own death and thus puts me into crisis. Death, usually content softly to whisper, now shouts. I must cope with devastation all the while sensing that my own demise is just a lack-of-a-heartbeat-away. "What if death is so treacherous as to come tomorrow?" queries Kierkegaard (1847/1962, pp. 23–24), hitting us in the heart with the bullet that we all must bite. The heartbreaking truth of finitude factually came today for my loved one. Tomorrow, it might be my turn. As common parlance puts it, my number might be up. Grief-work, done in crisis, cannot be accomplished with a clear head and settled emotions. In *Seven Pillars of Wisdom* T.E. Lawrence (1926/1966, p. 197) writes: "An individual death, like a pebble dropped in water, might make a hole; yet rings of sorrow widen out therefrom."

Sigmund Freud's grief-work: The bond

Freud's pioneering work gives the seminal and decisive picture of the ties that bind us, of how the work unfolds, and what gives it its moving power and thrust. What does bind human beings to one another? Freud uses a homey, down-to-earth German word, *besetzen*, to capture his insights about the power of the *trieb*. *Besetzen* means *attachment*. It signifies everything vital in terms of bringing up a child, and grieving. It expresses the bond between a mother's nipple and an infant's mouth, between a penis and vagina. It means *investment*, as a capitalist donates to Wall Street. It means *occupation*, as an invading army seizes a helplessly conquered country. It signifies any and every sort of *bondage*, ranging from raw sexual sadomasochism to the most subtle spiritual form of master–slave relating.

Freud (1921c) also employs *trieb* and *besetzen* as cardinal notions to account for the formation, cohesiveness and staying power of groups. This book will unveil grieving as relational, familial, and social. Please read the following picture of group dynamics within the context of a death in the family.

Remember! Freud is a denizen of 1900 Vienna. Whenever he says "group", the natural next word to roll off his tongue is Leader (*Fuehrer*). Members of the masses are tied to their leader and bonded to each other by libidinal bonds to their leader. The energy/meaning is sexual, both vertically and horizontally: duty-cum-sex. Between group members, fraternity and solidarity persist in their dedication to a cause or devotion to their leader. But intense libidinal forces of jealousy, envy, competition, back stabbing, and betrayal—sexual and homosexual longings—always potentially sabotage the team spirit. Toward the leader, members feel reverence unto love … when all is well; but the passion blazes to hate-unto-mutiny and assassination … when it all comes undone.

The dynamics of hypnosis, falling in love, belonging to a religious sect, or believing in the military, one's military leaders, or one's political party exemplify Freud's position. The hallmark of these phenomena is self-prostration before a higher power, surrendering critical judgement, and yielding personal will to the collective will of the herd or to the whim of the Leader. In terms of the theme of sorrow, a powerful *trieb* tie makes grief so exquisitely painful that even death does not break its seal. Pathetically, *The English Standard* Edition translates this pivotal word of linking with the term *cathexis*—which means … nothing.

Individualized labour done in crisis, bit by bit

Grieving is the process of gradually coming to terms with a loss, mitigating or surmounting it, overcoming it, transcending it … . This litany of words is not a vocabulary exercise; the process takes many forms, drifts in many temporal rhythms, and endures many different emotional surges. The process is like ocean waves rushing to the shore, breaking against the rocky cliff.

The work of mourning exacts a high cost. In Freud's vocabulary, "work" is not a word to be taken lightly. Dream-work is basic to understanding and eventually interpreting our nightly visitors;

working-through is so pivotal to his psychoanalytic therapy that, without it, emotional abreaction, catharsis, and intellectual insight fall to the wayside. Work carries the same special aura as with Karl Marx, more closely knitted to liturgy than to grunge labour done by the sweat of one's brow.

Is Freud's emphasis his peculiar quirk? No. Grief demands work because nothing programs us to let go, to end, to say goodbye, especially to lose what is "good", satisfying, and enriching. Even letting go of "bad" relationships is complex—a matter that does not engross us herein. "Good–Bad," within the psychoanalytic context, always refers to the libidinal standpoint of pleasure and satisfaction. It is not a moral position, even though often both converge.

Apropos the point under consideration, nothing in our genes, chromosomes, Deoxyribonucleic Acid (DNA), or Ribonucleic Acid (RNA) facilitates the release of love-ties. If biological-medical bases ever are helpful in the negotiation of psychological chores, they have nothing to contribute to the algebra of loss. We hang on. We cling. We clutch. Sometimes we grovel. Whenever we finally let go, it is not because some enzyme or hormone kicks in. And it won't happen because we swallowed a pill every four hours for seven days. It is an achievement, an accomplishment.

The labour is not mechanical, hum drum, routine, or repetitive. We are facing the natural and 100% inevitable crisis of life. Commitment costs us dearly. Love and Death are two faces of one coin. Pain, the other side of joy, is also Life's imperative. While we work, we ache, wonder, struggle, and ponder the price tag of commitment. All the while, we yearn to mend. All the while, we worry also about others' needs—our dear ones or those under our care who need to heal. Not surprisingly, grief breaks the heart and rightfully is accused of being a killer.

The upsurge of grief raises at least four barriers between the mourner and everyday life: 1) painful dejection; 2) abrogation of interest in the outside world; 3) inhibition of all activity; and 4) temporary loss of the capacity to love (Freud, 1917e [1915], p. 244). Freud easily clarifies this powerful psychological and existential constriction. The significance of the lost object to the self of the mourner is strengthened by a "thousand links", he tells us. These must be withdrawn "bit by bit" (Freud, 1917e [1915], p. 256). It is so easy to picture the humanness of it. Bit by bit. It is so simple and straightforward that it hits us right in the hearthead. We understand immediately that absorption in the labour of mourning pre-empts the capacity to adopt a new love object. In C.S. Lewis' (1961/1980, p. 9) description, "an invisible blanket between me and the world ... Part of every grief is misery's shadow or reflection—the fact that I not only live each endless day in grief, but live each day thinking about living each day in grief." Consciousness and self-consciousness bless and burden us. We reflect and we hyper-reflect—we think about our thinking and we think about how we are inserted in the field about which our thought thinks. Our life or existence is an issue for us. "Man is the shepherd of Being" (Heidegger, 1954/1991, p. 245); the only being that in its being questions its being. Eventually, we might reflect to the point of being trapped in obsessive thinking. Lost in thought or held hostage by it, we dwell in warped time. Time is a careless, cunning, and cruel thief.

A Norwegian father, who had lost his daughter to death, worked out his grief over time by taking an axe to the trees on his land and hacking his grief, chop by chop. Can you not just see the wood chips flying, one hitting his cheek, stinging and reminding him of the Greater Sting? Chop-by-chop!

Bit by bit also shoots right to the hearthead, because it captures another human quirk concerning grief-work. Since we grieve what matters to us, we resist premature replacing of the one mourned. There is no quick-fix. We let go strand by strand.

Passionate emotions

What starts the process of mourning? It engages all the traditional faculties of body and psyche, mind, soul, spirit, heart, and head. In this first phase, the phenomenon of emotion is cardinal. By promoting pathos, I am not giving a soft, boohoo humanistic pitch or invoking some vanilla, syrupy human capacity. As part of the Western culture's faculty psychology, emotion wears a flimsy rationalistic-dualistic costume. Our philosophy and medico-social sciences water it down it to a second-class citizen, one which requires apology. Is not emotion a failure to reason logically? Does it not impede judgement and decision-making? Wrong: Emotion jump starts the long and arduous grief process.

We too lightly call grief an emotion. It is the raw power to e-mote, to move, to stir. Irritation, frustration, and annoyance are emotions; they do not kill. Passion kills. Grief challenges us to change the valence of the ordinary word. Make it intense. Make it matter; make it precious.

Emotional expression is particularly important in light of the fact that shock and disbelief characterizes the initial encounter with death. One is numb, dazed, empty, and cold. Pre-reflectively, one erects a barrier to overwhelming sorrow. "This-is-not-happening ... when will this bad dream end ... where is the other side of this nightmare?" Although my world is in chaos I must not collapse; a mess is caving in, but I will not discombobulate. I am stunned, protected from having to absorb the impact of this loss in one fell swoop. I wander in a daze, almost floating in remove from this stark reality. I must partly tune-out. Who can swallow it all at once?

Eventually, the shock gives way to free floating anxiety. One feels like screaming, is nervous all the time, or fears having a breakdown. In short, responses shift during this period dramatically, drastically, and fluidly. On an emotional roller coaster, I go from one extreme emotion to another.

The literature also lists a multiplicity of physical symptoms, implicitly affirming that—in spite of the omnipresence of Western dualism—the psychesoma co-inheres. Tightness in the throat, shortness of breath, sighing, loss of appetite, sleeplessness, waves of emotions flooding us for twenty minutes to an hour, lack of muscular power, empty feeling in the pit of the stomach, fullness in the chest—as if the expanding heart would soon burst. Grief is a killer. Even this scattered list is easy to interpret: The heart is at risk—both the anatomical, physiological heart and the living heart. Broken heartedness!

Emotions as meaning detectors

In Husserl's (1929/1973) phenomenology, emotion carries a different force than the usual way we think about and value the phenomenon. Emotion is a form of intentionality, a meaning-detector, not a flimsy knee-jerk reaction. In the "moment" grief strikes, emotions reach the "object" directly. They tell me about the situation or predicament. Logic fails. My illusions or self-delusions dissolve in the face of the changes wrought by death: "I don't understand." "Why?" Honest answers about my standing in the matter come in the shape of emotions. Each answer is personal and unique. Jean-Paul Sartre (1957) alleges that emotions transform the world by magic. What does he mean by that?

The objective world does not change because I am emotional. Sartre is talking as a phenomenologist. But my standpoint toward the world alters. Meanings change. Sartre elaborates the point. As long as other forms of intentionality are operating quite nicely—practical pursuits and conscious logical activity—then emotions do not show. But as soon as rational pragmatic movements run into a brick wall and go missing, emotions erupt. Whenever they do emerge, they are meaningful. They reach truth, belying the conscious ideas that we entertain with massive convictions. Picture the woman telling her therapist how happy she feels, even as tears stream down her face, making her pancake makeup run and her mascara smear. Emotional expression reveals the lie of our ideas and conscious beliefs. Emotions do not always show us what we want to see, but they do provide individualized and personal answers.

Heidegger's (1927/1962, p. 172) German words are *Beflindlichkeit*, "How are your feeling?"; "How are you faring?" and *Gestimmtheit*, "having a mood or being attuned". *Dasein*, the human's essential being, is moody. Life's chord of circumstances and blows out of the dark bring us before ourselves such that we find ourselves in the mood in which we are. Passion evidently terrifies Western consciousness, nonetheless, because mainstream philosophy and psychology only "squint at it" and demean it (Heidegger, 1927/1962, p. 175).

Alfred, Lord Tennyson (1849b, p. 353) provides colour:

> Home they brought her warrior dead;
> She nor swon'd nor utter'd cry
> All her maidens, watching said,
> She must weep or she will die .

In this important first phase, emotions break through denial about the loss. This is especially true when we cannot view the corpse because the dead body dramatically vanishes, for example, during tsunamis, floods or war, or when the casket of a suicidal parent is kept closed such that a youngster never sees dead ... dead.

The "moment" of grief is as peculiar as one's fingerprints; it is a personal answer to an individualized situation; there is no recipe for it;

it is one-in-a-row every time. ("Moment" is a cardinal concept of this book and will be kept in quotes.) In life, all we have are "moments". It is, or should be, the starting point of all psychological studies. T.S. Eliot (1936a/1963, p. 95) puts it precisely: "And what is actual is actual only for one time/And only for one place." Furthermore, he describes "a lifetime burning in every moment" (Eliot, 1936d/1963). That is to say that any given "moment" might die on the vine in an eye-blink, or build into an encounter, then become a genuine meeting, and possibly evolve into a relationship—even a lifelong one.[1]

Concerning the "moment" of grief, who knows what emotions will erupt? Tears of sorrow will raise no eyebrows. Some emotions, however, do not honour our cliché that we should speak well of the dead. Maybe anger bordering on rage surfaces, not just that he died on me, that he left me alone, but that he left me with debts, and died wantonly and stupidly in a drug-related horror.

How does one grieve the death by suicide of a dear one? Is not self-murder a judgement on me? Should I not have done something? Will not the social others implicitly blame me, even if they only wonder out loud, "Why?" Was the suicide really a mis-aimed act of murder, as we shall see that Freud alleges? Was the actual victim supposed to be … me? In the face of those questions, might a myriad of feelings emerge, ranging from guilt to disgust to fury?

In *Last Tango in Paris* (Alley 1973), Paul's wife, Rosa, cuts herself with a razor blade and crawls in the bathtub. In a powerful scene of grief, Paul sits and talks to her in the casket, surrounded by flowers. He berates her, calling her every name in the book, protesting to the cold corpse that she had crawled away and hid from him. He screams at her that their marriage was just a "foxhole". Then he breaks down sobbing (Alley, 1973, p. 170).

What about feeling relief that someone died? One might be glad that it's over. Glad to be unburdened. Maybe the death was lingering, and the dying one demanding. It is easy to castigate oneself for feeling glad that the other is finally gone. The emotion does not fit our hypocritical culture of being polite at all costs.

Authentic grief-work is complex. It is the task of severing the links between the self and the lost object, strand by strand, bit by bit, chop by chop. Not one pill at a time. Optimally, we use whatever spontaneous emotions surface in order to get the business underway. "The heart has reason that reason never knows about," writes Pascal (1670/1981, p. 277). "One sees best with the heart," writes Saint-Exuprey (1943), "What is essential is invisible to the eyes" (pp. 64–71). From the perspective of rationalism, such lines are mere poetry. Poor impoverished reason.

Going to excess

If ever it suffices in matters of the heart merely to cope, mourning is beyond coping. By saying this, I am not sponsoring confusion and wanton chaos. Who would gainsay that it is a basic value to stand on one's own two feet in the face of outrageous misfortune? We all have to make it through the night, through the dark night, and the darkest of nights; however, to accomplish this, more than one narrow perspective or any one exclusive tactic is necessary. The superficial, one-dimensional cognitive behavioural view that dominates in our culture needs supplementing. Health professionals must learn to honour excesses by including the uncommon sense of a second-dimensional depth approach, and the extraordinary sense of the comprehensive, existential third-dimensional vision. What balances calm and composure? Is it not the act of cursing?

Alfonso Lingis eloquently and trenchantly writes about the place and the power of "excesses" in human life. Repeatedly, he unmasks the failure of our ascendant pragmatic-rationalism to comprehend the vast majority of human practices that do not fit under that statistical artifact—the bell-curve. Even as our dominant ideology makes us first-world privileged lot feel that we are safe and secure, it also tyrannizes us. This is not the place to articulate or argue for Lingis' overarching vision. But he pens a chapter incredibly germane to our theme of grieving. We are born in a nourishing environment, he reminds us, and generate "forces in excess of what [we] need to adjust to the environment and to compensate for ... periodic lacks" (Lingis, 2000, p. 67). In the face of death, we tap into our deepest reserves of intense excesses:

> There is no grief that is strong that does not act by casting curses. Curses are not impotent reactions to the mindless blows of adversity; they are the forces of grief that know their power to pursue the malevolent into its lairs ... . The forces of grief that curse the human and cosmic villainy are the source of all

the religions and ethics there have been and are in the world (Lingis, 2000, pp. 73–74).

There is no laughter without tears. There are no blessings without curses. This is death we are talking about. This is confrontation with the Void. You are choking on the anguish of nothingness. You are gagging on what you cannot see or put your hands on. You are sobbing sore. You are balling your eyes out. You are shaking like a leaf. What is called for to express the ravages of grief? Fluffy feelings, vanilla emotions, and marshmallow Mickey Mouse reactions—modulated, measured, and composed? Of course not! Should you be mealy mouthed? Do you put on your best face and freeze it there? Harden your stiff upper lip? Speak in docile tones, soft, solemn, and sensible? No: You rage. You rant and rave. Malevolent forces have paid you a visit, have they not? So you curse the drunken driver who killed your child. You blaspheme the gods who struck your woman with cancer. You spit your spite and venom at the puppet of Power and Money whose business venture, called "war", took your husband to his death in Iraq. The ways to meet adequately the villainy of these figures, and to match these fiendish forces, is to flail your arms viciously, sling your fists into the air, flip your finger, and shriek vituperative curses.

In the west, worship of abstract, pragmatic reason cools our hearts and modulates our reactions. We find excessive grief in the Papuan culture, abiding as "a deeply troubling attraction for blood, putrefaction, and corpses" (Lingis, 1998, p. 63). A grief-stricken individual tarries in a zone completely alien to our consulting rooms and clinics. Lingis (1998, p. 63) elaborates:

> The Papuan woman who cuts off her own finger upon the death of her child or lover throws her own body outside of the sphere of work and reason and consigns her body to decomposition …. It continues to suffer and to be rent …. The space of split blood … is visible and sacred.

Western medicine … dispenses drugs.

Pill-poppers

In this "hour", Western culture sedates the bereaved, as if pills were some gift of the gods. Off the wall—or off the bell-curve—go the stats on the use of alcohol, tranquilizers, sedatives, muscle relaxants, sleeping pills, and illegal substances. At this precious time of life, we are medicated or we self-medicate. Tell a physician that your mother just died, and you have a prescription in your hand before your sentence ceases, or your first tear falls. If you break a leg, crutches are surely called for. But relying on anti-anxiety anti-depressive medicine as a crutch is a mistake. Although momentarily useful, in the long run pills are grief-impeding. The inveterate medical value of alleviating symptoms glares in its inadequacy. We cannot sleepwalk through our grief. In Shakespeare's (1937/1955, p. 91) Macbeth: "Give sorrow words; the grief does not speak whispers to the erfraught heart and bids it break." Notice: The Bard did not say: "Give sorrow Prozac."

Mainstream terminology

The grief literature calls this the "initial phase", and sandwiches it between "when death occurs until a few weeks after the funeral". The parameter of this time-box gives a practical guideline. But it is flawed. Findings on "anticipatory grief" show that the initial phase of mourning might occur much earlier, perhaps as soon as one senses that loss is imminent. People can feel the "moment" of loss creeping, like experiencing the chill of an early arriving autumn.

A woman waiting for her man to return from Iraq, terrified that he might die on her, grieves him ... unto closure. He either reads his "Dear John Letter" somewhere in the hot desert sand, or hears the words of goodbye soon after the hug when he de-planes stateside. A child in a family, learning that mum or dad has cancer, begins to grieve as soon as the diagnosis (death sentence) is uttered.

From another perspective, however, this time frame is very accurate. Because why? Necessary funeral arrangements usurp time. The corpse must be disposed of. Depending upon one's cultural mores or sub-culture-religious sentiments, wakes, viewings, funerals or processions engage the mourner. Most likely, the values that surface for the grief-stricken individual in daydreams or night dreams will jostle and collide with traditional Jewish rituals, Muslim death rites, Catholic ceremonies, or Hindu traditions. These collisions between the individual and group customs carve out ample space for the eruption of emotion. Rituals are precious and useful because they express emotions too deep for words. Too deep for words! We must dig into this.

Rituals

Saint-Exupery's (1943) *The Little Prince* grants us a moving description of the power and necessity of rituals or rites. The prince and the fox meet. The latter explains the necessity of observing the proper rituals, and chides "men" for neglecting them. Rituals promote the "taming" that builds friendship. They also give sure footing in doing the work of grieving. Our de-ritualized culture lacks these natural social-cultural facilitators.

Arnold van Gennep's (1975) *The rites of passage* provides a broad framework for understanding the values embodied in non-Western rituals. Funeral rites for the deceased and mourning rites of the survivors run parallel and co-constitute each other. For the entire community, death summons forth a protracted period of transition for both the dead and the living. While the deceased voyages to the land of the dead, the survivors journey through the country of grief (Van Gennep, 1975). In Vietnam, the family visits the tomb again three days after the burial for *le mo cua ma* (worship). They open the grave in order to make sure that the deceased departs along his or her journey. After forty-nine days, on the day of *le chung tsat*, the family returns to pray, but no longer brings rice for the dead. The community now accepts that the deceased has embarked upon his final journey. After 100 days, the family celebrates *tot khoc*, the end of the tears. Finally, after three years comes *le xa tang*, when mourning comes to an end. The family burns the white gauze garments that they wore at the funeral. Life goes on (Toan Anh, 1976, pp. 496–532).

The Arctic Lapps of Norway, Finland and Russia, reindeer herding peoples today called the Sámi, "took care to kill reindeer on the grave so that the deceased might ride it during the difficult journey to his final destination" (Van Gennep, 1975, p. 134). The Vietnamese put money into the corpse's mouth, preferably gold coins (although the actual money depends upon the family's financial situation). The money, as in the case of the Egyptian practice of mummification, both pays the expenses for the trip to the "other side", and signifies that the departed is going to a better life.

In *The Road Home* (Sun, 1999), Luo Yusheng returns to his village because his father, a revered teacher there for forty years, has died. Upon his arrival, the mayor promptly presents him with a problem. The authorities have decided to bring back the corpse by car from the hospital morgue in the town where his father had died (while fundraising for a new schoolhouse), but his mother is stubbornly insisting that her beloved husband be buried in the traditional Chinese way. She wishes to honour the ancient belief that carrying the casket the long distance by foot is the proper way to return the body to the earth, assuring that the deceased will never forget the way home. During the trip, the pallbearers shout and yell to the deceased, giving orientation and directions. (Similarly, while walking with the casket to the grave, the Vietnamese[2] throw money to the left and to the right, bribing ghosts not to impede the journey.) Luo Yusheng's mother insists that her son drag out and repair an old loom, so that she can weave the shroud to cover the coffin. She will walk the road to accompany her beloved.

Love is served, not only tradition. Luo Yusheng unfolds his parents' tender story of a marriage not arranged, but the village's first ever based on love. The road is a cardinal part of their story, a concrete symbol of their tie. It is also a metaphor that connects the village and the outside world and links Life and Death.

It happens that their love and the deceased's forty years of dedicated service are served in the most beautiful way imaginable. Enacting rituals inevitably stirs up essentials of the dead person's life and rounds out the life of the community—in this case of several generations of students. Love–Death! Who can separate it?

Judaism exemplifies another ritualized sub-culture that confers maximal respect for the dead and provides a communal structure for the mourner. In the "hour" of death and "moment" of grief, it helps those devastated from splintering and from falling apart. Specifically, rituals provide a nomenclature, a temporal structure, and clear prescriptions for wholesome actions. They also involve and implicate the community as a whole.

During the crucial period between learning of the death of a dear one and the interment or burial, the Hebrew names the mourner an *onen* and the interval itself is called *aninut* (Isaacs and Kerry, 1991, p. 20). Immediately before the funeral service, the mourner performs the *keriah*, the ritualistic rending of the garments or tearing of a ribbon attached to one's clothes (Isaacs and Kerry, 1991, p. 27). The act, a concrete symbol, rips open the living heart so that it might express anguish and rage. It is a socially sanctioned sacred destruction. Since the mourner stands up while performing the *keriah*, the confrontation with death is excessive. We are not going to take this outrage lying down! Stare death straight in the eye, we will, both accepting its reality and simultaneously affirming the precious sanctity of life.

At the grave site, the pallbearers carry the (prescribed) wooden casket to the hole in the ground. Once it is lowered, family and friends shovel the covering earth over it. The clang of rocks, ping of stones, and the thud of the dirt drive home the same message of Ash Wednesday when the Catholic priest rubs black soot on the individual's forehead: "Ashes to ashes, dust to dust ... . Remember man thou are dust, and to dirt thou shalt return."

The Analects of Confucius (Waley, 1989) also reveals the topmost power of ritual in China and other countries, such as Vietnam, that have been influenced by the sage's "transmission" of ancient Asian wisdom. Confucius describes a "way" of life rooted in and oriented by rituals. They grant people a place "to put hand or foot", in stark contrast with the haphazard way of doing things "after a fashion, in a hugger-mugger way" (Waley, 1989, pp. 172; 66).

Confucius anticipates the bankruptcy of our superficial de-ritualized, short-term, quick-fix, pragmatic "ways" of trying to forget quickly and to cope. Cognitive-behavioural solutions only create a patchwork, full of holes. For Confucius, abstract concept-driven functional strategies are said to be *kou*—which term Arthur Whaley translates as "fluked". This is a sobering idea. Insofar as we spurn ritual, we function by happenstance, by fluke.

Under ritual prescription, the Confucian mourner leads a life apart. This pattern of thinking is so sane. Death has paid a visit, wrought its irrevocable change, and created its "taint". One would not "feel at ease" in their ordinary garb, eating the food they ate before, and doing habitual work. So he or she retires from routine, withdraws from acting as usual in the public mode, wears special clothes, eats special foods, and refrains from typical pleasures (including sexual intercourse). There is even a prohibition against singing on the same day that one has wailed at a funeral (Waley, 1989, p. 124). As little room as possible is granted for conduct by ... fluke.

This description is not a prescription, but a pause for reflection. We will never imitate ancient Chinese practices in our 9–5, "Shop till you drop", "Image is all", "Just do it", "Only success matters", outcome-oriented society ... where moolah is King. But we can learn a style and set of ideas that we can adapt to our Western "way".

At the very least, we can allow ourselves to make the period of grief a time-apart, creating our own symbols to acknowledge to ourselves and to alert the outside world that we are going through a special and difficult time in our life.

Music

Music is a powerful component of ritualistic mourning. Arthur Whaley, a Brit, states that we Westerners have a peculiarly "abnormal" attitude toward music and dancing. "Our view of music is an agreeable arrangement of sounds, listened to for enjoyment," he writes, "and dancing is a means of social distraction combined with mild bodily exercise (Waley, 1989, p. 68). Of course, with a residue of Victorian hypocrisy concerning sexuality, he leaves out the erotic, sensual, and seductive use of these two modes: the élan of love-sounds, and the rubbing together of two bodies. Nevertheless, he does unmask the lingering Victorian hypocrisy. For non-white people the world over, song-and-dance exercise "a magic power not only over the heart of man, but also over the forces of nature" (Waley, 1989, p. 68). Confucius esteems music as an instrument of education that promotes virtue. In terms of the matter of grieving, the *Songs* incite us and give us firm footing. The Hebraic generous use of the Psalms during the funeral rites serves the same purpose as well as placing death in a religious context.

The Roman and Orthodox Catholic churches are also intensely ritualistic, employing incense, icons, stained glass windows, statues, and especially music to evoke mystery, to present tapestries of beauty, and to provoke emotion. The wedding of the Latin language and Gregorian Chat is peerless, matched by the similar wedding in Eastern orthodoxy. The music of the Roman "requiem" calls forth tears in believers and non-believers alike, especially within the context of the "Mass of the Angels" on the occasion of a young child's death. "*Dies irae. Dies illa ... Requiescat in pace ...* . These are days of anger and wrath. May the rest of peace visit us come to us" (*The Liber Usualis*, 1959, pp. 1, 810; 1, 815. My translation.)

The closest secular counterpart is playing taps at the grave site of a soldier's burial. The music of the horn cuts right through the listener. Often, if one in grief has not yet cried, taps will unleash the flood of tears.

Emotions jump-start the process of grieving. Rituals and music are ready-at-hand modes for stirring and perturbing our emotional registers. Within a Western secular context, we can use the requiems of the masters—Bach, Mozart, Mahler, Beethoven, Verdi, and Faure—to drink in and press out death's impact. We all have our favourite musical genre and favourite performers that touch our hearts. This is a good time to slip in the CD and let him, her, or them ... wail. It is of supreme importance in the "moment" of grief that something would touch our hearts and perturb our souls, so that whatever must well up in us would indeed gush forth. I underline the point that shoots throughout the standpoints from the *Analects* to the *Talmud*. In the "moments" of journeying when we most might flounder, rituals provide firm, sure footing.

The meal of condolence

The after-the-funeral meal also helps to put the death-event into perspective. Life must go on. Life will go on. Solemnity has held sway during the burial ceremonies, whether they are marked by a simple procession or an elegant cortege. In the immediate time after death—the Jewish *aninut*—grief duly has been coaxed out into the open. Henceforth, grief must work itself out within ordinary time. People eat. Mourners must be nourished. The mourners leave the cemetery and come to a banquet. Nourishing them is a concrete metaphor. It matters not how simple or elaborate the feast, whether the meal is prepared by church members or neighbours in highly traditional groups, small towns, or closely knitted communities, whether delivered by an expensive caterer, or whether the family hires a restaurant to feed their guests. The meal's mood is ordinarily festive. The communal action switches from respectful interment of the corpse to the celebration of a life and of Life.

In the traditional Jewish "meal of consolation or condolence" the food served is "hard-boiled eggs ... cooked vegetables (lentils) and a beverage" (Isaacs and Olidzky, 1991, p. 33). The roots of my raising orientate my sensitivity and understanding. In a later chapter, I will draw upon my experience, mentioning the final meal at my mother's death.

Telling stories

The meal is a farewell party. Food and drinks are served. There is music. There is laughter. People trade stories about the deceased, both funny and sad. Some individuals have only a few words to say. Some fall silent. Others are storytellers who are able to bring the corpse alive again with colourful tales. Some of the stories are incredibly precious. The son or daughter—even the widow—may not know something about the dead father-husband-grandfather that an old army buddy narrates (or someone who worked with him, "back when", before the company closed down the factory and left town). A stranger might show at the wake, but shun the farewell party. She/he, who does not belong to the core group, might have told rich stories, but those would have painfully true and destructive (Alapack, 2008).

Weddings and funerals bring out the best and the worst in families. Sometimes the farewell party gets rowdy. Sometimes bones of contention get picked. After whatever efforts they had expended to give a dignified burial, estranged family members grumble, bad mouth each other, argue, and quarrel—especially after being lubricated by the fruit of the vine, with brew made with barley and hops, or with harder liquor. Such divisive—even vicious—actions dampen the party, but rarely ruin it. More importantly, it expresses ambivalence that the family members need to face and work through in the coming weeks and months.

Are not our lives stories? We *are* how we are *held* in the words of those who know us. So the information passed along to the mourners, and the tone in which it is passed, and even the ire with which it is sometimes delivered, helps round out the picture one has of father, or grandfather, or spouse. It helps forward the difficult work.

Death happens within a certain social fabric and rends the communal cloth. Grief does not take place alone. I repeat: The ongoing debate in the current literature about a possible causal relationship between continuing bonds and adjustment merely perpetuates the rationalistic dualism that hinders holistic death-grief studies. Within the group and in living time, continuing bonds are necessary to shelter the social fabric and to hold the community together. As a people, we must not forget.

Happenings in the immediate aftermath of the body being laid to rest give the survivors a glimpse of metaphors they must face as they begin the long task of grieving. At the condolence meal, they get a subtle or raw peek at it. In one way or another, they can use it as grist for the mill of grief. When you boil it down, the human is a network of relationships. Everything in life is interrelated. There is no other way to get the work done.

In closing the chapter

Emotion is the *lead* phenomenon during this first phase when the importance of the bond between the lost object and me is at stake. If I do not get in touch with my deep emotions, feel them, express them, perhaps name them, I do not yet begin to grieve. As should be evident by now, it is not emotions-in-the head that I am talking about. Emotions are embodied, which is why music, a meal, and stories evoke them.

Are we not tired by now of being reminded that we are neither angels nor apes? The emotional body expresses our grief as more than embodied. Rather than smile at me for using what sounds like double talk, ponder instead that the Western dualistic-rationalistic way of conceiving reality confounds our understanding of the act of grieving just as it foils every other human experience. Such is the situation of the individual who shows no emotion when his mother dies, or his sweetheart exits stage left never to return. Six months down the road, a late Saturday night re-run, *Lassie, Come Home*, flashes on the TV screen. Suddenly, our fellow is balling his eyes out. In the immediate moment, he doesn't even know what he is crying about. It will take between an eye-blink and forever to realize why. The timing of his awareness and the outcome will make all the difference. Maybe this is the start.

Better late than never, of course; the sooner the better, of course. This is not a matter of mouthing one cliché after another, or trading them. In transitioning to the next phase or "moment" of grieving, one gets a preliminary handle on the meaning of the bond with the lost object by mobilizing the heart. Otherwise, the labour of mourning sputters.

CHAPTER TWO

Phase II: Over-binding: Memories and the voluptuaries of grief

Mainstream literature calls the second "moment" the Intermediate Phase. It starts after the leave-taking ceremonies have ended and day-to-day activities have resumed, lasting roughly three weeks to one year. For Freud, the task of this first year is hyper-investing, excessively harping on the bond, over-doing it.

The Jewish tradition fine tunes the time. *Shiva*, from the Hebrew word for "seven", refers to the period from the burial until seven days have lapsed. It is a socially sanctioned time for intense grief, the time for rending your garments at any time the urge should strike. Jewish tradition encourages the mourner to stay at home. Friends make visits to share your pain, to offer comfort and support. Such comportment is played out with the limits of being human, so almost never are the visits perfect, and rarely does anything earth-shaking happen. But structure encircles the mourner.

Grief is as natural a part of life as joy. Here comes the echo: grief also kills. Voodoo death demonstrates that falling out with the community leads to an early, premature and—from a Western perspective—wanton demise. Colin Parkes (1996) demonstrates that a widow, who lives past the anniversary of her man's death, goes back into the normal distribution for life-expectancy—if graciously you would grant that there is a normal distribution of anything existential. The statistics for widows dying within that first year—if graciously you would grant that statistics ever are *psychologically* relevant—are staggeringly high. Whatever the death certificate reads—and be assured that it will not read "died of a broken heart"—nevertheless the widow (or the tribe member, who the Songoma had banished from the group for some transgression), do die heartbroken. One loses the key figure of his life: he falls out with the community permanently; she or he loses heart. This second phase, therefore, is so important that negotiating it poorly might be ... lethal. The grief literature names three styles of excessive comportment that characterize the first year of mourning. They mesh nicely with Freud's ideas.

The obsessive review: Remembering-forgetting

The mourner uncontrollably dwells upon a certain idea or scene. For example, one re-lives the moment the tsunami waves swept his child out of his arms; sees again the Twin Towers flop like cakes in an oven; watches dad keel over while shovelling the driveway snow; sees again mum draw her final breath. One replays it, and replays it again as if hooked on watching a horror movie. Seized, tortured, and haunted one feels compelled to review the scene. If emotion is the key register within the first phase, in this phase memory looms most important. More exactly, it is the memory-forgetting dimension that comes into play. "Do I have my memories, or do they have me?" Good question! Who knows? Nevertheless in whatever genre of music one prefers, "If only ..." is the theme song. If only I had gotten to the hospital in time. If only I hadn't asked him to shovel the snow. If only I had told her that I loved her. If I had it to do over! If only ... not.

Such lines prey upon one's mind. The obsessive review, therefore, is necessary. Memories have to be dredged up, examined, and appraised ... for their beauty and their pain. The drug cartel sells no pill to balance the subtle dialectic of remembering-forgetting. Only by experiencing the range of one's own registers is it possible to find an even keel between what one must remember, and what one should forget. A thorough and honest review will strike a balance.

Trying to go to sleep does not work. Like a delicate butterfly, sleep must descend. Likewise, we forget naturally as a result of first thinking through, facing something important, and letting it be what it was and is and probably always will be. Trying-to forget and trying-to-remember boomerang.

What's "good" about goodbye? How does the ending transpire, and why? The balance between remembering-forgetting is fragile. Often we skew it by equivocating. With a half-hearted desire to forget, I tell my psychotherapist that I can't even remember if she and I said the unwanted phrase, "goodbye". I even give flimsy excuses, saying that I only miss her every now and then, in "moments: when the soft Pacific wind blows across my cheek". My therapist says, "Breezy, eh?! Who are you kidding?" So I halfway own my guilt. Somehow I provoked the ending. Somehow I made her cry. "But 'goodbye', I don't remember the 'moment' of saying it." My shrink reads between his lines and challenges me: "How could you forget ... or not forget *that*?" "What hurtful words did you use?" "What promise did you break?" "About this relationship you can't afford the luxury of amnesia."

Then I spill the beans, letting the painful truth trickle. First I cry. The word sticks in my throat. "Goodbye, goodbye, goodbye."

Healing hands of time?

Emily Dickinson (1924/1993) has written the definitive lines dismantling the idea that the sheer passage of objective-clock-calendar time confers necessary relief and heals wounds:

> THEY say that "time assuages,"—
> Time never did assuage;
> An actual suffering strengthens,
> As sinews do, with age.
> Time is a test of trouble
> But not a remedy.
> If such it prove, it prove too
> There was no malady (pp. 226–227).

What is easy to forget or easily slips away was never grave to start with. A serious wound transmutes into longing.

Keepsakes

The keepsake is a precious memento. It keeps memories alive. Usually, it is a small item that is insignificant to anyone but you. In you, it rouses an emotion with strength to devour you. "Everyone knows the power of things," Simone de Beauvoir (1964/1965, p. 98) writes, "life is solidified in them" You gave the deceased a gift, a locket that she always wore. Or you both picked out a souvenir on your trip to Romania and Dracula's Castle. Or you stumbled upon a beautiful seashell on the shores of the Black Sea in Sochi. It is precious, not in the world where the market economy is "top dog", but within your psychological economy. It is dad's pocket watch, mum's scissors, the hussif your Aunt left you, or the pretty pink barrette your daughter wore in her hair. Lying on the table, the item looks "orphaned, useless, and waiting to be turned into rubbish" (De Beauvoir, 1964/1965, p. 98). His wedding ring is waiting "to find a new identity". To you, it is a treasure.

Simon de Beauvoir's mother, during the month that she was dying, wore a black ribbon around her neck. As "they" undid the simple piece of material from the dead woman, Poupette, Simone's sister, began to cry. "It's so stupid and I'm not a worshipper of things, but I just can't throw this ribbon away." Simone replies, "Keep it. It is useless to try to integrate life and death and to behave rationally in the presence of something that is not rational: each must manage as well as he can in the tumult of his feelings" (De Beauvoir, 1964/1965, p. 98).

The dictionary says lightly that a keepsake evokes memories; it is more serious. It is memory concretized, realized, and congealed. It is the residue of loving. It marks your history of affection and reciprocal desire. It betokens your broken heart. As often as not, it is something you wear or touch: a medal, a medallion, a bracelet, a ring, or a necklace. Or it's a stone you finger, a silk scarf, something she embroidered for you. It is your grandmother's rosary; you remember her telling her beads endlessly. Seeing them piled on the table, surrounded by a ball of wool and the unfinished mittens she was knitting for you, makes you weep. Or it is a bottle of perfume, the starlet's *Poison* that you used to tease her about. You know you will open it, every now and again, so that the scent might bring her back, although without her taste or touch. It is a catalyst for your memory to bring back the scent of your woman.

Keepsakes hold emotions. Only our dualistic Western thinking dares to separate emotion from memory. Keepsakes cradle the two together.

When your mother was dying, she told you that she was giving you the linen tablecloth on the top shelf of the closet that she had spread out for so few festive occasions in your life. She knew that you would give away the rest of the contents of the apartment—her furniture, kitchen utensils and clothes—to the Goodwill or discard them. The linen tablecloth was the only thing that her peasant mother has to give her when she left Lithuania to make her way to America, alone, because her widowed mother would not leave ... these woven flax fibers a century old caution your fingers to touch them lightly. They speak of your grandmother and her love of the marshes of that northern land and the leaves that danced about her and whose fibers clothed her. They tell why she would never leave that place (Lingis, 2005, p. 122).

Families fight over little mementos after a death. It seems petty. One family member, caught up in grief, does not even think of things during the wake, funeral, and the aftermath. Later, he finds out that a brother, or sister, or niece—like a vulture—scooped up items while the corpse was still warm. It becomes fodder for a family feud. Blood kin will hold a grudge for the remains of their days over a keepsake item that one took that the other thinks she should possess. All-too-human!

As often as not, a member of the family wants one thing or another, and takes it. I am not talking about a big-ticket item pertaining to the setting of the estate, to the bickering and contesting of a will. I am talking about the little things that money cannot buy. The little "nothings" that are the life-blood of love. Within the family, when the matter is discussed, everyone will have an opinion about who should rightfully have which particular item. Only something so small and worthless can be so valuable.

Our culture as a whole is obsessed with NASDAQ and the Dow. Proponents of dynamic systems theory distinguish between "open" and "closed" systems, and thereby explain why "we" talk about the "market" as if it is a living subject. Yet simultaneously, our dominant cognitive behavioural technology, enamoured with abstraction and objectification, describes living people as if they were objects, computers, or cyborgs. But is not the tender keepsake pre-eminently relational? By definition, it refers to something that withstands the ravages of time. The neglect of the keepsake by grief researchers highlights the a-relational and quick-fix character of its basic paradigm. Ron Cornelissen (unpublished manuscript) puts it succinctly: "Our culture is too busy trying to forget everything to remember anything. The heart grieves to remember, even as the mind grieves to forget!"

The fragility of keeping promises

My promises are easy to remember while the totality of my conscious and unconscious power is dragging me through a torturous review. What good am I if I didn't even keep my word? A statement like that is hard to gainsay. What can a friend or a therapist say in response to one who makes such a scorching indictment of self?

Making a promise is a capacity that differentiates the human from the animal. My living word, *parole* in the French language—as in "I give you my word"—differs from the other word for word, *mot*, which is the dead word of the dictionary or lexicon. Promising is one of those acts that hold a community together; and it is pivotal to an intimate bond between parent and child, between woman and man, and between friends. We feel awful disappointment in self when we can't fulfill our promises.

Promises-not-kept, nevertheless, are part of the inherently unfinished business of death. Again, what do I mean? A promise or a vow requires a future. We don't promise something that we can do here and now. We do it! We promise what is to come down the road, around the bend, when something might come to pass that I plan and hope for. Letting go of an unfulfilled promise, big or small, important or trivial, is necessary to get the monkey off our backs. I promised my loved one I would stop smoking/finish my master's degree/do an El Camino pilgrimage. Well, who can gainsay that such a promise is a sharp motivational spur? Maybe keeping it is in my best interests; maybe not. But it persists as an interpersonal pledge. If doing the act truly expresses my heart's desire, splendid. But the promise might have been made mostly to please her. Any resolve that fundamentally aims to keep the promise to the dead is at best ambiguous. C.S. Lewis says it plainly and simply, "Keeping promises to the dead ... is a trap" (1961/1980, p. 8). We must strike a balance between the promise as absolute or merely contingent.

Broken promises

Broken promises surface in our obsessive review. If a spouse dies—or divorces you—one issue that multiplies guilt is infidelity. If I had crossed over into the land of broken promises—whether or not my now "gone" partner consciously knew of the deceit and treachery—I have a heavy load of the broken vow to carry. "If only not." The peculiar poignancy of this situation is that forgiveness is now impossible, since the other is physically dead. If he is a living ghost—your ex-husband who insists that you return to him—forgiveness is possible but not very likely. At least from where you are standing—or crawling—it does not look forthcoming. Erik Erikson (1969, p. 154) writes, "We mourn most dramatically where, with the death of someone, an unlived chance of reconciliation and inner enrichment is gone forever."

Broken dreams

Shattered dreams fit (un)comfortably under the banner of "gone forever". Whenever infidelity enters a man–woman relationship, broken dreams follow in the train of broken promises. A new beginning requires repair. It necessitates picking up broken pieces and mending broken dreams. We rake through ashes, hoping to find a spark. This is not sheer poetic justice. The phenomenon of innocence is vital to authentic living. We prefer to plead we are innocent; we know the times when we are not. Loss of innocence is as much a part and parcel of life as making love, having babies, or futilely marching with banners to prevent your government from immorally invading a beleaguered country. After every loss of sexual or spiritual innocence, healing comes with the regained capacity to see innocence again whenever and wherever it might flower. After death, or if estranged lovers do not reconcile, the survivor must pull the weight of the past alone. Forever has come to stay. Dreams remain shattered. How can we cope with it?

The illusion of closure

There is a crack that lets the light in. A cardinal sliver of truth gained by harping on the chant-lines of regret is to see the dead end it leads to. I am referring to what I name *the illusion of closure*. Seemingly, it would be so easy to imagine that if one had paid a last visit, finally asked forgiveness, or broken down and cried, then closure would have occurred. I could wash my hands of it, right? This god-awful guilt and pain would never have come to hang around my neck, right? Wrong! If the moment of forgiveness comes, if saying, "I love you," passes your lips, the interaction would only open the relationship anew, not close it. So clobbering ourselves for what we had or had not done—our guilt-riddled reason for failing to end—is simply a pipe dream. The presumed ultimate "moment" would create a new beginning not a final resolution. It would evoke a new promise or create a new dream. The sooner we realize this, the sooner we can silence those two incredibly powerful words: "If only." Innocence is there for the seeing, if only we have eyes to behold it.

Freud's hyper-investment

This obsessive review interfaces almost perfectly with Freud's second phase of over-doing it. The mourner is vulnerable to belittling, derogating, denigrating, and castigating self. Freud's (1917e [1915], p. 246) phraseology is priceless: the struggling griever expresses guilt without shame. Is Death's robbery my own fault? My initial memories and associations are guilt-tinged because of my actions or omissions. Freud, with tongue-in-cheek, comments upon the self-castigation and ugly self-disclosures of the shameless mourner. Why, he rhetorically asks, does it take such dire straits for us all-too-human humans to admit our pimples, warts, and scars? So strange! Usually we hide from others even our minor blemishes, the speck in our eye. Yet here we are, yelling from the rooftops, airing our dirty laundry, telling the whole world about our worst dirt and biggest beam. Guilt without shame ... .

Within Freud's framework, the over-bonding or hyper-investing is necessary. We devote ourselves to our mourning, indulging in the pleasure of the pain. Alfred, Lord Tennyson again makes the point beautifully. We glory says the Lord, in the "voluptuaries of grief" (Tennyson, 1849a, pp. 378–475). Ah, indeed, there will be no premature letting go of the beloved. I will resist letting go too soon; I will hang on even if it kills me. Sometimes kill me it does.

Over the self of the mourner, Freud (1917e [1915], p. 249) says, "The shadow of the lost object" has fallen. Just as one cannot punch one's way out of the proverbial paper bag, one cannot blink away this shadow that drapes us. So we overdo it. We play the old love song over and over, the one we fell in love to; we read old love-letters, the one's on which we have underlined in red precious words; we return to our old haunts only to find ourselves haunted there. It hurts. It hurts again. This is the only way, says Freud, to sever the thousand links, strand by strand in service of freeing the energy/meaning necessary to go on with life. For the time being, my self is empty and poor. By hyper-occupying the loci between the lost object and me and by activating memorial intentionality I move forward the process of release. We do not fail to overturn every stone under which pain might be hiding. We find it.

Seeking answers

The second comportment of this intermediate phase, closely connected to the brain-racking review, is seeking an understanding of the death or loss. "Why?" Beyond blaming self for what I did or didn't do, and beyond struggling with my own regret, this is the quest for bigger answers. It is not the answer to a *Trivial Pursuit* question that is bugging us. This is Life–Death we are confronting. Why did it happen? Why the hurricane? Why the tsunami? Why the accident? Why the Twin Towers? Why an illegal invasion? Why bomb my country to rubble? Why do the "good" die young and the tyrants live longest, the selfish, heartless, greedy ones, the power-mad politician who sent my son to battle? Why does God allow "bad" things to happen to "good" people? Yeah, God! Goddamn it! Why does God allow badness in Her world? Whenever the death of a dear one provokes a crisis of faith; the struggle either solidifies one's religious creed, or one's faith falls away. C.S. Lewis (1961/1980) arguably gives the best description in English literature of religious despair in the face of the death of his Joy.

Searching

The third comportment of this second stage, searching, is looking precisely for the missing one. We anticipate meeting our dead beloved. The blue Toyota that just drove by, wasn't it his car? She will show up any moment now. Hope against hope, maybe he will return with the first fall of snow. Even the whisper of the wind sounds like she's singing to me, as she often did. A letter arrives, and for a minute there I thought it was her scrawl. The phone rings: this is the precise time he used to call me, religiously. "You've got mail!" the cyberspace machine chimes, and you startle. God, you might as well cancel your SMS account! You won't be getting any more of her quirky messages!

The specific aim of searching is finding her who is gone, of conjuring him up. To that degree, I at least still keep his memory alive. What have we here? This is near the end of the first year, remember. Things are supposed to be back to normal. Most folks, if you bring her up in conversation, are apt to look at you or speak as if meaning—no matter what they are trying consciously to say to sooth you—"Haven't you gotten over her YET?" No matter which way you turn, or who you turn to, it's the same. Low and behold, enters from stage left to centre … loneliness.

Loneliness

What is loneliness? Obviously, it cannot be pigeonholed precisely and absolutely. Operational definitions—if they ever have any significance beyond the theoretician in love with his theory—are useless in pinning down loneliness. But in the context of grief, we can say what it means to be lonesome. Loneliness is the reaction to the deprivation. It is the attunement to the gap, being acutely aware of the Hole in the Whole that opened up and still gapes. The loss of the loss is now poignant. Loneliness is living with the loss of the loss. That is why longing will come soon; longing: a searching that is a reaching.

My lost beloved is a referent of my meanings. She is the target of my emotions and passions. Without the target, there is nobody on whom to put certain feelings: my tenderness, perhaps, or my worry. To try to express those emotions now would be expressing them in a vacuum (Searles, 1965). The beloved, gone now, had been my companion, my listening ear, source of inspiration, sounding board, source of stimulation, my sexual partner. C.S. Lewis (1961/1980, p. 12) conveys the loneliness in these terms: "The worse spot, if spouse or physical lover is my own body." Without her, I do not have the same lived body. My body feels like an empty house now. There is an empty vacant spot on my bed. I ache. There is the pillow where she laid her head. I can smell her perfume emanating from the pillowcase ... that I have washed at least a half dozen times. Ah, the fabric of loneliness.

Love is a many-splendored thing (King, 1950/2003)

Mark, an American war correspondent during the Korean War is involved in an "outlaw relationship" with a Eurasian doctor (Alapack, 2007a, p. 89ff). She is a widow. He can't get a divorce. Her tradition-dominated family disapproves of their forbidden love. In addition, strict racial laws in Hong Kong in that historical "moment" criminalize their indulgence in sexual love. Mark and Dr. Suyin must sneak like thieves or beggars to meet to be together ... alone.

In the climax of the film, Mark gets blown to smithereens in the field, thus suffering the war correspondent's ultimate occupational hazard. During the final scene, after she learns of his death, she is hurriedly climbing to the top of the high hill above the hospital. It was there, by a lone tree, where they would meet, touch, kiss ... and make the world go away.

Dr. Suyin knows he's dead. But frantically, she hurries to their windy love-spot. As she stumbles along, crying bitterly, she looks up. In amazement she sees him, solidly etched against the sky, standing near their lonely tree, waiting for her just as he always did, with a face full of love ... patiently waiting.

When she blinks, of course, he's gone. The facial expression of the actress shows sheer ache, agony, and longing. When Dr. Suyin reaches the top, she stands blown by the wind, buffeted, and bent, appearing almost broken. Devastating grief explodes around her, attacking her with endless waves of anguish, like Twin Towers that could not move out of terror's way. As if in a moment, she would go up in smoke.

The missing touch

Lady Constance Chatterley and Mrs. Bolton are talking about the death of the latter woman's husband, twenty-three years earlier:

> One part of my life ended there. One part of me went with him ... . It was as if I could only feel his arms round me, an' his

body against me, an' his legs against my legs ... . And I kept waking up thinking: 'Why, he's not in bed with me' ... . My feelings wouldn't believe he's gone. I felt he'd have to come back to lie against me, so I could feel him there with me, warm. And it took me a thousand shocks before I knew he wouldn't come back, it took me years ... . I've never got over the touch of him to this day, and never shall. And if there's a heaven above, he'll be there, and will lie up against me so I can sleep (Lawrence, 1928/1983, pp. 175–176).

Concerning a man and a woman, Connie asks the basic existential question: "But can a touch last so long? ... Can a man's touch on a woman last so long ... such that you can still feel him?" Mrs. Bolton gives the root existential answer: "Eh, my Lady, what else is there to last? Children grow away from you. What else is there to last?" "When he touches you?" Connie asks. "Yes, my lady," the older woman replies, "once you've been warmed by a man" (Lawrence, 1928/1983, pp. 175–176).

Longing

The lingering of loneliness is longing. I yearn for what is missing, for the one who oriented my existence, he who gave me direction, she who kept me from slipping away. I reach for her. The deep passion of longing harkens back to the past, ransacks through old memories and—as if playing cards—shuffles and cuts them, divides and deals them ... with no end. Longing arcs toward the future, too. Out of that seeming impossible mixture of past and future, it wants to install a temporal structure that provides something to live by— what is typically referred to as "someday". "Marriage gave me a constant impact of something very close and intimate yet unmistakably other, resistant, real. Is that all undone?" (Lewis, 1961/1980, p. 20). How do I get my pivot back, or my rock solid foundation? I devote the last chapter of this book to longing.

Absence is a mode of presence

In an incomparable phenomenological analysis, Jean-Paul Sartre captures the gist of this entire phase. Borrowing lines from Heidegger, he writes that "Absence is a mode of presence" (Sartre, 1956, pp. 61–63). You enter a café looking for Pierre. He is not there. By rumour, he is in Algiers. The music is loud. From one side, comes the fragrance of wine; from the other, the smell of espresso and butter on the croissant. There's lots of laughter and many folks are dancing. You hear, see, or smell none of it. Pierre is not here. And it is Pierre to whom you are present.

A teacher stands before a room full of students. She thinks she is delivering the best lecture of her life. She looks out at the group for a moment and stares at the faces. She can see that half the class or three-fourths of the class ... most of the class ... is not there. They are at last night's soccer match, last night's love-tug ... who knows where? Western thought since Plato is plagued with the primacy of substance and presence, unconcerned with and ignorant about "the nothing". That bias, as expressed in our times, has hindered the development of a *psychological* psychology that would embrace the whole person and the fullness of Life-Death. Instead the ruling (cognitive) behavioural technology bequeaths to us superficial abstractions befitting only a one-dimensional man. In the lifeworld, absence is a mode of presence. Grief cannot be grasped and dealt with without opening to the second and third dimensions. C.S. Lewis (1961/1980, p. 11) again, "Her absence is like the sky, spread over everything."

Visiting the garden

The work of this phase is over-attaching, in order to detach and let go. Memories have to be dredged up. You dwell upon the various and sundry heartfelt hopes bound to the dead person. In some sense, he was the bearer of your future. Comes the moment when you sift through her belongings, or must decide what to do with his clothes, his book, papers, and music. Eventually, you find out that the places you did not think you could go back to visit without her accompanying you ... are no better or worse than any other spot on the globe. Eventually, you visit her grave to see your beloved chiseled in stone.

The sociologists/anthropologists Francis, Kellaher, and Naophytou (2005) have interviewed visitors to the cemetery. They found out that the full spectrum of mourners, adults and children of all ages, people of all religions, ethnicities, and income level visit cemeteries.

Some attend daily, others yearly. They bring flowers, tend the grave, clean the stone, and pick weeds. They talk with the beloved, chat with other visitors, and reflect upon weighty and lingering issues. In the light of such findings, lingering doubts about lingering bonds is ridiculously abstract.

The story in the garden ... alone ... is a long and deeply personal tale all by itself. Do you talk to her? Do you ball your eyes out? What's the story?

The Garden is a splendid place to find answers to pressing question. Tears, of course, are part of the discovery. It takes some of us a long time to visit the cemetery. There are individuals who refuse to go. There are those who go religiously, even daily. Joe DiMaggio would bring Marilyn Monroe a flower each day. There's an eternal flame flickering in Washington, D.C. Some individuals—Sigmund Freud is a prime historical example—get vertigo or faint at the threshold of the cemetery gates. While looking at the tombstone, reading words you know so well you'll never forget them, it's a good time to talk; it's a good time to listen; it's a good time to pray, or reflect. Etched in stone makes it very concrete—no pun intended. It cuts through unrealistic fantasies and liquidates useless denial. Unvarnished loneliness = carvings on chiseled granite.

D.W. Winnicott (1965a/2005) explicates that "the capacity to be alone" (pp. 29–36) so necessary for health, develops because the growing child learns to take for granted the presence of the care-taker.[3] The young child plays comfortably and at ease knowing that mum is there. Sometimes she checks back. If she sees dad or mum reliably available, then the child can play without fretting, as if under a rainbow. The parent is in eyesight and earshot, and in reach of my heart. The child relaxes and gives self over to the play world or school tasks.

What's my point? Our grief-work must de-literalize presence. To accomplish this, it is necessary to liquidate our Western bias that privileges presence, substance, and observable measurable variables. Absorb instead, I propose, the phenomenological idea that absence is a mode of presence. If I don't see me in your eyes anymore, but see instead "a far away look in your eye", then absence is a more authentic presence than physical nearness. Instead of reading a "self-help" book, visit the Garden. It might be upbuilding.

Keening

The Irish is one ethnic group that soon after the death promotes the necessary emotional excess. Irish keening drags raw emotions into the open. Paradoxically, the wailing brings everything close and simultaneously helps create a distance. How? Keening generates energy and prompts movement by stirring one's body and quickening the group.

You watch the Irish mother, whose precious son is stone cold in the casket. In a moment of keening, she almost disintegrates. It pierces you. Then she sits, half-composed. In an eye-blink, she stands to greet a condolence visitor who just walked into the parlour. She talks coherently and calmly to the one paying respects. He takes his leave. They share a hug. She watches his back for a second. Then she runs to the casket, falls on her knees and wails again. The shriek goes right through you.

William Faulkner (1987), in his tale of the run-of-the-mill-madness that characterizes any burial and the events which splice it, lets Dewey Dell do the deed:

> Leaning above the bed, her hands lifted a little, the fan still moving like it has for ten days, she begins to keen. Her voice is strong, young, tremulous and clear, rapt with its own timbre and volume, the fan still moving steadily up and down, whispering the useless air. Then she flings herself across Addie Bundren's [the corpse] knees, clutching her, shaking her with the furious strength of the young before sprawling suddenly across the handful of rotten bones that Addie Bundren left, jarring the whole bed into a chattering sibilance of mattress shucks, her arms outflung and the fan in one hand still beating with expiring breath into the quilt (p. 44).

The clearing is necessary. Distance is imperative. If something is too close to us, we do not see it. Faulkner closes the chapter after Dewey Dell gets up from the corpse and smoothes the quilt clear up to the deceased woman's chin. Then Pa, the husband-father, approaches the bed, touches the quilt too, and with nothing but futility in his actions tries to arrange the quilt the way the woman who keened so ferociously did. At length, he ceases and desists. As he mouths his snuff against his gums, he says through breathing that is both quiet, yet rasping, "She's taken and left us ... God's will be done ... Now I can get them teeth" (Faulkner, 1987, pp. 46; 48). Dead is dead. One family member protests it with fury; the other sounds the inevitable: life goes on.

We must court Tennyson's "cruel fellowship of sorrow". We must over-do it, howl to high heaven even if only to whisper one's agony to self. One looks at Edvard Munich's *Scream* and identifies with the horror; one plays Mahler or Mozart and sorely sobs.

Memorial consciousness

World War I, the "war to end all wars", failed. But it did succeed in staining our consciousness with the conviction that the dead have the right to be remembered. Ever since in the USA, Memorial and Remembrance Days have dotted the calendar year. On Memorial Day, visits to the cemetery are common, planting flowers, cleaning the tombstone, remembering.

United States cities also proudly house War Memorial Auditoriums. Originally built as cathedrals to memorialize our veterans of foreign wars, most have been renovated and today serve their cities profitably as state-of-the-art performances centres, premier sports facilities, venues for trade shows, gun and rifle shows, and so on. They are venerable old buildings (the "Aud" in Buffalo, for example, dates from 30 November 1939). The Fort Lauderdale structure, close to the beach, sports ornate marble and bronze statues. Its atmosphere fosters serenity and patriotism. Some things we must remember; we cannot afford the luxury of forgetting. While travelling from shore to shore across the USA, therefore, visit one of the country's heritage buildings in Worcester, New Haven, Richmond, Nashville, Chattanooga, Greensboro, Louisville, Charlotte, Rochester, Syracuse, Columbus, Kansas City, Des Moines, Pasadena, San Diego, San Rafael, Sacramento, San Francisco ... .

The anniversary

Now draws near the anniversary date. At the anniversary time, the story comes back. She died in the spring. Now the flowers are a-blooming. You whisper to her, reminding her that she coaxed you into helping her make a bed of roses the very day you took possession of your matrimonial home. You both searched to find the best plot, and with a make-shift spade you broke the ground. Then you drove into town to buy the seeds.

Working under the brutal Southern sun, she got her face smudged with dirt. With a shared smile followed by a kiss, you wiped her cheeks. She finished her planting pleased and optimistic. You had doubts, then. But now, gazing through a lovely sun shower from a hammock on the deck, you'd give your eye-teeth and all the tea in china if she could just see those roses blooming.

On some days, you sit endlessly staring at those roses, so young and vibrant. But you're already anticipating the change of seasons, and know that they'll wither covered with an early autumn frost. The seasons of your own life preoccupy you, too. The only thing that seems certain is that the roses will bloom again come spring time. But your beloved is gone.

You pick one of the prettiest. It pricks you back; your tears water it and you wipe the blood. Under your breath you say, "If only I can make it through December," figuring that if you get past the holidays and her birthday, then your life might hang on for a few more autumns. You hum, as much to yourself as to her, a song you are writing about the Little Prince and his rose, lyrics about memories, nostalgia, and love, about spring decaying into autumn. And winter looms.

With the reminders flooding at anniversary time, it is incumbent upon us to see "it". Seeing it is hard. Most of us prefer to avert the eyes. Most prefer to remember selectively. "Truth is akin to death," writes Lacan (1966a/1977, p. 145), "and all in all a bit inhuman. We prefer the real." Start searching.

CHAPTER THREE

Phase III: Recovery—The power or failure of the imagination

Accrding to mainstream literature, the conscious decision that dwelling in the past is fruitless inaugurates the third stage. Life must flow forward into a new future. If you are smiling at this vain hope—that the rational brain plus self-aggrandized willpower can put a stop to the grinding grief-machine—I share your dubiousness. Freud's language puts teeth into that marshmallow description, one vague enough to mean almost anything. He also demonstrates that the detached brain has precious little to do with it. The key is that the bereaved is able to imagine a new future approaching like a snow storm.

For Freud, recovery means that the overwhelmed individual, who had psycho-spiritually beaten himself half to death, finally has severed the link and is capable of re-investing in life, and even of forming new ties. In a nutshell, the individual regains the capacities—Freud's hallmarks of maturity—to love and work.

When can I stop grieving?

Of all the ambiguities generated by our de-ritualized culture, top-shelf is the acceptable time to cease grieving ... publicly. When can

41

we say, "It's finished. Get ready world! I'm back." If I desire to date again, for example, or to initiate another intimate partnership, when can I go back into circulation without tongues wagging? Especially if I'm a ... woman! Since I'm back in "circulation", I must be "on the prowl" right? Our culture has no acknowledged time of mourning. In traditional cultures, the period is as rigid and as simple as taking off the black dress of mourning that you had been wearing for a year. In Vietnam, traditionally the widow and her children are prohibited from marrying until three years after the death. Don't hold your breath. In the West it will never be that simple again; a throwback is not even desirable. But a peek at some tradition-bound ways will give us a frame of reference, some realistic parameters, and help to put the matter into a historical and cross-cultural perspective.

The Confucian period of grieving is three years (Waley, 1989, pp. 86; 106). The managed care companies that pay the cost of grief counselling would never hire that guy, would they? Three years! The System case managers typically authorize four sessions (to start with) for clinical psychologists to treat grief reactions. The Jewish community allots one year for the grief process, still a scandal to our quick-fix, outcome-oriented, evidence-based health care system. Within that year, the Jewish mourner socializes minimally. More importantly, the son and daughter have the significant obligation to recite the *Kaddish* for the deceased parent. (One may also opt to say the Kaddish for another loved one.)

> The *Kaddish* is a strong statement of faith; it is moving and emotionally powerful. It is a poetic declaration of belief which echoes from the soul of the Jewish people and therefore has the potential to reflect your deep pain as a mourner (Isaascs and Olidzky, 1991, p. 36).

Moreover, you repeat it at selective intervals, ritualistically. It is an anchor, especially in times when nothing else seems stable. You also recite in a public forum, becoming one with all mourners of your people throughout history. It "helps to move you from the intensity of grief at interment to the less intense emotional mood of the various periods of mourning" (Isaascs and Olidzky, 1991, p. 36). The recitation of the *Kaddish* provides an existential index of progress.

The Jewish people also ritualize the custom of erecting a monument or marker over the grave. Normally, close family and friends unveil the tombstone near the end of the first year. A rabbi may or may not officiate. The ceremony includes the recitation of psalms, brief remarks about the deceased, uncovering and reading aloud the stone's inscription, and reciting the *Kaddish*. The community gathers once more to remember and honour the deceased, and to meditate about the meaning of Life-Death. It signifies that the ritualistic time of mourning is winding down.

"Graduation" is the word that nicely captures these rituals. The individual takes clear and distinct steps in the presence of a community. You are on a path with evident markers. Step by step, bit by bit, chop by chop.

C.S. Lewis writes about the gradual ending of his pining after Joy:

> At the moment I mourned her least, I remembered her best. It was something better than memory: an instantaneous, unanswerable impression. To say it was like a meeting would be going too far … . It was as if the lifting of the sorrow removed a barrier. I remember her better because I have partly got over it. You can't see anything properly while your eyes are blurred with tears (Lewis, 1961/1980, pp. 52–53).

Lewis depicts "mitigation", a levelling and toning down of the whole grief-drama. Mitigation means to mollify, to alleviate, and to reach an even keel. But the curtain does not go down all at once. Nothing about this agonizing adventure, this experiment of Life with itself to create new forms, can go quickly or be hurried. Short-term therapy, if it is ever effective or useful to any besides the HMO that saves money for the System, is useless when it comes to grief. Oh, it will educe some surface modifications, but it facilitates no genuine transformation. Stop and think about it. What do the words "transition", "transformation", or "turning point" mean? Whatever we might agree upon, doubtlessly death is the number one transformer. In Zora Hurston's (1998, p. 84) lovely image, we have had an appointment with Death "that strange being … with-the-square-toes … flashes like a 'glance from God' … comes and bids us to watch and to listen". This Death has changed your life. Does it make any sense to face that creature with square toes with a time-lined and measurable … quick-fix?

Mitigating occurs slowly. It is not forgetting, as Lewis says, but remembering better. You have gotten over it partly, let go a little, and grown past the pain. Now you can prepare for re-investing. Showing us his steps to recovery, Lewis (1961/1980) describes his:

> concern for turning her into an imaginary woman—my ideas, my selected memories, my impressions settling down like snow-flakes when it is going to snow all night ... settling down on the image of her. The real shape will be quite hidden in the end ... Ten seconds of the real .... He would correct this (pp. 20–21).

The distinctions between grief and depression

Freud's (1917e [1915]) essay kills two birds with one stone. He articulates the process of normal mourning and also distinguishes it qualitatively from the grief that does not abate, that hangs on, protracted, unremitting, extreme, excessive, and complicated. Melancholia—what nowadays we term depression. The following table gives a snapshot of the three issues by which Freud distinguishes the two soul-states.

Categories that differentiate depression from normal grief

Depression (*melancholia*)	Grief (*mourning*)
Unconscious	Conscious
Loss of self	Loss of object
Ambivalent	Ambiguous

Conscious

In smooth flowing grief-work that goes to its end, my loss is conscious; I am both aware of what I lost and of its meaning or significance. There are no bones about what is at stake in the loss, the whys and the wherefore of it, or of what I must endure in the face of it. I will deal with the truth and find the courage to transform the loss into—if not a great gain—into something meaningful and endurable.

Unconscious

What does it mean that the loss may be unconscious? Some dear one has just died. What could possibly be more obvious and more consciously harrowing? Here's the rub. I know that I lost and who I lost, but I don't know what I lost in the losing. The significance in some vital way eludes me. Jean-Paul Sartre calls it "bad faith". I know the fact of the loss, its details; but I don't grasp the meaning, the essential significance. By dying or leaving me, the other took to the grave something of me, something from me. I don't know what. "Oh," I say rightly and poignantly, "You took my heart. Give it back, please." But if I am unable to grieve, then how he high-jacked my heart escapes my comprehension. "What power does she still have over me, even from beyond the grave?"

A third party—one's therapist, family member, or friend—eventually sees what is at stake, sees that which was lost in the losing, and thus how my heart got pilfered. Some vital psychological nerve connected me to the deceased or lost object, dependency perhaps, or support, or definition. She had been my veritable right arm. My psychological economy required his validating presence. My rock or pivot is now gone. As depressed, I am empty, poor, and living in a vacuum. Psychically, I lack. I need. I moan and groan. I belittle myself, criticize and complain about myself.

"Splitting", which I will elaborate on in-depth in a subsequent chapter, comes to bear. A part of consciousness splits off from my essential core self and criticizes me. A new structure has been installed in the "I". "The shadow of the object fell upon the ego, and the latter could henceforth be judged by a special agency, as though it were the *forsaken object*" (Freud, 1917e [1915], p. 249). This is the first place in Freud's oeuvre where he names an agency that later he will call *uber-ich* or superego (the over-I, the upper-I). He puts it more prosaically two years later: "A special faculty is slowly formed there [in the 'I'] able to oppose the rest of the ego with the function of observing and criticizing the self and exercising a censorship within the mind [*seele*]; and thus we become aware of as our conscience" (Freud, 1919h, p. 235).

The superego berates and punishes the self. I ooze guilt without shame, with a love that lacks pride. Split, I aim my "love" at the "lost object" and my "hatred" at myself. The complaints against me, Freud teaches, are really plaints against someone else in the legal sense, precisely against the other whom I have lost. I have twisted them, disguised them, and inverted them—just as the dream-work camouflages the dream and jokes tickle with double meanings. Instead of honestly expressing negativity toward the lost or missing object, I build her up, make her better, idealize, idolize, and glorify her. "The ego debases itself and rages against itself" (Freud, 1917e [1915], p. 257). We pronounce ourselves to be scum, but honour our lost Beloved, our fallen Hero or deceased Leader that psychologically stands in the place of the Ego-Ideal/Superego. Maybe he is the Benevolent Father (*Meher Baba*); or she is the Divine Mother.

Matters were never clear, honest, or resolved between me and the other while she was still alive. Now that she is dead, the issues remain obscure. Perhaps both of us had colluded in such a way as to keep the decisive matter veiled. C.G. Jung (1954/1977) describes this as the dynamics of the "container and the contained" (pp. 189–201). We had supported each others' convictions, excuses ... lies. What now? I am alone on the teeter-totter. The other is dead. Western civilization enjoins us, commands us, to honour the deceased. This constitutes one more reason to keep matters obscure or hidden. I live the lie. Still, I am stranded. I launch my protest, not at the appropriate other but at myself. No one commits suicide without first having the desire to kill someone else. Suicide and depression, from Freud's standpoint, result from the convoluted work of falsifying unconsciousness.

Loss in the ego, not of the object

Freud learned very early that psychological meanings are promiscuously convertible. Sadism turns into masochism; the exhibitionist also likes to look; scratch a prude and you find a whore. Nylons stand for the woman (a fetish). Freud, instead of talking about the person or the relationship, uses qualitative algebra, referring to anything and everything that binds us as an "object".

In ultimately successful grieving, the mourner attends to and comes to terms with the lost object. I miss her and all that she meant to me. Thus, bit by bit, I let go of her. In depression, it is a loss within self that bogs down the grief-process and obscures it. It is not what or who I lost, but it is the fact that *I* have lost. The accent falls on the ego. If *I* am preoccupied with myself, it is impossible for me to let go of *her*. Simply characterized, a depressed person is stuck with herself; or he is stuck on himself. I throw a pity-party which I alone attend. I'm the only one who knows what motivates the party in the first place.

Link this with the preceding discussion of conscious–unconscious. Although I can see that I lost and who, nevertheless I cannot see clearly what I have lost in the losing—precisely because I am standing in my own way, blocking my own view. I interfere with grieving and with its getting accomplished.

Ambivalence

The third facet of this differentiated picture between normal grief and depression is also based upon the splitting. The ego splinters and takes itself as a target for emotions that it would prefer to disown, deny, or suppress. This process is more profound than just the projection of emotions. Ambivalence has to do with love–hate, the fundamental stances toward existence. Ambivalence means that the matter is at a passionate level. I aim my hatred at myself; I hold safe, secure, and innocent my love as abiding. That other, whom I would like to kill, is protected from me; instead the superego punishes me. This launching often goes the distance, all the way to suicide. Mostly, it crystallizes into depression. The monkey on my back, the internal saboteur, the assassin, the smug, self-righteous, hypocritical executioner says, "I'm only punishing you for your own good; don't you know that I ... love you?"

The unconscious loss of the meaning of the object is thus smothered within ambivalence. Grief-work, therefore, is jammed from the start. The dynamics of depression take its place. I treat elaborately the "depressive position" more fully in Chapter nine.

Ambiguity: Anticipating the imagination

As opposed to ambivalence, Merleau-Ponty (1964, pp. 96–155) writes, "ambiguity is a phenomenon of maturity". It consists of the awareness that something can be correct from at least two different points of view and about these two I might have a divided heart. Simultaneously, it is the realization that the same person who is kind and generous can also become mean, selfish, and under certain circumstances unbearably cruel. A challenge faces the human lover: I must learn to love and hate the same person at the same time, even if I depend upon him. This acknowledgement reveals the truth. Truth liquidates guilt, especially if we had been lying to self. The alternative is to live with cognitive confusion and emotional ambivalence, a pair that always go hand in glove. The brain is not excluded from the work, but it is not the logical, analytical, abstract act of ratiocination that contributes. It is consciousness as imagination that comes to the rescue. Imagination is the power to de-literalize and to see possibilities necessary to put matters in perspective, gleaning truth. Facing truth promotes clarity and the courage to forgive the imperfect other and thus to tolerate my own flaws and foibles. It fosters the courage to let go. Succinctly, if a loss remains fixed as a self-centred, unconscious and ambivalent soul-state, it cannot be mourned. But using a negative capability, one can see that things are hopeless but can still carry on without lapsing into despair.

Freud's fade-out

How does grief come to an end? We all want to know. If it is not the $64,000 question, maybe it should be. "You'll get over it, in time" is the sage advice we most often receive. What can I say to that? "In time," I ask, "In time for what? Do you mean tomorrow?" And then I laugh, "Tell me what to do about today!"

In this long, arduous work, do we just wear out our grief-garments over-time? Or does not the imagination see something brand new to wear? Freud (1917e [1915]) juggles *energy* and *meaning* and appeals to "reality-testing" to explicate the move of re-investment or re-occupation (p. 255). Like a naturalistic process, he lets grief burn itself out or run out of steam. Clunk! Thud! Ker-plonk! Plop. The loss put the self in a masochistically vulnerable position. The "Upper-I" was employing a sadistic machine to punish the self in service of protecting the hallowed dead loved–hated object and of speaking no ill of the deceased. Freud just lets the libidinal thrust splutter and fizzle until the sadistic chastising engine runs out of gas and simply peters out. Psychological self-flagellation wears me down, Freud surmises. There is a limit to how much one can beat oneself up—albeit that "line" is as peculiar to each of us as our fingerprints. Eventually, we stop punishing ourselves. We quit.

Reality passes its verdict. Dead is dead. The person is gone. Her life is over. The "object" no longer exists ... for me ... in this world. Grief-work, from this perspective, comes to an end for "economic" reasons. Within the libidinal economy of the self-punitive griever, one becomes saturated with psychological self-abuse. In today's lingo, I "give myself a break". Serving the "real", we let go and get on with it. Freud ends with a whimper and not a bang.

Always a master with his concepts, Freud finds a way to support this economic view. He appeals to narcissism, another concept he is always trying to understand. Paul Ricoeur (1977, p. 132) says Freud writes as if narcissism alone terminates grief:

> The 'I', confronted ... with the question whether it shall share the fate [of the lost object], is persuaded by the sum of narcissistic satisfactions it derives from being alive to sever the attachment to the object that has been abolished (Freud, 1917e [1915], p. 255).

He makes it a matter of survival, the cheapest excuse on the intellectual scene, the rationalization given for racial cleansing, illegal invasions, and dropping bombs. Darwin would love it. But is this even the penultimate answer to how we finally end our grief-work? "I've had enough. I accept the heartbreaking truth."

Such an ending shows Freud's blind spot and opens him to the charge that reductionism, materialism, and naturalism stymie his analyses. His suspicious critique of religion and spirituality as cradling the idols in an infantile way, limits his vision. In Life, grief never just fizzes, yields to coping strategies, or vanishes after a superficial cognitive reappraisal. Freud does not even applaud his own conclusion. He notes that this explanation leaves dangling the phenomena under investigation: "In the meantime the existence of the lost object is psychically prolonged" (Freud, 1917e [1915], p. 245). At the end of a clarifying piece of writing, a gem, Freud starts to flounder. The ballgame isn't over yet, and he knows it. We shall see in Chapter eight that Freud lived the protracted agony.

He stopped loving her today

What does George Jones sing?

> He said "I'll love you till I die." She told him, "You'll forget in time." As the years went slowly by, she still preyed upon his mind. Kept her picture on his wall; went half-crazy now and

then. He still loved her through it all, hoping she'd come back
again (Braddock and Putman, 1990).

One might simply fail to get the picture and never see the writing
on the wall. One might never let go of the possibility of a second
chance. I'll get my Princess back, won't I?

"Hope springs eternal," he would say. Stacked on his night table
by his bed were letters from 1962 with each "I love you" underlined
in purple. When I went to see him today, he was dressed for a journey. He wasn't crying today. In fact, it was the first time in many a
moon that I saw him ... smile.

The woman in the song is gone, departed. It makes no difference
why. Maybe she died on him. Or maybe she abandoned him to be with
another man. Maybe she just left in order to be on her own. He's hanging on. And it hasn't resolved with time. In terms of time, it's perpetually 1962. At length, the ultimate change occurs: "He stopped lovin'
her today. They put a wreath upon his door. Soon they'll carry him
away. He stopped loving her today" (Braddock and Putman, 1990).

It turns out that this is not a physical death but a break-up that he
never let ... break. She is still around. Everyone wondered if she'd
made it to the wake. She did. Her presence made it clear. "This time
he's over her for good."

The cliché goes, "It's not over till the fat lady sings." In his inimitable way, Yogi Berra puts it, "It ain't over till it's over." However
you express it, we must grant that sometimes grief does not end ...
until the griever dies.

Doctors of broken hearts

Who writes these lyrics? And who croons these tunes? Are these just
individuals who want to defy reason, reject the sober scientist's findings that dismiss as illusory true and lasting love? Or do they have
genuine insight into the human predicament? In a culture which
privileges cold scientific objectivity, not surprisingly singers of sad
songs refer to themselves as doctors of the broken heart.

If we slacken our absolute convictions, isn't it a value judgement
whether the choice to persist in one's grief is healthy or unhealthy?
But it goes against the grain of the narrow paradigms that dominate
health care nowadays. Only you can decide for you what about this

drama belongs on the natural plane, and what is psycho-spiritual. But in everyday life, never-ending ties are a fact. On this patch of warm earth, it makes sense to invoke forever.

Working without a net

Picture this. You are on a trapeze, swinging on the bar, holding on with two hands. The object is to let go of the bar that you're hanging onto and to take grip of the other one that just this moment swings ever so close to your nose. To accomplish that move you must let go. See the two hands open, free, and groping. Watch then as the hands take hold again. Simple, but not so simple! It takes a risk. There is no net below. You are working without one. Anything can happen ... if you let go of that bar.

Don't we all prefer holding on to the rod with one hand as we reach to secure the other? How many self-help books have you read that advocate taking a free-fall? Don't laugh! The self-help genre fosters getting your "ducks all in a row". It teaches you strategies, tactics, how-to-do it "tricks". But in everyday life, hanging on to one firm structure while trying to latch on to another rarely works. Successful grieving requires making a leap. In "fear and trembling", Kierkegaard tells us, the alternative to suffering is despair—the "sickness unto death". I offer a statement of qualitative algebra to depict the predicament: So blessed to know; so devastating.

Forgiveness

How does grief finish? Can depression be cured? The two questions are one and the same. The authentic resolution to the drama of grieving and the agony of depression is the acceptance of the loved "Other" as fallible and flawed. Radical healing requires forgiveness. Forgiveness heals splits and liquidates ambivalence. Forgiveness is an eye-opener. Forgiveness opens the door to atonement, to making reparation, and to spiritual reconciliation. One does not just fall into forgiveness. It is an achievement which takes imagination, truth, and courage. The capacity to forgive the imperfect "Other" has a wonderful correlate. Insofar as I genuinely forgive and forget whatever offense I have suffered at the hands of the imperfect "Other", to that degree I accept and tolerate my own imperfections and flawed fragility. I can tolerate my own foibles, weakness, my real or merely imagined crimes, and god-awful mistakes. I receive absolution, and I bestow it. Like mercy, forgiveness is twice blest Love need not be—cannot be—perfect. Still I am loved, without deserving it. It comes to me by gift, as a grace. Humility does blossom in the face of this basic realization. I do not forget my lost love or distort her, but I remember her better. Love abides.

Love lingers! Isn't that keeping matters open? No: I accept death and the changes that it has wrought. I must carry on without the dead object—my Beloved—at my side. A chapter of my life has closed. It's over. But I can't say strongly enough that grieving successfully does not mean that all of the energy and meaning that attached me to the missing object must dissipate into some Black Hole. I urge calling a halt to the Western obsession to end grief with haste. The experiential fact of continuing bonds provides the foundation for health and wholesomeness. Successful grief converts into sorrow.

Sorrow and restorative surmounting through the eyes of Kierkegaard

In 1850 Copenhagen, Kierkegaard was expressing the power of sorrow: "Sorrow always contains something more substantial than pain ... . Sorrow does not lie in me, but it lies in the tragedy" (Kierkegaard, 1843b/1971, pp. 229–277). Every study which indicates how bereavement is affected by weather or hair colour, while simultaneously ignoring sorrow, is at least half-empty. To fill the vessel, we must add sorrow to grief-work. In saying that, I am promoting synthesis not just analysis, and pursuing depth-life, not superficial adjustment or coping. These moves draw us into the realm of meanings, not numbers—into the place where Freud also abides.

> I have no right to harden my heart against the pain of life, for I *must* sorrow ... yet neither have I the right to cease to sorrow, for I must sorrow. So it is with love. You have no right to harden yourself against this emotion, for thou *shalt* love (Kierkegaard, 1847/1962, p. 57, original emphasis).

Søren Kierkegaard, in terms of sorrow's profiles, is a breath of fresh air. He weaves together the many dangling strands about the labour of grieving by eschewing a premature pulling of the final knot; instead he ties a flowing bow.

In sorrow, we keep our love alive. Unresolved grief—which converts into depression—hides in guilt the truth of what pertains to the lost object. In sorrow, the issues are undisguised. Sorrow safeguards and preserves the truth about my Beloved and our bond. Living with sorrow is not succumbing to what is too hard or too painful to bear. It differs also from inauthentic resignation, the mere capitulation in weakness. T.S. Eliot (1936c/1963, p. 209) writes: "People change and smile; but the agony abides. Time the destroyer is time the preserver."

Common parlance, alluding to the bible, has it that the truth will make us free; however, it makes us miserable first. Such it is with Kierkegaard, too. Do not construe him as pulling sorrow out of a hat like a magical rabbit to blunt our agony. Rather, picture sorrow knocking on our door. We must summon the courage and resolve to let her in. Teacher and taskmaster, she springs the tap on what memory distorts and hides. She makes us docile. Under her tutelage, we recognize our pain and remember it without being bowled over by it or wallowing in it. It is not in the cards that we would overcome our sorrow. To call for the healing of sorrow is absurd. Instead, the genuine resolution to the grief process is a deepening, a *restorative surmounting*. What do I mean?

When an open wound closes, it leaves a scar. Restorative surmounting converts the psycho-spiritual scar into a mark. Sorrow, to repeat, springs the trap on distorted memories. Whatever had been lost in the death, something has been preserved and something restored. In Nietzsche's oft-cited aphorisms: "What does not kill me makes me stronger"; "When I stand atop my pain, I am a bigger person". Neither Nietzsche nor Kierkegaard pictures us floating like a balloon to this mountain summit where we stand and gloat! No: Sorrow must be sorrowed so that it can endure its own truth. The endurance that sorrow shelters is not resignation; the word that best suits is "serenity". Sorrow and calm fit nicely together. Federico Garcia Lorca describes pain-sorrow as "a little brown girl sitting in the dark, wearing shoes that pinch her heart" (Lorca, 1954/1991, p. xiii). Seeing Freud though Kierkegaard's eyes broadens our picture of grief, lets us see it from the perspectives of both the cellar and the stars.

The power of the imagination

The process of grieving is not linear, but breaks like ocean waves against a rocky shore. At each new surge, one or another phenomenon is salient. At the "moment" of closure, the imagination underlies the important shift. Imagination de-literalizes my loss. Imagination evokes the possible. It disengages the specifics of my pain, casts them in a new light. I see the death-event within the context of my life as a whole, and of the whole human predicament. The imagination gives perspective and scope. It grants a future; it grants freedom.

A passage

Grief, successfully worked through, creates a passage. I will be different now. I have just endured what I thought I could never bear—something that I feared might kill me. I negotiated the crisis. I navigated the Scylla and the Charybdis, even though most of the time I could scarcely see the dangerous cliffs and rocks but only feel them as the sea of pain spat me out and bruised and bloodied my psyche. I could feel all the forces of self-destruction well up within me too, with no awareness of what the boiling-point was, without assurance that I could put the lid on what was bubbling over, and without knowing if—in a case like this—a serviceable lid might even be found. We don't rehearse for grieving, you know, none of us. It's all ad lib, a free-fall.

One more time: an additional Jewish ritual that minimizes the free-fall in the negative sense of a crash landing. On the anniversary of the day of death, a commemoration takes place known as *yahrzeit*. The ritual year has come to an end. The mourner lights a twenty-four hour candle. A service of reading, chanting, and remembering the deceased closes the year. There is no illusion that grief has totally abated. But there is a strong message that the community has done all within human limits to promote closure. Whether or not satisfied with her position, the mourner knows where she stands.

If the construct of "identity" has any existential meaning, then now I have a new one. I am not only different, but stronger. I must take a smidgeon of credit and a peck of pride in the fact that I got the job done, don't I? In spite of almost losing my legs, I am still standing. The matter demanded, at a time when I was feeling like half a man, that I find in myself resources—strength and courage—that I did not know I could access or muster. My legs are not only under me again, they are firm.

Like the Phoenix, I have emerged from the ashes. To borrow Heidegger's statement of qualitative algebra (that comprehends an almost limitless number of human predicaments): "The dreadful has already happened." This is not the way I would have orchestrated this music. Oh, no. But that does not matter now. If it was not this music at this time that I was forced to listen to, then it would have been another tune at another time. Nevertheless, I could not have escaped death. It is simply the lot of humans to meet it. It is life's basic imperative. Authentic grief-work creates a transformation, sometimes a metamorphosis. Religious folk call it a resurrection.

If one indeed lets go of the loss, one finds that the other is not gone—except in a physical sense. I still have the "Other" with me. One does not have to take refuge in any particular religious credo to feel and know that he or she is still with me. Only the stark stubborn hostility to life's spiritual dimensions balks at the lingering presence of the gone other. Only gross naturalism and materialism insists on a total deletion of the other. Dead is dead, doubtlessly. But it is also only the beginning. Love lasts.

Back to the garden

The visit to the cemetery, so potentially helpful working through the grief during the time of intense investment, also plays a powerful role in the transition back to everyday life. The anthropologist G. Holst-Warhaft (2000) writes that a powerful sense of physical proximity takes place when the survivor confronts the deceased via the coffin, the grave site, the very bones or ashes of their gone loved one; it is "a way of drawing closer" (p. 103).

A man visits her grave regularly, she who had given his life meaning. He brings flowers, picks the weeds around her tombstone, and wipes the marble clean. Comes eventually the visit in which he tells her he is finally replacing her.

He talks small talk, first, working his way to telling her what he figures she already knows. He insists that he never wants to hurt her, that he still loves her, but that a radical change signifies that the time is at hand for letting go. Awkwardly and apologetically, he explains that he met by chance a woman who reminds him of her. It was in the library, of all places. "I've been seeing her regularly," he says, "and I told her all about you." Before telling her the gut-wrenching truth, he mumbles that a storm is brewing and the gatekeeper looks miffed because it's past closing time. "I told you I'd love you for always. I never thought today would come, the day I hav' ta' break my promise. See, darling, she can give me now what you can't anymore."

He shuffles over to his Volvo. The car seems to drive to the exit by itself. Through his rear-view mirror, he watches the caretaker close the gate. At the sound of the clang, his tears flow freely. Death has closed the door. How, too, do you and I close it?

What's essential is invisible to the eye

The conversation takes place between Saint-Exupery, the pilot who has landed in the desert in need of repair, and the little prince, his alter-ego. The little prince, who soon will die in order to return to his asteroid, tells Saint-Exupery, who is insisting that he wants the little fellow alive and musically laughing, "The thing that is important is the thing that is not seen" (Saint-Exupery, 1943, p. 70). He gives the pilot the stars. He will be on his star laughing after his death. Whenever Saint-Exupery looks to the heaven, he will experience what his confers will never know. They will see stars from a myriad of perspectives; but he will experience the presence of the absent prince, perpetually. The two of them will "play" a joke on the rest of the world. The imagination wins.

At this "moment" of resolution of grief-work, all the registers we have reflected upon come to bear. The other is alive in my emotions, memories, and imagination. If we truly want to live life as fully as possible, not encased in a tiny bubble, we must factor death, loss, and joy into the equation of our life. Life is given as a lush, temporal tapestry. We have contemporaries, predecessors, and successors. We never see the whole kit and caboodle of those pertinent to our lives. Sure as shooting, we cannot co-exist with them all! It is impossible. Some accompany us on our journey though life; others prepared our way; hopefully, we will build a road to the future for those who will follow us. There is no other way to walk on whatever path we are walking on. It hurts like hell to suffer the inevitable implications of the human predicament. No one can gainsay the grief over those implications that bid us, nay force us, to labour. But the grief-work lets us behold the "more". It helps us to put the miracle of aliveness into perspective. It helps us to be able to tell the inside from the outside and the top from the bottom. It helps us to get an even keel. In *Lies My Father Told Me*, the Rabbi answers the boy's question why Yahweh allows death with the simple statement that Death gives Life its meaning, that nothing would be precious if it lasted forever (Allen, 1975). There came a Hole in the Whole. By crawling into the nothingness, we are able to create a Bigger Whole.

Good grief

Laughter returns. For what seems forever, you thought you would never smile again. You relegated laughter to the zone of gone, almost forgotten. Finally laughing again is enough to make you want to cry. In the chapter on regret, I will come back to humour. Making yourself the butt of the joke is especially vital to escaping from the Black Hole into which you had fallen. I ended a personal episode of grief by writing a song that ended this way: "Good grief ain't no better than bad grief / Bad grief ain't no better than good grief / new grief ain't no better than old grief / and your grief ain't no worse than my grief."

The ongoing presence of the lost object shows in Freud's concept of identification. A young man loses to death his father. Perhaps they had been at loggerheads. As part of growing into manhood, the fellow had rejected his father's way of life. Over what and why does not concern us here. It is common. Grieving takes place. Maybe it is more difficult because of ambivalence pertaining to the rift. The young man gets the job done. He finds peace. In my preferred expression, he forgives his imperfect father and tolerates himself. Time continues its relentless passage. People notice and start to say, "He is more like his father all the time, isn't he?" It will be especially evident if he has a child of his own, and maybe particularly if it is a son. So where is death's sting?

The circle of life …

CHAPTER FOUR

Gone crazy

The previous three chapters focus on the general pattern and typical processes of grieving. The "moment" of mourning elicits extraordinary happenings too, reactions to loss that truly are "once only" and often "one-in-a-row". Life hands the mourner a baton and says, "Go ahead, orchestrate." The individual gets caught up in events seemingly totally out of character. Such episodes are part of Life's run-of-the-mill-madness: indiscretions tinged with vague despair.

One goes on a binge. At the end of the spree, you wake up in a strange place on a strange bed with a strange face on the adjacent pillow. Turns out, fortunately, that you're not pregnant, and you didn't contact any sexually transmitted disease. While under the influence, luckily you made her no false promises. After the week's bender, now you're wearing an orchid tattoo in a place that, thank goodness, your dead beloved will never see. So what? You'll replace the money that got pilfered. Small potatoes, eh! You'll never cross the border into Tijuana again. No more will you engage in unprotected sex. Another drop of tequila might never pass your lips. "I was beside myself," you tell yourself and to anybody who will listen. "What came over me?"

Wild and crazy, these things happen and then pass with minimal consequence. Like nightmares, they visit and dissipate. In the throes of grief, however, we also do horrible things, unthinkable things, things that ripple widely and destroy.

You suffer an injury beyond injury, a wound to the very bone marrow of the soul. Your pride is mangled. You lose face. Darkness descends. In Kierkegaard's true and challenging statement, no matter how low we sink, we can further debase ourselves and more horribly degrade others. Such tales of destruction ought to be told in a portrayal of grief. This chapter mentions a few.

The kite runner

In the wake of losing to death his loving–loved wife, Baba (in *The Kite Runner*) "betrayed someone who would have given his life for him" (Hosseini, 2004, p. 226). He has sex with and impregnates the wife of Ali, his servant. Ali is sterile, so there is no ambiguity about paternity. It is the absolute worst thing an Afghan man can do to another, especially to someone you love. And Baba loves Ali.

The act seems totally out of character. It is something Baba will regret for the rest of his life and will try to atone for with charitable deeds. He personally designs an orphanage for his town and pays out of his own pocket for its construction. But the vile act remains a secret, kept hidden from his lawful and illegitimate sons who never know that they are half-brothers. They grow up together as master and servant, but with a twisted and unbalanced brotherly love. Amir always jealously senses the special affection Baba feels for Hassan; and he is always trying to win his father's respect. The hurtful repetition comes at precisely the "moment" he gains that respect. Amir, in cowardly fashion, betrays his loyal and beloved Hassan. It is not an act, but a failure to act. It is invisible. Amir tells no one. The secret haunts him throughout his life. The treachery shatters both their lives.

Baba's deceptive failure to speak, therefore, doubles and triples his crime, makes it a soul-murder. Even after his death, it will ripple even into the lives of the next generation. In the face of formidable obstacles, Amir will have to take care of Hassan's son. The sins of the father, visited upon the son.

Does not Baba remain a "good" man? He was only trying to punish himself, wasn't he, by lashing out in the original sexual assault? Are not the circumstances mitigating? Who considers, in a "moment" of painful rage, that he is about to kill innocence? Grief, however, does not justify extreme action, and typically the whirlwinds of life swoop up self-punishing behaviour and ensnare it. We humans are a network of relationships. Others are always affected by what the individual does. The act of self-punishment radiates and spills over into the lives of others, unbeknownst and undesired. We inflict hurt. The innocent suffer. Damaged people are dangerous. They hurt themselves. Unwittingly, they hurt others. Cycles of repetition destroy.

We think it's a secret; we spend our life mute about it, suffering in silence. Come the occasions when we consider spilling the beans, unburdening ourselves. The gain seems to outweigh the cost. Or we simply lack the courage. A vicious cycle grinds. I describe in "Vigilance for Life on a Deathwatch" (Chapter five) that only when dying does one finally unburden. Indeed, the phenomena of making a deathbed confession or of someone confessing to the dying person are two more common happenings about which mainstream sociomedical science is unconscionably mute.[2]

Exotica

In Atom Egoyan's (1994) film, *Exotica*, the protagonist reels under the weight of multiple losses. Francis' beloved daughter, Lisa, goes missing. Volunteer searchers, Eric and Christina, meet while combing a grassy knoll. They find the body. Subsequently, they become lovers, but split up at Christina's insistence.

During the murder investigation, the police inform Francis that his wife and brother were having an affair. They make him a prime suspect with doubt regarding paternity the motive. The actual killer, however, is discovered. Francis, in spite of the infidelity, remains with his wife. Three months later, she is killed in a car accident; his brother is in the car, left partly paralyzed.

We can imagine horrors as terrible, but none worse for a man. Grief consumes this ordinary Revenue Canada tax accountant. He muddles through daily life, aided by a nightly routine. He hires Tracy, his niece, the daughter of his perfidious brother, to pretend she is babysitting Lisa, his dead daughter. While Tracy "house sits" and practices on his baby grand piano, he visits *Exotica*, a local strip joint to which he is irresistibly drawn. There he creates a fantasy world, mesmerized while gazing upon Christina, the female who found the dead girl along with Eric. Most significantly, Christina as a teenager had been Lisa's babysitter.

Her act consists of provocatively shedding the little-girl costume she wears onstage. In hours of ritualized table dancing and conversation, she and Francis act out a repetitive drama. Psychologically, the promiscuous overlap sustains and protects them both.

Eric, Christina's ex-lover, is the club's DJ. Nightly, he scrutinizes the strange intimacy between Francis and Christina, insanely jealous of the invisible interweave. Eventually, he manipulates Francis into touching her—an act which Club rules forbid. As soon as Francis lays hands on her, Eric literally throws him down the stairs onto the rain-drenched street.

Banned from the club, Francis blackmails Thomas, a gay pet store owner, whose books he is auditing. Thomas is running an illegal import business raking in $200,000. Thomas enlists Christina's services, wired to record the conversations so that Frank can listen in. She lap dances, but mostly they talk about her and Francis. Eric also tries to set up Thomas to touch Christina. Death, decay, and the fall from grace hang over the convoluted saga like persistent shadows. At the crossroads in the film, Francis, in twisted grief, blurts out to his niece, Tracy, that he did not ask to be born.

The mother

May, the mother, has been a working-class housewife all her life (Michell, 2004). The movie opens with her and her husband (suffering from a heart condition) making a tedious trip to London to visit their son, daughter, and grandchildren. Their daughter-in-law greets them with no warmth. Their son, Bobby, welcomes them with indifference. He is a crack coke yuppie, self-absorbed, and lacking the human touch. Currently, he needs to sell his affluent house because of financial problems.

Paula, the daughter, is the classic "neurotic", an emotional wreck, a self-defeating woman–child who blames everyone else for her woes. She is having an affair with a married man, her brother's friend, Darren, a handyman with an autistic child and—to use USA street jargon to characterize his unreliability—a loser without a pot to piss in. His life centres around coke, weed, booze, and sex with any available and willing woman. He is currently renovating Bobby's white elephant, unaware that his job is almost over.

Before the visit—superficial, awkward, strained and conflicted—might end, May's husband dies of a heart attack. Bobby drives his zombie-like mother back to the matrimonial home in the suburbs. She has fit dutifully under her husband's thumb the entire marriage. He didn't want her to have any friends, for example, so she has none. Contemporary parlance would mock: "Get a life!" She refuses to stay in the house, now a concrete metaphor of the wasted, empty years.

Reluctantly, Bobby brings her back to London. His wife, who can't stand May, goes ballistic. May ends up staying with less successful Paula in her small, cramped flat. Bottom line: she is a built-in babysitter for Paul's young son. She sleeps there, wanders around London during the day, and visits Bobby's house daily because of a growing sexual attraction to Darren.

Paula carries a special big chip on her shoulder for her mother, and randomly lashes out at her. Her relationship with Darren is a blended mess of no trust, mistrust, and distrust. When May accidentally witnesses one of their sexual trysts on the living room floor, the ensuing fight, and then Darren storming off, Paula asks May to confront Darren and ascertain his true intentions.

This shy, dowdy, frumpy, unattractive, newly widowed grandmother past sixty initiates a sexual relationship with her daughter's lover, half her age. Darren complies, anticipating siphoning off her money. The pandering comes to light, because May draws sketches of their sexual acts and leaves the pad lying around. Instead of grieving the death—which would be grief for never having lived—May orchestrates a last gasp symphony of passion that creates crazy music of degradation and contempt.

The summer of '42

At puberty, the days of sand and shovels yield to the mysteries of life. The fledgling adolescent begins to look at the world through new eyes that now seize upon the erotic. Hermie says, "It was like getting a third eye that saw sex and only sex" (Raucher, 1971, p. 6). Night dreams rival daydreams to merit an X-X-X rating. One young male client expressed his malaise saying, "Do you know what's wrong with me, Dr. Alapack? I've got boner worry." Childhood symbols assume double meanings. Playing "ball" translates into "balling" and into a hard on; the throbbing topography of comic character, Sheena the Jungle Queen, "drives a guy mad for a dime" (Raucher, 1971, pp. 28–29).

Oscy, Benjie, and Hermie, "the Terrible Trio," are chronologically fifteen years old, but at very different developmental psychological levels. Benjie is still a baby. When he gawks at the medical ency- clopedia showing picturesque stages to intercourse, he says, "My parents never did that!" The cool dude, Oscy, is at the technical level. He scours the book for instructions about the steps to proficient sexual skills. Hermie's new lust-filled eyes, however, also glimpse what eludes the physicality of Einstein's $E = mc^2$: the One, the Good, the True, the Beautiful, and the possibility of Peace on the planet. Hermie is a dreamer. Soon he will learn that the two phases of the ontological revolution, the Magic and the Tragic, are flip sides of the same coin (Alapack, 2007a, p. 81).

While his friends are playing, Hermie sits gazing into the unknown, into the future. His stare filters through women's underwear hang- ing on the clothesline. Bras and panties wave in the breeze, luring and tantalizing him, making him both restless and hard. When- ever he thinks of Dorothy, however, he sees her as a woman, as a person, and he glimpses the invisible of the visible. Sex-cum-love; love-cum-beauty.

Dorothy and Pete live on the island. They are married. Their love openly shows when they kiss in public and even in the way they look at each other. Hermie marvels at their man–woman inter- actions, understanding enough to understand that he ... doesn't understand. Nonetheless, their love-bond intrigues him more than the mechanics of putting on a condom, figuring out how to cop a feel, or finally getting into that elusive ... hole.

Pete exits the Island in military uniform, off to one of the thea- tres of World War II. Hermie is keenly sensitive that Dorothy is dis- traught and in longing. He gets on speaking and then friendly terms with her by doing errands—even offering to mail the letters that she writes to her man, faithfully.

On the fateful evening, he has dressed up spiffy to visit her. As he approaches, he senses the "foreboding" and feels the "foreshadowing". Knocking on the door and "Hello" are in vain. As he enters the room, "an odd rhythmic scratching" greets his ears. His eyes land on a half-empty bottle of scotch, an empty glass, and an ashtray filled with half-smoked cigarette butts. His call, "Dorothy!" evokes no response. Moving forward and scanning the room, he spots the portable phonograph and the needle making the sound, "sker-ratchety", "sker-ratchety". He also notices Pete smoking a pipe in a photo inscribed with, "All my love forever." Then, from behind the bottle of booze, a "dull yellow ... telegram" assaults his eyes, "cruelly crumpled and then painfully smoothed out ... 'We regret to inform you that your husband ...'" (Raucher, 1971, pp. 254–255).

Dorothy appears and gives a smile of recognition through eyes "damp and red ... with a 'look of lonely vulnerability'" (Raucher, 1971, p. 255). Hermie wants to hold her and "cup her cheeks to his hand", the way his mother used to wipe away his childhood hurts (Raucher, 1971, pp. 254–255). They greet one another and fill the awkward "moment" by sharing a quick exchange about whether she looks "nice" ... under the circumstances.

Hermie has no idea what to say. Dorothy breaks the silence by singing softly, low and sorrowfully. And she puts the record back on. Intuitively, he knows it is "their" song, perhaps the one they fell in love to, a song now that measures "the distance between love and death ... the calculator of impossible separation" (Raucher, 1971, p. 257).

With a housewife's busyness, Dorothy empties the ashtray and tries to scrub clean the filthy soil of ashes, scouring the tray in defiance of the truth. Hermie follows her into the kitchen and says, "I'm sorry." She walks away from the sink to touch this alive and caring boy. Tears trickle down his cheeks. She reaches to catch one on the tip of her finger. Suffering the rest to drip onto her hand, she stakes claim to them because, then and there, she is the "rightful owner of all the tears on earth" (Raucher, 1971, p. 259).

After collecting and letting them all slide off, she puts her head "within the hollow of his shoulder, just to rest ..." The burgeoning man in Hermie emerges. He enfolds her. They find themselves dancing, almost motionless. In the dark shadows of grief, the haze of alcohol, and the swan song of innocence, who can decipher how in the world this music continues to play ... since the needle again has come to the end? And about the lyrics of love circling like silhouettes, touching her and then touching him, who can say between whom

are they swivelling? Only the Universe knows the true names of
these two dancers.

Dorothy looks at Hermie with studied seriousness, fingers his face
like a blind woman groping for what is always beyond reach. Ah,
but she knows him, smiles, gives a little laugh, and tosses her hair
before stretching her "unembarrassed arms" towards him (Raucher,
1971, p. 261). With their kiss, the room spins, "Touch and Whisper"
warm the chill of grief and colour bright its sombre blackness. They
enter the other room. Time stops. The world goes away.

"(F)or it was summer ... and he loved her so. Dorothy, I love you,
Dorothy ... and because it was his first time ... he'd remember it
forever ... in a very special way, Hermie was lost forever" (Raucher,
1971, pp. 262; 264).

The next day, he hears her voice whispering the words to the letter she left him. He tastes and smells every word, as if they were
etched on her skin, as if her legs again were drawing him down.

> *Dear Hermie,*
> *I must go home now, I'm sure*
> *You'll understand. There's so much that*
> *I have to do. I will not try to*
> *explain what happened last night*
> *because I know that, in time, you*
> *will find a proper way in which*
> *to remember it ... .*
>
> *What I will do is remember you,*
> *and I will pray that you be spared*
> *all senseless tragedies. I wish you*
> *good things, Hermie, only good things.*
> > *Always,*
> > Dorothy (Raucher, 1971, pp. 272–273).

He never saw her again.

No dress rehearsal

I repeat my most fundamental presupposition: All we have in life are
"moments". Often, they are "one-in-a-row" and "once only". We act.
A ripple ensues. Sometimes, we have consciously planned our moves

thoroughly, hoping to exercise at least a modicum of control. At other times, our action is purely spontaneous. No doubt, most of what we do falls somewhere in between. Whether our personality style typically dictates our "moments" or the situation steers them, we can say one thing with assurance about our responses in the face of death: we have not rehearsed them. Something will "go down" in a given encounter, things will unfold, and events will transpire. The ongoing and long-term repercussions are beyond our ken and outside of our control. The effects that ripple might surprise, shock, or horrify us.

It only takes an instant: the defiant act of committing adultery with your friend's wife; or an hour: Dorothy and Hermie making tender love; or a few weeks: May and Darren having an affair behind his wife's and her daughter's backs. Clock time be damned! What we participate in or orchestrate might haunt us for a lifetime.

A human lifeline

The major task that looms in the aftermath of a significant death-loss is letting go. How does this transition, or transformation, or de-coupling happen? Remember, a thousand links bind me to the lost object. How do I release, bit by bit? I already have spelled out the psychological issues at stake. Even though I showed the impact of outside realities, such as rituals, music, or the cemetery, still the stages and phases of grief-work smack of the heroic individual getting the job done. Atlas holding up the world ... But, alas, even Atlas needs to shrug. And as often as not, it is actually an interpersonal encounter that jump-starts the process and even shepherds it along. Someone, purposely or unwittingly, extends a helping hand—to name one possible body part. Priests do that, funeral directors, grief counsellors, friends, and family members. I am propelled forward by a human spur that may come randomly, come out of the blue, and right off the wall.

Imagine a screw that needs a driver to loosen it. Imagine a joint that needs to be unhooked. Imagine a way of living that must end so that another might begin. We need a rope, a cable, a bridge across troubled waters. Ron Cornelissen (unpublished manuscript) names this by the enigmatic term, "a cipher". Enigmatic, because the etymological root of the word means "zero" and its main sense is "nothing", "nobody", a "non-entity". But the word also refers to a text written in code, a code in which the letters of a text are replaced with others in some systematic way. By a reversal, Cornelissen makes trite and trivial details elegant. He makes the "little nothing" matter; makes it a lifeline.

Dorothy receives Western Union's fatal telegram and deadens the pain by almost killing a bottle of Scotch whiskey. Who should show up almost immediately but a sensitive and innocent boy, enchanted and enthralled with her? A cipher out of the dark! Making love clips an indelible cable between them fastens a link that will haunt Hermie for the rest of his life. It is also one twist of the tool that helps her to unscrew her attachment to her dead husband. It builds the bridge, too, across which Hermie strides from boyhood to manhood. They are ciphers for one another. Together they build a bridge to span their troubles. Neither will ever forget the "moment".

Crimes of passion

... are fatally outrageous responses to unbearable betrayal, wounded pride, or a broken heart: love or lust murders. The full diapason of mankind kills with love-gone-wrong as the reason. Ordinary men and women of all races, colours, classes, and creeds commit such crimes: the rich and the famous, the poor and unknown, the high and the mighty. An interloper, with his fast talk and money, has shattered my life, high-jacked my dreams, and swiped my sanity. A trespasser, with her peroxide hair and hourglass figure, has trampled my emotional core and pushed me right over the edge. The one I most loved has deceived me. I find out that from the start she has been telling me lies and lying even while telling the truth. Her lips now are babbling, "I never loved you." In a New York minute, you feel like a leper. You feel like a fool. The acid burn of humiliation makes you lose face. Something snaps.

The experience of such destruction is beyond envy, jealousy, or indignation. It is not just a violation; it is the most serious one on the scale of treachery. This act isn't just off the scale that indexes pain; it breaks it. Humiliation drills into the bone marrow of your soul. This is your encounter with pure evil. It will exact the ultimate price. There is no crass consideration of financial gain here, no taint of the marketplace, or of reward: only release of your anguish. As often as not, it turns out horrendously ugly, a bloody murder ... followed by suicide.

Preventive murder: The anticipation of goodbye

A woman begins to grieve the loss of her marriage as soon as she receives her first letter from her husband stationed at Camp Liberation, just outside Baghdad. A daughter starts to mourn the death of her mother when the tests are positive for cancer. Within one's love-situation also, you feel hurt begin to creep. The System isn't even counting, so we do not have a clue about how many murders, suicides, or murder-suicides happen in response to loss or anticipated loss of love. Likewise, we have no stats on who dies of a broken heart. Remember, there is no diagnosis to code the failed living seat of affection. The scientific establishment thinks it is poetic to talk about heartache, a broken heart, or the lovesick blues. The heart is banished to a colourful page in a thick anatomy-physiology text-book. Within narrow Western conceptual paradigms, love is not a 19th-century natural scientific concept. Even those most adept at reducing everything to a measurable designation have not come up with an operational definition of it that pleases everyone. In daily life, however, on the ground and in time, the common man knows that grief motivates killing. And just as a nation justifies its illegal invasion of a sovereign nation by calling it a "preventive war", so too do individuals.

An ounce of prevention

It was the way she kissed you—or didn't kiss you—that make the fear crawl. She actually utters, perhaps, the one word that ends your world: "goodbye". You have long been suspicious. You even know who the other man is because, on the sly, you read her email. Your pride shatters. You shout that it's not over yet because it isn't over for you. You want to hold her close and never let her go. You do go "over" her, forcefully, in what the System calls marital rape. It gets worse. You threaten that she'll never leave the room alive.

What are you going to do to prevent it? Hide the keys to the car? How long can you lock her in your bedroom? You can't keep it up perpetually, can you? Now that's a crazy thought, isn't it, even if you are now ... crazy? You are afraid of what you may do. You hadn't planned on any of this. Thoughts about her evil mind and unkind heart plague you, and about her lack of gratitude for your great love.

Your blood is boiling; your heart is breaking. You will stop her from leaving

Every "preventive war" seals our fate and that of those we battle. Seeking security randomly backfires.

Seduced, defiled, and abandoned

I was naïve, innocent, and trusting. I was green as grass. Dah 'ya get the picture? I was a dewdrop. And I had been preservin' my virginity, saving it for the right one. Then he came to town.

The wayward west wind blew him into Anniston, sure as shootin'. He sang me songs picturing scenes of the big, wide, exotic world. He fed me gypsy lines: "You're purttier than a cherry tree at blossom time." He turned my head every which a-way.

Out of a brown paper bag, he pulled a bottle of wine and grinned. I drank too much of the fruit 'av the vine. It was lethal. The alcohol was lethal too. I got giggly and goofy. He laid me down gently on a blanket ... over green grass ... under the Alabama sun. Then he turned into an octopus. I'd never been touched 'there' before. It sent shock waves all over my body. I was floating! Once I was open and wet, he paid a visit. It hurt at first. He kept a-pumping me, rhythmically and real slow ... until I started to writhe. Then he got like lightening. I was a-lovin' it! Out of my mouth popped, "Jesus, Jesus." Hearing that, he started to bang, roughly, as if he were trying to rivet me ta a patch of hell. It hurt me like the dickens. Then it turned vicious. He pinched my nipples, bit my shoulders, pulled my hair and wrapped his fingers 'round my neck as if choking a chicken. Before you could whistle Dixie, I was nothing but tears, blood, and pain—a fallen woman punished by the pounding, the abuse, and the humiliation.

When he finished, carelessly, he tossed my pride and dignity to the breeze. Trash, I was, litter like the brown bag and the empty bottle strewn on the lawn. He laughed at me, as if I was a fool. "Jesus, Jesus," he mocked, killing my living soul just as he had already defiled the living temple of my body.

I shuffled home, barefoot, my blue cotton sundress soiled and torn. Under the cover of darkness, I snuck into my bedroom, avoidin' mamma. She'd av' questioned me ta death if-in she saw me in my disheveled condition. Daddy would' av whupped me ta within an inch av my life if he knowed what I'd just done. So I just got down on my knees an' prayed ta Jesus. I begged him fer forgiveness. He didn't answer. I knowed he'd never answer me again.

Instead the devil whispered something in ma ear. Shocked, I whispered back, "What?" I could smell him. My whole body just reeked of his now caked man-juice. I was gagging. "What youse saying ta me, Satan?" "Death" was the only word the devil either knowed, or else at that very moment was fixin' ta use. Sniffing the fumes of hell, jism, and death, I puked.

I knew where daddy put up his guns. I knew how to load a pistol. Daddy had taught me how to use it. He told me, "You're good at it, Amy, real good." The gypsy-octopus-devil-man also kept a-moaning, "You're good, babe, ah so good" ... until he came, stopped a-twisting and thrusting ... and went away ... leaving me sobbing sore and a-hurting. So I knowed the Gospel truth: I was "bad". And he was plumb evil. I flushed the toilet, wiped my face, and started walking. I knew where to find him.

I found him. I aimed between his legs first. Then, I shot him between the eyes. If-in he had had a heart, I would 'av pumped the remaining bullets in and filled it with metal. Instead, I just emptied the cylinder by spraying the shots into his hollow chest. "No more gyrating." I heard the word said from somewhere. I don't recollect ever sayin' that word. So's it must'av been the devil expandin' his vocabulary. Gyrating! I chewed on the word. But I didn't know if everything was movin' or standing still.

The police came. I slouched on the couch. I hadn't removed my ripped underpants. I spread my legs. "Take me," I said, "The both av ya. Com'on." Hankering was written all over their faces. I just slid my hands down there, forcin' 'em to look. Then they took me ... away."

Humiliation reverses the blessedness of mercy and forgiveness. It kills the one humiliated ... who, in turn, kills.

Complicated grief

The measurable concept of complicated grief is as close as the professional grief literature comes to addressing such everyday happenings (Neimeyer, 2006). The term balances the usual "one-size-fits-all" approach to grief assessment and treatment.

Complicated grief shows many faces. It might appear either as a complete absence of mourning, as an ongoing inability to express one's normal grief reactions, or as delayed, conflicted, prolonged, unremitting grief. A plethora of factors spur it, including suddenly shocking and seemingly preventable or traumatic death, horrifying deaths by suicide, homicide, or a fatal accident, events that evoke shame, embarrassment, or social stigma, and an intensely ambivalent, or excessive dependent relationship with the lost or dead person. These happenings can provoke an intense cluster of overwhelming feelings: rage, humiliation, or a desire for revenge. It is a moot point whether "gone crazy grief" is of a different ilk from complicated grief or just an extreme form of it. My purpose is to showcase that, in the face of something that rips to shreds the fabric of one's life, grief takes on a twisted hideous face. Sorrow breaks even the best man or woman down.

Confrontation with the shadow archetype

From the perspective of C.G. Jung (1953/1966), the individuals who orchestrate a gone crazy episode are not acting out of character at all because outlandish grief releases my "shadow" side (pp. 96; 233-239). The shadow embodies my underdeveloped, unrealized self. I see it, first, in another person who, in a flash, I detest. Everything about her irritates me or turns me off. I recoil with strong and instantaneous aversion. It is hate at first sight. But I am spooked too. Are we not all initially afraid of our own shadow in the "moment" of facing our greatest weakness or what we most fear about our nature?

The heinous act we commit, therefore, forces us to confront our darkness and weakness, the unrecognized and thus opaque side of ourselves. In the service of wholeness and authenticity, we must come to see … that the villain is me … too. It is a dimension of ourselves that we might never otherwise acknowledge or own, even though we live our lifetime with the shame and humiliation of it.

Facing self

None of us know how we will handle the loss of a loved one, or cope with a serious threat to our love-bond. Facing such boundary situations teaches us something indubitable about self. If the tragedy also breaks my heart, leads me to feel like a lost soul, and fundamentally disrupts the foundation of my world, then my response might be extreme and what I discover about self most deep. The "crime" or "sin" that eventually I commit is a metaphor of self. I am what I do to others.

Getting our hands dirty

What over-arching meaning can we glean from these eccentric, off-beat situations? Otherwise "good" men and "good" women inflict pain and destruction as a result of their grief. We always engender more than we anticipate or realize. What we intend and how it plays out fail to mesh. Jean-Paul Sartre demonstrates in story after story that there is "no exit" from having to decide; we are condemned to freedom. However, there are no guarantees that our choices will not boomerang, and leave us with "dirty hands" (Sartre, 1943/1955).

That is not a phrase of judgement; it is a piece of qualitative algebra. Grief-work would be easy if we were innocent. But we are not perfect, none of us. We are flawed, fragile, and prone to foibles. None of us sport lily-white hands. Our lack-of-innocence is a huge stumbling block to grieving. Concerning sorrows' faces, does not the arrogant, self-righteous, hypocritical literature of medico-science hijack the human heart? The Occident hesitates to admit that it has dirtied its hands. It assumes the high ground. It professes that its saving the world: in Iraq, Afghanistan, Darfur ... History shows the truer picture: two centuries of ugly descent into the horrors of Imperialism and Slavery; the barbarism of Hiroshima; Auschwitz, My Lai; Cambodia, Dresden, Nicaragua, Abu Grahib, Lebanon, July 2006 ...

> We have to acknowledge the wrong we have done to another by our actions or omissions but also the wrong we ourselves did not initiate or foresee, the wrongs done by the government we elect and obey and which never acknowledges the harm done by domestic policies and foreign wars conducted in our name, the wrongs done to children and neighbors and people in far off lands whose ignorance and destitution are maintained by our prosperity ... Here to speak truthfully is imperative (Lingis, 2007, p. 117).

Can I live with my dirty hands?

PART II

THREE CONCRETE STUDIES
ON DEATH IN THE FAMILY

CHAPTER FIVE

Study #1: Vigilance for life on a deathwatch: One mother's dying and death

"The heart's testimony is better than a thousand witnesses."
—Turkish Proverb

Personal roots

How do the roots of my raising pertain to the themes of this book? Prior to any philosophical "choices", upon which existential platform have I stood to see—in the way that I behold—sorrow's profiles? Here comes a snippet about where I came from to help you assess my approach.

I was born and raised in the hard coal or anthracite region of Northeastern Pennsylvania, specifically in Wyoming Valley. The region was a magnet for peoples all over Eastern and Western Europe. They came in droves to work the coal mines. The valley was a melting pot during my formative years. My mother was Polish; my father Croatian. After a drunken driver killed him—when I was three and a half years old, to the day—my grandmother moved her family to Binghamton, New York. But I grew up in the valley, in daily contact with Russian, Ukrainian, Irish, German, Slovak, Scottish, Welsh, English, and Lithuanian ... with Bohunks, Pollocks, Krauts, Litvaks,

Croats, Wasps, Limeys, Spics, and Shamrocks ... with friends and neighbours.

The local radio station, WBAX, named us "The Valley with a Heart". Ours were a hard working people. They manifested all the pettiness of common folk, but all the warmth, too, of big hearted people. They reached to help in times of need. Two major floods devastated the valley. I was in Pittsburgh in 1972, writing my doctoral dissertation when Hurricane Agnes flooded the valley, wrecking havoc. When I visited in the aftermath, I witnessed or heard about the way the locals pitched in, shared what little they had, and took care of each other while waiting for the government's snail-slow response in forking over money for reconstruction. If I had had any doubts, they would have been erased then. It fit: The Valley with a Heart.

For my mother and Aunt Nellie—my two "Good/Bad Mothers"—it was a serious matter of respect and human-Christian duty to attend wakes and funerals of friends and neighbours. Nellie checked the obituary in the daily newspaper and listened to the noon recitals of deaths in the valley on the WBAX. Our modest home waked three family members, and hosted many more after-funeral meals.

At age seventeen, I remember waking up in the middle of the night when my uncle was lying in the casket in our parlour. My tiptoe walk down the creaky stairs preferred not to meet or engage another family member about my late night foray into the room of the dead. I smelled the flowers in the dim-lighted room, but it occurred to me that I was totally unable to distinguish what would be the smell of the flowers, already beginning to whither and decay, from the smell of death. I found my uncle, of course, in the same pose in which I had seen him last night before I retired.

Steve, a mechanic and body repair man by trade, had basically shut down after returning from Burma in the Asian theater of World War II. He didn't speak a lot. He and I rarely spoke. Whenever he would take me with him to American Auto Parts to buy something for a car he was fixing, he'd stop at the local watering hole to down a few. I'd sit on a bar stool nursing a coke or 7-Up, neither of which I was particularly fond of. The regulars would engage me in discussions about sports, always amazed that a little tyke could be so knowledgeable. I would turn the talk to the New York Yankees, the team over whose fate I suffered—until George Steinbrenner made a mockery out of the sport and the team that I loved. During January, we would discuss baseball in what was a vibrant "hot stove" league in those days—before the Super Bowl became capitalistic American's chief religious feast.

You won't be surprised that I smiled, therefore, when I told Steve it was time for an overdue chat. I thanked him for doing his best, given how broken he was, how difficult my Aunt Nellie was to live with, and how little money came into the house. I especially told him that he was a good "father" to my younger brother, Nick, who in my perception had accepted him more as a father-figure than I had. It was simple. It was natural. I even reached to stroke his hand, touching the place where his pinkie was missing, having been chopped off in a mining accident. The cold felt ... warm.

All in all, my mother and Aunt took me to more death-events than any boy—who would rather be playing baseball, football, or reading a book—should have attended. I witnessed many ethnic wakes and funerals. In my adult years, deaths of family members were handled in the same fashion. With the common people, death is as natural a part of life as being born. These grassroots people, with smiles, dreams and oft times petty ways, saved me from exile in the Ivory Tower and from choking on the rot of high-altitude thinking.

Mother's death

Earthlings and death-bound, sooner or later we find ourselves on a parental deathwatch. You're a son or a mother to one; or a daughter with a particular relationship to both parents. Perhaps you're a father. If an old enough parent, maybe blessedly you are a grandparent and part of the most ambivalent-free relationship on the planet. If *your* mother has died, then you can resonate with a descriptive-reflective tale about the portentous event. If she's living still, one question remains: Who will die first? If she should go and you remain, how do you imagine it will transpire? However it might happen, it will tumble the balance within your entire family. In a world of global crises, both natural and man-made, still the primary crisis occurs when a parent or sibling dies—most especially when mamma dies.

On a deathwatch, one's entire network of relationships jostles and collides. Like playing a piece of music, gestalt psychology's principles demonstrate that if one transposes the melody into a different key, you and I are merely treated to beauty that suits the artist's wishes or best fits her voice. But if one changes just one note snap dab in the middle of the work, we lose the original song. It is not the same tune. Likewise, when a family loses one member, the Hole in the Whole opens, and the entire family must re-organize and re-gestalt. In whatever way your particular family's bonds tumble, overlap, crisscross, dovetail—or splinter and divide—that constitutes your story, your song.

It is a truism in the everyday lifeworld that weddings and funerals bring out the best and the worst in families. Expanded psychological awareness about dying and death can foster the best. Instead of only focusing on coping after a significant death and with how to pick up the pieces, we can also heed Heidegger's call to anticipate death's visit. Heidegger does not mean that we so live with the awareness of our inevitable demise that we sit around moping about it, and brooding. Paralyzing preoccupation is as unhealthy and inauthentic as evasion and denial.

Heidegger bids us to advance in thought, imagine our end, live with it, and go forward toward it. Living in truth about all matters of Life-Death promotes calm and resolve. Concerning the structural dynamics of a deathwatch, we can anticipate and influence what in retrospect we eventually come to see. As I demonstrated in Chapter three, the power or failure of the imagination is cardinal in the successful negotiation of grief.

Certain "moments" emerge in life that make the possibility of death more possible, even announce ever so subtly that the impossibility of continuing to live is now probable. In a sane and wholesome way, we can start immediately to deal with dying. A husband relates, "I overheard her talking to an old friend, 'I don't know how to tell him, but it's out of control. He'll be so helpless. I'm starting to feel guilty just imagining the way he will flounder ...'" In that instant, the husband begins to struggle with the realization that his reason for living ... is leaving.

In the narrative that follows, I use the word "vigilance" to refer to being aware and paying attention to what is happening in the aftermath of hearing death's whisper. It is qualitative algebra. Look at the word, please, from the angle that Life has now put us on a deathwatch. How will we endure it, in a daze or by sleepwalking through it? Will we be medicated up the kazoo, or will we be vigilant? Vigilance also serves as a metaphor for altering our Western denial about death and our craziness of trying to beat death at all costs. It also counters our crazier craziness of trying to concoct an anti-aging cocktail so that we might endure endlessly ... in Never, Never Land.

Death is 100% certain; yet it always catches us by surprise. No amount of Heideggerian pleading is going to erase that all-too-human ambiguity. We will slip and slide within the gray zones. We will muffle the soft sounds that assault our ears. We will hum to ourselves the wish that our lying eyes be wrong. But it is also possible to imagine Death's visit, to face it, and thereby optimally to negotiate it when it comes.

Taking inspiration from Kierkegaard and Nietzsche, I searched my own hearthead concerning my mother's dying and death. My self-reflective search co-constitutes the following narrative which I hope you will find tenderly passionate and also touching upon the general core of the phenomenon. By way of anticipation, you must know that my narrative is maximally personal. As a piece of writing, how do I name it? This is not the place to quibble and quarrel with the intellectual status of personal reports, narratives, or autobiography. I do not even want to whip the various horses that are competing in the methodological field of psycho-medico-social science. Insofar as I do relate to these academic disciplines, however, I call my method an existential hermeneutic. Here comes my tale about what might trigger the first family crisis, or the most poignant one: mother's death.

My myth of vigilance

"You should come home, dad, it's time." My daughter loved her grandmother dearly and is no alarmist. The terminal moment was close at hand. Before we got off the phone, I was making travel plans and mentally packing.

Glue perpetually saturated the hyphen that connected my mother and me. No need for Nicole to cement this particular mother–son bond. She just evenly spread the gobs of paste that her grandmother and father had already poured out between them. My daughter spans the bridges that joined the three of us ... translating the mutual love ... flowing in the currents below ... where still water runs deep ... love's upsurge and its drift ... .

Isn't that what the "translator" does? Express the murmur of silent affection between the generations, the music gurgling beneath still waters ... scrape the rust off the handrails that bind together the Earth Mother ... who remained on the common shore ... and the Son who wandered wide ... and far away from home.

Every time I talked with Nicole about Bertha, I felt love swirling and crackling like an electric current. "She loves you, dad. She just doesn't know what to say to some of the things you write to her ... or talk about."

I'm convinced that Nicole had the same effect on my mum whenever she talked about me. "You know how daddy is ... with his books ... and his big words ... and his odd ideas. Lots of times I don't understand him either, Grams ... But he loves you."

At length, Nicole told me. On the night before the final hospitalization, she had helped her Grammy prepare for bed. They chatted in the moments before sleep descended. Sleep: the nightly surrender which rivals the helpless little scream in its power to remind us of our mortal flesh and bone; sleep: an unmistakable whisper of death.

Bertha told Nicole her deepest secrets, her greatest source of guilt and shame. My daughter was only twenty-two at the time, fresh and vibrant, with the grace and élan of the dancer that she was and still is. And she's an emotional sponge, is Nicole, just like her own daughters are today. Sophie: who is always on a mission; a bubbling fountain of ideas; an active volcano of creativity, emotion, and vital magnetism. Sophie: who while engaged with task A shuffles plan B and C on her plate while D is cooking on the back burner. Sophie, a beautiful child who catalyzes equally both children and grown-ups, who feels the feeling of everyone's feelings ... even emotions that are lost in their heads ... who at age three and a half responded, when asked if she misses her grandfather whenever he leaves for work in Norway, "Olivia says 'Where's my grandfather?' *But I don't have to miss him, I love him.*"

Olivia! Ah, she is a light-skinned, blonde-haired, dark-eyed, tiny lethal beauty. A focused laser beam is Olivia. She knows exactly what she wants all the time and wants only that and is receptive to no substitute. Olivia absorbs the vibrations of the entire Universe. At age seventeen months, she zeroes in on the one she wants, grabs your finger, yanks you to stand, and then commands: "Come. Walk." Or else, when she doesn't want to walk anymore, "Try your shoulders, grandfather." Olivia, using the personal pronoun before reaching the ripe old age of fifteen months, says when she wants *you* to pick *her* up in order to snuggle and cuddle her, "*I* hold you ... I hold *you*."

To whom can you tell your darkest secrets, if you can't tell Nicole? Someday I'll be writing that about Sophie and Olivia ... or both.

Did I know? Could I figure it out? The content is of no consequence. What matters is that Bertha broke her inclosing reserve. Bertha who, when I cornered her and pumped her with questions while driving sixty-seven miles an hour on the Pennsylvania Turnpike, clammed up: "I don't know ... I can't remember *that*. I don't even know what you're talking about, Son. Anyway, *I'm taking my secrets with me to my grave*."

Bertha gave her secrets away. Before the final hour, she let them go. She put them into Nicole's heart ... for safe keeping ...

On the night Nicole told me of the conversation, before I started to ... count sheep ... I lay marvelling that the flesh of my flesh had been her privileged listener. And I was supremely glad. Even in the dark, I could see myself grinning from ear to ear.

Nicole never spilled the beans. The words are hers to cherish. I never asked. I dwell in amazement and with gratitude. The *saying*, not the *said* is of utmost importance[2].

Life had been ebbing away for months. Bertha was dying as slowly and painfully as imaginable. Once a chunky woman of Polish stock, she was a bag of bones when I had visited a few weeks earlier. Now, "they" hospitalized her so that "they" could respond immediately to her pain. My cynicism surged. " 'They' know the number of billable days for in-patient treatment. We are approaching the millennium," I muttered to myself. "At stake is corporate profit!" Still, Nicole had said, "Time to hop the plane, Dad!"

One goes because one finds oneself compelled to go, Alphonso Lingis reminds us. We go in response to life's directives, urgencies, and imperatives. I flew ValuJet.

My mother never commented upon my fathering. No surprise. The glue between us wasn't goop or sticky molasses. Endlessly, she would talk about the children, both my brother's and mine. As shamelessly as I now rave on about Soph and Livy, she would

brag about her grandkids, amazed at how beautiful children are ...
and how lively. Whenever she commented on how well they behaved,
it was more lip service than preoccupation. Mostly, she was amused
by their antics, their imaginative expressions, and their precious sin-
gularity. She laughed with them ... far more than she reprimanded.

I never asked, either, "Do you think I'm a good father ... mother?"
... as if unscrewing a jar of honey. It wasn't reticence on my part, or
fear of her disapproval. By the time my kids came into my life ...
bursting with Life ... I was beyond looking to see who was looking
at me, especially as far as my family was concerned. I don't want
to go on record saying that I was immune to the sting of rejection
at the ripe old age of ... thirty. But by then, already I had chosen an
intellectual path that would walk me to the lonesome edge of the
cliff of my profession; would slowly but relentlessly fork away from
the trails blazed by my mentors and teachers; and would separate
from paths safely trodden by my family members and friends. It
would have made nonsense, simultaneously, to crave approval and
recognition.

I can close my eyes anytime to see moments during my life when
I walked around in the hall of mirrors like most others in society,
trying to catch the eye of one *here* ... or one *there*. About my children and me, however, I sought no outside confirmation. What was
"between" each of them and me concerned *us*, pure and simple.
Nobody knows your child better than you do. Nobody knows you
better.

I'll never forget the way Nicole looked at me shortly after her
birth, after the nurses finished with their rigmarole. The "moment"
changed my life. Her wee presence polarized my entire existence.
It was less dramatic with Richie and Boo, but just as powerful and
just as real. I have tried my best to dwell on the arc that continually
swings back and forth between each of them and me; have tried to
focus on the Rainbow under which we play together ... and under
which they sometimes played ... absolutely alone. Only the opinions
of their mothers I let matter. Looking back, I conferred with them too
frequently and in too much detail. That's another story. Another story
would include my awe-fully agonized decisions and dismal failures.

I never asked my mother. But as a father, spontaneously I tell Nicole
the way I see her mothering her girls. Thus far, it's been a cinch. I'm
genuinely proud of her. I hope I'm not invasive when I bubble, and

pray I'm not obnoxious when I write ... very reflectively ... taking care to express myself with the right ... biggest-small words.

To the very day, I was exactly three and a half years old when a drunken driver killed my father, and he gave back to Life the Death he owed it. How do I say it? I lived my entire life without a father? Or, that my life has always nested under the silhouette of Death?

Parallel lines plague my vision as these old eyes see the way Nicole is raising Sophie and Olivia. The bonds I have with my two granddaughters give me fresh insights into my daughter. It is a Chiasma, is it not? We live the overlap, the pervasive inter-twining and the emotional reverberations before thinking about them. While watching my kids with me, I'm sure my mum experienced much the same, even though it never came to words. If Nicole and I ever need someone to clear crud or clutter from the bridge between us, or to sandpaper a rusty rail, it will be Sophie or Olivia ... or both.

Somebody called it "the circle of life". In one's grandfatherly years, who wouldn't come to the point of cherishing ... repetition?

Like singing a lullaby to your Precious, words scarcely matter. Saying something ... anything ... is mandated. The content could be gibberish or word salad. Tone counts and texture: sound and reso-nance ... the music of your voice and its echo. That the eyes meet matters ... and that you touch.

You put your hand in her hand. You caress her arms to spread your warmth, careful not to irritate by rubbing the same spot over and over and over again without pause.

You make fleshy contact, with eyes and hands, and with the mate-riality of words. You hum and whisper, with warm liquid rolling down your cheeks. You flounder. Your words stumble. Your voice breaks. It seems strangely necessary that you trip and totter. This is not something you've rehearsed. There is nothing to accomplish. Nothing rational is happening, and yet it all makes sense.

She is busy dying. She must do it alone. Sometimes it's a snap to die. This one is a chore. She's in labour with this one, with giving birth ... to her very unique death.

On the other side of this deathbed, your daughter is fussing with the sheets and blankets, energetically attentive, oozing care. You are glad. She's better with the chitchat. You take clue from her talking.

She knows the lingo and the code. She sees her Gram regularly. She knows what to say.

An *implicated alien*, you rebound off her. The words ricochet. The gibberish crystallizes as the emotions career. The three of you constitute a living sandwich *here* in this hospital room: your dear dying mother, laying in pain ... in-between your pride and joy ... and you. The image flashes of three Slinky toys, caught within a rhythm, dancing in this antiseptic hospital space ... separate but related.

It feels like sharing a meal. You toss the salad freely, putting air under the ingredients, remembering that you were always the apple of her eye. This is the Last Supper. These are moments that you will never forget.

You glance at your daughter. Such a flame she is! You remember again the unforgettable moment of gazing at her across the delivery room, convinced that she was looking back at you. It transformed your world. Now, it is about to alter again.

Time becomes warped. How could Western man have imagined it is a straight-line? Inaugural and terminal moments collide. *She* is your flesh and blood *there*, dying. And *she* is your flesh and blood *there*, so vibrantly alive. This has never happened before. This will never happen again. Tenderness hovers and floats ... so palpably that it hurts. You have never hurt this way. Nobody ever warned you. You never imagined it. If you could now, you would pour yourself out. That's what it feels like, as if all of you were overflowing. If only you could, you would go ablaze. That's what it feels like, as if in this portentous moment you were a candle that is burning ... flickering brightly ... but burning itself out.

Your brother bounces in with Barbara, your sister-in-law. They are your other dear ones, family members whom you cherish. They are the steadfast ones ... who stayed home, tended the home fires, cut the grass, and shovelled the snow. Nick and Barbara are the salt of the earth. They harbour big hearts too, they do, hearts vulnerable ... hearts always at risk.

Barbara's family's reunion is scheduled that weekend. You insist that they attend. Until now, they have visited the hospital daily, faithfully. You promise to notify them instantly ... if the urgency should become ... urgent.

Nick chimes out, using *his* nickname for *our* mother, "Hey, Mabel, what 'cha been doing while I was gone?"

"*I've been dying*. For Christsakes, what's it look like, Son? I'm dying."

Everybody *almost* laughs. It is truly funny. It is more real than real, and therefore hilarious. Instead, we smile. We look at each other and share a grin so wide that it fills the entire room … acknowledging the humour … and the truth.

What is there to say? Wouldn't anything be babble?

She's working at it, real hard. The strength crowded into her slight bag of bones, as she tosses and moans, boosts every one in the room. She who had been so meek in life, so apparently dependent, is blowing us away with her courage.

Looking back, I wish we had laughed out loud. Methinks she would have laughed, too … at having reminded us to *pay attention* to what was happening … at pricking *our vigilance* so that we would not miss a trick. Probably, her laughter would have goosed the morphine, too, with which "they" were feeding her pain.

You have the premonition it is going to be a very good wake and funeral.

Weddings and funerals bring out the best and the worst in families. A few members were disgruntled during this one. Some people desire the impossible: "water from the moon" is what an ancient Japanese saying names it. They insist on being placed *first*. In this boundary situation, I marvelled at the way Death slices and dices, showing us who will hang together and who will be pulled asunder … Death who puts all of us in *second place*, absolutely.

Barbara, Nick, and I stay in synch throughout the whole ordeal. Certain moments both reinforce the old concrete edifice of our relationships and re-forge new links that I will cherish … for the remains of my Day.

Nicole had to perform one more *bridge-feat* before the post-burial meal was complete. That, too, is another story, more hers than mine. All in all, for the core family … for those of us who rode in the first limousine … on the trip to the cemetery … who made the serious joke, "All roads lead to Centre Moreland … and to a hole in the ground" ... it was an unforgettable time of both *loss* and *celebration*.

At the Requiem Mass, you stand at the pulpit with written notes in your pocket ... in case you need them: You begin, "Anyone who knows Bertha has heard her say: *'It's a great life, if you don't weaken.'*" Instead, you could have spouted gibberish. The crowd in the church came to honour Bertha, a Polish *Pani*. What matters is the *saying*, not the *said*. When you finish with the repetitive phrase, "don't weaken", and look out toward the pews, you can't see a dry eye.

After the funeral we share a lovely meal catered at *Perugino's*. The restaurant proprietors, classmates and friends of Nick and Barb, put out a feast. Outside, in order to recycle the summer humidity, it starts to rain. Inside, we enjoy each other and celebrate, satisfied that we had given Bertha a "good" goodbye, quietly thrilled that she did not die a meaningless death. Someone repeats the Polish adage. *"Cry when they're born; laugh when they die. Cry when they're born; laugh when they* die."

Epistemological presuppositions: Existential-phenomenological hermeneutics

What are the conditions for and the possibilities of knowledge? These questions haunt the entire book, especially since I reject outright the classical ideal of "pure" scientific objectivity[3].

"Hermeneutics" means to interpret from within the circle or spiral of Life. What does it mean that natural science psychology pretends that we are studying human phenomenon by getting distant, staying uninvolved, and not becoming implicated? It is a rational-dualistic trick, leftover baggage from Platonic and Cartesian thinking, leftover wine from the drunk-with-optimism heydays of the 19th-century natural scientific revolution. We are "in" the spiral, not pristine observers of it. We are not in like a square peg in a round hole, nor like a cigarette in a pack, not like hand-in-glove. We are at-one with our world and our lives. The whole kit and caboodle is a Chiasm, intertwined and meshed. Our task as researchers is not to exit the hermeneutic circle so as to study, but to get in it in the right way. We must enter with intellectual awareness—with fore-understanding, fore-sight, and fore-conception—with our heart already attuned (Heidegger, 1927/1962, pp. 194–195). If we are going to make sense of life, we'd better be earnest and we'd better become engaged. Psychology, if it would be a psychological rather than a technical discipline, must enter what Kierkegaard calls a heart-room, must therein form a heart, and then exhibit what Nietzsche refers to as "the heart's genius".

The "existential" methods of Kierkegaard and Nietzsche are the basic nerves that quicken my research. Subjectivity is the gold standard for reaching knowledge. Existential, in this study of my mother's death, indicates radical uniqueness. Comprehending it is best accomplished by someone speaking in the first person singular. Each family member describing my mother's dying would nuance something different, something that particularly struck or impressed them. Indeed, it would make nonsense to collect and collapse data about the death of an anonymous mother. The relevant research questions are "Which mother?"; "As experienced by whom?" Average trends, and nomothetic data, if they ever reveal anything about psychological matters, mean nothing here. But I am not merely substituting an idiographic approach. In what scandalizes conventional, orthodox research, I adopt Heidegger's revolutionary approach to gaining knowledge. I put no gap between what appears to me and what I communicate about it. I assume the existential self-sameness of the disclosing with what is disclosed.

> Knowing is not like a bridge that somehow subsequently connects two existent banks of a stream, but is itself a stream that in its flow first creates the banks and turns them toward each other in a more original way than a bridge ever could (Heidegger, 1954/1987, p. 83).

The fundamental image that depicts my entire approach to research—especially concerning death and sorrow—is the Chiasma. In the beginning is relationship. Life is a promiscuous overlap. Mankind is a network of relationships. As soon as one sees the human predicament this way, the dualism of isolated, detached substances-subjects melts down and volatizes.

I have written from the viewpoint of the oldest son, the first of a new generation. Nobody else could possibly see the "moment" in the way it filters through my subjectivity. I am a "preferred researcher" for this study (Alapack, 1972, p. 257). My narrative scrubs out the stain of pseudo-objectivity of detached, uninvolved, measurement-generated knowledge that our culture privileges. Kierkegaard is adamant. Ignoring subjectivity leads only to abstract information. What one sees depends upon how one sees. Who one is matters. Passion gives perspective and validity to knowledge. Kierkegaard and Nietzsche advocate the deep act of writing in one's blood. One reaches authentic objectivity, not through cold reason, but by being objective about one's subjectivity (Nordentoft, 1972/1978). The heart, holistically not scientifically understood, is the mind ... warmed. The heart and head are ontologically identical. We have known since Aristotle that certain truths are self-evident: "[I]t is undereducated not to have an eye for when it is necessary to look for proof and when this is not necessary" (Heidegger, 1969/1993, p. 449).

By affirming the immediate truth of that to which I have been a direct eyewitness, I am not endorsing a promiscuous intimacy between the disclosing and the disclosed. Kierkegaard's ontological-epistemological principle supports my studies. "Unum noris omnes." If you know one, you know all. All understanding is self-understanding. The deeper one penetrates into one's experience, the more one finds—not an isolated individual—but our common humanity. Of course, balance is required. If we stand too close, we cannot see. There has to be distance. Across a clearing one must see our seeing and what that seeing co-creates. Specifically, I put poetic distance between myself and my story by adopting the "mask" of an insider–outsider, an "implicated alien". My experience should be nothing than what Kierkegaard calls a "vanishing occasion" for you to tap into your own hearthead.

Considerations from the literature

Harold Ivan Smith (2003) canvases the entire ballpark. Mother's death in the most mundane matters, he reminds us, scrambles our schedules, priorities, agendas, and commitments. Too often, it even makes shambles out of our most important and intimate relation-ships. Always, mother's last breath changes you and me.

In Western culture, mother is typically the centre of the family, its primary caretaker (Lazear, 1994). She is the one who observes holiday rituals, shepherds family traditions, remembers special days—such as the birthdays of her children or grandchildren—and organizes their celebrations. Like the keepsakes that she will leave behind, she holds family memories. Her death leaves a massive gap. Family members experience an intense crisis when she departs. More matters are left dangling than are tied together.

It matters little as to our personal chronological age when mother dies; her death is devastating (Myers, 1997). Complex and intense emotions surface, even though there are qualitative differences between the effects of her sudden death versus a slow decline. In the immediate aftermath, the corpse must be disposed of, funeral arrangements made, the last will and testament read, and personal property divided. All the while, lingering and unresolved feeling plague the survivors. What happens so quickly and so spontaneously will bear long-lasting implications for each individual and between and among family members. Concerned friends, for the most part, flounder in talking about the matter, because it cuts too close to the bone (Myers, 1997). They ask, "How is your father taking the loss?" but rarely do they ask how *you* are feeling. As we will see in Chapter seven, it is similar for the sibling when a brother or sister dies.

While discussing the resolution stage of grieving, I stressed that our lost Beloved is gone physically but remains alive in meaning—as long as we keep our heart open. Sinclair Browning (2003) presents dramatic instances of this possibility. He has collected more than 70 stories from a cross-section of daughters whose mothers have died. The stories testify to after-death communication between mothers and daughters. The contact happens in dreams, in vivid daytime impressions, or via the presence of certain special objects—keepsakes—and even the simple matter of finally getting one of mum's cooking recipes down pat. Browning's essential message is that whatever had been the relationship between the mother and daughter in life, this after-life communication comforts the surviving women. His evidence throws into a different stratosphere the debate about continuing bonds. He offers penultimate proof of the incredible impact of a mother's death: the reach of longing and the infinite-spiritual dimension to grief so hard for Western materialistic culture to fathom or swallow.

The classic account of the death vigil is Simone de Beauvoir's (1964/1965) *A Very Easy Death*. She records the four week post-operative timeframe within which her 78-year-old mother is dying of cancer. Simone is superbly reflective about the theme, and her ironic title deliberately alerts us to its inherent ambiguities. She pitilessly exposes the raw nerves of her complexly conflicted bond to her mother, expresses the shock of seeing her mother's nakedness, and reveals the unexpectedly pitiable surges of love and hate at the bedside.

> When my father died I did not cry at all. I had said to my sister, "It will be the same for Maman." I had understood all my sorrows up until that night: even when they flowed over my head I recognized myself in them. This time my despair escaped from my control: someone other than myself was weeping (De Beauvoir, 1964/1965, p. 31).

De Beauvoir perceives that her dying mother undergoes remarkable, growth-filled, changes in her way of relating to others. Eventually, this brilliant woman who refers to herself as a "dutiful" daughter, writes: "I came to like this woman who was dying" (De Beauvoir, 1964/1965, p. 76).

Simone also unmasks the humiliation of the dying patient. The events occur in 1963, in a historical time before our modern palliative care. Since then, our capacity to meet challenges in health matters has progressed significantly. Elisabeth Kübler-Ross (1970), for example, has revolutionized the System's approach to dying. Her pioneering research provokes thinking and opens hearts. Kübler-Ross has promoted transparency, honest communication, and the awareness of the rights of the dying individual. Nowadays, we feel we control symptoms adequately. We are convinced that we possess skills in communicating with patients sensitively and with clarity. We prefer to think that the medical profession no longer simply exercises license to perform its duties arrogantly. We are cognizant of the tension between disclosing to the patient the true diagnosis and practicing deceptive collusions between physicians and the families. We refuse to believe that the hospital can be equally a cathedral of the living and a house of lies about dying and death.

However, the very best lessons we learn from *A Very Easy Death* is the easy deception practiced by the individual and the System. De Beauvoir alleges that bourgeoisie ethics ride roughshod over the human touch. One can find elsewhere as harsh, but not harsher, complaints and criticisms about the politics of patient-betrayal. She rails that a conspiracy of silence hides the truth from her mother. The doctors deceived the dying woman. Simone expresses her own guilt and disgust that she was an accomplice. She did not refuse to play the game—to cite the phrase with which her friend Albert Camus starts his novel, L' Etranger (Camus, 1957). No: De Beauvoir pretended until the bitter end. What Simone shows us, the readers, is more ironical than her book's ironic title. Her well-articulated and well-written text oozes the truth: Maman KNEW that she was dying. Collusion with the family's evasiveness and the medical lies consti-tuted a major part of her burden. It was acute, Simone's betrayal.

My mother, Bertha Halas Alapack, died on 23 June, 1994; Ruth De Vizia, my mother-in-law, whose death is the theme of the next chapter died in June 1976. My beloved sister-in-law, Barbara—who you met in my myth of vigilance—died in June 2009. I was an ocean away, and not witness to her final days. Therefore, I do not know with blood-certainty if our health care system has transcended the atrocities that de Beauvoir unmasks and that I lived through with my mother, Mother-in-law, and my Aunt Nellie. Are the issues still raw? Provoke a debate over euthanasia in almost any gathering, and you will be listening to the fire crackle whilst watching the sparks fly.

Death: Natural or unnatural

De Beauvoir's raw recording of this momentous four week inter-lude in her life is peerless. We smile at her wit, ache with the pain, hers and her mother's. Our blood boils, too, at the reduction of a human life to an interesting experiment. Nevertheless, I have a bone to pick with de Beauvoir. She ends her moving account philosophically:

> You die from *something* … There is no such thing as a natural death: nothing that happens to a man is ever natural, since his presence calls the world into question. All men must die: but for every man his death is an accident and, even if he knows it and consents to it, an unjustifiable violation (De Beauvoir, 1964/1965, pp. 105–106, original emphasis).

My standpoint is 100% otherwise. We die of life. Death is Life's first and most fundamental imperative. *The Blind Owl* affirms, "Only Death never lies" (Hedayat, 1957/1997, p. 83). Death does not violate, it comes; it visits. Nothing in life is an "accident".

Gleanings from the parable

I eschew the possibility of picking apart analytically my own myth. However, general reflections upon it are in order. The "hour" of death and its aftermath is, above all, a family affair. A thorough-going, integrated, and comprehensive picture of mum's death must acknowledge contemporaries, predecessors, and successors. We die alone. It is the quintessential human act. No one can "pinch hit" for us. Our dying is our most personal "decision", our own most "moment". Death, however, also weaves a tangled web of relationships. Who dies? And who survives? I focus upon the family in a thorough-going, holistic way. Surviving my death will be my wife, my children, my parents, my siblings, my friends and colleagues— or the "stranger" at my wake (Alapack, 2008). This cast of characters comprises the ground upon which the dead person forms the figure. Nobody has the power to erase them.

Into "Vigilance", I truck four generations, spanning the central figure in the drama, my mother, to my father—who died when I was a young child—to my brother and his wife, to me, to my children, and thence to my grandchildren. This large cast of characters, each one relevant, comes to roost on a deathwatch. An entire family is undergoing an event that will render impossible its former way of conducting itself.

Although I jotted down journal entries at the actual time of my mother's death, I was not impelled to write my narrative until Nicole, my daughter, became mother to Sophie and Olivia. One might dig within my psychological make-up or biographical predicament for reasons for that delay, but they would be of little relevance. I watched the wagon wheel of life make many rotations. It seasoned me, disciplined me. The spontaneity of the writing, its untamed sense of control, is based upon that platform.

It is dubious that anyone would find significant or interesting the leaden particulars of my myth. Hopefully, I do not excessively suffocate the reader such that I obscure what is beyond my own conscious experience.

As I Lay Dying is William Faulkner's classically precious novel about a mother's death and its aftermath (Faulkner, 1987). He tells the story through the eyes of each and every one of the characters, one by one—including the dead woman. He invites the reader now to see it this way, and then to see it as another person sees it. We have no evidence that William Faulkner was making a theoretical statement about the best way to showcase a mother's demise. Intuitively, his artistic genius makes us listen to the various voices, and thereby he drags us along the journey to its climax. If the hilarity and significance of the repeated phrase, "My mother's not a fish," does not "click" with some reader, then she or he has not been paying attention with ... vigilance. And I would wager that, if nothing else, my myth shows that vigilance is demanded.

"Vigilance" exemplifies death's many interpersonal, familial, social connecting bonds. In this part of the book, I simply offer concrete studies, addressing the individual's sorrow-filled heart, and particularly accenting the over-arching presence of the family. In this section, I start with my mother's death. In Chapter seven, I will unfold the predicament of a sibling in grief. Now turn the page to hear about the innocent predicament of the child.

CHAPTER SIX

Study #2: The first talk to one's child about death

"When Nana died" (Alapack, 2001b; 2005b; 2006a) is an intimate study. It is a triple first: my first conversation about death ... with my first child ... whom death was visiting for the first time. Nicole, my beloved daughter, was four years two months old at the time of this first "appointment". Ruth, her Nana, her mother's mother, died of cancer. Since this death also mattered fiercely to me, the universe scheduled me an appointment. About this "imperative moment", I feign no neutrality or disinterest. I am a living witness. Coiled within the spiral of events, I never pretend to stand outside them. *The data itself is the story.* My narrative hides nothing. Its warmth and transparency showcase Aristotle's affirmation: one is wise to seek no proof about what is self-evidently true. Like "Vigilance", this story is existential, but not a myth or an interpretative story. I wear no mask of an "implicated alien", not by a long shot! Here comes an unvarnished account of a fragile father, flying by the seat of his pants, reflectively highlighting its sense and drawing from it general psychological insights.

Brief context

When Ruth died, Nicole and I talked on the nights before her wake and after the funeral. In my flawed way, I met her questions, spontaneous utterances, and concerns. Immediately after she fell asleep, I jotted down our chats. My notes comprise the raw data and record of this report. I am holding the two now-faded-to-yellow and ear-bent pages written in red pen. They are my original notes of our conversations. You can see them anytime you care to. Cradling my precious treasure, I tell my story.

The first conversation: The night before the wake

Picture this scene. It is night time. A father is putting his little girl to bed. He has just finished singing to her ... her lullabies. She has exhausted all her "tricks" to stall the moment when her eyes should close. She has negotiated the last "one-last-time" before surrendering her head to the pillow and drifting into sleep. Instead, she asks an innocent, albeit pressing, question. Daughter and father begin to talk.

When Nana died

> *"Daddy, where's nana?"*
> *"She's with God, Nicole, like mommy and Lucy told you."*
> *"How is she going to be at the funeral if she's with God?"*
> *"Honey, it's the pretend nana that's gonna be at the wake and funeral. We'll see her corpse in the casket."*
> *"What's a casket, daddy?"*
> *"A casket is like a long box, except it's shiny, and has silky material inside it. Nana's corpse will be in the casket, but the corpse isn't your real nana. It won't even look like her. The real nana, nana with the light in her eyes, who smiles and talks to you, is with God."*
> *"How did she get there, daddy?"*
> *"She died. That's what it means 'to die'. God takes the light out of your eyes, and leaves a corpse."*
> *"How does God do it?"*
> *"That's God's secret. The only way we know is to die. Nana knows how because she died. We haven't died, so we don't know."*
> *"Don't the doctors know?"*

"No, the doctors only think they know the reasons nana died. But they don't know how God
took the light from her eyes with him."

"Will God take everyone?

"Yes, Nicole. We all die."

(Pause) "Then nana must be with the angels. They know about God and they are happy."

"Nana's just like an angel now. She's happy. Her feet aren't swollen any more and she doesn't have to have her bandages changed either."

"Daddy, I'd like to see the real nana again."

"I would too, honey." (By now, my eyes were tear-filled.) "But we won't until we die. That's the way things happen."

(Pause—as if she were stretching.) "If Jesus died and came back to life, how come nana can't?"

"She did, Nicole. The light in her eyes is alive with God. The real nana did come to life with God."

"But not the pretend nana?"

"No, not the pretend nana. Not her corpse."

"How come, daddy?"

"That's God's secret. We'll know when we die."

"Good night, daddy."

Fragments of conversation: During and after the wake

Ruth was waked at a funeral parlour in Wilkes-Barre, Pennsylvania in both the late morning and early evening. We, the immediate family, visited before the morning public viewing. I approached the casket holding Nicole. Her mother, Ann Marie, knelt at the casket and began to cry.

Saying there was no resemblance between Ruth and the hideous corpse sounds ridiculously obvious. Ann Marie quickly began to comment about flaws in the undertaker's dressing of the body. Almost immediately, Nicole said, "Daddy, Nana looks like a dummy." Our child's innocent words touched all nerves of grief. The moment was tenderly sorrowful. I was glad I had at least anticipated the difference between nana, warm-eyed even when shrunken to a veritable bag of bones, and the absent-eyed corpse—the "pretend" nana.

When I put Nicole down, she alternated between running away from the casket and then running back to her mother or me.

I remember a protracted interval between the time we paid our respects and the coming of condolence visitors.

When my Aunt Nellie and mother arrived, whom Nicole called "Grammy", she hugged them and then continued running back and forth. Nellie said, "Stop running around like a rambunctious boy without a tassel, you little piss-pot. Sit down and be still." Simply, but with anger-tinged authority, I said, "Leave her alone, Nellie! Her nana is dead. And she's a ... girl ... who I allow to express herself anyway she wants to." Uncharacteristically, with no further debate, these few words sufficed to silence my otherwise irrepressible Aunt.

At one point, Nicole came to me and said, "Nana looks too long." I picked her up, walked to the casket, and pulled down the blanket so that she could see where the corpse began and ended. "There's nana," I said. "That's nana." she replied. We shared a smile. I set her down and off she pranced.

After the first viewing, Ann Marie went to lunch with family and friends. On the way to my mother and Aunt's nearby home, Nicole asked me from her car seat:

"How is Nana going to sleep in that casket, Daddy?"
"Remember, it's the pretend nana in the casket. It's just a corpse. A corpse is a dummy. It doesn't sleep."
Then, using her 'bossy' tone of voice she pronounced,
"Grammies are better than nanas."
"Why, honey?" I asked, grasping her meaning but not wanting to assume.
"Nanas get sick and stuff."
"Are you mad that Nana died and left you?"
"Yes Daddy."

Spontaneously, I began talking about life as a dynamic flow of predecessors, contemporaries, and successors. "Honey, some people live before us—like your grandfathers. Nana died when we are still living; babies will be born after we die. That's the way life goes. Your Nana and your Grammy buy you toys and clothes, and they play with you, and take you to the park. They both ..." (In my notes, I never finished that sentence. I probably repeated that they both love her very much.) When Nicole said nothing more, I terminated my ... mini-lecture. Regarding recollections of the second viewing, I have no jottings.

The last conversation: At bedtime after the funeral

Nicole attended the funeral mass and funeral. I have only notes about the conversation at bedtime.

> *"What was Nana wearing when she died?"*
> *"A hospital gown, I think."*
> *"Was she wearing slippers?"*
> *"I don't know, Nicole. Let's ask mommy."*
> I yelled, *"Amer, did your mother have slippers on when she died?"*
> *"No, her feet were too swollen."*
> *"Nicole, are we ever silly! We forgot that nana's feet were swollen. She didn't have slippers on."*
> *"How come she had blue ones on in the casket?"*

Obviously, Nicole had perceived that the corpse was shoed at the time I pulled down the blanket so that she could see the relative proportions between nana and the casket.

> *"The corpse wasn't swollen. So they put nana's favorite slippers on for burial."*
> *"Did they bury the slippers?"*
> *"Yep, just like they buried the pillows of flowers that you, Tania and JoJo [her cousins] got*
> *for nana's wake."*
> *"Oh." (A long pause.)*
> *"Daddy, when I look through blankie, I can see nana and grandfather and all the people in heaven." ["Blankie" is what D.W. Winnicott names a "transitional object".]*
> *"That's good, honey," (I said through tearful eyes.) "Honey, that's really great. Now, go to sleep."*
> *"OK, daddy. Cover me." ["Cover me" was her phrase for asking her mother or me to massage her back.] "Cover me."*

The ripening

For 12 years, I put my notes into cold storage. I waited until Nicole was 16 years old before I read to her the two pieces of paper. We were sitting in my Chevy van in Kingston, Pennsylvania. She cried. I cried. We hugged. It was a warm moment. Then I put the text away again.

Relentlessly turns the wheel of life. On 8 August, 1999, Nicole gave birth to Sophie Elizabeth Stasio. By invitation of Professor Rex van Vuuren, later that autumn I travelled to Pretoria, South Africa to teach a doctoral clinical course, "Life-Spiral Development". A special chemistry developed between the students of this group and me. Rex had hand-picked a group of bright and very human individuals. They were already ripened clinicians, and therefore privileged listeners to what I would say. Against the backdrop of my more reserved students in Norway, I was motivated to pull out the "waiting" pages. Besides, I was a fledgling grandfather now. I decided to share with my South African students the tale of Nana and Nicole.

Twenty-five years after the original death-event, on 1 July, 2001, Nicole delivered Olivia Philomenia Stasio. My two granddaughters' four grandparents are all still living. Therefore, Sophie and Olivia will likely first face a significant death when the first of the four of us dies. For me, the time is ripe to present my tale. First and foremost, I write it for the eyes of Nicole and Dean, my son-in-law. Someday, they will have the awe-full privilege of conversing with their precious girls about death. Psychological research and writing should concern not theoretical gobbedly-gook and methodological dribble drabble, but raw, irrepressible Life.

Discussion

To repeat, "When Nana Dies" requires no interpretation. It is transparent, as plain as the nose on your face. Analyzing it would be like pulling the petals off a rose, one by one, to try to show the essence of the flower. I will not so indulge. I offer instead my reflections on the implications of what I learned while living through this "visit".

What can I say about such a conversation? What general ideas can I express about the "moment" to inform the nearly 100% of the population of readers who have been or will be in a position to talk with a child about death? How do I interface what I learned from the experience with the "advice" given in the mainstream literature?

C.G. Jung spoke about his experiences with archetypes, especially his anima, with a conviction beyond all shadow of a doubt. Nietzsche, however, reminds us that the difference between a conviction and a lie can be as thin as a grey hair from one's balding head. Therefore, I take a softer stand than Jung. There is no better evidence, nevertheless, than what you learn while speaking with your four-year old daughter, totally openly, spontaneously, and honestly ... in the dark that precedes sleep ... when time stops and, as T.S. Eliot (1936c/1963, p. 206) puts it, "the past is all deception and the future futureless ... and a lifetime is burning in every moment". If some other type of evidence would compel you more, then the following passionate reflections are not your cup of tea.

1) Fidelity to the relationship in the moment
You are talking to your child, whom you know better than anyone or anything. Whatever happens, trust the intimate living space between you. Whatever comes up, out of the blue, off the wall, or from whatever corners of her innocent soul, be your regular self. Whatever she asks, answer out of the total context of your shared lives. The two of you have your "way" together. Let it rule as usual. Let it dominate this "moment".

To name my chats with Nicole spontaneous and surprise-riddled does not even come close to the way I experienced them. I did not expect the words that came out of her mouth, nor could I anticipate what she was going to ask next; and I did not plan my responses. Such raw unrehearsed dialogue, however, is no idiosyncratic happening or mere personal quirk of our relationship. A free fall is the optimal way of holding such tender conversations.

This is truly a singular and unprecedented interaction that lacks time for delay or a reflective pause before giving the "right" or "wise" answer. Such "moments" quickly transmute into a lively personal exchange, or else vanish into the realm of missed chances (Lacan, 1966c/1977). It lapses into the unconscious, gone, but not forgotten, apt to return in disruptive ways.

Music is playing. You are not composer or conductor. You are the musical instrument. You must follow the melody and avoid all false notes. Fidelity to the immediate process, the multi-level exchange taking place between your child and you, transforms the "moment" into a significant episode and memorable encounter that contributes to cultivating a deep, rich, warm child–parent bond.

2) *Value-infested dialogue*
When Ruth died, I was teaching a summer course in Waterloo, Ontario, Canada. Almost immediately, I drove the 100 miles to Buffalo, New York. By the time I scooped Nicole into my arms, hugged her, and planted a peck of kisses, she already knew about the death.

Anticipating that she would spend most of the time with me during the next few important days, immediately I asked her mother what she had told our daughter. Above all, I did not want to contradict what my little girl already understood. Ann Marie had used the Christian viewpoint that Nana was with God in heaven. I oriented and co-created my ongoing responses on the basis of that explanation.

What is significant about our God-talk? The question is pivotal concerning the outlook of my entire book. At base, it is relevant to Nicole and me. In the "moment" in which it took place, I was circling within the orbit holding together my daughter and me. Nicole is all I was concerned about. However, in sharing it with you, I disclaim that I am an evangelist proselytizing you, or a card-carrying member privileging a particular religious explanation. The question rests on another one: Is there a difference between telling a child a "fairy tale" in the face of death, and tapping into a mytho-poetic or religious Vision, especially insofar as within that Vision shines all the particulars of one's socio-cultural-ethnic identity? I allege that a difference there is.

To grasp death in an honest and authentic way, the child does not need a fairy tale, not in the sense of an unreal picture filled with pure fantasy images, vain hopes—in a word: lies. When one wants to shield their child from the hurt that that child is experiencing, and feels at a loss to handle the emotional situation, it is easy to resort to a fairy tale in the pejorative sense. I prefer to banish from death-talk such fairy tales linked to fear, awkwardness, or ideology. Neither a religious nor a secular ideology can cut the mustard. What is the difference between an angel and money? Pin your hope exclusively on either, and you are on your way to La-La Land. The child suffering her first loss must feel the sting and the weight of ABSENCE; she must also feel the wonder of lingering PRESENCE. These are the values I am trying to preserve. Both-and. Not either-or ... or neither-nor. There truth abides.

It is a fairy tale to say that nothing survives death just as much as it would be vain to promise the little one the false consolation that nana will hug her again on the "other side" some day. Fanatic religious thinking, naturalism, and cocksure atheism leave a remainder. In this matter, as in the politics of Turkey or the USA, how does the individual or the nation balance secularism with faith? Myths, and especially poetico-religious myths, historically have addressed death and mourning. We are back to the quandary which, like a shadow, trails modern bereavement. We have no rituals or myths anymore; we have instead slogans, sound-bites, inframercials and SPAM. "Shop till you drop" does not cradle a mythology. Each of us must decide for self which words are empty and which full.

You miss the essential point of our talk if you conclude that I "mouth" a Christian theological vocabulary. One's personal vision or belief-system always grounds such talks. No matter what or how we say it, the conversation is value-infested and value-laden. We are condemned to ooze our ultimate values, the ones we live by and, perhaps, for which we would die. You and I believe in something, even if it is only the meaningless void of power ... or money. Our child will absorb whatever we radiate, consciously and less than consciously.

Values always shine forth when professionals write about grief. For example, Edgar N. Jackson (1983), whose work on children and grief has gone through multiple editions over four decades, infects the situation with secular values, specifically the values of medical homeostasis and pragmatic behavioural adjustment (pp. 52; 63: 75). Under the guise of helping the child cope, he writes a materialistic fairy tale:

> If children learn that death is natural for the aged but unnatural for the young, they have gained a resource for learning caution and valuing health; Granddaddy became old and his body had aches and pains and he was uncomfortable in it ... His body did not suit him anymore so he moved out of it; In India, it has long

> been the practice to have a ceremonial burning of the body that
> is no longer needed (Jackson, 1983, p. 75).

I appeal to Nietzsche again. The difference between a conviction and a lie is nada, zilch. Apparently, the above statement reflects Jackson's conviction. It is not only misguided, but mendacious. We tell a fairy tale either by telling our child that Grandfather is asleep not dead, and equally by saying that his body got tired, broke down, and he moved out of it. Death, in truth, is equally natural and equally possible for all ages. Jackson is just exchanging an old lie for a new one. He makes the common mistake of making science the new religion. Whenever my aching body calls it quits—let me be clear in advance—I am going to die, not change my address.

3) Originating speech

A child talks when she needs to, when for her the time is ripe. She initiates at the *kairos*, the right time. Once the child begins and the adult responds, the conversation should flow naturally. Originating speech is preferable to recipes, formulae or the party line of constituted speech. Several times, words coming out of my own mouth surprised me. I had to dig deep and later reflect to discover their over-arching significance.

This dynamic-structure is not peculiar to the relationship between my daughter and me. One cannot prepare or pre-plan such unprecedented conversations. Moreover, "canned speech" outside of and extrinsic to the momentary flow would ring false. Better to bluster and babble spontaneously, authentically, in tune with your emotions. Death, a blow out of the dark, creates a bloody mess. That daddy flounders is fine; no cause for alarm. The child has already felt the slashing of the twisted and convoluted chords of the circumstances of this death. Your raw emotions and genuine ignorance express existential chaos, thoroughly congruent with what your little girl has already registered. Truth comes as no shock to her system.

Instead of valuing flawed, fragile, human vulnerability, Jackson advocates self-righteousness. "Children are apt to be startled at first when they see an adult cry. It may shatter their idea of adult superiority ... Little children are confused when a parent cannot meet a crisis with complete mastery" (Jackson, 1983, pp. 18–19).

The opposite is true. One cannot even dignify such statements by calling them fairly tales! They are bald face lies.

Maria Trozzi (1999), renowned for her involvement in the acclaimed "Good Grief Program" in Boston in 1999, has attempted to stamp out the pernicious viewpoint that death is not a part of living, and that children do not mourn, and that we should shield them from the truth about loss. Unconscionably, she calls such statements, "myths", thus showing the typical medico-scientific intellectual myopia about embodiments of deep cultural wisdom. Moreover, she repeats the bereavement literature's desire to depict grown-ups with an aura of superiority when she says it is a major function of parents and caregivers "to be role models of healthy mourning" (pp. 6; 11). Is not that statement smug? Truth be told, our children show us as much as we teach them about mourning. Grown-ups would contribute a lot more if they would get off their high-horse and sit on the floor where they might be eye-level with the child.

Even stronger! A parent who must posture as "perfect" perforce performs as a mental-moral bully. The child does not need a superior parent, but a loving one. She benefits most from interaction with a parent challenged and humbled by life. Indeed, the assumption of the mainstream, namely that the adult's task is unilaterally giving to the child, spoils any attempt to help. It boomerangs. The child needs to know and feel that she is giving back to her parents, that the relationship is what optimally it should be: a two-way street. The only way to bring up a child is to be brought up by her. In this inaugural event of death, you and your precious one are in the same boat, floating down the same river. Don't pretend that you are on the shore watching and directing. Share experiences with your wee one. Share life. In this case Life … about Death. Share the richness of emotional meaning and the logic of the heart. It's like breast-feeding: the infant needs nourishment; the mother needs relief; they both need tender closeness. It's personal, eyeball-to-eyeball equality in spite of contingent inequalities. The gift given is the gift received.

4) Relational speaking
Everything between Nicole and I happened at the relational level. Her questions, the words we shared, and my responses, make logical sense. However, the logic of the heart runs deeper. The full meaning roots in our bond. Talk with a young child about death is never how

the professor lectures from the podium, nor how the rabbi or priest preaches it from the pulpit. Likewise, it is never the cool, calm, collected talk proposed in the traditional literature, one with practical–rational "keys to helping" (Johnson, 1999, p. 5), replete with hints about proper timing, correct mood, and due consideration of the youngster's developmental stage ... or with a list of coping strategies (Heegaard, 1988, p. 1) and expressing the "beautiful way" to explain death (Mellonie and Ingpen, 2005, p. 1). You may be a recognized "expert" in the world of academia or the clinic, but you are a humble father when your child says, "Daddy, where is nana?"

My conclusions fly in the face of mainstream's "helpful hints" that merely reflect politically correct jargon. I argue that intimate speech should neither degenerate into "advice" using the proper do's and "wise" pauses, nor avoid the don'ts which the "experts" fear might provoke guilt or magnify anxiety. They should be natural and spontaneous. By no stretch of the imagination am I pre-empting anticipation! Nor am I expressing opposition to education, preparation, or reason. When death actually enters your child's lifeworld, her questions are ripe and real. You should shoot from the hip. You must speak from within the eye of the hurricane. Around that eye, everything is whirling at 200 kilometers per hour. So-called facts, proper information, rational ideas, and filtered emotions are abstract and at best meaningless. Far preferable that a child cry together with a parent, or on the spot share a scream concerning the vicissitudes of the situation. Flying by the seat of your pants redeems the ambiguous predicament. The freefall blows away the most reasonably honed but pre-framed ideas. Instead, out of your mouth come necessary words ... truthful and tender.

Words are always important. Not the "dead" words of the dictionary, but living words, the words between us and especially the words between my child and me. She and I use words as part of our being together. In the formative years, using new words is everyday fare. We share verbal adventures, because she loves learning them. When death "strikes", I must introduce a new vocabulary so that we might frame its arrival. How unmistakably ordinary! Trozzi and Massimini (1999), however, caution against the use of everyday terminology about the event by saying, "Remember that words like wake, funeral, coffin, and casket ... they might be unfamiliar" (p. 49). On what platform must one be standing to say something so foolish? It is absurd to refrain from using words with your child that she hears all the adults using in their moment-to-moment banter.

Above all, let the words be your own, lifeworld real and therefore right, even if they fly in the face of expert advice. What could be less helpful to a parent reading about children and grief than absorbing ideas which warn him to be careful about using words like "corpse"? For a hesitant and unsure parent who doesn't want to say the wrong thing, such unwise advice is a recipe to become tongue-tied. The self-assured parent would read the above caution and laugh. Because why? Every ordinary devoted parent knows that words are always secondary to the relationship. My conversations with Nicole resemble the structure of the lullaby. The music counts, the rhythm, cadence, and flowing moments of silence. Content or lyrics pale in significance.

5) Priority to truth

Doers and thinkers from very distinct disciplines chide our culture's death-denying paradigm and unmask the insanity of using equivocation, evasion, secrecy, or lies to shelter. Silence shouts and inauthentic silence roars. Allowing mendacity to worm into the "hour of death" enshrines a life-destroying value. Unconscionably, some "expert" advice shields the child from truths about our human condition with boldface lies:

> Old age ... is a time of life when the emotions are less active and the physical organism is beginning to run down; Many of the conditions that surround the mystery of death can be relieved by giving information that dispels the unknown" (Jackson, 1983, pp. 67–68).

Age doesn't dull but rather sharpens the polished point of emotion. Some people do not become radiantly passionate until their later years. Information cannot dispel the mystery of death. Deceiving a child by pretending to explain (away) the unknown is irresponsible.

Catholics pray at night, "Now I lay me down to sleep/I pray Thee, Lord, my soul to keep/if I should die before I wake/I pray Thee, Lord, my soul to take." E.A. Grollman (typically a champion of the child's rights to hear the truth and to grieve openly), takes a perversely "tranquilizing" approach to the verse. Theorizing on the premise that the prayer creates anxiety which the young child cannot handle, he revises it. He deletes the "anxiety-ridden overtones" and re-writes the last two lines to read instead: "Thy love guard me through the night/and wake me with the morning light" (Grollman, 1976, p. 38). What is this unwarranted translation? Is it the Jewish Rabbi dismissing a prayer of a rival religion? Grollman pens a "white lie". The price tag is the evasion of the down-to-earth existential truth. Kierkegaard writes the wholesome words: "suppose death was so treacherous as to come … tomorrow" (Kierkegaard, 1847/1962, p. 148).

Truth is a difficult food to digest. We repress truth because, ironically, it is "akin to death"; we prefer the "real" (Lacan, 1966a/1977, p. 145). Nevertheless, whenever we teach our child something she will have to unlearn later, who does our fib appease? A child is never too young to know. Never! Shielding her from anything existentially real is psychospiritually lethal. Beyond facts and truth, caretakers need wisdom to approach each child radically individually. One talk does not fit all. Throw away your recipes.

6) Children are excellent perceivers but poor interpreters
Nicole perceived that her nana in the casket looked "too big". She also noticed that Nana was wearing slippers, the very ones too small for feet swollen with edema. Nicole simply and solely typifies the perceptual excellence of the young child. Kids are the eyes and ears of the world; they do not miss a trick. However, she lacks experience to interpret her perceptions. She requires the more seasoned adult to provide a context so that she might put her experiences into perspective and understand them. The child is doubly handicapped whenever an adult, instead of clarifying her perception, employs deception that vitiates, invalidates, or obfuscates it.

Our only adult advantage is that we've inhabited planet earth longer. We're not smarter, wiser, or better prepared. We just have had more chances to succeed and to fail. This is another reason why a lie is deadly. When we talk to our wee one, it behooves us to dismount our perch and pedestal and be ready to show our flaws and foibles.

7) Deconstructing the bias against passion and emotion

Platonic Christendom is terrified of passion and tenderness. The Occident privileges abstract reason. Our philosophy disparages emotions as *de jure* pernicious and *de facto* dangerous. Psychological theory apes this prejudice. While discussing the first phase of grief, I indicate that mainstream psychologists apologize for emotions as failures to uphold standards of reasonable comportment or for sabotaging decision-making. Psychological research focuses on how to overcome them or, since we cannot eliminate them altogether, on finding the means to use them positively.

Writers on children and death mimic the bias and perpetuate ideologically based soul-deadening ignorance: "Emotions are rooted in lower levels of consciousness … If your own strong emotions get out of hand, your child should not be subjected to them but should have his [*sic*] communication with you after you have collected yourself and can share your strength rather than your weakness" (Jackson, 1983, pp. 37–38).

Perniciously, Jackson advises us to tyrannize our children with the hypocrisy of pragmatic science.

> "Only the solid rock of fact is an adequate base for the structure of life. Only when the most difficult facts of human experience are met with serenity and sound judgment can the events of life be properly judged and the adjustments of mature thinking and feeling be made" (Jackson, 1983, p. 76).

To the contrary, excesses are necessary. Put no lock on heart or tongue. Let all hell break loose!

8) Vitalize death; do not deaden it

Death is death, not sleep. Nana won't wake up. She will not climb out of the casket to come back. Her warm flesh has turned stiff and cold. Her eyes are gone. These are the facts … the irreversible, heartbreaking truth.

By no means am I advocating that you bluntly hit your child over the head with stark realities, or expect her in one fell swoop to absorb the total human predicament! However, she can learn equally death's finality and its vitality. Death is the quintessential individualizing "moment". You and I are death-bound. We live on borrowed time. *Gilgamesh*, our first Western epic, states, "When the gods gave life to man, they also gave death to man." Death makes life precious. Nothing would be precious if it should last forever. Death is the last arc in the circle of existence, granting unity and wholeness. Do not our precious children deserve that we vitalize death, not deaden it?

> Death does not represent destruction, evil, meaningless oblivion or the dark forces of man. It is the quintessence of what man has always desired most, and what has been the chief motivational factor in his [*sic*] life: the search for, repetition of, the spontaneous unification experiences he has encountered sporadically and at random during the course of his life and existence. It is the final, ultimate, external experience of unity (Gordon, 1972, p. 109).

CHAPTER SEVEN

Study #3: When home shatters: The death of a brother or sister

The tale of sibling grief implicates you and me. If you are blessed with a brother or sister, you are vulnerable to loss. Unless he and I die together, by fluke—or in a nuclear holocaust—Nick (whom you already know from my "Vigilance" myth) will survive my death, or vice versa. But my brother is still alive and my only sibling. Therefore, unlike my downright raw presentations of my mother's dying and my talk with Nicole at her Nana's death, this chapter is based upon my experiences once removed from being a participant. However, I gained knowledge and absorbed sensitivity as advisor to Freda Woodrow's (2006) doctoral dissertation at the University of Pretoria, South Africa.

Like unto the above mentioned portraits, nonetheless, my narrative communicates the experience with my hearthead. I tell the whole tale in a nutshell, using ordinary speech. Everyday language captures its emotional resonance. It also spits out, as it were, all the ambiguities that plague sibling grief. The story reads fresh. It's full of noise. If you have experienced the death of your sibling, I will only judge the story adequate if it should draw you into your own grief episode such that you lose your place in my text ... to find your place within your own. If it provokes memories, may it also evoke emotions, even trigger tears. Although Woodrow shares the credit for this earnest and engaged chapter, she deserves none of its blame.

Orienting remarks on sibling loss

Life's imperative announces itself. The one summoned to death leaves behind a sibling. How does one depict the experience of the one who lost a brother or a sister? What is it like being left behind in this way?

Palimpsest: The suitable mode of expression

The story of losing a sibling is a palimpsest. Lickety-split, here comes the meaning. A palimpsest is a manuscript written on a surface from which an earlier text has been partly or wholly erased. The word captures the complexity of sibling grief.

I might say instead that the story of sibling grief consists in three different chapters in one book, or three testaments of one Bible. That doesn't capture the story accurately enough though. Three chapters imply three separate wholes, woven together and integrated. But the "moments" at stake in this peculiar mourning are not separable.

I might call sibling loss a phenomenon of syncretism, one in which three "moments" merge. That is not adequate either. One "moment" does not assimilate the other two, thus creating a single form. This is not like two rivers merging into one, as in Pittsburgh where the Monongahela and Allegheny Rivers meet to form the Ohio. Not like one religious sect gradually assimilates and accommodates to another, such as the Israelites—staunch worshippers of one god, Yahweh—allowed the Canaanites, who worshipped El and Baal, to infiltrate them. The resulting syncretistic religion later Prophets rebuked and railed against.

Freda Woodrow (2006), trying to capture the stillness and the flow of the phenomenon, writes that sibling grief is layered. Depending upon my mood in this instant, I can picture pulling off layers of clothing or putting them on. So her image is dynamic as well as structured. But I can also image a cake, with three layers, chocolate, white and marbled ... covered in pink icing with the Disney Princesses atop: Jasmine, Ariel, Snow White, Cinderella, and Sleeping Beauty. And that doesn't capture the phenomenon at all.

Woodrow also portrays grief as waves that slash the coast, break, recede, and return. It is a superb image to capture the unpredictability and maverick quality of the phenomenon. I offer instead the image of a palimpsest, of writing and erasing, and then re-writing over that erasure, and then another erasure followed by another re-write. The three pages continually shift; the texts appear and disappear and appear again. It is a textual scrawl. It's messy. The meanings are hard to decipher. Nothing stays. Nothing goes away. Everything flickers, yet you can't seem to get a handle on anything. Palimpsest most adequately depicts this complex, textual promiscuity. In what follows, the meaning will be self-evident to you. If you want Life presented linear and boxed, measured and objectified, you are in the wrong book.

Run-of-the-mill madness: Ordinary grief

As if the dreadful ordeal of grieving the loss of a significant other wasn't bad enough! You lost a loved one, so close that he or she is your own flesh and blood. You're mourning her or him, cold now in death with the lights in the eyes gone out. You are savvy enough to know that grief is a process which, although individualized as snowflakes, follows some typical patterns. You are about to pass through the work of mourning as any loss demands. You are as ready/not ready to start as anyone who ever embarked upon the journey. By itself, that is the quintessential swift kick in your butt, a vicious blow to your living heart. It is a veritable amputation of a limb from your family's flesh! What else could be more brutal than that your kid sister, older brother, identical twin has been delivered over to death?

Parental bereavement

You have got your parents to contend with, that's what. First and foremost, the loss is in-the-family. Your parents' grief is a mountain. You not only lost your sibling, you lost your family unit, your "holding" place within it. You have lost your parents in the old familiar way. As surviving sibling, you watch them flounder. Their text splices yours. It is blow number two to your living heart.

Undoubtedly, you see it better than anyone else. They are not climbing this mountain with adroitness or alacrity. In fact, they are hardly moving at all! You saw it first at the funeral as you tried so hard to support and protect them. Now a protracted period after the burial, a million emotions surface as you watch them discombobulate and see the different and often opposite ways each copes with the horror.

Their pain is palpable. Like a heavy mantle, you wear the garment of responsibility for it. If you are still living "at home", or are the only surviving child, the burden is especially atrocious. Having other brothers or sisters might lessen, but does not remove, the load. A married sibling is not as marginalized as you. He or she has a partner who sees the chaos of the predicament and acknowledges the pain. Whatever the family configuration, you coax and urge them to bounce back to the world, to forge a new beginning on the other side of death's threshold.

It's not working. Often you want to scream! You'd like to shake them. But then too, you want to hold them tight to make their pain go away. Especially mum; especially dad; especially both of them! Kiss away their hurt is what you'd like to do, the way mummy and daddy used to snuggle and cuddle you, and then kiss away your childhood cuts, bumps, and bruises.

You can't. They could not usher you into adulthood. They lacked the power to pick you up on the youthful side of Life's Great Divide and then to set you down safely on the grown-up side. But still, you would prefer to pole vault them and their grief on your back ... up, up and away; soar two meters plus for a woman's gold medal! You'd prefer to goose their mourning, and watch it spring out of its gloomy tomb. In some deeply significant way, and you are the privileged witness to it, they have psychically died with the demise of their precious child, their pride and joy.

Dimly you realize, however, that no matter what healing might occur, still such a glorious passage will not happen. For them, it has been a phenomenological death of self. For them "the dreadful has already happened". The unimaginable already took place. The uncanny entered their life-space. The most unnatural of disasters visited them. Horror of unspeakable horrors, they have outlived their child.

They ushered him or her into the world, cradled, raised, and gave of themselves their all. Letting go—*this* letting go—slices up the phrase it-must-be-possible-to-accept like a razor blade slashing through ribbons.

Maybe it is true—and you hate to admit it—he or she was the favourite, the "apple of mum's eye" or "daddy's little girl". A part of each parent was buried with your dead sibling. You feel it in your gut. Everything of him or her is *gone*, and yet a part still remains ... which is to say that everything has fallen a-part ...

From the point of view of *now*, it does not seem possible that they are going to let go. Not easily. They are clinging with all their might. It's been several months. Nothing in her or his room has been moved. By default, they are in the process turning it into a shrine. It frightens you the way they obsessively visit the cemetery. In death, your sibling seems to have shed all flaws, been transformed into a saint or an angel! Your parents are indulging in Tennyson's "voluptuaries of grief" as if they coined the phrase. By no stretch of the imagination will there be a premature mourning of this death. To put it mildly, they will resist any easy sliding of meaning into the zone of the forgotten. You are stuck with their refusal as stubborn as the plastic trash bags that will not decay. That stubbornness lassoes and entraps you.

This death, however, did not necessarily bring *them* closer together as our naïve perspective would have it. Mum is "pissed" that dad doesn't talk about it and shows little emotion. He is frustrated with her brooding and with her inability to respond to him—especially in "that" way—as if death has closed each and every one of Life's ... "gates". You hope against hope that this road will not lead to the divorce court. If "against" should win out, how in the hell will any of you cope with that destructive wipe out? You feel helpless.

Even if they do "hang tough", if healing happens and edges toward resolution, and then finally tiptoes towards acceptance still henceforth everything will be different. If the day should ever come when they finally see again a rainbow in the sky above, it will be a miracle. But on this good earth, a dark hole unable to be thoroughly filled will remain. That emptiness will remain a cold, hard, fact of life.

You see all of this. Not all at once. You see it through the Biblical glass, darkly. But you feel it incessantly. In response, your emotions shoot out. Either they flash in a laser beam of anger, or bubble like a fountain and proliferate. You couldn't freeze one in order to slap a label on it, not even if hell would freeze over. Maybe freeze is precisely what will happen next. Why not? *This* has happened. This death that turned your family life upside down, inside out ... turned it squirrelly. Hell, the basketball player George Girvan called himself "the iceman". Maybe there is such an animal as an "Ice Woman?" Or is not that an oxymoron? Don't answer. Instead, pray for warmth to conquer.

Your tale becomes a palimpsest. As soon as you start to grieve, you are pulled into their grief. Your grief gets smudged. You erase whatever you were marking for yourself to survive. Responding to their needs instead, you fall hostage to their grief.

A cipher in the snowy dark night

As if two blows out of the dark were not enough! You have lost your kid sister and lost your parents in the old familiar way! To loan a phrase from baseball, the American "pastime", you have two strikes and the proverbial curve ball is coming at you. This "pitch", particularly tailored to you, will strike you out if you are not alert. It's your individual cross to bear. How so?

Whatever your parents are feeling, or whatever emotions are being carried by your dead sibling's spouse-children-lover-friends, they don't get thrown at them the final curve that is twisting your way. Whatever is peculiar about their grief-process, they do not see the odd and wicked toss that you have to take a whack at ... What?

Your grief is a molehill. It doesn't count. It doesn't even have any geography. There is no room for it on the page. Oh, every night at minimum, trying to count sheep as part of trying to sleep, you calculate the algebra of your grief. But outside of you, it doesn't even exist. It is only within your own experience, within your own consciousness. Although your heart is breaking for your "gone" childhood companion, aching too for your parents who have vanished in the sense in which you previously always had them—still in this predicament, no one is even taking your psychological pulse.

Woodrow (2006) writes that paradoxically you are both intimately a *part-of* and strangely *apart-from* your family. You are the involved-outsider ... overlooked, taken-for-granted, and ignored. By "outsider" she means that you are relegated to the sidelines where you freeze your pain in order to sustain your parents. You become a silent, invisible, forgotten mourner.

Not surprisingly, you begin to wonder if you even have the right to grieve. Why should you have been granted survival? Do you even deserve to be alive? Waves of anguished emotion rush and undulate, relentlessly crash. All the words on the text run together. Your grief-work is postponed, held in abeyance. Sounds of your sorrow stay muted. Eventually, your deferred emotions knot and freeze. Sadly, it might take many, many years before they thaw. It will come as a grace when finally your enclosing reserve opens, silence cracks, grief overtly gushes, and healing begins. For the time being, picture yourself in suspended animation, a cipher in the snow.
In "Home Burial" Robert Frost (1914?/1979) puts his poetic pen on the sore truth:

> One is alone, and he dies alone.
> Friends make pretense of following to the grave,
> But before one is in it, their minds are turned
> And making the best of their way back to life
> And living people, and things they understand (p. 54).

In this case, there is not even the pretense. In their legitimate concern for your parents, condolence visitors never "pet" you, never offer you comfort. You parents are the bona fide sufferers. Others freeze you out. One young Norwegian woman tells me, "I got a bouquet from my class a few days after my sister died. But when I came back to school, no one except my Spanish teacher talked about it." She clarifies the "moment". "All I wanted was people to see me. Know I was there. But they were afraid." She elaborates as follows.

> I can not begin to describe how much the conversation with my Spanish teacher meant to me. She was the only one who could talk about *it*. The only one! Spanish class was like a free zone. It was out in the open air and not taboo. Everywhere else, a conspiracy of silence reigned.

It's even worse. A bizarre reversal takes place. As if you didn't already have enough to think about and agonize over. Whenever you do meet people, you have to stay composed. It seems up to you to start the conversation, steer it, and in general facilitate the exchange. You have to put them at ease. You have to take care of them. Lock up your own grief. Put it into cold storage. The loss of your brother or sister, therefore, is a triple loss. The waves keep breaking. An elusive palimpsest the remainder ...

Voices

I direct the interested reader to Freda Woodson's dissertation, available on the Internet, in order to confront a work that is solidly scholarly, both comprehensive and integrated. It both engages one's head with theoretical scope, and quickens one's heart with poignant narratives. It thoroughly canvasses the literature both on siblings and on sibling grief. That search reveals how shoddily and shabbily the phenomena have been treated over the decades. She writes that when we see the way a grieving brother or sister is marginalized in the existential forum, and how the the academy and medico-psychology understudies sibling mourning, we must simultaneously note that WE are the people and professionals who practice such un-benign neglect. This chapter does only partial justice to her readily available work.

Instead of ending with a reflective analysis, I present words Ron Cornelissen (personal email message) shared with me, words about his sister's death.

> I lost my sister less than two years ago. The empty space in the family left by the death of a sibling is different than the loss of a parent or even the loss of both parents. In many ways, this loss hits closer to home. Given a short range of years in either direction, a sibling's death is a "parallel" death of my own. Growing "up" together, my brother or my sister and I are gauges for each other. In the course of each others' lives, we share each others' pain, sorrow, joy, defeat, and good fortune. We rival each other, equal each other and, yes, compete with each other. Sibling rivalry is just another expression of love, a way for us to find ourselves in and through each other. My brother and my sister are there for me to "bounce off" of, to stretch and grow and discover life. Through our daily exchanges, scuffing, disagreements, disappointments, and support for each other upfront

and "behind the scenes," we move haphazardly forward. In a moment of heat, I can hate my sibling but, even in the same instant, don't anyone else touch him or her. Blood is thicker than water. I may not get along with my brother; I may not like my sister, but if needed I would risk my life, give my life for them! ... Losing a sibling, I lose a part of myself.

Mommies and Daddies don't die. Neither do siblings.

PART III

CHAPTER EIGHT

Foundation and framework

The life and work of a luminary: Sigmund Freud

Nobody has to agree with Jacques Lacan in order to agree with him ...
that Sigmund Freud is a "luminary" irreducible to a medical positivist.
Agree with him, too, that we must read Freud on his own terms and
remove from his texts both medico-biological glosses and ideological prejudices. It behooves us to see the luminary in the correct light.
Lacan puts it simply: Read Freud and get him right (1966a/1977).

One bone of contention between Lacan, the International Psychoanalytic, and Freudians in general—is the status of the *todestrieb*.
Was Freud falling victim to an avalanche of grief when he turned
from hysteria to depression? Was he especially sorrowful when he
wrote *Beyond the Pleasure Principle*? In 1920, his beloved daughter,
Sophie, his "Sunday's child" dies after a four-day illness at the age of
twenty-six. Something in him permanently died, he says. He writes
to Ludwig Binswanger that he had never gotten over "the mon-
strous fact of children dying before their parents" (Derrida, 1987,
p. 331). In a few short years Sophie's second son, Heinerle dies at age
four and a half. He is Freud's favourite, his preferred grandson, "the
preferred son of the preferred daughter ... the most intelligent child

125

he had ever encountered ... Heinerle dies. On 19 June 1923; Freud is seen to cry. For the only time" (Derrida, 1987, pp. 333–334).

Two short months before, the cancer in Freud's mouth shows itself malignant and fatal. In April 1923, he undergoes the first of thirty-three operations of jaw and palate. This pain, too, plagues him for the remains of his Day.

The horrors of World War I had already injured Freud's sensibilities and perturbed his agile mind. During this short time-span, he suffered his most heart-rending personal losses. Derrida says it plainly: "In the most crushing psychobiograpical style, there has been no failure to associate the problematic of the death drive with Sophie's death" (Derrida, 1987, p. 327). Lacan alleges otherwise. This confrontation with death ushers in a period of fantastic creativity, one during which Freud rediscovered the unconscious. Most of his contemporary disciples chose to dismiss his explanation of Eros–Thanatos as the over-arching conflict in human life. Subsequently, most revisionist-Freudians have excised the *todestrieb* from their interpretation of the psychoanalytic vision. Lacan and Norman O. Brown (1988) are two strong voices who argue that the amputation of death from Freud's vision is an unpardonable loss.

This book does not aim to sort out which-is-which about what per cent is pro or con about the matter or the whys and wherefores. From his correspondence with Wilhelm Fliess, we have evidence as early as 31 May 1897 of Freud's (1985) foreshadowing of the relationship between self-reproach and latent hostility in mourning and melancholia (p. 250). An academic quibble about the matter is not even interesting. I simply bracket any and all ideological, theoretical, and metapsychological debates in order to confront death and grief unalloyed. Heeding the phenomenological call to go to the phenomena themselves, I listen to what Freud says about their place in human life. Such labour will both unearth unparalleled riches in his thought and reveal gaps and his weakest spot.

Nowadays, the amelioration of both global and mundane human happenings cries out for a holistic, integrative, comprehensive standpoint, one that eschews surface in favour of depth and broad scope. Death-themes ache for Freud's touch. At the same time, they yearn for an interface between Freud and other luminaries. I orchestrate the cross-fertilization of his ideas and meanings with Kierkegaard, with whom he was apparently unacquainted; with Nietzsche, from whom he borrowed copiously; from Heidegger, Camus and Levinas who he could not have known.

The pivotal interface is between Freud's pioneer work and the Nietzschean-Heideggergian deconstruction of Western rationalism. At the crossing point, we find a sufficiently broad context within which to locate Freud's seminal ideas on death and grief. Heidegger so privileges time and death that he accuses the West of "forgetting" and ignoring them. Western forgetting is as fresh as yesterday and as recent as tomorrow. Freud's early works on dreams, errors, jokes, and so forth, anticipate the science of linguistics (eventually shaped by Ferdinand de Saussure). Likewise, Freud anticipated much of what was to become phenomenology and postmodernism. In matters that impinge upon the human soul, Freud was and still is ahead of his time. Mainstream orthodox psychology, preoccupied with behaviour and especially cognitive behaviour, has sidelined Freud as a relic whose science is not scientific on its terms. Nevertheless, from the perspective of the history of ideas, a one-dimensional approach to everything from love to death is still pre-Freudian.

Doubtlessly, Freud belongs to the psychoanalytic community, to those who embrace him and defend his vision in the face of an academic-professional world that prefers to consider him passé and irrelevant. Open any mainstream American Psychological Association journal. Witness how vociferously the mainstream positivism ignores him and his legacy. The psychoanalytic community also must endure the continual attempts to "kill" Freud, even though analysts would be the preferred ones to flash meaningful smiles at the irony or absurdity of continually trying to murder someone whom you have already pronounced dead.

Freud, however, is also a man for the ages. He belongs to other circles, to those who refuse as ultimate values contentment, superficiality, common sense, coping, adjustment, conformity, safety, security, and survival. We understand and honour him properly by interfacing him with other luminaries and by placing his writings in the midst of other heartfelt and clear-headed texts.

"Thoughts for the times on war and death": The death drive

In an appalling historical context, Freud (1915b) tells us that "the unconscious cannot imagine its own demise" (p. 296). The atrocities of World War I had become common knowledge. They disgusted Sigmund Freud. At the time, he was making a "turn" from the repression of hysteria to probing the self-punishment of depression. Already, in February 1915, he presented to Karl Abraham his first draft of what became his classic 1917 essay "On mourning and melancholia". Already, he was anticipating his 1920 book *Beyond the Pleasure Principle*, his 1921 *Group Psychology*, and even the 1923 *The Ego and the Id*. His thoughts turn to war and death.

With tongue in cheek, Freud (1915/1958) discusses the common *disillusionment* of that "moment" in history. Was it not rooted in the debasement of moral standards and the brutality practiced by the "great ruling powers among the white nations", ostensibly, preeminently civilized? (p. 276). With psychoanalytic vision, quickly he unmasks the hypocrisy. The *trieb*, undomesticated, lurks always beneath the veneer of culture. In times of war, therefore, we respond with savage "cruelty, fraud, treachery and barbarity" toward the enemy we consider ... barbarians or savages (Freud, 1915b, p. 280). Torture is run-of-the-mill madness. Do a reality check, he advises, and then temper all your disillusionment: "our fellow-citizens have not sunk so low as we feared, because they had never risen so high as we believed" (Freud, 1915b, p. 285). By clinging to mendacious attitudes toward death and war, Western man is "living, psychologically speaking, beyond his means" (Freud, 1915b, p. 284). Freud challenges us shepherds of the social order to grow up, cast aside our illusions and hypocrisies, and thus live within our psychological means. Citing the classical Western ruse invoked to justify establishment-initiated aggression—"If you desire peace, prepare for war"—he re-translates it: "If you wish life, prepare for death" (Freud, 1915b, p. 300).

In 1920, Freud rediscovers the unconscious when he makes Eros versus Thanatos the fundamental conflict in human life. The *todestrieb*, although rejected by most of his then disciples and almost all of his subsequent ones, is cardinal to understanding and judging the overall merits of psychoanalysis. The notion is inextricably linked to the "compulsion to repeat". It converges with the Heideggerian understanding that places death at the core of human life. His stunning assertions are that "the aim of all life is death", that human comportment is merely a "detour" on the way to death, and that the direction and orientation of our life—our life style and our choices—are in service of guaranteeing that we would die in our own chosen way (Freud, 1920g, p. 65). We "follow our own path to death, and ward off any possible ways of returning to inorganic existence other than those that are immanent" (Freud, 1920g, pp. 72–73).

The insights packed into this essay clarify our global-political predicament of today's world riddled with conflict. Cycles of revenge and counter-revenge ceaselessly swirl, spinning out in alarming rates worldwide, and forcing beleaguered individuals to grieve as newly created widows, orphans, and paupers. Freud's seminal and decisive ideas are both prophylactic and healing. Daily, we witness the severe handicaps of dominant mainstream rationalistic-dualistic thinking to halt the geopolitical madness and forestall the horror. In terms of everyday life concerns, behavioural analyses and cognitive homework simply lack the "guts" to remedy the less-than-conscious and non-pragmatic dimensions of revenge, regret, humiliation, love-pain, and melancholy.

This essay written during World War I—the war to end all wars— and Freud's later correspondence with Einstein published as "Why war?" are historical time-warps that come to us as an old letter as if from the future. They could have been written today, or yesterday— or tomorrow (Einstein and Freud, 1933).

Getting Freud "right", that is, reading his avowed intentions with fidelity, is a mammoth task. Genuine thinkers wail at the distortion of Sigmund Freud's seminal concepts and the way his choice, rich words have been butchered in translation. Freud's language reverberates in the soul of every German speaking person, from the child who misses her parent, to the old man who longs for his lost love. Merleau-Ponty accuses the guardians of the established order of clipping the Tiger's claws to blunt his revolutionary edge (Merleau-Ponty, 1960, pp. 6–7). Lacan scatters criticism and corrections of warped translations throughout his Seminars, telling us that the French have mangled the translation even worst than the British. In *Freud and man's soul*, Bruno Bettelheim (1983) does his utmost to right the wrong before he commits suicide. Bettelheim also concludes that the motives for the awful translation into English are to create distance from Freud's emotional meanings and to present him in a way that smacks of positive science and protects capitalism. If you have read Freud, and have been put off by some of his terminology, note well that the terms are not his. My aim is to give you a more faithful orientation.

CHAPTER NINE

The depressive position

A myth of human growth

In this chapter, I present a myth of human growth in order to elaborate and demonstrate the significance of the cardinal notions of splitting in the ego (self), the depressive position, and forgiveness. Historically, myth and stories are mankind's most common way to make knowledge-claims. The current preference for positivistic natural science merely expresses modernity's myth. That myth, unfortunately, shrinks the psyche and freezes the living heart. It narrows the human being to a one-dimensional creature by privileging non-involvement, the sur-face of humanity, and the superficiality of (cognitive) behaviour. This modern scientific myth, nonetheless, has become our sacred cow and our new religion. Currently, voices mount to challenge its hegemony as the standpoints of Nietzsche and Heidegger now gradually seep into our postmodern culture. However, the structures of Power and Money shelter it.

Herein, I present a more adequate myth for comprehending the two (psychical) and three-dimensional (spiritual) faces of sorrow. How do I compose it? The myth, "Felix culpa", the happy fault, starts with a Kiergegaardian self-search or psychological autopsy. Such reflective work yields a preliminary understanding of my own personal experiences with my three children, three grand-daughters, and with clients. The pivot of this work is this: I can verify what I say within my own experience. Then I seek other neutral input, weaving scholarly knowledge into the myth. Specifically, I integrate key anthropological facts, clinical data from psychoa-nalysis, and experimental psychological findings. In the most comprehensive sense, this myth provides the framework for including moral and spiritual issues within psychotherapeutic work. In particular, it clarifies both the power of forgiveness in the drama of grief, and helps us to comprehend the dynamics of regret, revenge, and suicide.

Felix culpa: The happy fault

Firstly, the myth eschews all dualisms. It begins with a self-evident truth that needs no proof. Except in abstract rationalistic theory, there is no such thing as an infant. There is no infant without a "mothering one". Nor is there a mother without her precious baby. In life, there is the mother–infant dyad. There is the symbiosis of a nursing couple. Conventional developmental psychology theorizes dualistically and thus studies an infant and a mother each unto self. Eventually, it intends to put Humpty Dumpy back together again. Tomorrow never comes.

Premature birth

A cardinal anthropological fact anchors my standpoint: *the premature birth of the human*. The human being is born at least nine months prematurely. She is absolutely helplessly dependent. Without her symbiotic partner, she would not thrive, and maybe not even survive. This premise authorizes my statement that there are only two irrefutable psycho-spiritual "facts": 1) All of us have experienced basic love; 2) None of us have had perfect parents. Our parents loved us with flaws, foibles, and fallibilities. The "dance" of life is to integrate the inherent ambiguity of flaw and scission characterizing our experience, consciousness, and relationships. Imperfect lovers: the stuff of which dreams ... and nightmares are made.

Unfolding the myth

Melanie Klein (1975) roots Freud's Oedipus in infancy, much earlier than he describes the nuclear conflict of problems in living, of the neuroses (at approximately three years old). She starts with the "schizoid position", the concept of splitting, and theorizes on the basis of the dialectics of the good breast-good me/bad breast-bad me.

Position

The word is basic. The psychoanalytic tradition uses "position" to indicate meanings that are more than a one-shot happening, especially within a relationship. Some "moments" come and vanish without a trace. Others happen, but linger. They form a pattern. They are ongoing and continue long after their first emergence. The names change, the faces change, the places change ... but nothing changes. The issues that I am raising, as starting in early infancy, endure. Based upon our best knowledge of developmental progression, we can date their emergence. But they are also un-datable. Actual numbers matter little. The issues at stake plague humans throughout the life spiral. Their meaning is not chronological, but psychological and existential.

Splitting

Any attempt to comprehend sorrow and its derangement remains shallow insofar as it fails to address the various offshoots of splitting. By splitting, the individual accomplishes several psychological feats—albeit in a defensive and less than conscious way. Splitting is the stubborn refusal to understand the truth of one's situation. It keeps matters obscure, manufactures ignorance about them, seeks security by twisting the viciousness lingering between the other and self, and relegates unwanted aspects of the core self to someone else: a sentient or insentient "enemy".

Within the soul (*seele*), a double emerges. One part of the 'I' (*Ich*) splits off and critically judges itself. Such splitting is a preeminently normal psychic activity. If nothing else, our nightly dreams demonstrate it. They parade before me many characters. But I am the dreamer; the dream is mine. All figures that enter and exit are aspects of me.

In the larger social arena, the same process accounts for a plethora of social, religious, and political phenomena: loyalty, hero-worship, prejudice; bigotry, revenge, racism. The flipside of adoration for the idealized, numinous "Other" is pure cold hatred for the Demonic Other, the Wicked Witch.

From the get-go

The infant, fresh out of the womb, is "put to the breast" (Erikson, 1959, pp. 56–57). She thrives and grows, integrates and personi-fies, by taking in and incorporating what is good (from a libidi-nal-relational standpoint) and by projecting—expelling, spitting out—what is relationally bad. Every one of us has experienced basic love, insofar as our mother was "good-enough" at "holding" and "handling" us (Winnicott, 1965c/2005). And loved we have been, insofar as our family and society warmly welcomed us. Loved we are, because of the *coordination* between the social world and my helpless dependency. Without this necessary human contact, this loving bond—Freud's *besetzen*—we would be relationally starved and end up a caricature of a human person.

There are two compelling bodies of evidence for this assertion. One is findings on feral children, for example, the Wild Boy of Averyon, raised by animals (Itard, 1962). The other is findings on children raised in isolation (Davis, 1947). This data teaches us that the human is incredibly malleable and compensates for many early deprivations; but a low ceiling hangs, due to the absent love-bond. Despite Herculean efforts at education, socialization, and encultur-ation, the isolated children never reach full human potential, and feral children never become fully human.[4]

Elemental awareness

From the beginning, the loved infant enjoys living within the dimen-sion of the elemental (Levinas, 1961/1969, p. 130). She enjoys a vital sensing feeling relationship with the Uni-verse. The infant lives and loves with her mouth; her mother lives and loves with the breast. Within the orbit of symbiotic relatedness, the wee baby drifts in and out of a world of Light and Night, of sweet and salty, of loud and soft, warm and cool, brisk and soothing. She knows no splits. She has ONE mother, not TWO. And she is a little unit, a psychesoma (Winnicott, 1965c/2005, pp. 43ff). The original posture and position of human life is at-one-ness and wholeness. I am loved and love back wholeheartedly, perfectly. At first entry to this good earth, we all have fallen into the hands of the Living God, into the arms of the Divine Mother, the Good Fairy, a bountiful source of all that is good. And yes, I adore her.

The schizoid position: The social smile at three months

The elemental drama shifts because of another anthropological fact: *the smiling response*. At approximately three months of age, the infant reaches a new level. The phenomenon that indexes the change is "the social smile". The infant smiles now, not only because she is passing gas or because you are tickling her, but smiles in recognition of a human face. Such recognition implies a structuring of experience; it indicates that there is a before and an after, a here and a there, a primitive memory, and primary consciousness of space and time.

Insofar as the mothering one is imperfect, she brings the not just the Light of love, but also the Night. She introduces the "stranger" anxiety into the feeding situation. Who could possibly know each and every nuance of distress that taints the dual union? Maybe mother just had an argument with dad. Maybe the stock market collapsed! But the infant becomes acquainted with the Night. From where does this alienating glitch arise? How do we understand this emergence of the smiling response?

I turn to Jean Piaget and Henry Elkin. Piaget (1952) demonstrates that for the infant aged three to six months, the object has no permanence. Out of sight equals out of mind. Take away an interesting object with which the infant is engaged, she will lose interest in it and not look for it. The existence of the object is still glued to her experience of it. Good and bad experiences are not linked to specific, independent objects.

What is going on? Henry Elkin argues that the infant, not yet conceptually developed enough to be aware of concrete, phenomenal, *material objects*, nevertheless has an awareness of immaterial presences. Elkin calls it the awareness of the "Primordial Other" (Elkin, 1966; 1972, p. 401). The infant is conscious of benevolent and malevolent presences. This is the anthropological ground of human ideas of God and the Devil. The schizoid position expresses that drama.

The drama displays the necessary fault, the flaw in the seamless fabric. This is the *Felix culpa* (from the *Exultet* of the Roman Catholic Easter Vigil liturgy), the "happy fault", the absolute necessities of human flaws and of love being expressed imperfectly.

The infant, therefore, lives with two totalized Presences. He absolutely loves the Divine Mother, or God, and totally hates the Bad Mother, the Wicked Witch, or the Devil. To express hatred and the desire to annihilate the Demonic Presence is as totally innocent and completely justified as to adore the Goddess. To use psychoanalytic concepts, the infant internalizes and fuses with the Divine and projects the Demonic. Never will the two meet.

If there is a break in the relationship, if the "mothering" one withdraws, the infant is in terror. Remember, the infant is absolutely and totally dependent. The terror of the terror, the despairing "moment", is that my love for the Blessed Mother drove her away. My love spoiled the Good Breast and ruined our loving symbiosis. Hey, I had a good thing going. I messed up. My very act of loving is bad. Yeah, my love is bad. My love destroys. Oscar Wilde is only one of the many artists who have communicated the awful horror. One kills what one loves. Whenever anyone can make me feel my love is not good, is indeed evil, I totter on the brink of despair. It is the "moment" of horror. It is the suicidal "moment".

Six–eight months: The depressive position

Maturational changes between the ages 6–8 months ushers in the depressive position. The infant enters the phenomenal world. Because why? Piaget demonstrates that the object is constant now. It is no longer out of sight, out of mind. Physical developments, with psychological consequences, occur. Teeth erupt, leading to biting and often prompting weaning. Lacan (1966c/1977) describes the emergence of the "mirror stage" at this "moment" (pp. 1–7). Twinborn emerge the *je*, the self as subject (partaking of spirit) and the *moi*, the objectified or alienated self. When presenting an infant in the mirror, the parent and little one experience *jouisssance*, the glee and jubilation of the latter's recognition of selfhood that is reflected back. And they "play" with the image. This "moment" is not possible for a highly developed chimpanzee at the same age, even though the primate is far superior to the human infant in terms of sensory-motor skills.

The key issue of this complicated developmental stage is that now depressive dynamics confront the more sophisticated infant. The little one has dropped out of heaven and joined the human race (Elkin, 1966). She is aware of one whole mother. Now she must come to terms cognitively with the fact that the Good Mother and the Bad Mother are one and the same, and find how emotionally to express the polarity of loving and hating the same person at the same time, the precise person that you are absolutely dependent upon.

On a daily basis, the "worse" that our caretakers actually minister to us (libidinally), the more we are plagued with what to do with our "badness", with our hatred, envy, and greed. The depressive position is the agony that our own "evil" destroys our good relationships. Psychologically, it is easiest to aim the ire at ourselves. We take the fall, absorb the blame, and ooze guilt ... shamelessly.

This subtle drama is never observable in the typical empirical sense. In a hypothetically perfect situation, I would express myself and my emotions spontaneously and unconditionally. But no situation is perfect. Every mum curbs her wee one's expressiveness. She draws her own inimitable line that curtails the negativity aimed at her. She balks at nipple-biting, perhaps, or at being slapped in the face. Human to human, even when it is a tiny one and the Giantess, there is always constraint. The human is a creature that creates boundaries. It is part of the socialization process. Pity the poor child whose mother sets no limits—because limits also set free. Pity also the child whose mother demands to be treated as if she WAS perfect, or who tolerates no expressions of anger, hostility—no biting, no scratching, or no outbursts! Under such circumstances the dependent infant has to swallow it all ... and BE "bad".

The saving grace is contained in a third anthropological fact: in human life, *mental-spiritual autonomy precedes, by many years, physical autonomy*. With the advent of object constancy, the child realizes that mother makes mistakes. She thinks I'm hungry when I'm wet. She thinks I pooped when I want the nipple. Ah, there is a secret part of me that momma doesn't see. She does not have eyes in the back of her head. She is not omniscient or all-powerful (Elkin, 1966).

This secret part of me that mother doesn't see is Spirit. It is vitally important, earth-shaking. I am not being over-dramatic. It means that we are granted a zone of freedom. I never have to be a slave. I can always say "No" and rebel. Human life is based upon consciousness, not instincts. If momma could read my heart, mind, and soul totally, I would be a slave … or paranoid.

Do a simple act, if you doubt me. Pretend we are face to face. I say to you, "Please contract your buttocks. Hold it for a second. Now release." Would I know if you complied? Could I ever know if you obeyed? Freedom …

Disposing of evil: Paranoid projection

The paranoid dynamic conjugates the act of splitting. Psychologically, it is easier for the weak one—the child and the slave—to make self conditionally bad. In the process, one cleanses the genuine bad object, makes the other object good, better than she is in everyday life. Here is what is at stake. If I am blameless and if you with power and might are evil, then I'm in big trouble. Ronald Fairbairn (1952) splendidly describes the predicament of needing a "moral defense" which in formula goes: "It is better to be bad in a world ruled by God, than to be good in a world ruled by the Devil" (pp. 65ff). Because why? If the Devil rules, innocence anticipates persecution; if God reigns, the sinner hopes for forgiveness, salvation, and redemption.

For the most part, most of us protect our abusive parent … or spouse. And we honour the dead one about whom we are ambivalent. We cherish our murderous Leader. We identify with the aggressor (A. Freud, 1936). We pat ourselves on the back for protecting our bad object, supremely pleased and proud for rescuing him from taint. We'd even die in defense of her! "No one kills himself," says Freud, "who first did not wish to kill another." Short of suicide, one lives an ongoing mutual seduction into games of guilt. Here come some descriptive lines: One is not grateful enough or sufficiently appreciative; the other party is demanding, never satisfied, takes me for granted, and acts entitled … What sustains such guilt-riddled games? It is the refusal of two parties to accept their respective imperfections and forgive them.

The inauthentic possibility: Projection

How do I dispose of badness—hate, greed, lust, self-loathing, and self-contempt? I project it. Instead of blaming myself, I locate evil in another. I find a person or ethnic group to dump the crap onto.

Get a juicy new target. Whenever one feels like the scum of the earth, weak as a dying flower, wicked as sin, then one way to find relief is the paranoid dynamism. I see with blinding clarity, embodied in the Demonic Enemy, what I can't acknowledge and own in myself. I experience both relief and worry. I crow that "they" are the problem, just as I always suspected. "They" embody the worst of the worse that I can hate furiously and with impunity—just as I could freely hate the Demonic Mother during the three to six months of life. In the social area, it comes out as revenge. I feel justified and vindicated in my disdain and contempt for the greedy Jew, the sensuous black, the sneak-attacking yellow-horde ... for "Charlie", those damn Viet Cong "gooks" that my country could not defeat! Brown, heathen, oil-rich or puffed-with-poppy terrorists! Wipe them off the face of the earth. Let's have a long and successful round of racial cleaning.

What "casts out our devils", heals our rifts, or cures our splitting? Melanie Klein (1975, p. 311) names it "making reparation". D.W. Winnicott calls it the transformation of guilt into concern. Henry Elkin uses a more anthropological term: forgiveness. All mainstream quibbles and quarrels about the relative importance of emotion, judgement and behaviour are abstract babble. Forgiveness transcends my feelings, my ideas, and my action.

Seattle University, Washington: Clinical dialogal phenomenology

Jan Rowe, Steen Halling (1989) and their associates present rare research findings on forgiveness as part of ongoing work done from a dialogal phenomenological perspective. They find a dearth of research on the topic, documenting that even the family therapy literature strangely overlooks it. They suggest that the basic reasons for the benign neglect might root in the choice of psychology, psychiatry, and grief researchers to imitate the approach, method, and content of 19th-century science. Since forgiveness is not amenable to natural scientific methods of study, it eludes the positivistic cast of mind. The disciplines avoid it, relegating it to religious studies or theology. However, the existential-phenomenological-hermeneutic tradition is suited to comprehend forgiveness.

The Seattle group locates itself within the hermeneutic tradition, favouring a dialogal approach as the preferred way to access the phenomenon. Finding mainstream academic-clinical literature impoverished, the team searches theoretically minded psychologists such as Fritz Heider, and psychoanalytically oriented thinkers such as Harold Searles.

The group's findings uncover key injuries that call for the need for forgiveness. That is, the origin of the need for forgiveness is a deep hurt or loss so intense that feelings associated with it fester over time into blame unto vengefulness or the desire for revenge. Only after agonizing soul-searching does one ultimately forgive and forget.

A glitch shows, however, in their published work. Rowe and Halling write a blatant error: "Heider's classic study discusses resentment and revenge at length but is silent on forgiveness" (Rowe and Halling, 1989, p. 234). In actual fact, on page 269, Fritz Heider (1958) writes: "Forgiveness does not always imply a passive acceptance of the implication of harm ... Forgiveness can affirm the power and status of the forgiver." Obviously, this idea is crucial to the Seattle Group's project. Why the unconscionable oversight? We can only speculate.

Henry Elkin: Forgiveness

Merleau-Ponty (1960) writes that a phenomenology which dares to descend into its own basement of necessity converges with the project of Freudian research. Of course, he is spot on. Even more than evolving a form of psychotherapy, the development of a science of the soul (*seele*) engaged Freud. Throughout this book, I repeatedly and relentlessly accuse positivism, as it is played out in mainstream theory and praxis, of decaying into destruction. I would be remiss to overlook flaws in the implementation of the Vision which I esteem as the most comprehensive for understanding and healing the human condition: phenomenology.

The Seattle Group puts a skylight in the roof to allow in the fresh air and brightness of revelation, grace, freedom, and clarity. "There is a spiritual dimension to forgiveness which creates the foundation for embracing a new future" (Rowe and Halling, 1989, p. 242). However, not heeding Merleau-Ponty's expectation, they keep the trap door shut to the cellar. They ignore the core drama around which forgiveness pivots—the cosmic clash between the Titans of Good and Evil. Forgiveness seems a soft humanistic gift. It is that, but is more. To find a phenomenology that does go into its basement, I turn to Henry Elkin. In one short paragraph, his insights dwarf the findings of both mainstream medico-psychological science and dialogal phenomenology:

> The capacity for forgiveness, complimentary to the capacity for concern ... makes possible ... an ongoing process of reconciliation not only with others, but endopsychically ... This integrative movement toward Selfhood brings that experience of mutuality in feeling, of participation in community, which is the foundation of authentic, nondefensive, joyful acceptance living in the world. Insofar as the capacity for forgiveness is lacking, the psyche is prey to *resentment [and revenge]* ... affixed to a cosmic picture of perpetual conflict between the *Divine* and the *Diabolical* ... Forgiveness that dispels *hatred* ... channels the libido into tender feelings of closeness that express reverence ... and serious concern for the well-being of others. Forgiveness is thus the foundation of whole-some love (Elkin, 1972, p. 409, my emphasis).

Mourning, to reach a satisfyingly cogent resolution, travels a spiritual path of courage, truth, and forgiveness.

CHAPTER TEN

Re-visioning death: In Heidegger

How do you explain death?

> Most of us do not know it, but unborn babies within their
> mothers' wombs communicate with each other. As a matter of
> fact, where there are several pregnant women in a neighbour-
> hood, the little embryos chatter daily about the news of their
> little world.
>
> Now it happened that in one neighbourhood, there were
> several pregnant mothers and one was carrying twins. And all
> the other embryos were very proud that they had twins among
> them. The twins, too, were very glad to have each other.
>
> But then, one of the twins was born premature, and the other
> twin was left alone in the womb. And when all the other little
> embryos in the neighbourhood heard of it, they quickly began
> to call the remaining twin, and all said: "We're so sorry that
> your brother was born."[5]

Sooner or later somebody in the Western world was bound to emerge
to give death its due. Somebody had to comprehend it, not just as
concocted in abstract arbitrary ideas, but in the way that we humans

actually live it. Someone had to wrest it away from the philosophers and theologians who had framed it such to support Authority—to protect the Power and Money of governments and the Church. Somebody had to arrive who was sufficiently gifted to express an alternative Vision. Such a thinker never could have emerged from within the Club of committed professional rationalists. In fact, Martin Heidegger appears on the historical scene. He replaces the Occident's substantive way of thinking with a relational one. He gives death ... a life of its own.

Moving and shaking history

The thrust that moves history includes both the genius-magic of a certain individual and the *zeitgeist*—the prevailing spirit of the times, the new climate of thought permeating the air. In Heidegger, both forces coalesce to change our understanding of death. His thinking penetrates to the core. He taps into the rich source of our Western way of comprehending the person–world relationship. He insists that philosophy did not start with Socrates, Plato, and Aristotle. And he learns from the seminal thinkers that, nowadays, professional philosophers prejudicially denigrate with the term "the pre-Socratics": Heraclites and Parmenides, and the Milesian philosophers, Thales, Anaximander, and Anaximines.

By piercing through Platonic-Christendom's other-worldly veil, Heidegger first turns philosophy on its head then puts it back on its feet. He puts it on this patch of earth, plants it in time, and brings it to the flesh. He makes decisive distinctions and anchors thought in concrete everyday life. He grants to nothingness, absence, and silence their rightful place.

Living death

Heidegger severely criticizes Western thought for failing to give death its due. He distinguishes cogently and concisely the differences between the Greek metaphysical and the phenomenological standpoints on death. The Greek view constitutes our run-of-the-mill, taken-for-granted understanding. Both the scholar and the man in the street in Western society *think* of death in Greek categories. The Greek standpoint levels down dying to a mere occurrence that happens to "nobody" in particular. We say cavalierly, "'One' dies' but that does not concern me. My number is not up." Such thinking legitimizes evasive concealment of death.

Heidegger's phenomenology turns 180 degrees otherwise. Both philosopher and layman *live* death in the way Heidegger describes it. His distinctions rest at the heart of my way of articulating the issues pertinent to death and sorrow. Therefore, this chapter—midway through the book—is at the nexus. It presents the crux of what has preceded and what will follow. I present the nerve of Martin Heidegger's foundational thought. It quickens topics that allow death and sorrow ... to live.

Humankind's title: Being-in-the-world-with-others

Is the human being best described by the metaphysical name "rational animal"? Not in Heidegger. He expurgates the arbitrary dualism at the heart of Platonic Christendom. He gives the human a new ontological title: Dasein (Heidegger, 1927/1962). Man is the "there" being, there where it is happening, where it is "at". Man is a being-in-the-world-with others. Heidegger cancels the traditional substantive account of man's essence. The human is a network of relations.

The "in" is not an insertion, like a plug in a socket, popcorn in a bag, or a bug in a jar. Heidegger contrasts "in" with "beyond". Meta-physics means ruminating about what is beyond the immediately accessible. Heidegger insists that we are "in" the circle of life a-becoming, in the spiral ever spinning. Out and beyond is utopia, no place, a meta-physical concoction. Heidegger's challenge is that our western thinkers leave the ivory towers and get grounded on this patch of earth, in living time, and in our bodies. That is, he accents the inherent earthiness, temporality, and mortality of human existence (Heidegger, 1927/1962, pp. 91ff; 383ff; Heidegger, 1950/1971a, p. 23ff; Heidegger, 1952/1971b, pp. 149–150). Our destiny is local, worldly, and in here-and-now time. We are intertwined in everyday life with such ordinary things as the hammer, the jug, the peasant's shoe, and the full glass of wine. Contemporary media jargon chants: "on the ground" and "at the end of the day". We dwell on this patch of earth, our home.

Heidegger simply brackets, puts into parenthesis, suspends belief in, puts out of play ... any imagined other-eternal world. We can only know of such a place-time by faith or abstract thinking. In the everyday lifeworld, we experience and co-create meaning with available finite spatio-temporal objects that implicate us and with which we passionately engage ourselves.

"World" does not signify a physical locale but my familiar horizon, a system of meanings interlaced with my modes of intentionality, correlated with my thinking and feeling and willing and desiring, and with my comings and goings. World includes the *umwelt*, or my surrounding world—the mountains, the ocean, the plains; sunsets, rainbows, and the Northern Lights; the homes, huts, or hovels where we dwell; the Twin Towers that have been levelled down to Ground Zero. It embraces the *eigenwelt*, my very personal life-space, the core of me, and my inwardness. It also includes the *mitwelt*, my being-with-world that I share with others … with my neighbours.

We also have our being among ready-to-hand "tools" which we wield and weapons that we brandish. We dwell within our private space, cherishing our singleness, the precious individuality that we are always in the process of pressing out. However, my unique core, my commerce, and my putzing around only make sense in the face of my co-existence with others. I comport myself always among my fellows—flesh, blood, bone and as finite as I am—and as fallible and prone to inevitable foibles. We are death-bound subjectivities.

How do we ek-sist or stand out to face our sisters and brothers? (Heidegger, 1947/1993, p. 228) We have an intellectual fore-understanding, fore-sight, a fore-hold and a pre-comprehension of our milieu and interpersonal network. We are also emotionally passionate and tender, or "moody". We have heart. We find ourselves always-already attuned to the stuff of life. We hear the music of the world and orchestrate it. We are never out of mood, but only go from one emotional disposition to another.

The care-structure

About our multiple networks of relationships, we "care" (Heidegger, 1927/1962, p. 158). Care is so central and salient that we "fall" into it, losing our authentic self in *das man*, the they-self. We wallow within a collective life, thinking-willing-acting like everyone else. We follow the herd, parade with the masses, mask as "one". In our solicitude, we forget our ontological vocation, lose track of time, and evade our finitude. We forget that we forgot. We give the whole kit and caboodle over to the "they". But the "who" of the "they", Heidegger (1927/1962) reminds us, is "nobody" (pp. 165–166). Nobody needs to take responsibility for anything. Is not this serious? Indeed, it is the destructive consequence of 2,500 years of nihilism, the kernel of what today is wrong with Western de-civilization.

What calls us back to our authentic self? What reminds us that man is "ontologically excellent", the "shepherd of Being", and not a dull bleeping sheep (Heidegger, 1947/1993, p. 245)? How do we recall that we are the *only beings that in our being question our being*, the only ones for whom our existence is an issue? What lifts our forgetfulness and shows us that we have forgotten even that we forgot? Death promotes us to awareness. Death is our wake up call to remembrance. Death is the eye-opener. It is **definite** *that* I will die; it is **indefinite** *when* or *how*. Our arch imperative happens 100% absolutely. Death is my constant companion, a permanent variable in all that I do or don't do. Giving death its due would change everything.

An uncanny ending

Not death is our death, as rotting oranges perish; not a halting, as the rain ceases. It is not a completion, as when we finally finish building the house, get our degree, or write our symphony. It is not the fulfillment of receiving our first real kiss, or hearing the right one express their appreciation, or finally getting into her jeans. All those analogies are "bad" analogies. Finite finishes to depict death miss the mark.

Death is rather an uncanny ending. It is the possibility of the impossibility of continuing to exist. No accident, fluke, or disaster will cause my death. The bullet that will snuff out my life, the tsunami that will sweep it away or the nuclear holocaust that will put out all lights—they only delimit the *when* and demarcate the *how*. The cause of death, if one must predicate a cause at all … is Life itself.

We die of Life. We'd better get a handle on that one! W.H. Auden (1991) gathers together and expresses concisely Heidegger's demand: "And life is the destiny you are bound to refuse until you have consented to die" (p. 353).

Resoluteness

As soon as I am no longer "lost", I hear the call. As soon as I stare into the Abyss, pierce through Nothingness, and endure the encounter with the Void, I am open to the call of conscience. Heeding the call and answering it promotes responsibility. I am responsible for myself. I stand alone. I must speak in my own name. I must act with resolve. I am also responsible for the others. I care for them. But my solicitude is not such to take their care away. Rather, I point out their care and show them what burden they are carrying, so that they may be free to shoulder it. This is duly called authentic solicitude.

We die alone. We live with others. Before the "hour" of our death, there is time to be for and with them. Even if we be granted only one ... night. Is there anything more natural?

Two fundamental standpoints on death: Greek metaphysics-phenomenology

Here comes James M. Demske's (1970) schema for contrasting the metaphysical and phenomenological approaches to death. I pencil in my own nuances and insights.

Separation-final unity

Greek metaphysical thinking defines death as *separation*, the dissolution of a composite creature into its two principles: matter and form or body and soul. The material body—a few dollars worth of chemicals—burns to ashes or decomposes into dust. Finite to start with, the body is nothing but a shell or prison of the eternal spirit. It decays into its inevitable temporal tomb of dust, darkness, and maggots.

The spirit or infinite principle, on the other hand, is released. It assumes another life and goes to the "other world". Insofar as Christianity—by baptizing Platonism—fuses the two into one, that other world is called heaven, hell, or purgatory. The soul begins an eternal life, earns its reward, receives its punishment, or waits in limbo.

Heidegger will have none of it. The human being is a *unity*, never dual to begin with. Death does not separate; it binds together. It is the moment of supreme unification, drawing the last arch in the circle of existence. During our lifetime, we have various and sundry "moments" of unity, times when everything comes together.

Sexual love can be such an experience, the feeling that with her … all-is-one … and it would be perfectly fine to die now.

Death is the quintessential expression of our longing for completeness. Until death, we are always be-coming. Something remains unsettled. Death finishes it. We stop becoming. We stop walking. Our can-be and can-do halt. The spiral of life stops a-spinning. Death enacts elusive wholeness. What Western rationalism calls death is death's end … the death of death.

Particular case or unique possibility

Secondly, Greeks metaphysics considers death a *particular case* of a general process of passing away. Death is what we have in common with vegetative and animal life. By analogy, we die the way everything that lives dies. Death is reduced, therefore, to a biomedical matter.

In Heidegger, to the contrary, death is a distinctively human phenomenon. It is precisely that which I do *not* have in common with animals or plants. Death *distinguishes* me from the rest of living creatures. I alone imagine my own demise, live with it always impending, and can advance towards it with calm and courage.

Since death sets me apart from all other levels of life, it co-creates my freedom. An Alaskan beaver does not awaken on a cold and rainy Monday morning in December, refusing to build a damn dam that day. Momma cat in heat in Pittsburgh does not ward off Tomcat, least she become pregnant. But we humans, from sea to shore and mountains to prairies, do make choices about our love, work, and sexuality. We choose in the shadow of death, which may be so obnoxious as to visit … tomorrow. Death cannot be reduced to biology. It is ontological and existential too.

My death is my unique, utmost, ownmost possibility. For the execution of any other affairs of my daily commerce, I can find a stand in, seek a substitute, or hire a replacement. But there is no pinch-hitter when it comes to death. I die alone. No one can die for me. It is my own most personal decision.

In "Vigilance", I make theme my mother's struggle to die. Though she was pain-racked and a veritable bag of bones, some strength in her clung to Life. It was a work for her to die, to give birth to her own unique death.

Artificial end of the line

Thirdly, Greek thinking conceives of time as a line. It casts death as an *event* that marks the *end* of one's life-line. Death is a terminus, the final limit of the time-string spanning my life history. Within this linear perspective, a straight arrow-like horizontal line can be drawn to depict my life from birth to death. The line further is pierced with vertical lines, locating events occurring on the way to the final event. Marker events litter the span: when I walked, talked, started school, came to puberty, got laid, got married, came out of the closet, won a gold medal, became a parent or a grandparent. So-called developmental psychology is precisely that discipline that chops up my "lifespan" into stages and phases: childhood; adolescence; early adulthood; the middle years; the senior years. It not only multiplies the slashes, it identifies them as the normal steps that I take. The verticals set apart and isolate as regular and predictable boxes into which I hop and jump out of.

The denial of death

Insofar as we are brainwashed by the locked-in view that death is a menace awaiting me in the future, we are prone to death-anxiety. Death spooks us. It is a frequent refrain of this book, in one way, shape or form, that death terrifies Western (de)civilization. We are a death-denying people. And in an unholy reversal, we torture, and kill, especially those who are not of our race, colour, creed, or country—especially if they are oil rich or popping over with poppies. Terrified of death, we Westerners promote instead the pornography of death. And we believe we are standing on the moral high ground.

The impossible objectification of my death

Is death my last stop? The Greek metaphysical account of death as the end of my line, merely describes the phenomenon as experienced by others, by the outside observers, by those who will mourn me— or be glad that I am finally gone. Death is objectified. I, who die, am nevertheless a subject. I am missing when they sign my death certificate and pick out my coffin; I never read my obituary or see my tombstone. I am out of the picture.

Heidegger makes intellectual mince meat out of the arbitrary notion of linear time. It is simply and solely an abstraction that lacks any basis in existence or grounding in lived experience. In nature, there are no straight lines.

The warp of time and the twist of death

Death is my present reality, not my future "maybe". It takes place in time, part of the spiral of life. It is as different from an event as one can imagine. And most assuredly, it is not an ending event. Rather, death is always on the horizon, part and parcel of all my comings and goings. Life-Death comprises a figure-ground structure in the "now".

Death shows itself in my choices, doubts, decisions, crises, and losses. One gives up the ghost with a knife in the back, with some major organ compromised, with vital signs gone, and with the body blood-splattered. Someone psychologically knifes me in the back. The treachery does not compromise my physiological heart. The betrayal draws no blood. My organs are still functioning, and my vital signs are fine. Still I have experienced Death.

Since death is my constant companion in the living present, I can enlist it as my consultant. Ordinarily, in the face of a major decision, we talk with friends, family members, a priest, rabbi, mullah, or "shrink". We can also confer with death. If this is the last decision I will ever make—and well it may be—what will I do? What would be authentic? We can listen to death's whispers and its shouts.

There is no framework on the intellectual scene like Heidegger's to make better sense out of our minor deaths, those losses and failures that require survivors to grieve a divorce or a relationship break up ... exactly as does one the assassination of our President, or the wanton rape and murder of a 14-year-old Iraqi girl by an American soldier expressing lustful revenge, or one raping a 14-year-old Japanese girl ... just to express lust ... Death is what I subjectively live. Heidegger is not indulging in philosophical analogy or lapsing into poetic metaphor or simile. Only Greek rationalistic dualism, with its head in the heavens, thing-i-fies Death and construes it as a substance that only others witness.

Death, as consultant *par excellence*, also helps us to put into perspective untoward events in our lives, and to balance the brain-racking, heart-rending madness of the slings and arrows of outrageous misfortune. Bobby Lane, a legendary professional American football quarterback of the Detroit Lions and Pittsburgh Steelers, reputedly said: "I never lost a football game. Time ran out."[6]

The beauty of commitment is compromised when I fix as absolute one possibility. Putting all my eggs in one basket prepares, should I drop the cargo, for a messy glop. But the sports team leader reminds us that there is always another "game" and another season. No one action defines me, irrevocably. No one love relationship is the be all and end all. In the face of death, I can slacken my stubborn control, my ridiculous insistence that I steer the wheel along one road only. Living with death, I can make changes, radical changes, even profound conversions ... right up until the moment I draw my last breath. Death helps me, therefore, to let it be. Søren Kierkegaard enjoins us to live as if we were already dead.

Ted Rosenthal, a poet dying of acute leukemia, describes how ordinary is Kierkegaard's seemingly outrageous statement.

> You can live a lifetime in a day; you can live a lifetime in a moment; you can live a lifetime in a year ... It's the sense of already being dead that makes you feel that you don't have to be just you, or an extension of what's in your hip pocket, but the infinite potential of the whole race. Man; first man; last man; all men. Because I had nothing, because I had no needs of my own, I wasn't self-occupied, so I had a feeling of love for everybody, unilaterally, unequivocally (Rosenthal, 1973, pp. 53–55).

What's next?

The metaphysical viewpoint logically leads to the question of the *future*. What happens after death? The body is disposed of, buried, or cremated. What happens to the soul? Where does it go? Since nobody comes back to tell us about it—whether or not we believe in "near-death" experiences or a Resurrection—the answer to this question is perforce speculative. The Christian answer is heaven or hell; the Catholics add purgatory and limbo; Muslims are convinced that those who die martyrs go to a blessed life; a plethora of ancient perspectives focus on the transmigration of souls and reincarnation.

This is not a place to delve into a history of comparative religions. Needless to say, Heidegger brackets all of this. Belief in any is simply that: an act of faith. He says instead that death throws us back to our present "moment". Back to Life! What are we doing with the time allotted to us? What will I do next, here and now, in order to love those precious individuals who are part of my life?

Think of it this way. We have *reveries* about the moment *before* our death. We picture the self dying a martyr in the instant the suicide bomb detonates; or peacefully drifting off into sleep; or as a hero who does not flinch in front of the firing squad; or in the "saddle" with the women with whom we were granted only … one night.

We have *fantasies* about the "moments" *after* our death: we picture our lover deciding that they cannot go on without us and committing suicide so that they can follow; I make myself the fly on the wall, watching and listening to those who come to prattle about me at my wake and funeral; or after the nuclear holocaust, we picture the earth empty and desolate.

Our reveries and fantasies are the things nightmares are made of, or novels. But it is playful, and we know immediately that it is illusory. But what is the true *image* of death? It is of the Void, the Abyss, of Nothingness.

Filling the void

What does one do now? Where does one go from here? We go back to life. We learn something rock bottom solid from a confrontation with Emptiness, and by unflinchingly staring into the Void. We realize that there is no divine or metaphysical first principle to sustain us, safeguard us, to ground our intellectual framework, to authorize our moral stance, or to support our practical activities. In the abyss, the grounding ideas and guiding principles vanish, those that were inculcated in us by our nourishing environment—by our caretakers, good shepherds, and teachers.

When Nietzsche (1882b/1974) utters the "word", "God is dead", he is not picking on the poor Crucified or on the lonely Prime Mover (p. 95). It has nothing to do with faith or religion. The affirmation dismantles Platonic Christendom's practice of legitimizing thinking-willing-doing by an appeal to a supreme rational principle, an *arche´*. After Nietzsche, such an abstract project is intellectually defunct. He challenges us: Learn to think. Open your heart. Create something. Heidegger shows us the ordinary way to reach

Nietzsche's insight. Face death. Crawl up the asshole of death and feel the fear (Alley, 1973, p. 170). Then leap into life.

This is no heroic move that I am advocating; nor am I bouncing wisdom off one of seven pillars. I willingly accept all criticism concerning this chapter or this entire book. But I refuse to stand guilty of the accusation that I am trying to make heroes of us all. The matter is plain, simple, and sane. When we die, we can take nothing with us. In the face of death, we are stripped of pretty ribbons or our Queenly Crown. And if we can see ourselves with nothing on, we've got nothing left to hide and nothing to fear. Is it ever truth, if it is not naked?

Heidegger brackets a foundational God-figure and a heavenly home. Remember your first course in algebra. You can take off the brackets and handle what you had suspended. When the final curtain comes down, perhaps we will see the Force that our faith convinces us holds everything together.

For all the careless ink spilt concerning Heidegger as godless and dangerous, you cannot read the man seriously, extensively, and in-depth without feeling the quickening nerve of Catholicism in his thought—no more than you can fail to shudder at the nerve that also quickened Hitler's National Socialism. It matters not what this little German man in the Black Forest—for the most part a failed human being with an incredible mind—genuinely believed. Heidegger's thought is beyond the hackneyed, dualistic rhetoric of theism-atheism. Martin Heidegger does not concern us; we are concerned with what's *in* Heidegger (Schurmann, 1982/1987). After him, there are only "echoes" (Sallis, 1990).

Heidegger reverses Pascal's wager. Instead of gambling in favour that there is a God, Heidegger gambles that He or She is absent. Obviously, if it turns out that God exists, acts to authorize everything, and provides us with a solid foundation, then fine and dandy. The question is simple: what have we to lose in suspending belief and acting as if there is nothing? *Nothing!* Our gain is the capacity to create meaning, be honest, be resolute, and act humanly.

Our civilization professes that Christian views and morals guide us. But open your eyes and gaze over the 20th century. The west has practiced spiritualized malice. The entire history of our Western, rational civilization is a long tale of racism and violence, acted out under the banner of the Cross. If the cycle of revenge and counter-revenge doesn't do us in, maybe greenhouse gases will terminate us, or a nuclear holocaust. What can be worse than our rationalistic chaos that has driven us to the brink of extinction? Again, nothing! What's the fear in letting go of an *arche*'? You decide.

Final punctuation

Paul Colaizzi (1978) draws out vividly the homey implications of Heidegger's oft times torturous texts:

> Death takes all of us too soon. No one whose death is evidently imminent is any worse off than another whose death is not obviously immediately forthcoming. None who die young are more deprived than those who die old; likewise, there is no guarantee that one who dies old has lived "more" than one who dies young. There is no one in comparison to self whose time of death is more suitable. In this regard we are all the same. Our disappointment at the realization of our impending death should not be aggravated by the false belief that others live longer than we do; nor have we grounds to gloat over the equally false belief that we shall live longer than someone else. Here comparisons are totally beside the point. No one is snatched from life earlier or later than anyone else. That another dies is grounds for sorrow; when another dies is irrelevant (p. 77).

Colaizzi (1978) also turns his reflections in the direction of the other:

> If I could choose the time of death of a loved one (as distinct from the cessation of his [sic] suffering), could I ever really be able to select an appropriate time? Is it better for him to be spared the tribulations of old age, or should he be granted a long, full life? The question is meaningless. There is no good time for death. The regardless-of-the-when-of-death provides the constant meaning and joy of life; the meaning of life springs from the inconsequence of its measured duration (pp. 77–78).

Nietzsche gives us a task. Some of us die too early: some of us die too late. The challenge is to die at the right time (Nietzsche, 1883b/1982, p. 71).[7]

PART IV

CHAPTER ELEVEN

Towards an alternative approach to intervention

Living in moral pain

Intervention is the right word. At root, it means to enter into the midst of what is happening. Whenever that happening happens to be grief, it is truly splendid to have someone come in ... intending to help and actually helping. The $64,000 dollar question is, "What precisely is the healing touch?"

In Chapter six, in the context of talking with Nicole about her Nana's death, I offer my standpoint on authentic dialogue in the "moment" of grief. The theme of therapeutic intervention, however, requires this separate chapter. I now expand my discussion beyond talking with my precious daughter. In a nutshell, I forge past the limits of mainstream medico-behavioural psychology's short-term, quick-fix approach, the drive to adjust and cope, the haste to forget, and the need to obliterate pain. The same standpoint that roots the entire substance and style of this book, both its research tactics and choices of writing-genre, inspires my viewpoint on care. Thinking and in-depth understanding must precede doing, so that therapeutic intervention would be sane and wholesome. I affirm that to approach grief without honouring psyche, *seele*, soul ... is insane.

Our culture tries to offer a healing touch. We have evolved as many varieties of therapeutic theories as snowflakes. To address the turmoil caused by various deaths, our certified grief counsellors treat the distraught individual; we dispatch emergency response specialists to zones wracked by the hurricanes, tsunamis, typhoons, floods, oil hemorrhages, or sites of murders—at a high school in the shadow of the Rockies named Columbine; at a simple school in Lancaster Co., Pennsylvania where the peaceful Amish hold court; at Virginia Tech University, a city-like establishment where a disturbed young man slaughtered thirty-two persons; in Fort Hood, Texas, a USA Army major kills thirteen of his fellows and also wounds another thirty. Survivors need help to deal with the madness both in the emergency "moment" and afterwards. The System provides it.

No doubt about it. Our hearts are in the right place. However, there is a lack. The more the flakes proliferate, the more they express one more variation of the same one-dimensional paradigm. Abstract rationalism, decayed dualisms, and crass pragmatism rule psycho-medico-therapy. Insofar as the resolution of shame, humiliation, grief, and depression involves forgiveness, making reparation, facing truth, and drumming up courage, our standard treatment remains off-target. It ignores the moral and spiritual dimension of psychic pain, what Edward Tick (2005) names "soul wounding and soul loss" (p. 16). Haste, superficiality, and busy-ness are ultimately counter-therapeutic. Boat loads of goals and aims, plans and objectives, sophisticated coping strategies, coaching models to manage symptoms, and thought-stopping techniques are woefully inadequate. They miss the Big Ship. It would be a pie in the sky hope that, in a book such as this one, I might overhaul the entire system or even convert our encrusted cognitive behavioural approach into a *psychological* psychology. Seminal and decisive thinkers—Nietzsche and Heidegger—have already tried and failed to dismantle the way in which we think in the West. My appeal is more modest. "Please, let's add one more very different snowflake to the arsenal of therapeutic approaches."

Arguably, the most damning article written about the bankruptcy of medico-cognitive behavioural therapy, insofar as it overlooks the moral-spiritual dimension of human existence, comes from an artist. Peter Marin (1991) is not interested in the marriage between psychiatry and cognitive behaviourism (p. 41). Nor does he give a hoot about their ideological positions or practical politics. He is concerned with the suffering of Vietnam vets. He cares about healing their pain.

A quarter of a century ago, a task faced him: to review and then critically comment upon the proliferation of films about the Second Indochina War, the American War in Vietnam. He took the job.

The conflict occurred from 1959 until the Fall of Saigon, 30 April, 1975. By 1981, filmmakers could listen back with distance to the shrill voices of righteous individuals who supported the war on a patriotic platform and to angry shouts of those who hated it with a passion beyond belief. Marin began to interview veterans as part of his brief. He quickly became more intrigued with the stories the vets had to tell than about the movies. He writes eloquently and intelligently about their plight.

Whatever one's political stance, no one can doubt that this was a war of liberation that successfully reunified the Vietnamese nation under a communist government consisting of the Democratic Republic of Vietnam (DRV or North Vietnam) and the indigenous National Front for the Liberation of South Vietnam. Today Vietnam, which Western politicians arbitrarily and foolishly had bi-furcated, is a united country. The slice of historical turf known as Cu Chi, a tri-leveled 200 km tunnel system, an amazing architectural and engineering feat, symbolizes Vietnamese ingenuity and heroism (Tran, 2004). Likewise, it was a humiliating defeat for the USA. In spite of the political rhetoric and mendacity about this unprecedented and not-yet-forgotten narcissistic blow to USA military might, by 1981 the general USA populace felt sympathy for those veterans who came home alive but wounded, maimed, plagued with Agent Orange, and suffering from a post-traumatic stress or delayed-stress syndrome. "More than 58,000 Americans died as a direct result of the military hostilities. Hundreds of thousands more were wounded" (Capps, 1991, p. 2). Stack that up against the number killed thus far in Iraq—4,258 as of September 2009—and the toll of life lost in Vietnam remains an unconscionable waste. However, the story of the survivors is the object of my focus.

Approximately twenty percent of those who served experienced deep and persistent emotional distress and psychological trauma. *More than twice the number of those who lost lives there*

have taken their own lives since returning home. Huge percentages
of America's homeless are veterans of the war (Capps, 1991,
p. 2, original emphasis).

That story is as fresh as ... tomorrow. In the *New York Times,* Tom
Shanker (6 April, 2008) expresses the USA military leaders "increased
alarm about the mental health of soldiers who would be sent back
to the front again and again ... in Iraq". One out of four non-
commissioned officers, an Army study of mental health reveals, show
signs of anxiety, depression, or acute stress ... exhibit symptoms of
post-traumatic stress disorders. The tale of the horrific effect of service in Iraq is on permanent hold as long as the occupation continues.
It is easy to anticipate: similar to post-Vietnam, the system will flounder concerning care for veterans of combat returning from Iraq and
Afghanistan.

Our young warriors were victims and scapegoats. Vietnam, remember, was "by far the most morally suspect war America had fought in
modern times" (Marin, 1991, p. 41). The entanglements in Iraq and
Afghanistan lack the shroud of moral taint that blanketed Vietnam.
Nowadays, we are hardened to the politics of oil and do not flinch
when blood is traded for the moolah of black gold. In spite of the
fiendish atrocities at Abu Ghraib, therefore, and in spite of the many
legal indictments and convictions of our military troops for crimes
of rape, torture, and murder against the people they are supposed
to be liberating, the populace welcomes home our troops as having
done their duty and served their country. We yap about the "few bad
apples" who make it difficult to win the hearts and minds of the Iraqi
people, but we decorate the rest of the "good stock" that fills the barrel. We will continually appreciate them, even if the war efforts in Iraq
and Afghanistan remain abysmal failures, and despite the fact that
we always had no more chance of winning these "wars" than we had
of defeating the bright, resourceful, and courageous Vietnamese.

No: Vietnam was the first time that the "boys" fought with ears
ringing from a furious protest against their efforts. It was the last time
that returning soldiers will be spat at instead of cheered. America,
collectively, will never dishonour again and humiliate its uniformed
warriors.

The homecoming troops came back to face disgrace instead of
returning as military heroes. They got a bad shake and a bad rap.

Sympathy for their wounds was skin deep. In fact, we dammed our combatants in several ways. First of all, victory eluded them. No surprise. They were not properly trained to fight the fight they had to fight—the "Bamboo-spike and nail-spike traps ... steel-pellet bombs ... 'dupling mines' ... primitive weapons that frightened to death the enemy ... and [had them] running for dear life" (Tran, 2005, pp. 29, 36, 50). Put cynically, their commanders forgot to discard the military manuals taught at West Point or the Naval Academy. And the treacherous freedom fighters in the jungles and tunnels of Vietnam outright refused to fight textbook-like battles, just as today the insurgents use roadside bombs and suicide missions in the deserts of the Near East, defying classical military strategies.

Coming home, the vets experienced a double whammy. Society blamed and adjudged them failures for being either 1) patriotic villains, or 2) anti-patriotic traitors. The radical left-wing viewed them as concrete symbols of a decayed nation that had committed genocide on a poor, underdeveloped nation, one reeling from many decades of French rape. For many born and raised in the "land of the free and the home of the brave", Vietnam was not just a "moment" of disillusionment but of blinding insight. The USA, in spite of the Lady in the Harbour, is a violent and racist country. "Spreading democracy" appeared to them as a code phrase for "opening new markets", for freeing the world so it might embrace capitalism. They took out their rage and moral indignation on the young men who carried the weapons, instead of calling to court the greedy military-industrial-political leaders who armed them. The embattled losers were only soldiers, not the architects of the pathetic misadventure, and not the ones who reaped financial profits from their agony and from the misery of the Vietnamese and Cambodians. With Iraq and Afghanistan, nothing has changed.

The far right scorned and detested returning servicemen as disgraceful mutineers, failing to distinguish the fact that only a small minority of the combatants simply stopped fighting and turned their guns on their commanding officers (Neal, 2003).

The indignation at this dubious moral enterprise pervaded the social milieu like an atmosphere that refused to let the next day's winds blow it away. The troops suffered the consequence. The politicians and the profiteering military-industrial elite went Scott free and laughed all the way ... to the banks ... and pinnacles of power.

Only the "fall" of Richard Nixon gave any shred of justice to the majority of Americans who opposed this war from pillar to post.

The above view gives one side of a complex matter. It is not a political commercial, but it provides the proper context for Peter Marin's (1991) insight: the surviving vets were "living in moral pain" (p. 40). If you do not grant that immorality, humiliation, and bi-directional outrage ate up the lives of our returning troops, then you only perpetuate the historical failure of our health care system to heal the "boys". From my standpoint, it is the same with treating grief. The tangle of shame, guilt, humiliation, and false pride cannot be understood on the natural plane alone. They are psycho-spiritual issues.

Back up a bit, please. The atrocities the soldiers witnessed, the heinous crimes they committed, and the composite horrors they experienced are part and parcel of all wars. Which war has ever been prosecuted without rape, pillage, plunder, and outrageous acts of wanton destruction? But in this case, the Spirit of the Age of Aquarius did not condone the evils. The *zeitgeist* did not slip it under the rug. With the help of the mass media, the spirit of the times stuck it in our eyes and spelled for our ears that the whole enterprise from start to finish was terribly ... wrong. *Hair, Woodstock*, love-beads, and the peace sign ... multiply the concrete metaphors of a generation that saw what was happening in Vietnam for what the judgement of history now sees: It was genocide.

Soldiers, sailors, and marines after World Wars I and II came home with scars. They also carried ugly memories which gave them sleepless nights. They needed to come to terms with their actions, and find a place within their hearts and heads for the brutality and insanity they had witnessed. The culture as a whole condoned their actions construed as saving the world for democracy, stopping Nazi evil, or winning a war to end all wars. That made it easier for most vets, or at least manageable. They learned to live with it, stood on their feet, and walked the streets of their towns with heads held high. Some merely shuffled, having simply shut down. They never talked about it, withdrew somewhere deep inside, and went cold. The culture commemorates D-Day 6 June, V-E Day 8 May, and V-J Day 15 August as if they are not just days of civil celebration, but veritable holy days. Until today, the veterans of both world wars are proud.

It was 180 degrees different after Vietnam. After the world wars, we built monuments and re-named streets to commemorate "victory". But our "boys" did not win in Southeast Asia. You have to travel 20,000 miles to walk the street with names you won't find anywhere in America. There never will be a street named the "Ho Chi Minh Trail" in Dayton, Ohio.

The boys accomplished nothing. No redeeming values washed the slime and the scum that covered their souls. No communal structure afforded them the luxury of legitimizing their actions. Instead, society indicted them for creating multiple layers of scandal. Robert Jay Lifton (1991) describes their paradox: Sent as intruders in an Asian revolution, asked to fight a filthy and unfathomable war, they return as invaders in their own society, defiled by that war in the eyes of the very people who sent them" (p. 62).

Thus, they bore the brunt of their country's hypocrisy. Moral pain ambushed them. In the face of it, they reeled, soul-sore. Marin informs us that the therapeutic establishment did not address the hurt.

Marin's insight into his own insight is that the established therapeutic modalities were as hamstrung to help the returning vets as the military brass had been inept in prosecuting the war. The therapeutic community not only did not help the returning troops, it hindered them. It magnified the pain by misidentifying it, ignoring its core, and treating it in a way that only rubbed salt into the genuine wounds.

Marin's insight into the insight of his insight intertwines with my outlook—which is why I have gone to lengths to spell out the predicament that generated it. Most discussions you read about therapy are written by true believers using buzz words and categories that are part of the rhetoric of club members. Looked at from the outside, however, the paradigm that dominates therapy provides a metaphor. Marin exposes this normative paradigm and its metaphorical implications. I use what he says algebraically. That is, the deficient approach to moral pain and soul-wounding of Vietnam vets applies with equal force to grief therapy. In a nutshell, Western thinking simply is ill-equipped to deal with the moral and psycho-spiritual issues that haunt the human soul ... in whatever way the soul is haunted.

Marin (1991) exposes "the inadequacy of the prevailing cultural wisdom, models of human nature, and modes of therapy to explain moral pain or provide ways of dealing with it" (p. 41). Edward Tick

(2005) concurs when he affirms that conventional psycho-medical models and therapeutic techniques are "not adequate to explain or treat" soul-wounding and loss of soul (p. 2).

The over-arching need for forgiveness was never addressed as a part of standardized treatment plans. Don't laugh! Can you imagine back in 1975 that a major treatment goal would be to address shame for committing crimes against humanity or for being complicit with genocide?[8]

"We seem as a society to have few useful ways to approach moral pain or guilt" (Marin, 1991, p. 43). Fortunate was the vet whose therapist showed the natural intelligence and wisdom to treat shame and humiliation as moral-spiritual problems. The following statement is so on target that it seems ridiculous even to call it a metaphor for the way we treat grief or post-traumatic stress:

> Our great therapeutic dream in America is that the past is escapable, that suffering can be avoided, that happiness is always possible, and that insight inevitably leads to joy. But life's lessons—so much more apparent in literature than in therapeutic [literature]—teach something else again (Marin, 1991, p. 46).

In Vietnam, we rained our bombs and splayed our napalm upon a yellow race for no reason rooted in truth or freedom. In the body-count announced daily on the Six o'clock news, Vietnam showed us that dead-is-dead-and-murder-is-murder. Ironically, it was this crass and boringly irritating litany of deaths (especially events like the My Lai massacre and the other countless scenes in which innocent women and infants were slaughtered) that helped to sour and incense the general USA public against the war. Ironical, I say, because in this most political of wars (until Iraq), one of the reasons that the troops started to shoot their commanding officers was because of the mandate they imposed upon the foot soldiers: to increase the body count (Neal, 2003, pp. 149–184).[9]

The truth ... about the stark truth ... of the evil of murder is so simple and self-evident that it should not have been a bitter pill to swallow. It was too bitter to even administer. Our arrogance, false pride, wounded ego, and penchant for abstract theorizing got in our way ... and maybe also did our guilt and shame. Tick's (2005) work taught him "that we do not even know how to think about war" (p. 3).

Genocide is hard to sweep under the rug. Nobody, officially, in the System would discuss it as a possible problem with returnees in distress. The effective and appropriate help for the Vietnam vets never did come to pass. The System qua System invested most time, money, and energy, not in rehabilitating and guaranteeing a good life for the vets, but in making sure that the decade of the 1960s, bloated with visions of love, peace, and revolution, would NEVER happen again. In that it has succeeded. Until now, the vision has not re-emerged.

Along the Seward Highway in south central Alaska, the closest settlement to the city of Seward is Moose Pass. The west side of the tiny town sits flush against the Bear Tooth Mountains. In approximately its middle, a flowing waterfall turns a wheel that the residents built there to harvest nature. Near the waterwheel rests an axe on a log, and a drinking cup. The sign above the wheel reads, "If you have an axe to grind, grind it here."

Most authors of medico-psycho-scientific books—with the possible exception of those bought and sold by the profit-ruled textbook industry—do have an axe to grind. Who, for example, would bother to write about death and grief with no message to disseminate? Even if the toil is mostly to carve out a niche in the field that would bear one's name, the author has a point to make. In whatever way she or he tries to hammer home that point—almost always with maximal integrity, neutrality, and a minimum of bias—a streak of passion spikes one's Vision. Passionate reflection—or reflective passion—marks a book as recommendable and relevant.

My basic intention is to track sorrow's profiles, faithfully. This book is a candle made of hearthead that, in order to throw light, burns. We lose; we suffer; we need to heal. To facilitate deep healing, I eschew the one-dimensional approach of cognitive-behaviourism, do not put stock in the self-help and pop psych genres, and am not embracing Freud either or the followers, developers, or revisionists of his psychoanalytic paradigm. My two guiding presuppositions clash with, go against the grain of, and turn 180 degrees opposite all of the above standpoints: 1) Understanding precedes explanation; 2) Thinking should precede doing.

In "When Nana Died" (Chapter six), I tender my ideas about partaking in genuine conversations. Not every act of intervention can be such a spontaneous free-fall; and 99.99% of the time you will not be dealing with someone you know as well as your own child. Still, in that chapter I communicate a metaphor about intervention, one that bucks the tide of the culture's dominant paradigm. I address the literature on grief therapy with the same vision.

Before hand a disclaimer. I am not dismissing as irrelevant the one-dimensional goals of mainstream rational, pragmatic medico-psychology. It is a genuine value to get back on one's feet—to recover, to cope, to overcome, to make it through the night, to survive. With a broken leg, one leans on a crutch. In dire straits, popping a pill might be the crutch most useful. Learning skills or techniques facilitates the adjustment that we all need to handle both the slings and arrows of outrageous misfortune and the ordinary demands of everyday life. To gainsay this surface value is to live in La-La Land. Even being cocksure that homeostasis is a limited value, and conformity a dubious one, still one cannot refuse whatever it takes to stop the bleeding, or reduce the fever, or to fit in (even if fitting-in is for no other reason than to try to change the System from within). My axe starts to grind, however, because the goal of the medical model, the quick-fix alleviation of symptoms is off kilter. Grind, too, because the System champions one-dimensional values as the privileged herd of sacred cows. As humans, we do not only behave or perform but we also have a depth-life of love and tenderness, of sacrifice and humility. Cross-examining with uncommon sense our sensible modes and levels of adjustment is as important at striking an even keel. For the sake of life living, we must be prepared to turn over the applecart. As human, we aspire to heights that have lured our kindred since time immemorial. Mystery also sustains us. Surface is never the be-all and end-all. Behaviour is just a tiny sliver of human existence. Superficial treatment, therefore, fails to cure a broken heart.

In the best of all possible eventualities, I would prefer just to grind out, with no criticism, my descriptions and reflections about sorrow's profiles. Bottom line, I want to communicate with those who labour to take care of those in grief and thus with those who might share my concerns. I wish there was no theoretical-practical crisis in psychology, and no fragmentation among the disciplines.

I would enjoy it if there was no reason to complain, criticize, and harp about the levelling down of the human spirit, about the dumming down of our mental capacities, the shrinking of the human heart, and the elimination of soul from a discipline that calls itself psychology. My own (borderline) contributions, however, must be put into context. They would not even stand out vividly, unless viewed against the backdrop of mainstream rational-pragmatic positivism. So I grind my axe.

In a work that aims to be genuine scholarship and serious writing, the thinker and/or doer will inevitably have an axe to grind. It is not of the essence *that* the woman or man picks up the axe, but *how* she or he does wield it. What matters is that the individual grind with care and not carelessly. One must not serve a purely private or selfish purpose. As common parlance characterizes grinding one's axe, one has a "bone to pick", a "score to settle", or needs "to set the record straight". Or one has been annoyed for a protracted period and, until he works it out, he's "got something stuck in his craw". In the extreme, the grinding intends to hurt or belittle, or aims to avenge a wrong by humiliating or destroying.

Authentic grinding, on the other hand, would serve the goals of emancipation, the betterment of humankind, and radical cure. It should be fierce work, leading to critical discernment. It should sharpen the tool in the sense of scouring dross or scraping off scum caked on metal. It would open windows and doors to distinguish what is supremely worthwhile from what is merely in vogue, from what is worthless, and from what is ultimately destructive. Fine lines face us. How does one deconstruct what one sees as destructive ... without being destructive?

Aware of this ambiguity and in an attitude of respect, I ply my pickaxe to the roots of two trees. First, I dig in order to uncover the glint of jewels buried under the hegemony of today's cognitive behavioural positivism. I grind my axe in order to turn psychology on its head and to shake the heart into it. Second, my grinding aims to dismantle or deconstruct the life-denying nihilistic metaphysics that steers all Western ways, from science to politics.

I see my axe through the lenses of a Vision that is holistic, integrative, and comprehensive, not dualistic, divisive, and narrowly rationalistic. I would misguide you, without doubt, if I would insist that our contemporary therapeutic disciplines do as bad a job in treating grief as they did while sacrificing the health of returning Vietnam veterans in service of protecting the System instead. We do a better job. Still, our work remains superficial. If you would graciously don my glasses, you might have a better insight into my reflections about representatives of the established therapeutic order. I seek the balance necessary for genuine healing. I turn to the current literature.

Points of convergence

Robert Neimeyer (2006) has gone to school on their findings of Selby Jacobs, Colin Murray Parkes, and Holly Prigerson, each of whom showcases the broad, complex, and highly individualized manifestations of grief. He has also appropriated George Bonanno and Camille Wortman's demonstrations that so-called positive emotions signify resourcefulness and predict long-term successful outcomes of mourning better than trying to eliminate negative emotions.

The blurb on the eye-catching brochure for Neimeyer's workshop on the experience of grief and loss does not advertise the typical cookbook approach. It focuses upon the "experience" of grief and loss. It seemingly eschews the one-size-fits-all approach to grief assessment and treatment. It states that grief impacts each person differently. No set formula exists for the length if time it takes to move through the grieving process. As I wrote in Chapter four, he distinguishes complicated grief from depression, anxiety, simple adjustment reactions, and post-traumatic stress disorders. The markers to differentiate the concepts are measurable, including the length of time of the symptoms, their intensity, and the degree to which they interfere with normal functioning. Differential diagnosis suits as a top priority, of course, since it leads to different forms of treatment. In fact, Neimeyer espouses no radical agenda. He has formed a panel of experts advocating the inclusion of complicated grief in the next version of the *Diagnostic and Statistical Manual of Mental Disorders*.

Such action by a mainstream scientist-practitioner is a matter of course. Equally naturally, this new twist changes nothing at root. The approach does not embrace the experience of the singular person as a full blown subjectivity. Neimeyer has sketched yet another constructivist model of questing for meaning in which the invalidation of Life's rational-logical premises constitutes the trauma of bereavement. The "narrative structure of our lives" is, at root, the way everything hangs together. Healing after loss, therefore, entails the conceptual reconstruction of meaning of the self and the world. Brief therapy, as a process of meaning reconstruction, will do the trick.

Robert Leahy, the President of the Academy of Cognitive Therapy, conducts a competing workshop. Leahy (2003) titles his routine, "Overcoming Resistance in Cognitive Therapy". In his brochure, Leahy criticizes Neimeyer as being simplistic, dismissive of emotions, and asking patients to do more than they are ready for (Leahy, 2003). As soon as we read that Leahy offers participants a regime for overcoming such resistance, we wonder whether we have not surreptitiously entered the realm of Sigmund Freud.

If Neimeyer would pursue his thematic intentions to their logical conclusions, he might dismantle the central dilapidated buildings of the mainstream multiplex. But his operative intention is the drab Kantian project of properly getting our cognitive schemata into order. He offers a new menu but serves the same meals. Cognition and emotion, the two horns of the Platonic-Cartesian dilemma, remain fractured, as do all the integrated and joined phenomena in this book. Likewise, the work manifests the self-same individualistic prejudice, focusing upon the isolated mourner. The family and the larger communal structures remain marginalized. Par for the course, the Darwinian evolutionary bias dominates: adapt, modify, and evolve a new structure ... survive. Western cognitive-behavioural technology does best when it appeals to biology—to reflexes, instincts, and genes. It soon exhausts itself concerning death-related themes. Their complexity inevitably eludes the reduction to biological explanations. Social constructionist thinking tries to replace the biological basis as the preferred mode of explanation. This conceptual turn, however, simply circles and repeats both the perennial penchant for dualism and its endless and boring debates about which horn is more valid: nature or nurture.

Continuing bonds

Alfonso Lingis (2007) states commonplace truths. The bond with a deceased loved one does not vanish into thin air when the casket is lowered into the ground nor does it go up in smoke when the corpse is cremated. It is healthy and healing to remember the good times, to visit the gravesite and to chat there with the one whose name is etched in granite, to maintain an internal dialogue with a lost loved one about hum drum daily concerns, and to continue to picture her face, or to imagine his reactions to current political events. The natural goals of grief counselling are not only gaining closure, or trying to say goodbye, but also supporting and fostering continuing bonds with one's deceased loved one.

A decade ago, one wing of grief-researchers began to focus upon the persistence of social-communal bonds. Klass, Silveman and Nickman (1996) prompted a debate on continuing connections between a survivor and the deceased. Nowadays, this persistent tie has become fashionable, the newest wave in the grief maelstrom. Even within cognitive therapy a movement is afoot to acknowledge the obvious. Ruth Malkinson (2007) now affirms that the goal of successful grief therapy is to construct a positive inner relationship with the deceased, even while maintaining high functioning in day-to-day life. Neimeyer (2006) also admits that the ongoing attachment of continuing bonds can empower the bereaved. The sacred cow of grief counselling is slowing dying a natural death. We who mourn have been set free to do it in our own particular way.

From the get-go, Klass and associates (1996) had clear and evident intentions: to overturn the common prejudice of the healing professions, the academy, and the culture at large. They wanted to dismantle the notion that ongoing interactions or continual bonding with the dead is pathological. Today's system-sanctioned perspective, the one with the scientific seal of approval, is nevertheless still a split-model: the "dual-process model of coping with bereavement" (Stroebe, Stroebe and Abakoumkin, 2005b, p. 2,178). Two stressors, "loss-oriented" and "restoration-oriented", impinge upon the bereaved. The former serves adjustment and confers relief from suffering; the latter perpetuates the "negative ... yearning and rumination" (Stroebe, Schut and Stroebe, 2001, pp. 395–414). No surprise. Western thinking is particularly incapable of comprehending and studying natural wholes, especially whole relationships. And it simply cannot subsume under its tiny positivistic umbrella what eludes measurement or direct physical, observable contact.

Dennis Klass (2006) puts it succinctly—but far too delicately: "In the contemporary hegemonic individualistic culture, community bonds and other wider attachments are weak, except in times of crisis ... . our view of attachment is too small" (pp. 843–858). He cites N. Field's article which, although assuming an "internal" connection between the living and the dead does not even broach the "idea that the bond remains integrated in the family or community bonds does not occur to him" (Klass, 2006, p. 851). Let's call a spade a spade. Field's ignoring of and debunking deep ongoing connectedness manifests myopia.

Ten years on since his seminal work, Klass still must make silly disclaimers to counter narrow-minded, heart-shrunken criticism. Describing continuing bonds, he clarifies, is not the same as prescribing them; and the support that such bonds provide the bereaved does not replace the need for adjustment to everyday life; a continuing bond is not "an antidote to loss" (Klass, 2006, p. 844).

The current debate in the literature bogs down in the typical morass of causal conceptualization, validation studies, and the protection of researchers' turf. The lip service paid to structural approaches, dynamic systems, and continual attachment stumbles on splintered syllables tucked within cognitive theories. Do continuing bonds between the bereaved and the deceased facilitate or hinder adjustment? Are adaptive functioning and continual attachment integrated, as if belonging to a web? Or are they fixed to two separate tracks, interacting but not identical?

In the everyday lifeworld, "on the ground" and in fullness of the day, a son grieves his mother, a sister grieves her sister, and a little girl grieves her grandmother. There is nothing anonymous or individualistic about it. And love endures.

Is would be absurd to have expected that mainstream grief theoretician or researchers who haggle about continuing bonds would have studied and been informed by Heidegger's radical standpoint on death. The following quotation from *Being and time*, however, renders the debate ridiculous.

The "deceased" [*Der "Verstorbene"*] as distinct from the dead person [*dem Gestorbenen*], has been torn way from those who have 'remained' behind [*dem "Hinterbliebenen"*], and is an object of "concern" in the ways of funeral rites, interment, and

the cult of graves. And that is so because the deceased, in his
[sic] kind of Being, is "still more" than just an item of equipment, environmentally ready-to-hand, about which one can
be concerned. In tarrying alongside him in their mourning
and commemoration, those who have remained behind are
with him, in a mode of respectful solicitude (Heidegger,
1927/1962, p. 282).

Sadness: Is healthy

Allan V. Horwitz and Jerome C. Wakefield (2007) give a much needed
thought-transfusion from outside their positivistic paradigm. Even
as the *DSM-V* revision looms, it is evident that it will merely expand
on rather than radically alter its predecessors. Clinical disciplines
and the caring sciences, to their detriment, will waste another decade following a bankrupt guidebook and practicing thoughtless and
heartless therapies.

Specifically, Horwitz and Wakefield (2007) accuse the mainstream
of pathologizing and medicalizing sadness after loss. They name a
danger lurking due to the domination, since 1980, of the *Diagnostic and Statistical Manual for Mental Disorders Depression* (DSM), the
psychiatric-psychological bible. What do the authors say is in peril?
Our normal emotional life, the ordinary human condition, and our
embracing sense of humanity.

As the *DSM* title indicates, quantitative indices determine diag-
noses in the handbook, specifically the number, frequency, and
duration of symptoms. Tucked within that limited framework,
depression has grown in epidemic proportions. Here is the kicker.
Under the dictatorship of *DSM*, run-of-the-mill events of loss due
to love and death are still treated as psychopathologies. The layman
since time immemorial and the physician since Hippocrates have
understood that situations of loss naturally evoke sadness. They are
emotionally charged, evoke pain and suffering, and demand struggle. With support from family, friends, and the community, we get
the job done and we endure.

The *DSM* has perverted this everyday reality. Randolph Nesse
(2007) minces no words: as an alleged vehicle of science, the DSM
is a "train wreck" that sabotages research, and distorts our experience both of our own sadness and the entire spectrum of our normal

emotional responses. As written and in the process of revision ... again ... it is incapable of differentiating between normal sadness and depressive disorder (Nesse, 2007, p. 35).

"Since 1980, the number of people in treatment for depression has soared more than 300 percent; making depression the most commonly treated psychiatric disorder" (Horwitz and Wakefield 2007, p. 5). Winston Churchill has given us the proper orientation to statistics, warning us that the only numbers we should believe are the ones we ourselves have made up. Therefore, please take such numerical information with the proper amount of dill seed and peppermint leaves.

What is behind this statistical juggernaut? Horwitz and Wakefield, with a mixture of truth and kindness, state that the desire for adequate scientific research motivates the dwarf-like approach to diagnosis. To tell it like it is, money spurs the *DSM*. Depression is a money-maker. Researchers use the cookbook to earn grants and to rake it in. But the practices only perpetuate establishment-violence. I refrain from citing statistics on the explosion of prescriptions for anti-depressants—which even physicians (at least in Norway) refer to as the "happy pills". Instead, I pose the question this way. Can we afford to cure depression? The answer is that the System could not bear the cost. An economic depression would ensue if nobody was diagnosed depressed. Wall Street would have to do a jig or a breakdance. We would have one more financial meltdown, a repeat of 15 September, 2008. Too many workers earn their daily bread by charging against the diagnosis.

What is the flip-side of this dwarfed labelling? The *DSM*, by no means person-centred, is nothing but an instrument of social control that feeds a capitalistic economy. The symptoms that merit a depressive diagnosis provide us with no relevant information about the suffering human being. It just gets her into the system and labels her for life! Some hackneyed questionnaire or a staff member trained to use the cookbook tease out these appropriate symptoms. These belong to no grounded context, nor are they connected to what happens at the "end of the day"; they have nothing to do with qualitative factors.

Not surprisingly, Horwitz and Wakefield (2007) affirm that psychiatry denies any benefit to intense sadness or that the feeling might be normal. I push their argument farther. Psychiatry today denies value to any intense emotion that comes from the depth of the human heart. Psychiatry renders sadness, grief, sorrow, and longing ... pathological; and it polices suicide.

We badly need a thorough and proper understanding of Freud's reflections on death and grief to ameliorate our global-political madness. But we need Freud equally to balance the tyranny of the DSM. Freud uses qualitative factors to distinguish between normal grief and depression. Likewise, Kierkegaard's insights into the human heart beef up the thin psycho-medical menu. The heuristic of each also preserves the dignity of commonplace human experiences. In context, sadness and sorrow are healthy, longing for a lost love is not a disease, and suicide can express dignity.

What is the link between the plight of the returning Vietnam veteran and grief therapy? How does one calculate the qualitative algebra? From my standpoint, grief responses are unique, sadness is sane and wholesome, and long-lasting lingering attachments are beneficial. They are self-evident truths which never needed any proof in the first place. We must add what is still missing from the mainstream cookbook: moral-spiritual dimensions to our work with mourning.

Does our culture give death its due? Or do similar dynamics operate nowadays that hamstrung efforts to help the Vietnam vets? Now as then, political prejudice, economic factors, and deep-seated theoretical biases confound death-related work. We privilege explanation over understanding and, in our obsession with outcomes, short-term success, and quick-fixes we still are not thinking. We are busy calculating financial costs instead.

Concerning the prosecution of the American War in Vietnam and its aftermath, nothing was officially more taboo than to acknowledge that the troops were given a morally-spiritually compromising task. Walter Capps (1991) writes that it exemplified the "dark night of the soul ... a personal experience ... so raw and debilitating that persons wonder if they'll ever be able to affirm anything again" (p. 3). Our dismal failure with Vietnamese vets is not a historical anomaly. We are as inept in helping returning troops from Iraq and Afghanistan. So Vietnam gives us a metaphor to examine the ways in which we treat death and grief.

Death is natural. Remember, I disagree with de Beauvoir. Death is Life's imperative, the ultimate terminator. Grief kills. There is no quick-fix. Short-term success is not the same as mending a broken heart. We need to give meaning to our pain and wounds, grapple with any moral interpretation of them, or struggle to repudiate the heavy judgement that we have been victimized by Fate. Genuine grieving that allows one to live, really live, requires that one be willing to pass through the hourglass of suffering-unto-understanding. Romano Guardini (1997) nails it: "Inwardly accepted suffering transforms the sufferer" (p. 35). One navigates the abyss, not through forgetfulness, but in loving remembrance. Healing takes courage. Don't expect to find courage treated in the mainstream grief literature.

You yourself can assess the predicaments pertaining to intervention that I have raised. You will appraise their merits. My appeal is simple. Bring the psyche and the heart into the consulting room of grief. Honour the moral and spiritual dimensions. Add one more snowflake, that's all.

CHAPTER TWELVE

Divorce

> Houses rise and fall, crumble, are extended,
> Are removed, destroyed, restored, or in their place
> Is an open field, or a factory, or a by-pass.
> Old stone to new building, old timber to new fires,
> Old fires to ashes, and ashes to the earth
> Which is already flesh, fur and faeces,
> Bone of man and beast, cornstalk and leaf
>
> (Eliot, 1936d/1963, p. 196).

Divorce is a man-made disaster. It is also a death experience from whoever's perspective we view it. For one spouse, the end of the marriage is a living death. For the other partner, divorce terminates death by granting a new lease on life. If there are children of the union, another can of worms opens. What does the divorce mean to the child? Debates rage furiously concerning the positive or negative consequences on children, short and long term. Always there is a settling of the estate, the dividing of durable goods. Never is there a way to divide the non-durable goods. It borders on mouthing a cliché to say that the topic requires a book by itself, or a library shelf of them. One chapter cannot do the topic justice, but

179

it would be ostrich-like to print a book on grief omitting it. How to address the matter?

I present a parable. In A Divorced House, I imbue a domicile with the power of consciousness, a depth of soul, and a tenderly passionate heart. My decision is neither arbitrary nor quirky. Grief is embedded in a network of involvements. A "For Sale" sign on the lawn concretely symbolizes that an entire network is tumbling and fraying. One parent or the other, one child or all, are deeply attached to the house. They don't want to leave it. It is full of memories. They have poured their very souls into it: painting it, making renovations, planting a garden. It has cradled their lives. It had borne their futures. Being ousted from it creates the core of pain about the break up. In the years to come, nostalgia about the old homestead will play like a song that won't fade away, one that captures the hurtful metamorphosis of a "home" into a "house". One still has the key that opens the door, but one's loved ones don't live there anymore.

A parable: A divorced house

An ordinary house, nothing to shake a stick about, that's all I am. I was built a plain and simple box with a roof and a tiny porch. Two oak trees in the front yard make me look spiffy, and the white picket fence that surrounds me identifies me as quintessentially American. Otherwise, no frills adorn me: no sprawling cedar deck, no California hot tub, and no built-in swimming pool. A "meat and potatoes" structure, that's me. That's all I ever intended to be.

Did I daydream of becoming a Confederate White Mansion, or a Castle along the Rhine? By no means! Within my modest confines, I never even aspired to encircle a spiral staircase. A humble brick bungalow, I was content to settle into a modest plot of ground on the mid-western Plains, smack dab in the Breadbasket of the USA. There I was prepared to endure the seasons, enjoy sun and shade, the raindrops and snow, watch my trees grow ... and age gracefully. Robert Frost (1914a/1979) writes: "Home is where when you have to go there / they have to take you in ... Something you somehow haven't to deserve" (p. 38). Gaston Bachelard (1958/1969) says home grants us protective intimacy.

My supreme privilege has been to be a "home". I have warmly sheltered a family.

Oh sure, I admired European cathedrals. No pun intended, but I looked up to edifices such as Notre Dame in Paris, Duomo in Milano, the Dom in Cologne and Nidarosdomen in Trondheim. I'm tempted to say that just like any other assemblage of squares, rectangles, and triangles I get awe-struck in the face of architectural feats such as the Taj Mahal, the Eiffel Tower, and the Pyramids. Truth is I have no awareness of whether any other barns and buildings have personal favourites. As far as I know, I may be the only house on the planet that is aware of the existence of other houses and huts, mobile homes and cottages, slum tenements, and high rise apartments. I might be the only assemblage of brick and mortar that wept when Terror melted down the Twin Towers.

I'll never understand how it happened, but I am plagued with consciousness. Instead of remaining a normal example of man-made handicraft, I evolved into a sensitive and alert dynamic-structure. I not only sit here on my foundation, but I *ex-sist*. I don't only exist, but I *know*. I don't only know, but I *know that I know* (De Chardin, 1961). What's worse, my rooms are empty now … and I understand what it means. My walls are bare … and I feel it. I am cognizant that I have been … abandoned.

Laughter once ruled here under my roof, while two children played. Later phosphorescent adolescents pranced aglow in the first blush of sensuality, desiring a jolt of the mighty force of life. The man and the woman, from the beginning, filled me with echoes of mad passion, the grunts and groans of loving each other as if at any moment the world might end.

"If these rooms could talk," a human saying goes. Ha! Doubtlessly, people know that secrets blare out of the woodwork. Why do you think people get spooked over a haunted house? "They" know that in nooks and crannies lurk horror. "They" are cognizant that creaking stairs and squeaky doors moan with painful memories. Teardrops also gather at the corner of windowpanes, fogging them precisely to blur all Vision of the Storm.

What do you think is the real meaning of Halloween? Halloween isn't just the holy evening before All Saints' Day in the Christian calendar. It's not only frost on the pumpkin. It's not even the Last Two Unicorns canvassing the neighbourhood—two pretty little costumed sisters dressed for trick-or-treat. Let's face it. The explication of all classical myths comes from white-Western-masculine-upper-middle-class-racist-violent prejudice. Halloween, too, has been presented only from the point of view of the biased Christian creed.

Halloween has pagan origins. It is the feast of man the wanderer, without a natural habitat, restless ... yearning for a home ... terrified by the spooks and spirits that track him over the tundra, the moors, mountains, deserts, savannahs, and ice fields ... trail him through vales, and valleys, and the rain forests ... sail with him the raging rivers, and the seven seas. It marks the celebration of basic truths: home is a penthouse, a skyscraper, an igloo, a tent, a cave, a castle, a sharecropper's shack, a mansion, or a hovel in a squatter's camp. The family domicile does not just stand, but breathes ... does not just age, but absorbs the Life within it ... doesn't only assimilate paint and wallpaper, but holds memories. Halloween reminds us, year after year, that every man is potentially uprooted ... a hobo, an exile, an ex-patriot, an asylum seeker, an alien. Everybody knows it when they say, "I'm lost. I can't find my way ... home." Halloween reminds us, year after year, *every family home is haunted!* Everyone know it when they say, "There are skeletons in his closet," or insist that they see ghosts hovering near curtains just below the ceiling, or hear voices gurgling in the cistern in the basement—the lingering echoes of the cry of the woman who, as rumour has it, drowned there.

What is the true meaning of the myth of Pandora's Box? As soon as someone opens doors, shuts windows, hits buttons, flicks light switches ... then echoes circulate and old tapes play. Opening a Pandora's Box means that when men or women re-visit a room, touch a banister, or smell some lingering scent, all the registers of their sensibility explode. Memories began to dance a jig with images, reverberating and amplifying. Howling is heard ... eerie shadows flicker ... moonbeams play, hide, and go seek behind wafting cumulus clouds ... the crisp air chills ... humans shiver in their shoes. Sometimes ... all hell breaks loose!

Gaston Bachelard's (1958/1969) *Poetics of Space* is an elegy to houses and homes. The brilliant French scientist-poet lures us into intimate living spaces, into our warm cosy childhood hideout, into the attic or the cellar. He coaxes us into the nook or corner where we curl up, perhaps to read ... maybe to enjoy his enchanting anima-tales of Earth, Air, Fire, and Water.

The house emits vibrations and exudes an atmosphere peculiar to the family that dwells in it. Its rooms cradle warm memories that quicken nostalgia. Some bedrooms smell of tenderness, bristle with passion, and sparkle with afterglow. But not all, by no means! The normal house also witnesses anger roaring, raging bedlam, and the wanton lusts of incest, marital infidelity, and marital rape. In some bedrooms, jealous-spilt blood has seeped into the walls. Visitors or prospective buyers can't see the stains under the paint applied to hide it, but he or she can feel it. Those who viewed the O.J. Simpson house in Beverly Hills, after he brutally murdered Nicole and her dream-faced friend Ronald Goldman, could smell and feel the explosive possessiveness of love gone rotten.

Houses house the forgotten too.

Lacking a tongue, I can't talk. But if I did have a mouth, I'd keep it shut. I wouldn't be like most humans with their penchant for gossip, rumour, and loose talk. I'd also eschew their aggressive style of interrogation, accusation, and condemnation. Definitely, I'd nix out their ugly practices of resentment, revenge, and lying. I'd prefer to let memories hide in my attic ... huddle in my cellar ... ooze through split planks ... seep through broken shudders ... or splinter like cracked glass. I'd prefer to let sleeping dogs lie. Some secrets should never be told.

Nevertheless, since I witnessed the Tide Turn, for the sake of truth I must pry open the only Pandora's Box with which I am acquainted. Don't misunderstand me. I'm not trying to become a storyteller, or spin family folklore. I just want to share what saturates my act of memory: *pain*.

The kids grew like weeds. The eldest, the mother's son from her first marriage, outlasted his baby fat and his troublesome easily provoked rage; the daughter stretched slim, a spitting image of her beautiful mother. By then, the husband and wife slept in separate bedrooms. They talked little to each other. When they did speak, mostly they argued. The boy stood at the edge ... on edge ... itching for his fists to do the talking. The girl played politics, armed with the distorted power and burden of the one perched at the apex of the Family Triangle. Even when she didn't dramatically cry, more dramatic were her demands and threatening tummy aches ... that bordered on emotional blackmail.

"Home" isn't just a word. It's a deep song. Sports fanatics know the word is numinous. Fans of the National Football League (NFL),

National Basketball Association (NBA), or Major League Baseball (MLB) believe it has the power to turn the *momentum*. Beware of the lethal force of the "home crowd".

I loved to eavesdrop when the Master of the House, a "couch potato" lying on an expensive piece of furniture, watched sports on TV—baseball, basketball, football, soccer, golf, and tennis. I was amazed at the sport world's fetish about "home court" or "home field advantage". Even if you've only wasted an hour or two chomping upon what Frank Lloyd Wright calls "chewing gum for the eyes", still you've seen the gestures and heard the rhetoric. If the Kansas Jayhawks block a shot, watch the fans wave off the action or shake a finger to nix the attempt. Should the St. Louis Rams make a goal line stand, my Master would join the mob of fans as they gleefully boom out as of one voice, "Not in our house, oh, no!" Like man, go do your dirty work somewhere else. You're not going to get away with it here. I wanted to scream at him: "In your house, only YOU do the dirt … which you sweep under the rug."

Meanwhile the Mistress of the House, sweating in the kitchen while mixing a cake, mimics: "Yeah, not in OUR house, no way!" She is longing for another man and torturing herself about what she can and cannot surrender. The day comes when she tells him she is leaving him. He asks, a typically possessive male, "Who is he?" She responds, "Someone you know. Someone you haven't talked to in a while." He shots back, "I bet I can guess." She almost laughs and … almost cries, "You're not even close. I'm leaving you for … *me*."

Before she had the courage to leave, the temper-riddled son, the family's "elected member", would be in the basement alone … vibrating his rage to the heavy metal of *Metallica* … or doing his job of expressing the family's distress by playing a blood-stained World Wrestling Federation computer game.

Meanwhile, the daughter would be scheming. At half-time, she knows that dad lowers the sound and pours himself a cold one. How can she lure mum from the kitchen to the couch … to warm up papa? Warm and cuddly, her unconscious household-job is to raise the emotional temperature, to put heat into an emotionally cold marriage. Helpless, I knew it wouldn't work. I knew she knew it, too.

Condemned to think, I have been alert. Since I don't suffer from Western man's disease of rationalistic dualism, I know I'm not alone even if I'm not occupied. I belong to this good earth, embedded in my milieu, and part of my local community. The "being" of a house is to-be-for-a-family. An isolated house is a madhouse, just as seclusion, sensory deprivation, and humiliation drive people crazy.

Whenever "The Boss" sings about home, I shudder with gratitude. The father tells his son, his pride and joy, to open his peepers and to behold his dying hometown. He learned today that the local factory is closing down ... for good. The foreman barks the death-sentence that the company isn't going to return. The lifeblood of the city is drying up.

With heightened intensity, Papa and Junior are cruising down soon-to-be-deserted Main Street. To drum up pride in his roots, the older man plays on his son's heartstrings, deliberately perturbing the lad's innocence and raw sensitivity ... even as dread crawls across the field of his own soul—like locusts destroying everything in their path. Hometown, where both were born and raised will soon be ... a ghost town.

In the face of this approaching death, the man is furious. He wants to scream, but at whom? Who will own responsibility? Which corporate executive? Which politician? Oh, man! What? There is nobody to rage at directly. So he takes his fury out on his car. He hits the ignition button, engages first gear, and burns rubber, leaving his jagged mark on the soon to be lonesome macadam parking lot. Then he turns up the tape player and sings at the top of his voice his anthem to home.

I'll always be proud of the tornado I endured ten years ago. When it whipped across our part of Missouri, it decapitated not a few of my fellow edifices. With inhuman resolve, I summoned such will-to-power that even Friedrich Nietzsche would have been amazed. I chased the raging wind just enough to the East so that, even though the storm levelled most of Joplin, it didn't even uproot my stately trees.

The hurricane within the household, however, broke my heart. In the master bedroom, I heard the Mistress tell the Master, "I'm out of here ... for good!" The Master snapped back, as he threw her on the bed and started slapping and ripping, "You made vows, goddamn it! You're *mine*! You'll never walk out of this bedroom alive, you slut you ... you'll never leave ... me."

After the storm, for a minute there, they thought they were pregnant and the calm of a cold war settled in. She would sit in privacy on the commode and whisper softy, "It won't stop hurting down *there*." And she'd unroll the toilet paper to wipe ... her tears.

After barren promises, and a long non-pregnancy, neglect set in. No: apathy is what it was, deadly cold indifference. Everybody paid the price, even me.

Isn't "homecoming" the finest word in the English language? After "racial cleansing", indubitably the most ugly of all phrases *in any language,* "homesickness" strikes me as the phenomenon most deeply and profoundly sad. On the day my Mistress walked out the door, in agony I had an epiphany of what had happened within my rooms. The ending transformed me from the family's "storm refuge", the man's "castle" and the woman's "love nest" into a "sick house".

Scandinavian languages call a hospital, a *sykhus,* a sick-house, and the nurse a *sykepleier.* How strange! "Hospital", rooted in the Greek *hospes,* means "stranger, guest, and friend". Did the Northern peoples just ape the inhuman logic of German Idealism? Or were they duped by heartless Anglo-Saxon pragmatism? A hospital should *welcome* potential friends that enter its portals, should it not? It should not rub their noses in the fact that now, like lepers wearing number-infested plastic wrist-bands instead of bells, they are ... unwell?

By now, what is the point of still asking questions? It's too late. I sit somewhere between refurbished and faded out. A few of my stairs are broken, and several creak. Some paint is chipped. My bricks could use sandblasting. I hold more than my share of putty, not a little of it applied to patch up holes punched into my walls. So, I sag. A tour of my rooms will reveal that not all presumed parallel lines are parallel, and not all the perpendicular ones form right angles. Marked and stained, that's what I am, inside and out, tattooed with Life's scars. T.S. Eliot (1936d/1963) understands:

> Houses live and die: there is a time for building
> And a time for living and for generation
> And a time for the wind to break the loosened pane
> And to shake the wainscot where the field-mouse trots
> And to shake the tattered arras woven with a silent
>   motto (p. 196).

Recent circumstances have expanded my vocabulary to include "foreclosure", "liquidation", "custody" and "access". I hate it. In protest, I want to shake in the wind. To borrow a human metaphor, I fear I am on my last legs. Am I about to crawl into my own cellar? Am I starting to descend from old and forlorn into terminal dilapidation?

You think I exaggerate? By no means! I ask you: *"Where does love go when love goes away?"* You laugh at me! Oh! It's not a scientific question, is it, and not amenable to quantification? You think only an old, worn-out, weather-beaten, scratched piece of decayed architecture would pose such a silly question. Oh, man! The joke's on you. Rationalism is a disease. Disinterested objectivity destroys households. So go stick your cold, abstract science where ... uh ... where the sun never shines. The truth about Love, buster, is always beyond statistics, 100% of the time ... with a perfect degree of confidence. What is done out of Love is beyond good and evil.

What's the answer to my existential question? I'll come right out and say it: *you can't kill love*. At first, the souls of humans siphon from Love all that they need. Then, they desert it. Lost love doesn't know if it's raining inside or outside. For shelter, it melds into my walls; for safety, it nests there; for comfort, it crawls under the covers ... licks its wounds ... and dies ... all by itself ... By itself, Love slowly dies.

Tell me, smart aleck. What happens afterwards to the house where love had lived, now that it's saturated with love-corpses? Can a house be meek while needing to mourn? Nobody figures that it shoulders heavy grief, even though it is ready to explode with pain. Who even considers that it has a right to grieve? Think about it. How does it commence its grief-work and see the labour to its end?

Don't tell me "Wait," for crying out loud! For what! Wait until my foundation cracks? Wait until the Terror-istic termites get me? Until a fluke fire burns me up? You're bonkers. Don't talk to me about "tomorrow". You humans even have a saying: "Tomorrow never comes?" Tell me, I beg you. What do I do about *today*?

"Moments", that's all we have. There come "moments" of "no return". There will be no "second chance", no "second time around", no time "for decisions and revisions which a minute will reverse" (Eliot, 1936f/1963, p. 14). Hey, after a tornado lashes, humans rebuild. The Phoenix arises out of its ashes. Although resurrection is a fact of Life, sometimes it's the heart-rending truth: it's *too late*, the truly saddest words in the English language. Sometimes it goes past the point of rescue.

Some contractors were sneaking around this morning, peeking at me. Actually, one taking my measurements was and—let me just come right out and say it—he was *inspecting* me. I heard him tell his colleague, "It needs to be jacked up." "*It!*" I slashed my shudders in humiliation. I was mortified. Rage swelled within all my square meters. If I had a tongue, I would have lashed him! I would have told him that maybe *he* needs to "jack off". I would have insisted that he not do it inside me, but that he go outside to do his ... wanking.

Did I say I was sagging? With contempt, Mr. Jag-Off also told his companion that I resembled an old grandmother—and I quote his exact words—"whose over-sucked breasts were hanging low". He could have said instead, respectfully, that like an old grandmother my walls were crooked and drooped because of my *promiscuity of love*. Listening to their macho banter, I doubt that "promiscuity' is part of their vocabulary. They use a slimy synonym, "slut", to describe the pretty Hispanic adolescent girl whom they wish they could "bonk". "Bonking"? That has the same meaning, does it not, as "For Unlawful Carnal Knowledge"? Man, I'm so furious. I feel I'm going to go through my own ceiling!

These guys just blow smoke while they talk, pretending they're "lady killer". Chances are, a close inspection into the noggin' of the one with the mouth would reveal that he *had* killed a lady or two in his time. His tarnished silver tongue surely has soul-murdered a few heartthrobs. No surprise that he is reading a cheap paperback about the O.J. Simpson affair.

Who but an old house can accurately read the human heart? Answer me that! You say "God!" OK. She can. But except for Her, who? I'm not only getting off topic now, I'm getting in over my head. Or I should say, "Over my roof?" This time, I wish I wasn't the only building on the planet with a heart. Damn it!

An appraiser was here today, too. His eyes flashed dollar signs. Market value was his only question. Now, it gets serious. Now it starts to unravel. Packing needs done. Stuff gets discarded. Decisions determine what to hold on to and what to keep—as if there were anything worth saving. History now, from at least two points of view, will be re-written.

Woe is me! I'm about to get stripped. Woe to each and every family member! Severe suffering approaches them, like a storm.

Divorce means that "they" put up a *For Sale* sign.

Divorce is death. I'm about to pay the total and complete price of being conscious. I'm suffering my sickness unto death. I'm in my death throes. It's the heartbreaking truth: Houses rise and fall ... Houses live and die ... .

CHAPTER THIRTEEN

Malignant currency

Natural and man-made disasters kill massively and randomly. Grief follows in their train. Daily, the media flashes words and agonizing images of *natural disasters*: floods in Bangladesh, India, and North Korea; tsunamis and typhoons in Japan, the Philippines , Vietnam, China and Southeast Asia; cyclones in Burma, Bangladesh, droughts-cum-famine in Darfur, Australia, and the former U.S.S.R.; hurricanes in the Caribbean, the Gulf of Mexico, the Atlantic coast, and New Orleans; earthquakes in China, Kashmir, Peru, San Francisco, Mallipo Beach in South Korea; fires in Greece and Southern California; Tornadoes in the Midwest, South, and Southwestern USA.

Man-made disasters also is riddle planet earth—oil haemorrhages from Valdez, Alaska, to Galicia, Spain, to the Guimares Strait in the Philippines, to the Shetland Islands off the north shore of Scotland, to Galveston Bay, Texas, to the San Francisco Bay, to the waters of South Korea. Miners trapped underground in China, West Virginia and Utah. Killings wrought by terrorism and counter-terrorism. The cycles of revenge and counter-revenge that spin ceaselessly worldwide. Plane crashes, trains de-railed, automobile accidents ... Murder; torture; suicide.

Mammoth rescue operations, cleanup activities, and emergency/crisis counselling take place to help ravaged communities and entire peoples. They are incredibly important. But still, the agony of the agony is the story of each family that has suffered a devastating loss ... in Taipei, Wenzhou, Lumpur, Muzaffarabad, Bangalore, Baghdad, Kabal, Kingston, Port-au-Prince, Cancun, Pisco, and Biloxi.

The above is a mouthful. As the saying goes, that ain't the half of it. The scope of natural and man-made disasters cannot be covered in a single chapter or even a single book. Each disaster, in a radical sense, is "one-in-a-row". Each type manifests its own peculiarities. But each also carries a metaphor of the rest. I will tell about one, the only one I know like the back of my hand. The story is my baptism by fire.

The Exxon Valdez oil haemorrhage in Seward, Alaska[10]

The Gulf of Alaska drank poison on Good Friday, 24 March, 1989 (Meganack, 1989). Shortly after midnight, the $125 million *Exxon Valdez* tanker rammed into Bligh Reef and oozed 11 million gallons (41.8 m litres or 40,000 tons) of crude oil into the waters of the Prince William Sound, contaminating 1,300 miles (2,080 km) of coastline. In the wake of this disaster, life in Alaska capsized. Sea-death always ripples to the land and into the souls of the people. Until 9–11 and Hurricane Katrina, the Exxon Valdez was the greatest disaster in USA history.

In the wake of this catastrophe, I directed the Seward Life Action Council (SLAC), an umbrella of clinical-community programs. My work included: 1) co-coordinating response to its aftermath along with medical, community, and law enforcement personnel; 2) supervising a team of substance abuse/mental health counsellors and domestic violence sexual/assault workers, a crisis intervention staff, and workers in shared and respite care; 3) writing grants to support our umbrella of programs; and 4) doing direct psychological treatment.

Although I argued to the State of Alaska that WE at SLAC were the appropriate body to study the psychosocial impact of the disaster on our town and the souls of our citizens, nevertheless the State of Alaska rejected my research proposal, and instead gave contracts to Seattle-based research firms. Initial damage assessment studies ignored people-related reverberations, despite the consequences it engendered, profoundly turning life upside down in all affected Alaskan cities, and especially putting into peril the subsistence way of life in native fishing villages. My Board of Governors, nevertheless, honoured my desire to tell "our" story, and granted me permission to do the research upon which this chapter is based.

Hermeneutics is the appropriate method. Because why? My standpoint was (dis)-advantaged. I was trying to understand the impact of that which I was simultaneously trying to heal and to change. Such engaged action does not disqualify me from generating the richest knowledge. My position, in fact, gave me access to data from all respondents of the disaster: clinical clients, city officials, professionals, scientists, clergy, and members of the governor's oil spill commission. Daily, I gathered sheaves of conflicting evidence through a kaleidoscope of personal stories, public reactions, professional narratives, official spiel, and obvious propaganda. I selected some of my informants; others I encountered randomly. Some found me.

Not unlike someone who had blundered into an ambush, my research task was grappling with fanatic emotions, raw prejudices, and vain opinions. It was necessary to hold in abeyance the split idea-forms about the disaster. Two groups vied with each other, each idealizing its viewpoint and deprecating the other. Environmentalists, loud in the politics of disgust and shrill in behalf of penitential ecology, were advocating reparation and trusteeship of the earth. Expansionists, equally shrill, linked natural resources such as gas, oil, and timber to the creation of Alaskan jobs and to American self-sufficiency. At this tensely sensitive historical "moment", politicians pushed to open the last wilderness of the Last Frontier: the Alaska National Wilderness Reserve (ANWR) for further fossil fuel exploration.

My experience served as a springboard to see what the outsider or detached, neutral psychologist would not even look for, much less notice. Nevertheless, I needed to balance passionate, committed praxis with sober reflection. Our graduate schools train social scientific researchers to use "received" tools, support their design with already formulated theories, and follow "known standards". An event such as an oil haemorrhage "dirties" such scholarly control. I functioned instead as an "insider", snap dab in the middle of the circle, zipping hither and yon within the spiral of daily events, and up to my eyeballs in it. Without "reducing" myself out of the fracas, or blunting the vibrant existential nerve which animated my work, I bracketed the subjectivism of my involvement, suspended it, or put it out of play. Said slightly differently, I keep taking steps back to balance such closeness, continually criticizing my own standpoint. By passing through my subjectivity, and not by by-passing it, I disclose, with minimal prejudice, objectively meaningful portraits of Seward.

I present the story until June 1990, capturing the freshness of how it was "back then". Everything was on the edge; nobody knew what was happening, would happen, and nothing—especially legally—had even begun to be decided.

The primordial North Country: A portrait of the unique milieu

Not every mile of highway or coastline is the same. To assess the magnitude and meaning of this disaster, one must first appreciate the physical beauty of the tainted landscape. The Prince William Sound, the Kenai Fjords National Park, and the Gulf of Alaska are majestic jewels in magnificent settings. Second, one must understand the psychological resonances of the northland: absolute permanence, sublime innocence, primeval loneliness, the cold, the dark, and the silence.

Scores of lakes, streams, and waterfalls punctuate the massively rugged mountains that cradle the Harding Ice field. The largest glaciers outside Antarctica and Greenland, "so beautiful they make you cry," inch down toward the sea from mountains capped by permanent ice fields (Lopez, 1987, pp. 224–225). In their descent, they carve intricate fjords and release to sea floating icebergs, implacable creatures of pale light, fearfully and austerely beautiful. The ice groans its prehistoric laments, the muted and forsaken moans of something deeply wounded and abandoned (Haines, 1989, p. 103). The waters of the Sound are abundantly fertile with 1) various marine mammals including humpback whales, Stellers sea lions, sea otters, harbour seals, and killer whales; 2) fish and shellfish: pink salmon, sockeye salmon, Dolly Varden and cutthroat trout, Pacific herring, halibut, and rockfish; 3) large birds such as sea ducks, loons, pigeon guillemots, cormorants, and majestic bald eagles; and 4) colonies of seabirds packed in breeding sites on cliff faces of the Chiswell and Barren

Islands (such as tufted puffins, horned puffins, black-legged kitti-wakes, murres, and black oystercatchers). The vast wilderness is also ample with varied terrestrial mammals: brown bear, mink, black bear, Sitka black-tailed deer, and river otters. Our eerie ties to the wildlife that live within this 850 mile arc pull at us like tidal currents, evoking root questions about our "human ancestry" (Lopez, 1987, p. 33). Each summer lush blueberries, and cranberries, fireweed and Forget-Me-Nots cover the rough terrain with delicately fragile colour. The aurora borealis, on wondrous occasions, unfurls its curtain of pale green and soft rose, then undulates gracefully across the winter sky. It throws the sky into a third dimension and caresses the viewer with such awe-ful tenderness that self-pity is impossible (Lopez, 1987, p. 211).

The stark vastness of the Northland, its extreme and unpredict-able weather, humbles us. Lopez (1987) describes the atypical and "numinous events" of this land: frostbite and permafrost, "a for-giving benediction of light and darkness so dunning it precipitates madness" (p. 7). Lopez (1987) writes further: "It is not that the land is simply beautiful but that it is powerful. Its power derives from the tension between its obvious beauty and its capacity to take life and from the feeling that this is the floor of creation" (pp. 351–352).

Dismantling normative, taken-for-granted terminology

The Exxon Valdez besmirched the beauty and demeaned the maj-esty. Pathetically, the language used to characterize the desecration adds to the blight and degradation. For the sake of clarification, adequate formulation, and deep understanding, it is imperative to deconstruct the normative terminology.

Oil haemorrhage

The Exxon Valdez is cavalierly and automatically referred to as an "oil spill" which is the unfortunate "tag" normally used to desig-nate such disasters. The phrase distorts, falsifies, and covers up. First, spill localizes and minimizes the catastrophe which affected 1,300 miles of coast along the expansive Gulf of Alaska and the lower Cook Inlet. The sullied coastline included portions of the Chugach National Forest, Alaska Maritime, Kodiak, and Alaska Peninsula/Bechar of National Wildlife Refuges, Kenai Fjords National Park,

Katmai National Park and Preserve, and Aniakchak National Monument and Preserve (Nicoll, Jr., 1991). Hardly a spill, eh?

Why is the common practice a ruse so to baptize such occurrences? Remember the day when your three-year-old accidentally knocked over her glass of milk? That was a spill. Our often-used English injunction not "to cry over it" implies triviality and invites putting the apparent crisis into perspective. The Exxon Valdez was a haemorrhage. Calling it by innocuous word spill obscures the fact that 10.8 million gallons, a black river rushing into the sea, is an environmental holocaust.

Equally importantly, the meaning of the event is the *spread* of the oil, not its discharge into the locale where it pored out—at Bligh Reef near Valdez. Caught by ocean currents and driven by 73 mph gale-force winds, the haemorrhage of black crude advanced relentlessly rapidly across 1,300 miles of coastline, a suffocating blanket of death, a "spreading pestilence" of terrifyingly immeasurable devastation (Spencer, 1990, pp. 8; 33).

From an economic perspective, the ruptured crude wreaked havoc on the $130 million fishing industry. From an archeological viewpoint, the cleanup activities themselves destroyed several Native and Russian cultural sites. From an environmental perspective, the disaster upset a plethora of ecosystems that toppled entire regional ways of life in south-central and southeastern Alaska. Viewed globally, the reduction of the event to simple "spill" condones the continuing greed that created the above ruination. To loan a phrase from Herman Melville, the event of the Exxon Valdez is a transcendental horror.

Accident or cancer?

Another "handy" explanation requires deconstruction. The event was not an "accident". From the perspective of the oil industry, the event was simply a fluke, the inevitable price tag of progress. Davidson (1990) attempts a keener insight. He calls the disaster a collision between the "politics of oil" and "our responsibility to the earth", and borrowing a ready-to-hand concept he names the Exxon Valdez a story of "addictions" to what destroys our natural and human habitat: power, money, alcohol, and energy consumption (p. xi).

This is true but facile. Is this disaster reducible to human foible, personality characteristics, or group dynamics? We treat addictions, avert mistakes, formulate and implement response plans. On the other hand, oil haemorrhages, twinborn with the essence of technology, are structurally inevitable. They will only vary temporally and spatially. As I indicated in Chapter ten, Heidegger demonstrates that there is no "cause" of Death except Life itself. Like death that will definitely happen but indefinitely in terms of time and mode; the only surprises about the next oil disaster will be time, place, manner, and magnitude.

How should we designate an oil haemorrhage? It is analogous to a disease. Siirala (1981) has demonstrated that the eruption of a major illness is not an accident, but rather each sickness bears a message to be heeded. My personality, character, or lifestyle co-selects a "fitting" disease: arthritis, cancer, heart problems, tuberculosis, or AIDS. Colaizzi (1978) also argues that each cultural epoch through its life and thought paradigms "invents" or solicits its peculiarly preferred disease. The Middle Ages, horrified by the flesh, suffered the Black Plague, a disease passed by touch—the similar issue surfaces nowadays with AIDS. After the 1929 stock market crash, polio assumed its place as privileged disease to manifest a crippled society. Cancer expresses our post-modern culture's chaotic coil of technology, mounting bureaucracy, excessive proliferation, and consumption of facts and goods. The Internet, with servers littered with Spam and Pop-Ups, exemplifies uncontrollable encroachment on all freedoms, especially by government agencies.

The Exxon Valdez disaster, inextricably linked with technology, is a *cancer* within the earth's ecosystem. Rather than picturing a tanker bumping into a submerged rock and making a spill, imagine a vessel moving chaotically and destructively, bearing a heinous cargo. Each time the tanker embarked from the terminal, it was carrying a plague.

Is there something peculiar about this political play-ploy that distorts language? By no means. It is the Western way. Western thought manifests a peculiar genius for covering up, for obfuscating. Take the vocabulary that blunts the harsh sting of death: "passed away", "just sleeping", "gone to her reward", "gone to the Great Beyond". Take the deceptive terminology that distorts torture and the murder of war: "collateral damage", "friendly fire", and "extraordinary rendition". It is no fluke that the presentation of this disaster for public consumption is mendacious. A lace of violence, racism, and mendacity is endemic in Western science-philosophy's nihilistic style. It behooves us to stamp it out right across the board.

Oil-slicked water, beaches, fish and wildlife[11]

From the original site of the haemorrhage at Bligh Reef, a black tide with death-tendrils spread inexorably across the Prince William Sound. By Easter Sunday, the wind-whipped sea churned the oil into a large, flat, foamy, bubbly residue that locals called "chocolate mousse" that Spencer (1990) describes as "a storm-beaten mixture of oil and seawater, reddish brown and very thick, full of debris, coiling around kelp and driftwood and shoreline like a boa constrictor" (p. 69). By the time the thickened crude washed ashore, it formed pools of "tar goop", "tar globs", or "black mayonnaise". Eventually, some oil evaporated and bacteria broke down lighter parts of it. The residue coagulated into "tar balls" (Spencer, 1990, p. 76). By the time the cleanup crews arrived, the balls had expanded into large, thick, crusted pancakes, two or three inches thick, one or two feet in diameter, commonly called "cow patties, the products of a "diarrheic cow" who had "wandered the beaches in confusion" (Spencer (1990, p. 77). The crude covered the rocks on the beaches with the consistency of "bearing grease, warm fudge, cold honey" or "blackstrap molasses" (Spencer, 1990, pp. 96–97). Endlessly, the oil kept moving and spreading to new areas, leaving behind filthy footprints, flowing back to spots once cleaned, marking and staining the land, leaving scars. One day workers would clean the rocks and shale on the beaches; on the next day, they found it washed black. The cancerous oil alternated between remission and relapse. Arresting it was impossible. Nothing would work, not booms, not skimmers, not absorbent pads. The process of bioremediation, using the controversial experimental substances Inipol and Corexit, also failed.

Psychosocial portraits of Seward: The psychosocial aftershocks, post-calamity, year one

During the spring and summer of 1989, Exxon heaped $2 billion on a mammoth and wasteful cleanup effort. This haemorrhage of funds from corporate coffers was the twin of the oil that gushed from the pierced tanker. As a result, a green malignancy metastasized in the souls of Seward's citizens. Uncle Sam's greenback dollars!

Seward (population 2,500) is one of the oil-slicked cities within the Gulf of Alaska. It sits on Resurrection Bay, the gateway to the 669,541-acre Kenai Fjords National Park. From July 1989 to July 1990, the atmosphere shifted in four distinct spatiotemporal moments: 1) the summer, during the height of the flurry of the so-called cleanup activities; 2) after 15 September, when Exxon halted operations; 3) during the dark winter months; and 4) near the anniversary date of the disaster, when the populace anticipated renewed cleanup operations. The following portrays the psychological repercussions of the disaster, the effects of the cancerous currency.

Summer: The height of the so-called cleanup operations

Throughout the summer of 1989, hustle and bustle characterized this city at "the end of the road", seven streets wide and sandwiched between Resurrection Bay and Mt. Marathon. Seward swarmed with life. Permanent residents had the disaster thrust upon them. An avalanche of transients, following the money, swelled Seward by eighteen per cent. Eventually, they filled apartments and flooded the beaches with tents, vans, campers, and trucks. By July, there was no available lodging in Seward. People simply "crashed" into rooms partitioned into makeshift apartments. Most property owners charged exorbitant prices. Folks felt fortunate to be paying outrageous rent for mediocre lodging. I know of only one property owner who did not raise his rent in the face of the influx. Inflation also marked the purchase price of houses.

Seward was also a hub of activity for cleanup efforts and for professional and scientific activities. By July, mayhem replaced the quiet, little, tourist town. The portable bird and otter rescue shelters concretely symbolized the physical changes. The helter-skelter pace equally indexed ongoing chaos, havoc, and pandemonium. Money was plentiful. The legitimate rate for workers, ranging from beach cleaners to chamber maids, was $16.69 per hour. By working overtime, folks typically earned $1,750 per week. It was difficult for the locals to resist taking a "spill-related job". Angry shopkeepers and resentful innkeepers helplessly watched employees desert their posts to take advantage of the artificial wages. Veco, Exxon's contractor, paid $5,000 per day to rent boats for the efforts on the water. At least one piper plane pilot was making $90,000 per week.

The locals viewed this money as more tainted than "Texas Tea"— the commonplace phrase denizens of the Lone Star State use to describe oil—and more marred than even "Black Gold"—the black crude pumped through the infamous Alaskan pipeline. Day labourers, city officials, and professionals shared the same belief: that Exxon lavished cosmetic money as part of an elaborate public relations campaign to solicit favourable press in order to frame the good image and to elude litigation. Nevertheless, the malignant dollars, tainted, tarred, greasy, and smelly, affected everyone by their presence or absence.

Sewardites are frequent eyewitness to frolicking otters, zany puffins, and majestic eagles. Many workers, who saw or had to handle the carcasses of these oil-coated creatures, simply walked away from the fiasco, either for ethical reasons or in disgust. Others cashed their large pay cheques ... with reluctant eagerness.

During the summer, the city was xenophobic. This is remarkable to report! Seward is a tourist town, accustomed to accommodating strangers and international tourists—most who arrive either by the Alaska Ferry System or by the Princess Love Boats. Three months after the Exxon Valdez event, resentment was festering towards those who had come to take advantage of the disaster. Tension and violence permeated the air. Smouldering anger and impotent rage burned slowly in the city. Getting a post office box was a two-week wait while the Postmistress checked to see if your address was a real domicile or just a spot on the beach. Arranging telephone service was tedious. The futility of disconnecting phones as fast as installing them had already frustrated the telephone company. The stranger, instead of being seen as guest and potential friend (the Greek *hospice*), was viewed either as an Exxon "company man" or an opportunist chasing the "fast buck". The locals used the veritable lexicon of pejorative terms: "drifters", "scumbags", "scavengers", "bar flies", "hooligans", "sleazebags", "rounders", "riffraff", "bozos", "bimbos", "dopesters", "low-life", and "white trash". The locals expected that these homeless, chronically unemployed, drunken drifters would ravage the city! Often destruction did happen, augmenting the pastime of bad mounting. Favourite targets of criticism and scapegoats included Exxon, Veco, and the Department of Environmental Conservation. Sour grapes about not getting a job or large contract underwrote many complaints.

By July, the phone company alerted us that our crisis line had the highest rate of busy signals in the city. We procured a new $7,000 phone system. The police reported a soaring crime rate. Our screens of DWI charges (driving while under the influence) nearly tripled.

The predicament of civic leaders

The mandate to respond to the disaster usurped the ordinary work routine of elected civic officials, health/social service professionals, scientists, administrators of multiple agencies, and the police. By the summer, they were living on adrenaline and suffering from our modern malady: stress. Their eyes looked chronically tired. Long, irregular hours and broken routine frazzled them. Too little sleep and irregular fast food meals harried them. By late September, they were edgy, jumpy, and on the verge of collapse—suffering combat fatigue. They were muffling their grief in order to ward off psychic disintegration. The disaster wrenched city officials in particular, because they knew its impact, implications, and reverberations. Daily, they faced the red tape of bureaucrats and the insincerity of "securocrats". Daily, they lived with the many levels of complexity and ambiguity related to the upheaval. They were brooding about the impossible tasks, the artificial situations, and the pseudo-problems. About the various ambiguities, they were ambivalent. The emotional splitting showed in the many shapes brooding took: depression edging toward despair, punctuated by nausea, infuriation, bitterness, and rage. These soul-rending emotions had no clear and distinct referents. Robert Kugelmann (1985) describes the process of diverting the passion of grief into seemingly productive work, of filling open-wounds of loss with busyness (p. 5). Each day their actions had the deceptive appearance of efficacy and goal-directedness. However, caught in the whirlwinds of pressure, tensions, and frustrations, many were "not themselves". Some became "vampires" who could not have shed their stress because the price tag, collapse, would have been too expensive.

> The vampire is a blood addict ... Stress is for people what blood is for vampires ... Modern forms of stress/grief allow for no resolution ... the position of loss keeps us energized, pining for we-know-not-what, feeling our inferiorities and helplessness and hence vulnerable to the demand that we take charge and flexibility adapt. So we willingly bite back on that which feeds us, hungry ... (Kugelmann, 1985, pp. 22; 29).

"The Spillionaire"

The disaster was also a boon for "the spillionaire", the nickname used to characterize profiteers who parlayed the tragedy into a bonanza. Some, who had prior standing in the community, and/or had financial resources, received preferential treatment. Not a few sold out, took payola, over-billed for services rendered, or otherwise made capital on the disaster. At least one owner "kick backed" one million dollars to produce a contract worth millions. The general populace viewed spillionaires with a mixture of envy and resentment, but basically recoiled at those who despicably took advantage of the misfortunes of their neighbours.

The run-of-the-mill worker

Many ordinary workers made more money than they could have ever imagined. Disposition of the unprecedented pay cheques varied greatly. Some used it wisely: they improved the present by paying bills, or buying a reliable vehicle, and built for the future by saving for the college tuition, or purchasing a fishing vessel. Too many, however, squandered it on "adults toys", or wasted it on legal/illegal substances. Some awoke in Anchorage after a binge with nothing ... or in Seward after a spree with a strange face on the adjacent pillow.

Unprecedented bonanzas do bring opportunity for fashioning new starts. But financial resources alone do not a new beginning make. Making a down payment on a house includes changing one's way of life, not just modifying behaviour. Too many could not muster the courage to turn a corner. They lapsed into familiar patterns, repeating waste and destruction. Money burned holes in too many pockets.

Darkening day of winter: Encounters with "fierce misfits"
and substance abusers

Exxon completed its operations on 15 September. We felt the impact first in our substance abuse programme. The court sent us "hard-core" alcoholics, whose sobriety pseudo-wealth had sabotaged. Several others became "hooked" for the first time, since it was the first time that they could afford the expensive habit of the "hard stuff". The phenomenon of "easy come, easy go", not unlike gambling away summer wages, repeated the "boom or bust" attitude that has punctuated Alaska's history.

Old Five and Dimers. The sudden confrontation with the artificial wealth of temporarily having income beyond one's wildest dreams forced most to confront themselves in a new way. In the real or metaphorical mirror, people saw something about themselves that they had never realized. Faces now reflected new appetites. Too many eyes now oozed greed. The oil disaster changed people irrevocably.

Domestic Violence. After the cleanup activities ceased, disillusionment took a heavy toll on the marriages of those who were "no better off" in spite of the inflated salaries. When the wind blew, the cold came, the dark descended, and the holidays arrived, all the seasonal issues of winter in Alaska were geometrically intensified. In the dark days of November/December, fierce misfits were mixing their drinks with the "blues" about lost riches and missed chances. Simultaneously, they were blaming others, lashing out, provoking each other, and hitting new lows.

The tumult affected the children of these fierce misfits, especially the wee ones with eyes still sparkling and bright. The youth, caught in the middle of their parents' war games, showed themselves all too familiar with the awful marks and stains of violence and abuse. The police figures showed a 167% increase in of violent crimes (from 32 in 1988 to 84 in 1989). These included seventeen cases of domestic violence. Seward General Hospital conducted six rape exams in 1989 and four in 1990. The local Division of Youth and Family Services reported fourteen cases of physical abuse. Our staff witnessed the truth of Søren Kierkegaard's assertion that no matter how we humans sink, we can always sink lower.

Living through an Ontological Revolution

The horror of the disaster provoked the negative phase of the "Ontological Revolution" (Alapack, 2007a, pp. 81–84). Idealists, environmentalists, and "political virgins" who had naively trusted the system experienced "crashes". At stake was the beginning ... of the end ... of innocence: coping with disenchantment at having witnessed the best and the worst in themselves and others. Typical dilemmas included: How to square the vision of the Whole with the cold hard facts of life? How to suffer the loss of lost innocence without losing hope? How to integrate one's newly discovered rage? How to regain the capacity to see fresh manifestations of innocence, such as to keep it alive?

Manifest horrors stunned white- and blue-collar workers alike. One woman had collected oil-slicked birds. As the summer of 1989 waned, her crew found less and less of the critters. She told me that the boat owner ordered the crew to "slick" any puffin encountered in order to prevent docking the boat, rented out for $3,000 per diem. The obedient crew played "rodeo" with the puffins to increase its daily "count". She, who considered herself jaded, who thought that she had witnessed or performed the worse acts while working as a prostitute, was infuriated and sickened. She vociferously protested the "bounty hunting", and lost her job.

Spring 1990 in the sound: Anniversary time

The interconnected and reciprocal impact among people within the community glared in spring 1990. The year had turned full circle. Warding off grief reactions was becoming impossible for civic leaders. The work of framing annual reports about events, in an effort to leave a historically accurate document, activated memories. The reappearance of certain people, the publications of books about the event, the return of certain sights and smells, or the hearing again of certain words and phrases, also brought back memories.

According to the phenomenon of the Zeigarnick effect, we remember best incomplete tasks. The Exxon Valdez episode left everything dangling in a state of irresolution. The crisis did not simply abate by the anniversary date. No issue pertinent to the disaster had been resolved yet; all matters were still changing daily. The future looked thoroughly threatening in its vagueness. Questions about survival of the salmon plagued the anxious souls of the fishermen. Pervasive helplessness kept mounting. The sense of victimization at the hands of mega-international corporations and governmental bureaucracies kept multiplying. The single diagnostic label for all of the above is ... cancer.

Those who had endured the unusual year craved an elusive, impossible closure. In the spring of 1990, few folks were proceeding smoothly through the normal phases of responding to a loss or to a natural disaster (Gist, 1989, pp. 13; 59). They were coping instead with a terminal illness.

The anniversary period coincided with the decision about another round of cleanup efforts. In March 1990, drifters geared for another bonanza. Seward swelled again. Civic leaders were troubled and concerned that the now-sullied wilderness was vulnerable to further taint. Even as they grieved the disaster, they had to cope with the unbridled greed and avarice of some citizens that craved another dose of the malignant money. Words spoken late at night in the bars, and written on the doors of tavern toilets, saluted Exxon for last year's dole and craved another spill.

Spring in Seward was tense. This time, Exxon conducted business differently. It used a select squadron of company workers in a focused $2 million cleanup campaign. Our caseload at SLAC, which had levelled in the early spring, increased dramatically in June and July as the ache for closure collided with swollen appetites. Greed, shame, and indignation kept rebounding off each other.

Discussion

A philosophical meditation on technology

Echoes of Heidegger have haunted this entire book. His works also provide the conceptual framework for grounding my findings and putting them into a Big Picture. In Heidegger (1927/1962; 1950/1971a; 1952/1971b), we find alternative "ways" to think about both technology and Death.

The inevitability of the Exxon Valdez is inscribed in the history of Western thought. Technology, the culmination of Greek rationalism, carries with it a lapse into forgetfulness. We have forgotten what it means "to be", and we are obvious of our very forgetfulness. We have lost track of time. We demean the earth, our home. We despise mortal flesh. We deny our mortality. We do not know how to think. In consequence, the coil of technology, scientism, and capitalism continually ravages the earth. Heidegger names this menace *Gestell* (Heidegger, 1950/1971a, p. 64ff).

Gestell names the essence of technology. It carries the senses of being "framed", "set up", or "duped". It connotes sterility, mendacity, concealed matters, or obscurity. It suggests scaffold, gimmick, and armature. The technological attitude blurs Being's radiance, renders it empty and tawdry. It underlines our provocative, imperialistic, dominating, engineering approach toward the natural world. We challenge nature and compel it. We rape the land, strip it of its ore and liquid; we move mountains; we try to coerce the sea; we aim to conquer space. Under the domination of technology, all beings whatsoever are disclosed as "stock": objective, calculable, quantifiable, and disposable. All beings are reduced to raw material or product, valuable only insofar as they serve the profit motive or contribute to the wealth of shareholders, or the enhancement of corporate power. And it is not only "things" which are at stake, but also the human spirit. The menace of this menace is precisely that the person is reduced to a mere commodity, a "human resource". We are not just Marxian cogs in the machine, but disposable pieces for the stockpile.

In our dual worship of profit and of efficiency for efficiency's sake, we harness, exploit, and destroy everything which, by vocation, we should shelter and safeguard. We blitz and bully, but we forget. Technology has become not only one point of view among others but the privileged perspective. Having collided with the 21st century, the natural attitude is the technological attitude. We take for granted the ultimate power, value, and goodness of technological solutions.

The double oblivion has edged the human race to the brink of ecological devastation and political suicide. With it, however, emerges the possibility of new choices. "Where there is danger recognized precisely as danger there grows the freeing strength of salvation" (Heidegger, 1946/1971c, p. 333). Holderlin's poetry is not just evocatively enigmatic. "The gig is up," street talk says. We are finally in an intellectual place from which we can see the nihilistic nerve of violence and racism that has been brewing in the Occident for 2,500 years. The ascent of technology to a dominant position in our era brings Western metaphysics to a "close".

Listen today to the speech of any politician, business person, or media correspondent. The criteria for assessing success, for valuing a plan or a policy, include that it be "on the ground" and solidly anchored in times ("at the end of the day"). This is not the language of philosophical rationalism or scientific positivism. No: this is the language of existential phenomenology, thinking that cherishes this good earth, our fragile flesh, and the "now" that circumscribes the time of our lives.

This "closure" puts us at a "turning". The time is over for our blind faith in reason, positivism, and quantification. It's time to jettison the attempt to attain neutral, distant, detached objectivity; time to stop isolating—rather than joining—mothers and their suckling infants; time to stop splitting communities of people and man from the environment. Closure, turning, and crisis offer both opportunity and danger.

Heidegger says, deadly seriously, that the future of the world might turn upon the proper apprehension of the verb "to be". Thinking alone will change the world. Heidegger insists that we have not yet begun to think. Science not only does not think, but the interlaced attitudes of science and technology are anti-thought. Heidegger summons us to liquidate metaphysics so that we might save the earth.

The original Greek term for existents, for the things that are, is *physis*. The word denotes "the process of a-rising", the "self-blossoming emergence" of being, its "inward-jutting-beyond-itself", its power to endure (Heidegger, 1953-1959, p. 14). The early Greeks thought that something was brought forth from hiddenness and unfolded unto its proper being in one of three ways: *physis*, *logos*, and *poesis*. Originally *techne* had a pivotal place. Authentic technique signifies the ability to plan and organize freely, creating and building in the sense of pro-ducing. Terms like "craft", "cunning", "knack", and "flair" capture this original sense. The rationalistic project of metaphysics debased *Gestell* is an attitude of provocation that does not donate to the earth, shepherd it, or accept its harvest.

Heidegger clarifies why technology which dominates us also dazzles us, such that we affirm and embrace it. It is "uncanny",

Heidegger (1969/1993, p. 312) says, but everything "works". Successful functioning pushes ceaselessly further toward still more functioning. The attitude of technology is efficiency for efficiency's sake ... mindless money-making action.

Heidegger, nonetheless, does not naively dismiss technology. "Salvation" will elude us as long as we either pursue technological solutions blindly, or "damn it as the work of the devil" (Poggeler, 1987, p. 200). The truly redeeming act would be to re-forge the broken bond between *techne* and *poesis*. How?

The pivotal balancing attitudes are poeticizing and dwelling. Originally, thought was poetic. Poetry, rooted in logos, gathers and grounds, initiates and preserves. If we should begin to poeticize, we would think in a holy/wholly way: docile, obedient, letting be the coming-to-presence, and withdrawal of things. To poeticize is to think; to think is to thank; to thank is to dwell. Poetry is "green", long before we became conscious of the lethal effect of greenhouse gasses, long before we began to stand poised on the edge of ecological disaster. If we who are "ontologically excellent" would dwell poetically, then we would shepherd all creation. Our "buildings" would shelter all the manifold and wonderful springs of being: the fourfold of earth and sky, divinities and mortals. Only such authentic edification would support a genuine Homecoming.

From a historical perspective, the circulation of Seward's malignant currency names the symbiosis between Alaska and the oil industry of which the 800-mile pipeline from Valdez to the North Slope is the concrete symbol.[12]

Alaska both readily "forgets" and easily overlooks human suffering. The history of the Last Frontier is a series of exploitative bonanzas: fur from otters and seals; gold from the hills; silver gold from the salmon runs; black gold from the pipeline. Alaska was ripe for the Exxon Valdez disaster, a tale that is a new version of an old edition: striking it rich at the expense of the Land or Sea.

Concerning the Exxon Valdez, the symbiosis drew a suffocating ring that encircled all respondents. Within the ring, perniciously neglectful complacency had festered. In the face of the disaster, lack of preparation by any system hamstrung any possible quick and effective response. Ready-to-hand conceptual and existential paradigms limited thought and action. Rationalism's chronic deficiency did glare: the inability to anticipate.

There are no demons in this affair. Nobody could claim exclusive prerogatives either of power and dedication, or sacrifice and avarice. *Gestell* rendered helpless both those victimized by gigantic corporations and governmental bureaucracies, and those supposedly in control of them. Apparent foes danced in the same ring, twins.

Concluding reflections

After two years: deniers, casualties and survivors

> Violence does not consist so much in injuring and annihilating persons as in interrupting their continuity, making them play roles in which they no longer recognize themselves, making them betray not only commitments but their own substance, making them carry out actions that will destroy every possibility for action (Levinas, 1961/1969, p. 12).

I published my original study in 1991. At SLAC, we were "cleaning up after the cleanup". Two years after the disaster, grieving had not ended, and the various cancers were not in remission. We identified three groups: 1) deniers, who still refuse to recognize that the disaster created any profound aftershocks; 2) survivors, who put into reasonable perspective all that the horror engendered, and moved on with their lives; and 3) casualties, whose devastation by the ordeal shows in the shapes of substance abuse, domestic conflict, stress, depression, and suicide. Some were still in an "an emergency mode", unable to shift out of crisis-thinking. I stated simply in 1991: "It is beyond the scope of this inquiry to anticipate the long term effects." I should have written: "Please don't tell me how the story ends."

Although it is beyond the scope of this chapter to trace the aftermath of the aftermath, some update is in order. The headline on the tenth anniversary of the disaster read: *Activists say wildlife has still not recovered at Prince William Sound*. Although Prince William Sound seemed back to normal, local fishermen and environmentalists insisted that it had been crippled. The bald eagles and river otters were the only species that had recovered. At that point in time, the number of killed creatures had increased to 250,000 seabirds,

2,800 sea otters, 300 harbour seals, 250 bald eagles, up to 22 killer whales, and an unknown number of salmon and herring.

On 19 December, 2003, fifteen years after the event, Richard Black, BBC science correspondent, reported ongoing danger. He cites conclusions in the journal *Science* that the environmental impact of the Exxon Valdez spill was more serious than previously believed. In addition to identified long-term damage suffered by many animals and plants—sea otters had recovered to only half of their pre-spill level, and several duck species were also significantly reduced—poisoning was still continuing. Significant amounts of crude oil remained trapped in sediment on the sea bed, poisoning creatures such as mussels and clams. Concentrations of toxic chemicals from the oil remain high enough to damage fish eggs, and the ill-effects pass along the food chain.

Some things never change. Exxon continues to contradict each damaging report of the damage, citing the support of scientific laboratories and academic institutions that resoundingly demonstrate the recovery of the Prince William Sound ecosystem. Each time I read that mainstream science continues to be bought and sold by meganational companies and the government, I did not know whether to scream or vomit. I do not remember if I laughed or cried after reading the conclusion of *Science* that "assumptions about oil damage have to be challenged" (Black 2003).

Some things never change. Efforts of activists to block the merger of Exxon and Mobile—at least until the former agreed to pay $5 billion in damages—failed. Until today, 27 May, 2008, Exxon-Mobil still tries to avoid litigation. Almost a decade on, its matter still dangles.

On 10 November, 2007, Governor Arnold Schwarzenegger declared a state of emergency to help fight the oil spill that threatened the coast of northern California. A tanker struck the massive San Francisco Bay Bridge on 7 November. It oozed 58,000 gallons of crude oil (228,000 litres) into the Bay. Inevitably, wildlife and beaches were put at risk. Worldwide, television cameras focused upon Alcatraz, the former (in)famous prison island, converted into a tourist attraction-museum, now disgustingly circled by the expensive scum.

The next day, on Sunday, 11 November, 2007, a powerful storm hit the Azov and Black Seas between Russia and the Ukraine. Four

Russian ships sunk, including an oil tanker. The BBC reported that "2,000 metric tons of fuel oil has leaked from the tanker in the Kerch Strait, which links the two seas" (BBC News). Nearly 6,000 tonnes of sulfur were also unceremoniously deposited. Some things never do change. The media still uses language that I insist aims to minimize the meaning of the catastrophe. In describing both events—at the Golden Gate Bridge and at the Black Sea—oil was merely "leaking into the water", and the System still minimizes the event by referring to it as a "spill".

Ultimately the Exxon Valdez tragedy of 1989 will be remembered as a marker event in Alaska's history, as the "accidental spill" which could have been averted, a happening which magnetized the resources of the citizens who, though victims, become their own rescuers. It will be a tale told to my children's children. Will the narrative unfold as another adventure story, a tale of heroics? Will it be the call Alaska made to the world to remember? Or will it unmask our stubborn oblivion?

Until the Exxon Valdez, consciousness was only marginal of the symbiosis between Alaska and the oil cartel. The disaster disclosed dramatically that all Alaskans had colluded in the unholy arrangement that menaces our homeland. The Exxon Valdez is another chapter in the volume of sacrileges against the environment.

Alaskan shame is the root phenomenon in this affair: present in those for whom the event was a revelation or an epiphany; present by its absence in those who, for whatever motives, steeled themselves against the horror. The Exxon Valdez, by sullying "The Great Land", desecrated its holiness. Alyaska! Alakshak! Alaksu! Alaska! The Last Frontier will never be the same. The event earned the name which Eskimos have given the white man: "The people who change the nature." We change society too ... with malignant currency.

CHAPTER FOURTEEN

On suicide

A lbert Camus (1954/1956) boils philosophy down to its core. The time has come to practice truly wise loving and love of wisdom. Should we not put aside, as mere cognitive play, such abstract concerns as language games, the problem of the One and the Many, or doubting that we can make knowledge claims from descriptions of experience? Such preoccupations merely ape decadent scholasticism which debated how many angels—if there are angels—could sit on this pin in my hand, if indeed it is a pin ... and if I really exist and actually have a hand in which to hold that pin. There are only two real philosophical problems: why not kill someone and why not take my own life? Camus is right. The rest of the wrangling and ratiocination are exercises—not of a hungry people—but of a stuffed, leisured people. Suicide and murder, the themes of this and the next chapter, may also be the root of psychological problems. They surely engender the keenest of sorrow.

Suicide means that the one who kills the self cancels the indefinite *when* and *how* of death. The individual exercises power over what is otherwise totally uncontrollable. "Stop the world and let me off" is the demand. And the individual does the halting. He takes life's ultimate ambiguity into his hands and sets the clock.

This reversal still begs the question, "Why?" Once again, the answer is as individual as the person's fingerprints. Remember, in 1915 Freud affirmed that nobody kills self who first of all did not wish to kill someone else. Suicide inverts murderous rage.

Implicit in Freud's heuristic is a dynamic-structural, dialogal understanding of the fatal act. Suicide sends a message. It is powerful communication. It is a desperate communiqué, however, one which signifies that other ways of reaching out have failed. This chapter makes explicit this radical dialogal understanding. I go to school on Jacques Lacan's faithful reading of Freud. For Lacan, the unconscious is structured like a language. Each word, gesture, or behaviour belongs to a chain of signifiers. The idiosyncratic chain of meanings constitutes the basic context for each suicidal performance. Each expressive action is radically interpersonal. Lacan (1966c/1977, p. 40) uses the term "interlocution" to clarify that there is no word without a reply, no expression without a response. I always express something to somebody. Building upon this dialogal-communicative viewpoint, I distinguish between two fundamental motives for suicide: a suicide gesture and a suicide attempt. The distinction arises from work within the therapeutic sanctuary, and thus it is decidedly not an experimental research finding. I claim that it is *existentially practical*. Nietzsche reminds us, however, that the difference between a conviction and a lie is nil, is nada. Thus, I share my viewpoint in the same attitude with which I share all the material in this book: with an equal measure of assurance and humility. Only you can decide if the distinction is of value.

Suicidal gesture

The person who performs a suicidal gesture does *not* want to die. He or she wants to live differently, or better. They crave a cardinal change in some component of their network of relationships. The gesture is an expressive act, a sign or signal. It is a cry from the living heart for redress, for help, attention, or for a need to exercise control over somebody or some predicament. In the language of Eric Berne (1967), the individual plays a "game" that creates a "payoff" (p. 48). The notion of gesture includes what the literature normally fractures into verbal and non-verbal data, into normal and abnormal communication, into conscious or unconscious intentions, and into the confusion about whether an act done alone can be ineluctably linked to the presence of a significant Other. The gesture intends, not death, but the reward of an interpersonal payoff. Although the act seems self-absorbed, it has a decidedly interpersonal referent. Someone else is implicated, whether or not either party is fully aware of it.

The modes of suicidal comportment hallmark the gesture and distinguish it from an attempt. Taking pills is a very ordinary way, and so is cutting wrists. It is common for the individual—either before, during, or after the act—to phone someone and say: "Guess what I just did!" Translation: "Help. Get your butt over here quickly and save me." Or—"Send the emergency medical team *tout suite*."

Don't misconstrue me. An overdose and a blood-bath are serious actions, too often fatal. The individual cuts self too deeply, takes too many pills, or help arrives too late. The dangerous gamble backfires, making it time to draw the curtain. But as often as not, the potential destructive consequence of gesture can be short-circuited.

Amelioration, however, requires mobilizing resources. The gesture orchestrates heightened activities in at least one "system" and usually in several. On top of that, the surviving individual, lying on his back in a hospital bed, concretizes the event by the tube in her mouth or by the bandage on his arm. These marks are vivid reminders that he had tried to end his life. They are accusatory signs. As often as not, the family member or loved one ... the husband who is standing looking down upon his wife draped in a hospital gown with her hair undone ... reads the accusation perfectly. "Did you think divorcing me would be easy?" "Aren't you sorry for cheating on me with that slut?" Whatever pain in the tummy the patient might be feeling as a result of a stomach pumped, or whatever pain she experiences as a result of the laceration, rest assured that the guilt hanging in the hospital room eclipses it.

The gesture is a manipulative act, a king size temper tantrum, an exercise in Russian roulette, a payback, emotional blackmail, or a high-stakes way to make another suffer. It is a manifestation of the tyranny of the weak (Fitzgerald, 1934/1995). In his classic work on suicide, Emile Durkheim (1897/1979) lists "egoistic" as one category of suicides. The individual, who feels left out, acts out against the one(s) who have neglected him. Someone else always takes the brunt of the destructive gesture. Or more accurately, the guilt experienced by the one for whom the other performs the gesture indexes its success. The coy ploy worked. The payback is the payoff. You have manipulated me and hurt me seriously. It's time to pay the fiddler. It's an act of revenge. My gesture is the first installment on the account due. A probe of the dynamics of the guilty interaction reveals the interpersonal structure of the situation: "I'm sorry. I'll never do it again. How can I repair the wrong?" Will a diamond ring, a new car, a new house, having a baby ... do the trick?

Although each drama has its own co-created script, the central point is that nobody can make me feel guilty unless I allow the tactic to work. Until I understand my own vulnerability and refuse the burden of guilt, a vicious merry-go-round keeps turning.

The gesture as adolescent

In developmental terms, the gesture is an adolescent act. It is a familiar tale in adolescent treatment centres that the fever of wrist cutting often permeates the milieu. I show you my scars and you show me yours. Oh how we suffer! Martyrs we are, aren't we? The rows of scars are identity-markers, substitute puberty rites. Performing them as part of groups dynamics leans upon massive suggestion and imitation. Nevertheless, the actions are serious-unto-death and cannot be dismissed. They must be met by the institution's "suicide watch". More importantly, they must be faced with intervention that confronts the truth. The issue is not to wrap one up or tie one down; it is to hit the button that stops the merry-go-round.

The gesture as hysterical

In psychiatric terms, the now defunct word "hysteria" also describes the suicidal gesture. The hysteric is the Queen of the Drama Queens; he is the Psychological Actor par excellence. In R.D. Laing's (1959/1990) vocabulary, hysterics pretend to be who they are. Usually that means dependent, needy, selfish, demanding, greedy, opportunistic ... but unaware of what they are doing! Who? Me? *La belle indifference* is the classical descriptive concept. His or her arsenal includes manipulation, ploys, psychological games, innuendo, insinuation, suggestion, teasing—and the suicidal gesture is the riskiest trick. High drama!

The suicide note

... requires serious interpretive study. A dozen years of research on the topic accomplished by A.A. Leenaars (1986; 1987; 1991; 1992; 1996; 1997) exposes only the tip of the iceberg. The work is more fruitful to help forestall another tragedy than to multiply actuarial studies and formulate plans to prevent another possible episode with pills or razor blades. Because why? The total situation must be interrogated, not just the so-called personality dynamics of the one who wrote the note, and then lived to read it. The note is usually as close to unvarnished truth as we get. Not truth in the classical philosophical sense, but truth in the lifeworld context, truth by which we orient our decisions.

It suits to discuss one more characteristic of the hysterical suicidal gesture. While discussing grief-work, I accent the significance of the anniversary of death, especially the first anniversary. But each yearly anniversary is also important. It is a day ready-at-hand for the gesture-prone person, apt to act in a hysterical lingering-adolescent way, to try suicide as an (unconscious) act of joining the deceased loved one. Maybe it is the person that he "loves" so much that he cannot let her go; maybe the person that he "hates" so much that he will take revenge by killing self; maybe the two "motives" are ambivalently one and the same. *A priori*, who can know? But it is that time of the year again. Watch out!

Suicide attempt

The line between the suicide gesture and attempt is permeable and thin. Holding me to an absolute distinction between them would be mixing up my thinking with the pedantic picayune rationalism and positivism. Nevertheless, I affirm that individuals exist who do want to die. They want out. Life is too unbearable. They have lost hope that their predicament will ever get better. They have lost face. They see a door that they might walk through to end it all. They do something drastic that opens and closes that door. This individual does not pop a bottle of pills. This individual jumps off a bridge, or loads a shotgun and pulls the trigger with the barrel pressed against his heart. Or weaves a noose and kicks out the step stool. Or turns on the gas and locks the door (Schivelbusc,

1995).[13] If this doesn't "work", it is a fluke! It is myopic not to see that the actor is getting a message across ... Sadly, these methods do work.

Despair: Sickness unto death

Despair is the phenomenon at stake in a *bono fide* suicide attempt. No measurement device exists to clarify the human heart's despair. We find such illumination in Søren Kierkegaard.

What makes up our culture's psychological literature? Self-help books, how-to-do-it texts, theory-supported and quantitative research-based texts, and pop psychology. Their common goal is to eradicate the evil of suicidal desire. Kierkegaard is not just the alternative but the devil's advocate.

Kierkegaard's works pricks us to look at self with searing honesty. He dares us to stop living like robots, clowns, cowards, or fools. He illuminates all dead ends, so that we can avoid living a provisional life. He is an especially terrifying character in terms of our millennium's mores. Not surprisingly, his approach goes missing from mainstream psychology textbooks. Mainstream thinking does not want to understand him. Psychology prefers to relegate this man—who is arguably one of the half-dozen greatest psychologists who ever wrote—to the theological dustbin.

Kierkegaard's viewpoint cannot be rattled off in a series of stylized, convenient, packaged, or politically correct phrases and buzzwords. He writes that most people are like school children wanting to look up the answers to life in the back of the book in the same way that they check the correctness of their mathematical calculations. But there is no short cut to the mysteries of human existence. Søren Kierkegaard instead gives us a penetrating analysis of the human heart.

Forms of despair

What goes wrong with my life? Kierkegaard is clear. Destruction comes from within. It does not come from without. We all have to endure the slings and arrows of outrageous misfortune. But what zaps us from the outside doesn't ruin us, corrupt us, or destroy us. Count on it. Events, circumstances, accidents, and political machinations will surround and engulf us. Disease, death, ostracism, rejection, broken promises, lost jobs, natural disasters, and accidents will knock us for a loop. People will deceive us, betray us, manipulate us, seduce us, bring out the worst in us, and die on us. These events present an occasion for us to face self and face life. They send us reeling, but none can destroy us. *Determinative is what we do with what comes our way.* Nietzsche's (1889/1982, p. 487) oft-cited aphorisms are: "That which doesn't kill me makes me stronger." "When I stand on my pain, I am taller."

Our ruination or demise originates within our own self-deceptive acts. Lying to ourselves corrupts and destroys us. Earthquakes swallow houses. Hurricanes sweep away our fortunes. But only we can destroy our own home and squander our fortune. Another person can do anything and everything to bring us down. Only we can put ourselves into despair. As often as not, the deception pivots around our convictions/lies about the most significant figures of our current existential predicament, or those caretakers who failed in our upbringing to shelter us lovingly.

What is despair?

According to Kierkegaard (1847/1962), despair is a faulty relationship, an improper relationship, "a dis-relationship in a relationship which relates itself to itself" (p. 54). The flaw is profound, basic, and central. Despair is not a feeling, an emotion, or an attitude. Despair is a *condition of existence*. It lets me know where I am truly standing and how I am fairing—whether or not I feel it, recognize it, or know it as such. We can be in despair without even knowing it. No wonder mainstream Western psychology ignores Kierkegaard. Those who cling to a behavioural ideology have no truck with invisible, intangible and not measurable possibilities.

In *Sickness unto death* Kierkegaard (1849/1974) writes:

> Is despair an advantage or a drawback? ... it is both ... The possibility of this sickness is man's advantage over the beast ... So then it is an infinite advantage to be able to be in despair; yet it is not only the greatest misfortune and misery to be in despair; ... it is perdition" (pp. 147–148).

Is this mumbo jumbo just the double talk of a thinker drunk on Hegelian dialectics? Is this man a fool, crying over the spilt milk that he lost his princess by his own hand? Or does he have a clear head and also lots of heart? I will simply present his superb gifts, gifts for the ages. They answer better than any argument.

Kierkegaard's insight is that the capacity to develop a self and the ability to despair are dialectically related, hand-in-glove. He does not mean "self" in the superficial sense of the statue that I polish, or the mirror-image that I shine to please the other with lip gloss or spiked hair. It is self as Heidegger terms "I-ness". Life demands that we become our own true unique self. Selfhood is both a gift and an obligation. Kierkegaard calls it an ethical imperative. What matters is what we do with this demand. If we should fulfil it, we are successful and authentic. When we have lost hope that we can realize our self in this world, we fail, we lapse into despair; we exit stage left.

Kierkegaard enumerates more forms of despair, as the old saying goes, "than has Carter little liver pills". This is not the place to detail despair as connected to each of two human dialectics: finitude/infinitude and possibility/necessity. I zero in only on suicidal despair, "the sickness unto death". In the New Testament sense, this means "a sickness the end and the outcome of which is death". Heidegger borrows it from Kierkegaard to indicate the definiteness *that* we are going to die and the indefiniteness of *when*. The act of suicide seizes this ambiguity and twists it. How so?

The torment of despair is: "To be sick unto death ... not to be able to die—yet not as though there was hope of life; no, the hopelessness in this case is that even the last hope, death, is not available" (Kierkegaard, 1849/1974, p. 150).

What does the Dane mean? Ordinarily, we dread death and consider it a great danger. But in hitting one's lowest bottom and realizing that one's self is sick, one discovers a more dreadful danger; then "one hopes for death". "Death, be thou my release!" Consumed with shame, I feel like a worm crawling in self-loathing and self-disgust. This is worse than death. I hope to die. But I cannot quit myself. So despair is the disconsolateness, the self-consuming impotence of not being able to die. Kierkegaard writes that the formula for this despair is "the rising of the fever in the sickness of the self" (Kierkegaard, 1849/1974, pp. 150–151). The pain gnaws; there is no possibility of relief. Kierkegaard's (1849/1974) formula is: "To despair over oneself; in despair to will to be rid of oneself" (p. 153). Jacques Lacan captures the "moment" by saying that the individual is in love with death. Lacan does not mean that being in love with death is the prelude to a honeymoon or a trip to Paradise. He means that the poor pathetic ego, always craving to be petted and polished, prefers the kiss of death to performing the mature task of developing a Self. And so all that remains is to tie the noose tight and set the step-stool; run the car in the garage and lock the door; fill the bathtub with water and slash the wrists; climb to the top of the bridge and jump; load the shotgun ... .

Mainstream suicidology

The mandate of the American Association of Suicidology is to promote suicide prevention and a better understanding of suicidal people. The *Comprehensive Textbook of Suicidology* of Ronald W. Maris, Alan L. Berman and Morton M. Silverman (2000) forwards these over-arching goals. The volume touches a plethora of bases about this most disturbing of man-made disasters.

Appropriately, as a medico-social scientific publication, the book first justifies its place on the clinical-academic scene in terms of its theoretical and empirical foundations. In part two, it treats thoroughly sociodemographic and epidemiologic issues. Part three presents medical and psychiatric matters. In a nutshell, the book basks in the glow of its natural scientific aura, or absorbs the criticism of that standpoint. About that judgement, we each bring our presuppositions. By now, mine are evident to you. The natural scientific perspective in the social sciences is incredibly rigid, cold, narrow, lifeworld distant, and of limited use.

This current wave of suicidology, nevertheless, represents a marked improvement over the work that was done at mid-century. Because why? During modernity, the clutches of quantitative research strategies hamstrung research. In terms of the neat and clean operational definitions necessary to conduct a quantitative study, a common experimental design would differentiate between "failed" and "successful" suicides. A fatal act was called a "successful suicide". Successful! This is the ultimate failure of a human life, and at least the penultimate failure of the community! Carelessly using the term "success" to designate the consequence of the act reveals a too heady social science with a badly shrunken heart.

My above remarks are not just snide. It is common knowledge that the highly funded research conducted using such terminology has done little to reduce the rates of suicide (Wolfersdorf, Keller & Kaschka, 1997). Is it not fair to ask whether the questions in the design are wrong? Indeed, the current research-community of suicidology has begun to alter it. Recent work includes an idiographic approach and the use of qualitative interviews.

In an effort to change the system from within, Birthe Loa Knizek and Heidi Hjelmeland (2007) try to expand the envelope. First, they cite studies showing that a large increase in the number of research publications over the last quarter century has "not resulted in a better understanding of suicidal behaviour" (p. 699). They also document that research in suicidology, by aping natural scientific quantification, has been methodologically too one-sided and narrow. In addition, they argue that the discipline lacks an integrated, comprehensive theoretical framework. Approximately every ten years, a new study appears accusing suicidology of suffering from the typical positivistic myopia.

Suicidology never reflects upon the scientific status of itself as a discipline. Knizek and Hjelmeland (2007) attempt a remedy by sketching a "functional model for interpreting suicidal behaviour as communication" (pp. 704–705). It aims to promote understanding by using qualitative methods, semiotics, and hermeneutics. Although they have done an Oman's job depicting the field as we collide with the millennium, their viewpoint is merely traditional-with-a-twist. Their model is run-of-the-mill, retaining all mainstream dualisms—idiographic–nomothetic, qualitative–quantitative, particular–general, and so forth. It also bows to natural science psychology as the standard by which one should measure one's work. For example, instead of encouraging researchers to let lifeworld happenings spur their work, they aim to develop a theory-based and-theory focused model. In consequence, Knizek and Hjelmeland show a glaring and disappointing preference for the arrogant erudition of high altitude thinking, not for thought grounded in the everyday, commonplace Lifeworld. They choose abstraction over raw life by nixing in their research "language that everyone can understand"; and they debunk ordinary speech as "the development of a debased pidgin language"

(Knizek and Hjelmeland, 2007, p. 699). The crude, warm freshness of the common people goes missing in consequence; their own discourse is so mixed that they flounder while trying to decide whether suicide studies should be "multidisciplinary" or a specialized discipline, an independent science with its own terminology.

Most relevantly, they succumb to the pragmatic nerve of Western thought, insofar as their key objective is to discover ways to enhance the communicative skills of potential suicide victims. Do not the members of the social order also need to learn to communicate better? Knizek and Hjelmeland totally ignore their own insight that the "Other" is at the heart of the matter of the suicide predicament. If we consider the whole picture, those who hold power must cease driving loved ones to the brink of self-slaughter.

Raj Patel (2008) cuts to the quick by saying that in seeking reasons for suicide, the "question is how far are we prepared to look" (p. 44). Knizek and Hjelmeland choose not to look very far. They protect the status quo. They embrace the reactionary goal of identifying persons at-risk of suicide, but propose no revolutionary change in the social-political arena. Solutions to the horror of suicide, however, do not reside in bureaucratic management. Policing suicide is as (in)effective as stalking streetwalkers. Authentic liberating comportment would be to help us to help people to make each precious individual life worth living. Social engineering serves death projects: the Holocaust and Apartheid. Social engineering rarely saves lives.

Gabriel Rossouw (2007) takes to task cognitive behavioural therapy, dialectical behaviour therapy, and psychodynamic therapies as limited and inadequate for understanding and alleviating suicidality (pp. 1–13). He either does not know the work of Knizek and Hjelmeland or finds them irrelevant. Like them, he bemoans the lack of a comprehensive theoretical framework. Unlike them, however, he builds no rationalistic-dualistic model that apes the mainstream. Instead, he seeks the ontological ground for understanding suicide in Kierkegaard and Heidegger.

Rossouw (2007) writes that cognitive behavioural and psychodynamic therapies are mired in Cartesian dualism and are "imprisoned by the cookbook-like dictates of scientifically inspired treatment manuals and the procedures of 'evidence-based practice'" (p. 3). He accuses technique-driven therapies of "forgetting the human", of turning both therapists and researchers into "dispassionate observers ... of behaving organisms" (Rossouw, 2007, p. 3). They "forget" flesh and blood existence in the everyday lifeworld, and instead fit the person into theoretical representations of human behaviour. Simultaneously, "they" put out of play the humanness of the therapist. Rossouw identifies the consequence simply and succinctly, "[H]ow do two nobodies meet one another as somebody?" (Rossouw, 2007, p. 3). On the contrary, "We can only begin to understand suicide in the relating with another human being, and in psychology this seems to have become a very difficult thing to do" (Rossouw, 2007, p. 9). He splices his essay with Heidegger's relational perspective, citing C.J. White's reading of homelessness so intimately connected to suicide:

> The person may find him or herself unable to resolve the situation. It is a crisis in which Dasein cannot resolutely accept the collapse of its world, its way of life, so as to be open to disclosing a new world in which the anomalies of living existence makes sense (Rossouw, 2007, p. 8).

Rossouw's views converge with my own concerning the philosophical presuppositions and methodological inadequacies of mainstream psychology. However, we diverge significantly insofar as he locates the problematic squarely within the individual's responses to the existential "given" of life. Like Knizek and Hjemland, he does not assign responsibility to the network of others within which the suicidal person is embedded. This point will become increasingly clear.

Clearly, this recent wave of interest in suicide has not heeded the eloquent plea that Thomas Szasz (1974) began making more than forty years ago. Stop it, is his cry! Terminate the witch hunts. Our "cruel compassion" (Szasz, 1998, pp. 4; 6) only succeeds in capturing potential suicide victims against their will, "disvaluing" them, and justifying "coercion" in the name of "compassion". The ethical or moral issue of keeping someone alive against her wishes is similar to the debate about euthanasia. Szasz (1974) and also Jack Kevorkian (1993) have trumped up similar arguments, championing individual freedom to decide in this most personal of Life's decisions: Death. Both scandalize medicine, theology, the American way, and Western mores in general: *dying is not a crime*. Szasz insists that if one sets aside ideological presuppositions, it is evident that the drive to prevent suicide ... only promotes it.

An individual prone to suicidal gesturing, of course, might profit from the efforts to wrap care around him. A witch hunt can succeed. But we cannot police despair 24/7. The genuine suicide attempt might take place while the husband or wife is taking a shower. Only the absurd idea that one can live the other's life for them might prevent suicide. In this case, would not the cure be worse than the disease?

The reader interested in the ethics and politics of suicide should read Szasz's anti-psychiatric position on mental illness and on the ethics of suicide in particular. He grants a necessary corrective to our normal madness of trying to beat death at all costs. For the purpose of this chapter, however, I evoke an even more radical point of view on the topic. Who best performs an *ontological reversal* that bleaches the stain of disgrace painted on suicide, and indeed dignifies the act?

For certain, the burgeoning discipline of suicidology does not touch with a ten-foot pole Antonin Artaud's (1925/1965) view on suicide (*Sur le suicide*) (pp. 135–163). I put it too lightly. Suicidology does not acknowledge the notion that *a man might be suicided by society*. The idea that suicide might manifest dignity is anathema to any system-sanctioned structure. From the point of view of the establishment, suicide must be eradicated.

In fairness, the discipline of suicidology discusses the legions of possible variables and causes of self-murder, and nods to family dynamics and socioeconomic factors. Artaud, on the other hand, challenges both mainstream and existential-humanistic therapeutic viewpoints.

Artaud (1925/1965) puts it indelicately. He calls van Gogh *The Man Suicided by Society*. Until I read Artaud, I had made a similar point by saying that an-other, at least implicitly, murders the one who takes their own life. I prefer Artaud's phraseology: Society suicides its victims.

Artaud spent nine years psychiatrically institutionalized. His interpretation of Vincent, therefore, is written in blood, not dusty ideas. Artaud writes in his blood. Society, running the gambit from the primary family to one's physician or therapist, snuffs out the life of the individual. Then "they" call it suicide. It's a whitewash.

It covers their butts. It absolves them of any responsibility. Artaud re-locates blame. He minces no words. He attests that Dr. Gaston Ferdiere, the head physician at the Rodez Asylum, "told me he was there to *reform my poetry*" (Artaud, 1925/1965, p. 137, my emphasis). Does not that self-righteous slice of arrogance make you bristle and your hair stand on end! What psychic warp authorizes Power to look a creative genius in the eye and say, "I will reform your art"?

Since Artaud uses his own experience to forward his views—plus the "case" of Vincent van Gogh—he pointedly accuses "the collective conscience of society" of punishing those who are visionaries, nonconformists, creative geniuses. "They" systematically punish "seers" during their lifetime, and eventually suicide them. His point also refers to suicide in general. Some significant other extinguishes the light and blankets the vital life spark of the suicide victim who did not fit in, live up to expectations, join the club, or sell out.

Artaud unmasks the heart of the matter of this essentially political process far better than the rest of us. How so? We grope to understand Kierkegaardian despair, so that we might cure it. But he trenchantly demonstrates that Vincent was not crazy. Or, to generalize beyond the insight into the "real painter's painter", nobody has demonstrated more trenchantly than Artaud that despair is not psychopathological.

In R.D. Laing's (1959/1990) qualitative algebra it is insane to be sane in an insane world. That touches upon it. But Artaud pushes it further. Those who fall out of the cuckoo's nest, who not only do not adapt and conform but who also divine another way, threaten the guardians of the social order. Artaud (1925/1965, p. 137) writes that society, to silence them for its own protection, strangles and puts into asylums those who "utter certain unbearable truths".

"Van Gogh ... thought that he was bewitched and he said so and ... died suicided because it was the concerted awareness of society as a whole that could bear him no longer" (Artaud, 1925/1965, pp. 147; 157). Notice the reversal. Artaud (1925/1965) is not saying that Van Gogh could not bear any longer the "deliberate dishonesty and downright hypocrisy of society, the deception and greed that goes by the name of 'feathering one's nest and providing for a rainy day'" (pp. 135–136). No: society could not bear with his sensitivity and lucidity. The genuine motive for the suicide is society's fear and weakness.

Artaud spells it out. He refers to Vincent's self-portraits with their penetrating, piercing eyes. We do not want to be looked at in the way Van Gogh gazes at us, sees right through us, "inspecting, and watching us, scrutinizing us with a glowering eye ... dissecting ... a man's face ... dissecting our soulless psychology and mendacious psychiatry" (Artaud, 1925/1965, p. 160).[14] It was only Nietzsche who had a similar eye, says Artaud, "who had the same power to undress the soul, to pluck the body from the soul, to lay the body of man bare, beyond the subterfuges of the mind" (Artaud, 1925/1965, p. 160).

Artaud (1925/1965) insists that Vincent located his illness better than any psychiatrist in the world, and

> chose the moment when the pupil of the eyes is going to spill into emptiness, where the glance, aimed at us like the bomb of a meteor, takes on the atonal color of the void and inertia that fills it (p. 161).

"Reform my poetry!" What is at stake in such a pompous project? If someone wants to re-shape the very core of me, and attempts the reform early in my life, they do dual damage. They humiliate me. They shatter something fragile and precious in me; simultaneously they evoke a root urge to recoil from the reformation they orchestrate. It leaves me damaged; and damaged people are dangerous. They are dangerous to others, oft-times. They are almost always dangerous to themselves. Try to cure me of who I am as a youngster, and as a result I can't rest at ease with myself. I can't live; and I can't die. I am hanging by a thread.

> Van Gogh was not mad, but his paintings were wildfire, atomic bombs, whose angle of vision compared to all the other paintings popular at the time ... doesn't attack ... conformity of manners and morals, but *the conformity of institutions themselves* ... if his way of seeing, which was sane, were unanimously widespread, Society could no long survive (Artaud, 1925/1965, pp. 136; 147).

In the matter of suicide, Artaud (1925/1965) alleges "a whole army of evil beings is needed to force a body to perform the unnatural act of depriving itself of its own life"; and "under the pressure of an evil spirit called Doctor Gachet", one of the "low scoundrels and patented shysters" of the medical profession—who detested Vincent as a painter and a genius—colluded with Theo, his brother, to terminate the painter's "terrible, fanatical, apocalyptic, visionary's imagination" (pp. 136; 144; 148; 161–162).

Theo had supported Vincent faithfully over the years. He was devoted to his brother's art. The wonderful record of their correspondence shows Vincent grateful in "moments", demanding at others, but always aware that he was a financial drain. Theo repeated that Vincent was not in his debt. Then Theo married; and he announced the birth of his son, whom he named Vincent. In late June 1890, a month before Vincent pulled the trigger, Theo suddenly was beset with problems. He writes "what for him was an unusually emotional letter" in which he "made his brother privy to his worries about his job, his finances, and his little boy's health" (De Leeuw, 1997, p. 498). The letter troubles Vincent. He writes on 7 July: "[H]ave I done anything wrong, or is there anything you would like me to do?" (De Leeuw, 1997, p. 499). On 10 July he writes:

> I feel very sad, and the storm which threatens you continued to weigh heavily on me as well ... *my life is under attack at its very root*, my step is also unsteady ... I was afraid ... that my being a burden to you was something you found intolerable ... I didn't have to put myself out very much in order to try to express sadness and *extreme loneliness*" (De Leeuw, 1997, p. 499, my emphasis).

Vincent wrote his final letter to Theo on 24 July. About things demanding discussion, he says, "I have lost the inclination ... and it seems useless to me ... [but] the peace of your household ... can be preserved" (De Leeuw, 1997, p. 502). "According to Johanna, Theo had difficulty making sense of the letter" and was taken by surprise when Vincent shot himself three days later (De Leeuw, 1997, p. 509).

Surprise! Surprise at what? That a life of utter sadness and loneliness, one under attack at root, might lead to self-destruction?

Those who prefer the security of rational logic and survival find it difficult to accept Artaud's diagnosis. On that fatal day, 27 July, 1890, Gachet sent Vincent off to paint from nature on a day when he should have rested in bed in solitude. Artaud finds a coil of complicity twisted within this complex situation: Theo and Gachet suicided him. The same status quo security-seekers will also not accept Artaud's twist, his insistence upon the integrity and dignity of Vincent's self-murder:

> Van Gogh condemned himself because he had finished with living, and we gather this from his letters to his brother; because of the birth of his brother's son he felt that he would be one mouth too many to feed. But above all, Van Gogh wanted to join that infinite for which, he said, one embarks as on a train to a star (Artaud, 1925/1965, p. 162).

> "One does not commit suicide alone" (Artuad, 1925/1965, p. 161).

Stuffed and starved

The system does not only suicide visionaries, poets, or those who refuse to play the game (Camus, 1958/1965). Nowadays, while bankers balk at limits imposed upon their bonuses, it suicides the poverty stricken of our planet. Specifically, it suicides the farmer. Raj Patel (2008) documents the soaring, rocketing rates of suicide of farmers across the globe, and gives basic motives (pp. 2; 15; 25). Today's farmers live on the razor's edge. They do not know where their next meal is coming from. They work themselves to exhaustion, scrapping to maintain a marginal standard of living. When the sheriff's sale sign goes up, or when the bank forecloses, they experience profound shame unto despair. A father bequeaths the family farm to his son. It has been in the family for generations. To be responsible for ending the legacy dishonours a man beyond belief. It is too horrible to bear.

> On 10 September 2003 at the World Trade Organization Ministerial meeting in Cancun, Lee Kyung Hae, a Korean farmer and peasant organizer, climbed a fence near the barricade behind which the trade meetings were happening. He flipped open his red penknife, shouted "the WTO kills farmers" and stabbed himself high in his chest. He died within hours (Patel, 2008, p. 35).

"The wind behind the World Trade Organization is the globalization of the capitalist system ... The WTO is a bomb to peasants" (Patel, 2008, p. 37). The modus operandi of the WTO polarizes the rich and poor. The rich get filthy rich; the poor descend into deeper dire poverty. Darwinian competition, struggle, natural selection, and survival of the fittest legitimize the injustice. "But if you're a human being with reason and conscience, then the WTO should be eliminated ... To live, people need to eat. You cannot commercialize this. It's such an anti-human behaviour, not just anti-social, but anti-people" (Patel, 2008, p. 37).

Parvarthi Masaya has a cropped short haircut, quite different from the hair of other woman in her village located five hours out of Hyderabad. On 11 August, 2004, her husband, Kistaiah, in despair over deep debt, killed himself by drinking poison, a pesticide called "phorate". "Parvarthi shaved her hair off on 12 August 2004 in a ritual of grief" (Patel, 2008, p. 25).

What killed Lee Kyung Hae? From the point of view of psychiatry and psychology, it is his psychopathological, unstable personality. Do not expect the System to get hung up on his lost self-respect, his lost dignity, and his humiliation. Should you and I blow out of proportion that he did not want to be a beggar ... but a creator?

Within hours after his death, the *campesinos* in Mexico chanted, "Lee no murio OMC lo mato ... Lee didn't die, the WTO killed him" (Patel, 2008, p. 47).

A rural autopsy: Did the WTO kill Lee Kyung Hae? How far will you choose to look?

CHAPTER FIFTEEN

On murder in Albert Camus

"The eyes do not shine, they speak ... Everyone will readily agree that it is of the highest importance to know whether we are not duped by morality"

(Levinas, 1961/1969, p. 21).

The partners in this chapter's dialogue are composite figures (Alapack, 1988a; 1988b; 2006b). To create them, I draw upon my experiences with both murderers and health care professionals. In order to challenge you and myself concerning murder, I imagine the real (Lynch, 1960). It is ordinary to draw from a wealth of personal experiences to capture an essential meaning. Ken Kesey (1980) taps into his work as an aide in an Oregon psychiatric hospital to depict pathological dependency in *One Flew over the Cuckoo's Nest*. Daniel Panger (1979) uses his intensive and extensive work with cancer patients and their families to write *The Dance of the Wild Mouse*, a fictional portrayal of the alienating impact of technology on a man facing a death-threatening illness and his woman reeling in horror that she will lose her beloved man. Only narrow, rigid positivist ideology disrespectfully reduces such heartlines to mere fiction.

Meeting murderers

I sojourned to the Ielase Institute of Forensic Psychology fifteen years after I had attained my Ph.D. Thanks to the dedicated and tireless leadership of Richard Asarian, Ph.D., the institute had mounted an out-patient programme and treatment programmes in all the minimum, medium, and maximum security prisons in the Greater Pittsburgh area. Richard, my friend and colleague, gave me the freedom of thorough involvement with the institute, including practicing in whichever ways I saw fit to create relevant and meaningful assessment, educational, and treatment modalities. I gained more than I gave from those with whom I toiled: from Richard, from his very personable and professional staff—especially Jim Johns and Barbara Williams—and from the men and women labelled "addicted criminals".

The cost was great, too. After I returned to the university, Dr. Asarian phoned to tell me that Philip, one of my former clients, had gone "on the lamb". Before the police apprehended him, Philip killed himself. *My narrative herein honours him* and a dozen other so-called thieves and murderers who shared with me their lives and pain.

My baptism by fire at the Ielase Institute came in handy during the Exxon Valdez disaster. At the Seward Life Council, we mounted a drug and alcohol programme in Alaska's only maximum security prison, Spring Creek Correctional Centre. This Ice Palace, then a brand-new facility, sits across Resurrection Bay with a magnificent Glacier sticking its tongue into its centre courtyard. Here, I met a few more murderers.

During twenty-seven months of service in Alaska, I lost my political virginity. Before I returned to my university post, I had learned that the politics of oil rules our world. In June, 1990, as I was presenting my description of the devastating oil hemorrhage, "Tore down in Seward" (Alapack, 1990), to the *International Human Science Research Conference* in Quebec City, Quebec, simultaneously several excellent pieces of similar journalism appeared. At the same time, the State released the official "scientific" findings that they had commissioned. These reports *glowed* with the "success" of the "cleanup". The State didn't want a "cleanup"; it wanted a "whitewash".

What counts as knowledge? Foucault's (1973/1979) assertion, that *power dictates knowledge*, whacked me in the face. Politicians buy and sell scientists to support their policies and programmes. In *this* historical moment, the State had "purchased" research findings to appease the citizens of Alaska, to protect politicians' jobs, and to support the oil cartel's elaborate publicity campaign for appeasing the world community.

Now, I was acquainted with the political night(mare). "You can't fight City Hall," the common folk say. The line is fine, thin, and permeable between those who administer the "prison" and those who rot away in it. More truly, they are synchronized swimmers.

Worldwide, governmental bureaucrats and "securocrats" trade in duplicity, hypocrisy, corruption, and the insanity of excessive rational-pragmatic assessment and planning. They fund research projects to protect the status quo, never to change it. More basic than making money, the goal of Western democratic political parties and university education is ... revolution prevention.

The Avalanche

Derek P.J. Dombrowski, nicknamed "the Avalanche", is serving a life sentence for killing his wife's lover. He had been a high-profile All-Pro middle linebacker with the Pittsburgh Steelers of the National Football League. After rehabilitation from knee surgery, he tries to continue his storied and stellar career. During the pre-season games, it becomes increasingly obvious that he has "lost a step". During his time away from the gridiron, his passion for the sport had also dwindled. On a doubly fatal August day, his coach informs him that the team is releasing him; his career is over. After an hour's drive, he reaches home to find, unexpectedly, a familiar car parked in his driveway. It belongs to his wife's artist friend. He sneaks into the house and finds them in the marital bedroom in the all-together, joined at the hips. He kills the interloper with his bare hands.

A highly intelligent, creative man, Avalanche did not attain a university degree as he left college early in the professional draft. While serving his life sentence, he does not become a jail house lawyer or "get religion"—as is so typically the case with bright incarcerated individuals. Instead, he decides to finish his B.A. in psychology and earn a master's degree in philosophy. Kierkegaard and Nietzsche, because they ground their thinking in subjectivity and individuality, become his intellectual heroes.

For twenty-five years, Avalanche enjoys learning for the love of learning, not stifled by the normal narrow demands of the university curricula: jumping through hoops, doing hackneyed projects, and sitting even sillier exams. Alone, he grapples painfully but steadfastly with the pertinent issues of Life and love, Death and ... murder. Along his journey of hearthead, he pierces through the social-conceptual "plastic" of Western culture and deconstructs the bull from its sacred cows. Most importantly, he learns finally to love.

The existential therapeutic dialogue: "Can YOU kill?"

I didn't consciously plan to pop the question, but it leaped out of my mouth in a session with Leonard, my therapist. The question is never out of my mind. "What's murder, Leonard?"

"To *whom?*" he replied.

"What do you mean, 'To whom'?" I did not expect him to answer my question with a question.

"Come-on, Avalanche," Leonard answered, sounding exasperated. "I thought we work this 'stuff' out together!" Then a complaint spliced his words. "I don't have the key to your heart's desire, do I, nor the answers to your mind's questions? If I were foolish enough to think I did, you wouldn't swallow them hook, line and sinker anyway, would you?"

I was taken aback. This was not Leonard's typical manner. "Well ... yeah ... Leonard. Ok ... Let's see." I began hesitantly. "For the one murdered, it's 'lights out' ... for those who loved and lost the ... newborn corpse ... it's crying time. For the one who did the deed, it's the beginning of everlasting questioning and emotional turmoil ... shame and remorse."

"Or satisfaction, if the murderer feels justified," he said, putting a period to my sentence.

I bristled! "Are you insinuating that I? ... You sneaky bastard, Leonard! You're playing 'dumb' just so that you can put words in my mouth ... What is this, some new fuckin' trick that you read about in one of your psychotherapy cookbooks? Go fuck yourself, Leonard! I'm not playing these psychological games."

"Jesus, I must of hit a nerve, Avalanche! You gimpy knee just jerked!"

"Oh, fuck, Doctor Doolittle. He hit a nerve, did he? Doctor-who-me-I-don't-know-anything! No, Leonard. You just hit a stone wall. I played middle linebacker, remember? I'm not easily baited. If you want to play mind games, find another sucker. Or go play with yourself!"

"For crying out loud, don't be so touchy, Derek. And don't personalize everything. It's pathetic to say, but self-satisfied justification for murder is mankind's most popular practice."

I closed my eyes, crossed my legs, folded my arms ... and waited.

"What's murder, Derek? It isn't just one more act, like any other. Murder is an 'infinite act'. Leo Tolstoy meditates on a tiny bullet and expresses the total disproportion between cause and effect. A tiny piece of metal can muffle our fragile breath and snuff out a life. There's no justification for bullets or 'smart' bombs either ... or any of our man-made weapons of mass destruction. No moral or political whitewash can legitimize the inherent ill-proportion."

I replied in a voice that didn't even sound convincing to me. "There has always been war, Leonard, and always will be. It's in our genes, part of nature."

"Is war ever 'just', Derek? I mean other than the good ole honest dyed-in-the-wool American game of football, that violent game of bombing and blitzing. You've heard of it, haven't you? 'Attack, sack the quarterback, bury him ... kill him!' Do you buy the sick arguments of St. Augustine and St. Thomas, splitting a cunt-hair in order to justify war ... on rational grounds? Or what about the Christian Crusades? Was killing justified because you happened to be wearing a uniform with a Cross emblazoned on your chest instead of numbers, and because your teammates carried banners with so many crosses you'd think they were cheerleaders with pom-poms? Wasn't Christendom just a cover for the white man's greed ... and perennial racial hatred of brown Muslim heathens? What about capital punishment itself, society's good ole use of the Talion Law? An eye-for-an-eye, a life-for-a-life ... 'Routine, ritualistic, even-tempered, assembly-line annihilation', a death row prison chaplain once called it. Do you condone capital punishment, Derek? Does retribution have any redeeming purpose?"

I'd never seen Leonard so animated nor heard him talk so loudly. Alert, I waited. All eyes, all ears.

"Hey, big boy," he continued, "You're just a rookie in this dig-ging-for-answers-about-murder-business. If you hit the panic but-ton at every new snap of the ball, some seasoned offensive lineman is going to knock you on your ass. So if you want to understand this game, of murder, you better start reading guys like Caryl Chessman (2006), Albert Camus, (1948/1991), and Edgar Smith (1968). The pros! Do you read me?"

He had my attention, big time! In a flash, I saw that we had entered Dante's darkened wood where immediately the straight way gets lost.

In response, I began: "You want me to see murder in as wide a context as possible, right, Leonard?"

"To learn something relevant, what's the sense of looking at it narrowly? At this late stage of your 'game', you're not about to turn into a ticky-tacky experimental psychologist, are you? Measure this ... measure that? How many killers use knives? Or how many guns? How many use their bare hands?"

"Fuck, Leonard!" I said. The phrase "bare hands" goosed me. Abruptly, I pivoted in my chair. "I should have kept my goddamn mouth shut. I don't want to get into this shit, not now."

"Hillel wrote," he answered, looking down at his shoes. " 'He who does not learn forfeits his life'" (Gross and Gross, 1993).

I recoiled at the verbal slap in the face and then went on the offen-sive, barking back at him: "What about you, Leonard? Could you murder?"

He spat out some Latin at me: "*Nihil humanum a me alienum puto.*"

"Huh ... run that one by me again, Leonard ... in plain English."

"I am human so nothing human is alien to me." We are all equally human.

"So you can kill, Leonard? That's what you're saying, right? You're admitting that?"

"Of course, I'm flesh and blood! If ever I'm with someone—whatever he's done—and I can't 'fess up to being capable of the same action, then I should walk away ... quit ... resign, stop doing psychotherapy. If I had been in your situation, Derek, or your cir-cumstances, I ..."

I interrupted. "Oh, right, the ole Indian dictum that bleeding heart liberals use: 'walk-a-mile-in-my-moccasins before'..."

He reciprocated the interruption. "No: *Wear them*! Don't borrow shoes to take a stroll, like a tourist visiting the reservation! Wear them ... everyday ... until you blister ... until your feet bleed."

A long, burning silence wafted over us.

"Notice that we both just interrupted each other?" he asked, as if gathering the silence into his palms and cradling it.

"Yes, what do you think it means?" I felt like I was dangling from a limb.

"You didn't want to hear that you and I might be in the same boat ... interchangeable ... synchronized swimmers in this game ... of life ... and death."

"That you don't do your job out of the goodness of your heart, like a 'perfect' father?"

"Or even a 'good' one. Sometimes not even a 'good' father."

"What about you ... interrupting me ... interrupting you?" I asked slowly.

"What do you think?"

"You flinched when I reduced your admission ... ah ... to a fucking cliché."

"That fits for me, Derek. I wasn't blowing smoke. The Cain and Abel story inscribes murder at the heart of human interaction. I wasn't condescending to you."

I got pensive. Automatically, my body lapsed into the posture of a linebacker waiting for the offensive centre to twitch his finger on the ball. Clearly, the game wasn't over.

"*What about you, Avalanche? Can you ... commit murder?*"

He blindsided me with that one! I was expectant, but I wasn't expecting *that* one. It's a wonder I didn't fall off my chair, or shit myself, because the question sent me reeling. I tottered and staggered to find my centre of balance, to get my feet under me or else be flattened to the turf.

While I floundered, Leonard waited patiently. To be perfectly honest, my first impulse was to escape to bolt to run away to fuckin' defy gravity! Instead, I looked him straight in the eyes and said, "Yes, on one occasion, amazingly ... horribly ... I terminated the life of a fellow-human. Somehow, by the grace of God, here I sit."

"Nice to meet you, Derek P.J. Dombrowski!" he said. "We'll pick it up here next time."

He stood up. Our ritual fifty-minute hour had expired. I stood up, too, a head taller. For the first time ever, in a gesture of mutual respect and support we hugged. It felt good.

I stopped at the threshold, before walking out into the corridors of this Alaskan Ice Palace. As Leonard was about to lock the door, I turned back to him. "'He who does not learn forfeits his life' ... Where the fuck do you find all these zingers, Leonard?"

"Wherever I need them, Avalanche," he replied, smiling as he turned to go.

I watched him walk away looking both more vulnerable and more real than I had ever noticed. I knew more than ever why I liked the little fucker.

Later, I lay on my bunk and closed my eyes. Yes, I could kill ... again. But I knew with rock bottom assurance I'd never. The gore in the bone marrow of my soul would never catch me by surprise again. If ever it surfaced again, I'd smear it ... and laugh ... and then I'd call an airport cab ... or walk away.

Avalanche's reflective synopsis of Camus

Albert Camus' (1948/1991) *The Plague* probes human-killing with conceptual, metaphorical, and poetic brilliance. At first, I howled at Camus' description of the small town mentality of Oran that reveals ordinary humdrum life of people all over the world. Listen: "Certainly nothing is commoner nowadays than to see people working from morn till night and then proceeding to fritter away at card-tables, in cafes and in small talk what time is left for living" (Camus, 1948/1991, p. 4). Ole' Albert wrote that in 1948. He should see today's TV and the Internet if he wants to watch life being frittered away. Anyway, next he unmasks the "mild habit of 'conjugality,' the way men and women consume one another in what is called 'the act of love' " (Camus, 1948/1991, p. 4). A biting period punctuates those words: "At Oran, as elsewhere, for lack of time and thinking, people have to love one another without knowing much about it" (Camus, 1948/1991, p. 5).

Not content to challenge love, he goes after death. He reminds us that dying can be very difficult to accomplish. Nowadays, we have been reduced to consumers who can only shop until we drop. We know not how to live, love, or die.

I wasn't finished digesting his view that society only encourages banal habits—not individuality, creativity, reflection, enthusiasm, tenderness, and passion—when he introduced *the rats*. I shuddered at their emergence, anticipating that Camus was about to display what we never pay heed to. I ploughed through the destructive events of the plague. Subtly but relentlessly, he unfolds a metaphor. By the time I got to his "picture of the criminal" on page 247, I thought I was ready for a punchline. When it exploded into a total vision about the horror of taking a life, I wasn't ready at all. By the time I waded through Tarrou's revelations, my spirit dove as deep as a Puffin into Resurrection Bay. I was ready to drown ...

"Each of us has the plague within him," Camus' character Tarrou states to Rieux, "No one, no one on earth is free from it ... It's a wearying business, being plague-stricken. But it's still more wearying to refuse to be it" (Camus, 1948/1991, p. 253). Pestilence menaces innocence, incessantly.

"On this earth there are pestilences and there are victims," Tarrou says, only that (Camus, 1948/1991, pp. 253–254). Our Western ideals and moral principles sanction death-dealings. Blinded by some half-assed cause that pleases and appeases us, we condone the death of others whom we don't recognize as human beings. Rendered brain-deadened and heart-emptied by some "great issue at stake", we sacrifice precious individuals to ideology. "I've heard quantities of arguments, which very nearly turned my head, and turned other people's heads enough to make them approve of murder" (Camus, 1948/1991, p. 254). The ideologists and the pragmatists alike splice their clamour for death with sermons condemning squeamishness. Tarrou couldn't stomach the impressive arguments they wanted him to swallow.

> As far as I was concerned, nothing in the world would induce me to accept any argument that justified such butcheries ... I resolved to have no truck with anything which, directly or indirectly, for good reasons or bad, brings death to anyone or justifies others putting him to death (Camus, 1948/1991, pp. 252–253).

"If you gave in once," he elaborates, "there is no reason for not continuing to give in" (Camus, 1948/1991, p. 251). If one can justify any murder, every murder can be whitewashed. The ones with the red robes offer the most compelling arguments to justify killing, Tarrou says, indicting the Roman Catholic hierarchy.

We are all innocent murderers. We should be disgusted at any form of killing. There is no "just war". The juxtaposition of those two words is a ruse of brain-farting ideologists and greedy politicians— members of the industrial-military complex who stand to profit from bombing and killing. In real life ... outside of meeting rooms with blueprints, battle strategies, and pseudo-ethical arguments ... in the world of flesh and blood and bone, there are victims: widows, orphans, the wounded and newly created paupers ... psyches permanently scarred by the experiences of slaughter and bloodbaths.

Tarrou clarifies to Rieux:

> Today there's a sort of competition who will kill the most ... The nations of the earth all are mad over murder and they couldn't stop killing men even if they wanted to ... Once I'd definitely refused to kill, I doomed myself to an exile that can never end (Camus, 1948/1991, pp. 251–252).

We all are living on borrowed time; everybody on the planet is serving a life sentence; each of us carries the plague within.

"Thou shalt not kill."

Preventive murder

In Chapter four, "Gone crazy", I presented crimes of passion as extreme acts to forestall grief. An over-wrought, heart-threatened individual who is coming apart at the seams nips grief in the bud. He is lucid enough to grasp that what is taking place, or what is about to come down, is unbearable. He kills to stop the desperately needed other from leaving. It's murder to prevent devastation to self.

Sling Blade (Thornton, 1996) depicts a preventive murder of a different ilk. For those who do condone killing another human for transcendent reasons, Billy Bob Thornton's film exemplifies a preventive murder. Karl Childers, in the stark, streamlined Norwegian way of expressing it, *ble satt bak lås og slå*, has been put away under lock and key and beaten down.

The universe dealt Karl a big, good heart with sensitivity, honesty, intuition, and the ability to "read" the hearts of his fellow men.

However, it did not grant him the "card" of advanced abstract intellectual ability. When we meet Karl, he is being victimized one more time, this time by a deinstitutionalization policy. To save money, the State of Arkansas has designated him for release. The State had decreed that twenty-five years in a rural psychiatric hospital has cured him. He had been housed there in lieu of prison.

At age twelve, Karl killed his small town's cruel sawmill owner's more cruel adolescent son. Alone, as usual, in his hovel in the backyard of his parents' poor shack, he hears uproar. His very attractive mother is making strange sounds. Going to the house, he catches her and his mean schoolmate "*in flagrante delicto*", or, in the language of the street, on the floor fuckin' like rabbits.

In an eye-blink, Karl acts to end abuse, believing that the evil boy was forcing himself upon his mother. "I picked up a Kaiser blade that was a layin' there by the screen door," he tells a pretty young high school newspaper reporter, interviewing him on the day of his release, "Some folks calls it a sling blade; I call it a Kaiser blade." With two swipes, he kills the lad, almost cutting his head off. His mother goes ballistic, screaming with fury that he had killed her lover-boy. Karl understands immediately that she condoned the lust, craved it, and had no virtue to defend. He promptly slashes her to death, too.

In the "moment", Karl has nothing but the sling blade and Biblical injunctions stuffed down his throat. In a radical sense, he never had the law on his side and never would. Spontaneously, he tells the reporter the tale that led to his commitment. When she asks him the innocent but cardinal question, he answers: "I don't reckon I got no reason to kill nobody." She sits there, ready to believe that he'll never kill again. But intuitively she realizes that something is wrong with the Big Picture. The State is releasing him only to follow a new policy aimed at saving money. She can see in an eye-blink that Karl will be like a fish out of water in the outside social world. When she asks what preparation and plan for re-entry to the outside world the institute made for Karl's release, the warden whisks her out the door.

What's a "Kaiser" or "ditch bank" blade? It features a hardwood pole with a wide, heavy steel blade with a half-hook point attached firmly to the end. It is usually kept sharp on both sides and is used for cutting earth and roots as well as heavier vegetation. A sling blade is a very lethal weapon.

Locked and beaten down during his entire adult life, Karl learns to read. During the movie, he repeats that he now possesses his own, albeit rudimentary and imperfect, understanding of the Bible. Released, he walks out a free man with an armful of books, including his Bible: his only treasures.

By bus, Karl arrives in his hometown. Disoriented, he moseys up to an outdoor fast food stand, recognizing from signs and pictures that it sells grub. He has no idea what anything means, and has no idea how to order. He asks for biscuits, an item that is not actually on the menu. The scene is painful and infuriating to watch. The counterman rattles off a list of the various burgers and wieners that he does sell. Karl understands none of the jargon, and asks what the fellow himself likes to eat. The counterman is as befuddled about dealing with Karl as Karl is in coping with the world that had passed him by during a quarter of a century. He says their French Fries are good. Karl ends up eating—with relish—a large order of them, smothered in mustard.

Having no place to go, he returns to the hospital from which he is now locked out because of liability laws. The warden takes him home where he is received with awkwardness. As a guest, he is given the daughter's bedroom. Uncomfortable at usurping the girl's room, Karl doesn't even turn down the sheets and sleeps not a wink.

The day begins. Since Ka has a peculiar genius for small engine repair, the warden procures him a job at a repair shop of a friend. In what is so familiar, he is offered space at the back of the shop. The owner even has a key made for him.

Sitting and eating French Fries in front of the town Laundromat, he meets a young boy, Frank Wheatley. Frank is dragging four large bags of laundry and Karl decides to help Frank carry the clothing home. Frank invites him to the dry goods store where Linda, his mother, works. The pivot of the movie is the tender preadolescent chum relationship that the two guys develop (Sullivan, 1954. Alapack, 2007a, pp. 7–53).

For Frank (whose father committed suicide because he felt he couldn't properly support his family), Karl becomes a father figure. They understand each other intuitively. "I like the way you talk," Frank tells him." And I like the way you talk," Karl replies. Their interactions make the lad feel calm. Frank is Karl's friend and the little brother he never grew up with. Karl moves into the Wheatley's garage out back.

What truly haunts Karl are not the murders he committed, but the hideous task his dirt poor, fanatically religious parents gave him when he was still a six-year-old lad. His father handed him his deformed, unwanted, newborn brother, the size of a squirrel, and told him to toss the towel and its contents into the trash. But Karl could hear whimpering. It was not garbage he was being ordered to dump. But brainwashed to obey, and in spite of an ache deep inside that it was wrong, Karl buries the child, still alive. Finding himself caring and cared for by Frank and Linda, he seeks redemption.

With anguish, Karl also repeatedly witnesses Frank's mother's boyfriend, Doyle, act abusively and aggressively. Doyle is a narrow-minded, bigoted, drunken, obnoxious, self-absorbed redneck, scared shitless of life but too stupid and afraid to admit it. He calls Karl "a humped-over retard", obnoxiously insults Linda's gay boss, and is especially contemptuous of Frank—jealous of the bond Linda has with her son. If Karl had available your words or mine, he would say that Doyle was a "certifiable wacko". With the wisdom of the heart, however, he sees what cognition might overlook: a grim fate for Linda and Frank, those he has come to love. Slowly, he also realizes that he is the only one who can bring about the necessary change to spare the boy and his mother ongoing pain, degradation, humiliation and, ultimately, destructive violence.

Near the end of the movie, this gentle man, locked (*lås*) in a bewildering world that he experiences as "too big", and which he would never have made such as it functions, begins to get his house into order and his ducks in a row.

After seeking and receiving baptism, he revisits the hole-in-the-wall shed to which he was exiled as a child. He enters the low class southern house, finds his abusive father sitting in a chair surrounded by cheap, tacky furniture and clutter. He tells him he is his son—which his father disclaims—and then he tells him that he thought about killing him. Awkwardness hovers. At length, Karl says that seeing him sitting there so broken makes him decide that killing him isn't worth the effort. Truth banishes the awkwardness. Karl walks out.

He goes out back to visit the primitive grave that he had made for his ill-fated brother. Later that evening, he arranges with Linda and Frank to spend the night at her boss's home. He gives Frank the present of his precious few books, including a bookmarker he made that reads, "YOU WILL BE HAPPY".

No time for dilly dallying. It is the propitious "moment". He goes to Linda's house. Doyle is sitting alone, sucking a bottle of beer. Frank asks him how to contact the police. Condescendingly, he tells him to dial 911. Frank twice whacks him with a lawnmower blade that we had seen him sharpening a few scenes earlier for the occasion. He phones the police dispatcher, reports the murder, and gives the location of the crime. Then he sits and waits.

Karl is no idiot savant; no wise fool, no mythic hero; he is no analogue to Forrest Gump, the Rainman or Norman Bates in *Psycho II*. Killing Doyle is not the act of an avenging angel, or a vigilante. Karl is just a man who loves and acts with anticipation spawned by tender passion. He understands enough of the Bible to know what must be done, beyond all moral, ethical, and legal standards of right and wrong. He has witnessed enough self-righteous hypocrisy.

His action blows away Immanuel Kant's moral imperative, the ultra-conservative idea that we must do our duty and simply obey. Karl had buried his dying brother out of invincible ignorance and blind obedience to his parents' command. He would never repeat that crime. Perhaps, he grasps the deepest implications of Kant's viewpoint, opaque to the philosopher himself, and acted upon it. How so?

Kant says that as moral agents we should act in such a way that our comportment would serve as a valid law for all mankind. The System has championed his views—in spite of the dreadfully written prose in which they are encased—because he supports the established order. Kant has us all toe the mark and walk the line. Karl's preventive murder sets a standard beyond such hypocritical morality. He kills the real killer. Beyond all shadow of a doubt, he truly protects his loved ones. Perhaps there might be peace on earth someday if all of us comported ourselves with love like Karl, instead of behaving like successful citizens but ... failed human beings.

After being exposed to "real" life outside the protective walls of the psychiatric hospital, Karl emerges with a stronger sense of moral ethics and self-awareness than before his discharge. Finally, he silences his fellow inmate, a sexual serial killer, who brags incessantly about his crimes: "Fact of business, don't you say another word to me. I ain't listening to you no more."

For twenty-five years, Karl had sat on the ward with nothing to recall but his murders. Now, he will sit with the good memories of his bond with his young friend, Frank. And he will now only listen to the liberating and authentic voice speaking for a more gracious humanity. He will heed the words of Nietzsche (1885/1955) who he could never read: "What is done out of love is always beyond good and evil" (p. 86).

The Seville Statement on violence

Twenty scientists of various relevant disciples from around the world drafted the statement on 16 May, 1986. It rejects the myths that violence is etched in human nature and, as such, cannot be eradicated. Specifically, the Seville Statement affirms that IT IS SCIENTIFICALLY INCORRECT to say:

1. That we have inherited a tendency to make war from our animal ancestors.
2. That war or any other violent behaviour is genetically programmed into our human nature.
3. That in the course of human evolution there has been a selection for aggressive behaviour more than for any other kinds of behaviour.
4. That humans have a "violent brain".
5. That war is caused by instinct or any single motivation.

The same species who invented war is capable of inventing peace. The responsibility lies with each of us (Adams, 1989, pp. 333–336).

"We do not torture" and other funny stories

In *Torture: A Collection* (Oxford: Oxford University Press, 2004). Sanford Levinson, professor of government at the University of Texas at Austin; Jean Bethke Elshtain, University of Chicago political philosopher; Richard Posner, judge of the U.S. Court of Appeals and senior lecturer at the University of Chicago Law School; and Alan Dershowitz, Harvard University law professor—all work on ways to justify and institutionalize the torture which had become policy at Guantanamo and at Abu Ghraib and other secret prisons and was advocated by later Attorney General Alberto Gonzales (Lingis, 2007, p. 143).

CHAPTER SIXTEEN

On Racism: Who is my neighbour?

Who is my neighbour? (Alapack, 2007c) Kierkegaard answers that question with incredible ease: *Everyone is my neighbour.* "One's neighbor," he writes, "is the absolutely unrecognizable distinction between man and man" (Kierkegaard, 1847/1962, p. 79). Without exception, my neighbour is each and every single solitary human being. "In being a neighbor, we are all unconditionally like each other. Distinction is temporality's confusing element which marks every man as different, but neighbour is eternity's mark—on every man" (Kierkegaard, 1847/1962, p. 97). Differences in race, colour, or creed are accidental contingent, flukes. The real mark of humanness cuts deep.

This robust criterion prevails as the gold standard for humanity's self-appraisal. Nowadays, we need such a clear-headed and warm-hearted appraisal of our brothers and sisters across the globe. Only you know in your heart of hearts whether you are a racist, discriminating against anyone because of race, colour, or creed. In terms of sorrow's profiles, xenophobia, racial hatred, and bigotry are major causes of man-made grief. I make no bones about it. Happily, Kierkegaard's Vision inescapably erases from our vocabulary the ugliest words and phrases in any language: ethnic cleansing, and genocide.

The political paradigms that have held sway in Western (de)civilization perennially ignore Kierkegaard's simple standard. Incredible lapses from it litter our history. Failure even to approximate it hallmarks modernity and post-modernity. Hideously heinous crimes against humanity make up the decisive stories of the 20th and early 21st centuries. These tales are blood-stained and shame-riddled. It suits to name at least the dirtiest dozen: the Holocaust, Hiroshima, Apartheid, My Lai, Rwanda, Kosovo, Darfur, Abu Grahib, Guantanamo Bay, Afghanistan, Iraq, and Lebanon 2006. Today, on 15 September, 2009, more than 201,000 million poor individuals are starving. As guardians of the social order, we have little to be proud of, do we? Whenever push comes to shove and the pressure is on, our courage to be human goes missing. We feather our nest instead. After meditating on the carnage encompassed in these historical events, who would fail to conclude that Western philosophy is fatally flawed and defective of heart? The Eskimo word for the white man, you will recall, is "he who changes nature". We have become masters of the most radical change of all: death ... murderous death, to be precise.

The events of 9/11 re-baptized our millennium. There is only one authentically healing response to the new dispensation that follows in its wake: a turning to love, forgiveness, and mercy. The de facto responses, pre-emptive diplomacy, a preventive invasion-occupation, and a contrived war on terror, are nothing but the terror of acting-out anti-terror, revenge written in capital letters. Under the cover of fighting "religious extremism", the West goes to extremes. In consequence, the wanton abuse of power and blood-for-oil-greed menaces the globe. War has become a business venture, amassing incredible profits for the warmongers. In consequence of the consequence, cycles of revenge and counter-revenge swirl across the globe, relentlessly and seemingly endlessly. A warped equation underwrites the numbers on the Big Board: the greater the financial profits, the greater the human cost in suffering, sorrow, and grief. This is a symptom of a sick society and a decaying civilization. Is there proof? 15 September, 2008.

For the last century and one quarter, the ruling paradigm of normal science has perpetuated the violence and racism originally etched in

Platonic Christendom. From our psycho-medical sciences, addicted to technology, the human touch is missing. Racism and violence originate, not in the passions, but in rationalistic detachment and positivistic pseudo-objectivity. Positivistic science, therefore, cannot contribute to the true solution to the world's woes. We, the people, must generate the power to replace cold abstract reason with a mind warmed by the fleshy heart. Nobody should starve. Everyone should be able to look anyone straight in the eye, acknowledged as an equal.

Apartheid and touch

What are the ground phenomena of our common humanity? One is the face-to-face encounter; the other is the exchange of touch. Emanuel Levinas writes "The eye does not shine, it speaks" (Levinas, 1961/1969, p. 23). Nothing is as naked as the human visage. Everything else is naked by analogy to the starkly bare openness, tenderness, and raw vulnerability of the human face. Each shared glance between two sets of eyes triggers the miracles of welcome, speech, hospitality, and teaching—Eros and ethics intertwined.

Immanuel Kant's (1949) categorical imperative never can provide the basis for an authentic morality (pp. 11–16). Remember *Sling Blade* in Chapter fifteen. Kant privileges duty. He expects each of us to act in such a way that our comportment would create moral laws for the entire social group. In a word, each of us ought to be a "lead" sheep attempting to recruit the rest of the flock so that they might follow suit. Kant justifies establishment violence.

Levinas offers the foil to Kant's rationalistic myopia. Infinity overcomes the tyranny of Western totality. "Ethics is an optics" (Levinas, 1961/1969, pp. 23; 29). We must see the others, listen to them, engage in dialogue with them, and touch them. Levinas tips Western philosophy on its head. Ethics ought to be the first philosophy. We should deduce our metaphysics from our morality, not vice versa. Life's first gesture is to show open hands, holding no blade or stone; life's primary words are, "Thou shalt not kill." Murder manifests a total disproportion between cause and effect. Remember the Avalanche and Leonard talking. A little piece of metal, called a bullet, can snuff out a life. Murder is an infinite act.

Touch, as part of the facing position, is a primary human "moment". Touch touches everything. We can never give away all our touches. Levinas bemoans that Western thought is *allergic to the other*. He pleads with us to overcome our allergies. Differences between peoples of race, colour, and creed are not *deficits*; they are just *differences*. If we are truly open to them, they can be assets.

Embracing the stranger is the most powerful way to dismantle social barriers. Is that not how to heal our sick and sickening allergies? When I lock eyes with the other, either I flow out in the welcome of speech and touch, or I turn away, avert my eyes, and refuse contact with alien flesh—whether out of shame, guilt, fear, anxiety, or disgust. Withdrawal avoids vital contact with the "terrible other". What essential message does the gesture of aloofness express? My fleshy recoil is the origin of prejudice and discrimination. It inaugurates the essential horror of racism.

Racism is typically articulated, in rational discourse, as mental-spiritual-religious disdain or disgust. Academics and intellectuals prefer to reduce the matter to "ideological" clashes. Existentially, however, racism is recoiling from natural wholesome touch. To repeat, racism represents Western man's most intense expression of his allergic orientation to otherness. But we also know that the avowed disgust with black-brown-yellow-red flesh perennially carries a double message. Sexual desire and aggression-unto-rape historically accompany racist ideologues. We kill, rape, maim, and plunder those who we hold as inferiors.

Alan Paton's (1953/1995) *Too late the Phalarope* presents a haunting tale of lethally forbidden love during South Africa's period of Apartheid. Within the bigger story, Paton poignantly describes bodily horror as core racial hatred. Into the mouth of Moffie, he puts the decisive story.

There is an accident in Cape Town. Moffie witnesses a car crashing into a telephone box. He sprints to the vehicle and is the first to reach it. Lo and behold, the door opens and a woman falls backwards into his arms. The light from the phone box is flashing on and off. At one flicker, while the light is still bright, he notices that the woman in his arms is Malay, "full of jewels and rings and blood", and at once he realizes that "he could not hold her any more; he lets go of her in horror, not even gently ... even though a crowd was there" (Paton, 1953/1995, p. 89). He simply drops her like a sack of potatoes, pushes through the crowd, and goes on his way. The coward flees. On-his-way!

Is not the "moment" pathetically evil? The biblical tale of the "Good Samaritan" rings in our ears. Yet what a simple, rich phrase does Paton use! "On his way!" On his way ... to what? What kind of "way" is he travelling along? Where is there to go? It suits that we follow, to see where this flight leads and see what we can learn from it.

Paton (1953/1995) writes: "For the touch of such a person was abhorrent to him" (p. 89). In self-defence of his gutless, inhumane action, Moffie insists that the disgust of brown flesh is "deep down in him a part of his very nature ... not learned" (Paton, 1953/1995, p. 89). He uses the lame excuse of biology. He insists that his primitive horror reveals him as a quintessential Afrikaner. Racial hatred is in his genes.

Paton, who is an eloquent anti-Apartheid spokesman, describes that when the group of Afrikaner men hear Moffie's story, they roar with laughter. *What does this laughter signify*? Does it not mask their shame? Paton (1953/1995) then nails the essential meaning of racism when he puts into the mouth of Pieter, his protagonist, who for the sake of love is violating the social codes: "to have such a horror is to be *safe*" (p. 89, original emphasis).

Moffie has fled to the familiar, to his group. His squeamish horror links him to the collective, to his clan of white men. He crawls into a psychosocial foxhole. He is a card-carrying, chartered member of the white race. He belongs to the brotherhood, to the *Broederbond*. Identification with his roots constitutes safety and security. By touching white-fleshed kindred spirits, Moffie finds refuge in the "sphere of the same", dwelling *chez moi*, "at home" with himself (Levinas, 1961/1969, pp. 37; 39). He abides as a smug, self-righteous, arrogant snob. A white racist!

Moffie has run away from his own humanity. His self-deceptive act is simultaneously the deepest form of other-deception. He is saying "nay" to life. It is ultimate irony that his horror legitimizes racial hatred. His alienation from self and other also reveals the life-denying, nihilistic core of Western rationalism. All theological-philosophical-psychological-sociological-biological arguments pile their ideological-conceptual malarkey on top of this bodily disgust and dread of touch.

The wounded woman dropped to the ground like a hot potato ... who is she? She is you; she is me ... .

The holocaust

The Final Solution is ultimate racism. The Holocaust is so dreadful that there are almost as many contemporary "humans" who want to deny it even happened as there are those who want to etch it permanently in memory. Six million Jews, two million gypsies, and one million Poles were led to slaughter. The scourge touched every country in Europe. Until today, the "Hitler virus' infects the entire Western world (Wyden, 2001). Our Occidental leaders, peddling democratic freedom, hide bloodied, dirty hands under a hypocritical veil: the unholy garment of complicity with the Third Reich. The USA with the money of Ford, Standard Oil, Texaco, Alcoa, ITT, and Eastman Kodak ... put Hitler into power; and Pope Pius XII was the first to legitimize Hitler's take over in 1933 (Griffin, 1974/2003).

D.M. Thomas' (1982) *The White Hotel* describes the attempt to implement the Final Solution on the Eastern front. It is set in the Ukraine, in the wane of the Third Reich's Thousand Year reign. Lisa, the protagonist, asks the pivotal question that haunts anyone who tries to understand racism: "Were not the Germans a decent civilized race?" Soon, she will experience Pushkin's "trembling of the sleeping night".

Thomas vividly depicts Nazi barbarism. It boggles our mind and breaks our hearts to realize the countless times that similar incidents were repeated. Daily, ordinary human beings were shamed, demeaned, skewered, gassed, burned, shot, raped, and pillaged. They are our neighbours! The author states incisively the truth: We can scarcely imagine, and it is impossible for us to comprehend the individual and collective pain. It is like trying to count the stars or the grains of sand at the seaside. Thomas (1982) writes, "If a Sigmund Freud had been listening and taking notes from the time of Adam, he would still not fully have explored even a single group, even a single person" (p. 295). Genius fails in the face of such horror. Martin Heidegger, C.G. Jung, and Knut Hansom are just a trio of the legions who "fell" when confronted with Hitler's voice and hands. Recalling that brute fact, none of us can read the following with clean hands.

Lisa witnesses Ukrainian Jews marshalled en masse to their deaths—unaware of what was happening—"quiet and well behaved, as if they were being told to go and have some supper", thinking it was an ordinary day just as a "spider running up the blade of grass thought it was a simple, ordinary blade of grass in the field" (Thomas. 1982, p. 295).

But no! The extra-ordinary beyond the extraordinary is happening: ultimate evil. Lisa hears shout an order to shoot the lot immediately. Walking in the macabre parade, she looks into the deep quarry to her left at a sea of bodies below, covered in blood. The soldiers are flashing their torches, shooting the bodies still showing signs of life. Then they approach like vultures, descend and bend over to loot the newborn corpses. Other soldiers, brandishing spades, cover the corpses with dirt.

An SS man bent over an old woman lying on her side ... There was a clatter of spades and then heavy thuds as the earth and sand landed on the bodies, coming closer and closer to the old woman who still lived. Earth started to fall on her. The unbearable thing was to be buried alive. She cried with a terrible and powerful voice: "I'm alive. Shoot me, please!" It came out as a choking whisper (Thomas, 1982, p. 293).

One soldier hears the plea and scrapes the earth off her face. He yells to his fellow that she is alive. "Then give her a fuck," comes a jovial response (Thomas, 1982, pp. 293–295). But for the virile killer, it is too cold for sex; he cannot get it up. Ah yes, of course! The real reason is the woman is old and ugly, right? So, the two soldiers pull the old woman into a flatter position and yank her legs apart. Then finding "the opening they joke together as he inserts the bayonet carefully, almost delicately" (Thomas, 1982, p. 294). By then, the still breathing old woman no longer makes any sounds. Guffawing loudly, they simulate the thrusts of intercourse "as the woman's body jerked back and relaxed, jerked and relaxed ... Spasms came; then her breathing stopped" (Thomas, 1982, p. 294). Before they carry on their inhuman chores, one grumbles that they are wasting time with the hag; the other "twisted the blade and thrust it deep" (Thomas, 1982, p. 294).

Who are the everyday citizens marching obediently to their death? They are us. Who is the old woman, brutalized beyond belief? She is you and me. Who are these monsters, masked as men, who perform the infamy? A searing question ... .

Nietzsche's "dynamite"

What is the peculiarly defining characteristic of humanness? To think as Nietzsche thinks is either terrifyingly dangerous ... or exhilarating. What? He says the multiple differences between one man and another are more significant than the differences between man and animals. From one perspective, his standpoint renders him vulnerable to the charges of aristocratism and elitism. But from another slant, it frees any and all thinkers from the materialistic, naturalistic, "mendacious race swindle of Darwinism" (Nietzsche, 1889/1982, pp. 522–523). The value of a human is not a function of race or of biological foundations. If it were, the consequences would be momentous: the chasm between the elite and the underprivileged, poverty-stricken, disenfranchised would be permanently etched in stone. Heredity would doom large masses of people and whole nations to an inferior and worthless fate.

Although Nietzsche concurs with Darwin that the idea of the human as pure spirit is bankrupt, he insists that evolving us from the animal is of little consequence concerning the future of mankind. Nobody better than Nietzsche unmasks Darwin's warped projection of British upper class values into evolutionary theory, baptized as "science". Darwin justified British arrogance, snobbery, breeding, and sense of racial superiority; he legitimized Anglo-Saxon violent conquest, the rapacity of British imperialism, and its evil trafficking in slavery.

Nietzsche incisively rejects Darwin's evolutionism. He offers instead the "overman", a new human being, the one who has struggled with self and has overcome his weaknesses, fears, and base urges. Humans do not evolve from natural stock; we cultivate, improve, and transfigure our nature. Self-overcoming, not uniformity and conformity, defines the essentially human. Nietzsche (1883b/1982) writes that it is painfully embarrassing—a laughing-stock—to compare the human to the ape as it is to compare the "overman" to man (p. 12). He bemoans mankind's usual choice to remain "the domestic animal", the "herd animal", or the "sick human animal" (Nietzsche, 1887/1969, p. 121). Like Kierkegaard, he privileges the singular, the unique individual, the one with courage and human power. Kierkegaard (1847/1962) says, "I have done what was mine to do … . Are you unique or have you existed only within the walls of your clique?" (p. 94).

Who is Moffie? He is a domesticated sick herd animal, less than human. Who are these soldiers of the Third Reich? They are lower than healthy animals: kin to the rat.

Nietzsche is correct. True human existence is not a function of race, colour, or creed. The ordinary man who courageously over-comes himself can ascend to the status that Nietzsche—using quali-tative algebra—names "artist" or "saint". Nietzsche is correct: the State is the "devil" that intimidates man into feeble conformity and prevents him from blossoming into his own unique self. Nietzsche is correct: The Church is the Antichrist that has perverted Christ's original call to perfection and freedom. Correct he is: Both State and Church collude to keep the masses under control. The gap between dire poverty and filthy wealth keeps widening. The greed that grounded 15 September, 2008 lingers. And revenge and counter-revenge swish and whirl.

Within Western ideology, *life is cheap*. Momentarily, the USA will send off one more of its youngest and finest to die to protect their nation's capitalistic way of life. Some woman is just now being changed into a widow in Iraq, and some child into an orphan in Afghanistan. The price of oil, $25.00 a barrel when the USA invaded Iraq, on the Big Board soared to $135.00 a barrel on 22 May, 2008. If one is not a sheep, the equation is easy to understand: oil is valuable; human life is … expendable.

What is the difference between Moffie, the Nazi butchers, and you … and me? *Nothing!* We are alike. To make a life-affirm-ing difference, we must confront the violent racist self within us and overcome it. And then with a warm heart reach out to touch our neighbours. I repeat Harry Stack Sullivan's (1953) one genus hypothesis: "Everyone is much more simply human than other-wise" (p. 32).

PART V

SORROW'S KINDRED PHENOMENA

CHAPTER SEVENTEEN

Mercy and revenge[15]

Check today's media. You will find ample evidence that revenge creates grief. Pathetic to relate, Western nihilistic metaphysics normalizes and makes revenge inevitable. Thomas Hobbes' Anglo-Saxon political ideology—fossilized in the dogma of *homo homini lupus*—justifies Establishment violence, imperialism, war, racism, and revenge.[16]

The cycles of revenge and counter-revenge that whirl across our planet are not naturally preordained. Revenge, like war and other forms of violence, have touchstones in human experience. Revenge starts with grief over loss. Afflicted with hurt, one howls to high heaven and then must go through a process of coming to terms with the loss.

Suppose your loved one is not just snatched from life by sickness, or disease, or by an act of God—the hurricane, flood or tsunami. Suppose instead your beloved is murdered. A drunk-driver did her in; the tragedy is senseless; and you know where, on the other side of the tracks, the perpetrator lives. Suppose it was a normal April day in 2007 at Virginia Tech in Blacksburg, turned crazy. Your daughter had morning classes. She is 1 of the 32 people killed in the shooting rampage. Rage-laced grief weighs heavy on your heart. You can't get out of your noggin the yen for retribution. Although you have never talked face-to-face with a person of Korean descent, you're not seeing red now, you're seeing yellow. Justice must be served.

Suppose it was a momentous day: 9/11. An entire nation reels with shock. Your husband was a fireman; you don't even know how he died. Your wife was a secretary, who apparently jumped out of a window. By now, you cannot even look one more time without wrenching at the footage of the Twin Towers, flopping like failed cakes in the oven. You don't even flinch when vets at your neighbourhood bar, after downing a few, loudly defend Abu Grahib, "Our boys and girls stuck it to the heathens." The Talion Law exacts a pound of flesh. Isn't it time to pay the fiddler?

Revenge is grief not worked through, but not transformed into depression. As such, it is always mendacious. Because why? Ambivalence anchors it. The concept of splitting returns for an encore. Revenge concocts a recipe for another disaster. In Dostoevsky and Nietzsche, we find a picture of the phenomenon, richly nuanced.

In Dostoevsky

Revenge is no simple response to an obvious, observable stimulus. It is lived as a fundamental orientating posture towards existence. Like phenomena such as jealousy, regret, or self-pity, *revenge* swallows us, poisons us, and eats us alive. It marks, stains, and smears all facets of our life-world. Fyodor Dostoevsky says revenge turns one into "a mouse not a man" (Dostoevsky, 1864/1960, p. 10).

Watch the mouse "creep ignominiously into its mouse hole". While he hides away "in his nasty stinking underground home", hyperconscious thoughts plague him (Dostoevsky, 1864/1960, p. 8). Revenge devours his inner being. Humiliation floods him. Abuse and ridicule have wronged and crushed him. He feels someone has mocked him, spat at him, flipped him the finger, or rubbed his nose in shit. He stews with hideous feelings of contempt, obsessed with vengeance and the nasty, stubborn, relentless drive to pay back the unforgettable and unforgivable offense. He "simply rushes straight toward the object ... as if possessed ... like an infuriated bull with its horns down, and nothing but a wall will stop him" (Dostoevsky, 1864/1960, p. 9). For the Biblical forty cold years, he remembers and embroiders every insult with everlasting spite. He recalls the injury down to the smallest, most shameful detail. Imaginatively, he replays his hurt, picking a psychological scab. Since his festering vengeful fantasies shame him, he must invent lies to legitimize his need to exact retribution.

The pretense does not work. With crowning brilliance, Dostoevsky reveals the inner malignant torment of vengefulness: the mouse does not feel justified in avenging, doubts its success, and knows before-hand he will suffer a hundred times more than the one on whom he takes vengeance. His revenge is his own worst punishment.

On his deathbed, guests visit to taunt and haunt the mouse about his regret, resentment, and despair for having buried himself alive in the underworld for forty years ... in the hell of cowardice and unsatisfied desires turned inward ... in the throes of madness con-cerning his endless vile project. The mouse psychologically grinds his teeth in silent impotence, brooding, and choking on bitterness.

In Nietzsche

In parable, Nietzsche shows us the tarantula, hanging on its web, in its hole, stewing with feelings of hideous revenge. "Touch it, see it tremble, and watch its poison make the soul whirl with revenge" (Nietzsche, 1883b/1982, pp. 99ff). In what follows, Nietzsche articu-lates a picture of the psychospiritual passage into revenge.

Anger

The offence takes place. I'm furious. Anger flashes like lightening, mercurial. A concrete and specific action triggers an immediate response. My anger is out in the open, showing on my reddened, distorted face and in my tone of voice, loud, shrill and harsh. If you are close enough, you will see the spittle.

Resentment

"Behind my back you slurred me. I saw red. My stomach is churning; I am fit to be tied." Draped in secrecy and bottled up, resentment is potentially more destructive than flashing anger. Nonetheless, it is concrete, limited by context, and bounded by circumstances. It is a situation-specific psychological itch or scratch. "You get under my skin!"

Envy

... is the true green monster. Spite, rancor, bitterness, mistrust, and hatred all pivot around it. The envious eye craves possessions or material goods, and hankers after good looks, talent, skill, or wealth. I envy your intelligence, your social status, or your lovely family. I wish I had your singing voice, your keen wit, or your gift of the gab. I wish I was sleeping with your husband, had your charm with women, or your spark that makes children readily take a shine to you. Envy is the kissing cousin to greed, avarice, covetousness, and ambition. It craves what the other already possesses.

Envy spoiling (Schadenfreude)

Failing to fill its own awful lack, envy spins into the mischievous delight of envy spoiling. With a "squint-eyed glance of contempt", it indulges in the secret joy of watching others suffer. "What I can't own, I'll destroy. I'll turn your treasure into scum .... I'll whittle you down a peg or two .... Then I'll gloat!" Life, however, exacts its existential-spiritual price: "My envy of you has destroyed me."

Ressentiment

The French word appropriately clarifies the more pervasive emotion. English has no equivalent word. Typically, the shallow term "resentment" translates it. *Ressentiment*, however, means "I hate your guts, the core of your being." No single deed but who you are galls me; what you stand for stirs my ire; what you symbolize casts a living judgement upon me and calls my very existence into question.

Sometimes we say and mean it: "When I grow up, I want to be just like you." Then it dawns on me that "it" is beyond me. I would always fail in the attempt to match you. I will always be less. *Ressentiment* seeps into my heart. *Ressentiment* is not an itch, but a psychological ache, a wound that festers with no possible relief by dab or scratch. It fills and darkens the soul. It eats out my guts.

Ressentiment cuts deeper than envy and burns more slowly then envy spoiling. I do not ache to steal your gorgeous wife, or wish to cheat you out of house and home. I won't spoil your good name or reputation. Rather, a super-ordinate virtue or quality of some significant other triggers *ressentiment*. Your vision, existential power, charisma, or wisdom cast a long shadow, making me feel small and insignificant ... eclipsing me. *Ressentiment* wants *nothing*: it hankers after the impossible.

Shame

Guilt is failure to live up to internalized criteria of social norms or religious conventions. We are guilty in the eyes of the other. Shame is the agonizing sense of failing in my own eyes to live up to my own standards or self-chosen values.

When I look appraisingly at myself in the mirror, at stake is not the reflection of my pretty face, my bulging biceps, or my Twin Peaks. At issue are my eyes! If they fail to shine with the integrity or power I witness in your gaze, I lose face. Then shameful *ressentiment* floods me ... grounds for revenge.

With grounds for revenge

Freedom fighters—branded insurgents or terrorists—literally cannot stomach what America symbolizes: power-wealth-military might-capitalism-materialism-secularism-mechanistic-technological banality. Such profound *ressentiment* demands annihilation of the "Beast". Suicide bombing is a miniscule price to pay for creating destructive chaos. "There is much that life esteems more highly than life itself ... Where there is life is there also ... not will to life but ... will to power" (Nietzsche, 1883b/1982, pp. 115–116).

Terroristic assaults on law and order frighten and infuriate the Establishment. Terrorists are worms of hidden treachery, perpetrators of sneak attacks. The events of 11 September hallowed subsequent invasions, the curtailment of civil rights at home, and torture in prisons abroad.

The transmutation

"White hot" emotions cool to ice, stop being passionate-personal, become detached and transcendent, then transmute into revenge. If resentment talks aloud, in perplexity it queries, "What am I going to do with you?" In passionate blood-curdling hatred, *ressentiment* wonders: "What would I do if I meet you again, kiss you or kill you?" Revenge, however, knows exactly what to do. With vicious vendetta, it brags: "You'll pay for this, regret it until your dying day, Maybe I will use slow torture ... or cut your throat, blow you to smithereens ... off the face of the earth."

Beyond retaliation

The Talion Law, an eye-for-an-eye, balances the scales of life. "It serves you right. You got what you deserved." *Ressentiment* transformed into revenge, however, lacks proportion or limits. Vengeance's labour is never finished. Every grudge aches to inflict suffering with an infinite depth of hatefulness, over an endless breadth of time. Like a coral reef, revenge accumulates, solidifies, and petrifies over time into a perverse strength. Psychospiritually stubborn and intractable, it is endlessly unyielding. Nietzsche (1883b/1982) laments:

> No deed can be annihilated ... the will cannot run backwards in a futile effort to erase time's "It was" .... I will hate you with an everlasting hatred. I will not let you rest in peace ... Existence must eternally become deed and guilt again ... No deed can be annihilated ... The endless spirit of revenge must devour its children (pp. 139–142).

Innocence

Pure unadulterated revenge defies death. Revenge is infinite. Is not this stance inhuman, especially bizarre when historical memory kicks in and groups bear grudges across generations? Nietzsche explicates the human core. Revenge presumes innocence—in the case of worldwide conflicts—the innocence and purity of one's people. "Blood is what they want from you in all innocence ... bloodless souls crave blood, so they sting in all innocence" (Nietzsche, 1883a/1970, p. 53). God is on our side.

God and the Devil

Our nightly dreams demonstrate that, at the deepest layers, the psyche is split. Splitting compartmentalizes the Good Breast/Bad Breast, God/Devil, truth from error, blessing from curse. Nietzsche writes (1878/1969), "In every morality man adores part of himself as God, and to that end needs to diabolicize the rest" (p. 172). Since my enemy is evil incarnate, my hate is perfect, pure, and gives me license to destroy with total justification. According to Nietzsche, hypocrisy easily occurs because the steps are small from a conviction to a lie to fanaticism. False pride comes before the fall.

Psychic weakness

The dynamism fuelling split-consciousness is impotence-inferiority. "You will pay for making a fool out of me. I will stalk you. Sleep with one eye open. Be careful when you open your mail! You won't know what hit you ... or where or when I'll hit again". "By invisible hands we are bent and tortured worst" (Nietzsche, 1883b/1982, p. 42).

Justice

White-Western-European-Christian-masculine-racist-violent-totalizing consciousness refuses to rest until justice is done and our thirst sated. Revenge and justice go hand-in-glove. "Justice justifies the seething *ressentiment*, the urge for retaliation and annihilation that hides under its own urgent demand ... a person single-mindedly obsessed by a wrong ... is a gruesome sight" (Nietzsche, 1883b/1982, p. 95).

Hot and cold blood

Hate, the flip side of love, is fleshy and hot. In rage, my body quivers and shakes. My lips quake when I say, "I'll wring your neck ... slit your throat ... cut your balls off ... tear you from limb to limb." Jealousy tries to scratch out the interloper's eyes, or pull out her peroxide hair. In fury, *ressentiment* hurts another human precisely as human.

Revenge, on the other hand, detached from flesh, blood and bone, trembles not. Terrorists, warmongers, anarchists, imperialists, exploiters, torturers, and assassins are convinced that they have God on their side. To that degree, they feel mentally-morally superior to the Devil's dumb scum, their enemies. Thus they kill with superior innocence, with "elegant coldness ... with ice in their laughter"

(Nietzsche, 1883b/1982, p. 212). Hitler slaughters six million Jews and two million gypsies not in passionate hatred, but with abstract calculation of the "Final Solution", a rational plan. Cruel, stark indifference sustains the yen for *racial cleansing*. In Hitler's apathetic psychological reductionism, Jews, Blacks, and Gypsies are nothing but vermin, germs, or parasites on the body politic of the Fatherland. Pimples, they were, on white faces ... lice in blond hair ... and dirty specks in the blue eyes of the pure Aryan ... Goddess. Innocence-truth-justice-righteousness issues the license to kill.

Mercy: In Aquinas, Nietzsche and Gandhi

Mercy is "beyond good and evil". How summon forth the "twice blest" quality that, as the British Bard describes, enriches equally the merciful one and the one who accepts mercy? How balance its "not strained" beauty with reason? (Shakespeare, 1997, Act IV, Scene 1) With a secular prayer, Nietzsche (1883b/1982) invokes the genius of the heart: "For that man be delivered from revenge, that is for me the bridge to the highest hope, and a rainbow after long storms" (p. 211). Nietzsche's analysis of revenge shrewdly reverses Western values. Since Platonic Christendom sanctifies revenge under the name of justice, clearing a path to mercy requires eradicating our obsession with bloodless constructs and anti-life values: sin, punishment, and vengeance. "Mistrust all in whom the impulse to punish is powerful ... Thou shalt not kill, even to prevent killing" (Nietzsche, 1883b/1982, pp. 212–214).

St. Thomas Aquinas

In the 13th century, 737 years ago, St. Thomas Aquinas penned with impeccable logic three brilliant articles. They identify the revengeful motive fastened to murderous violence, anticipate the twisted dogma of religious terror, and analyze the mentality of power and greed (Aquinas, 1272/1990). Three key interwoven convictions warp Christ's message of mercy: evil is irreversible, lurks everywhere, and requires punishment, retribution, and eradication at any cost (Merton, 1965, p. 12). Leaders obsessed with revenge cannot shower mercy on others. Their "rage and daring aggression" prompts them to frighten their people with threats of lurking danger, an evil "they" intend to prevent (Aquinas, 1272/1990, pp. 534–535). Likewise, the proud, arrogant individual lacks compassion. He despises "evil", and assumes that evil people deserve to suffer mercilessly (Aquinas, 1272/1990, pp. 534–535).

To the contrary, Aquinas melds heart and head, demonstrating that mercy (*misericordia*) is a moral power. Mercy integrates reason (intellectual appetite) with sensory-emotional passion (sensitive appetite). The compassionate heart (*miserum cor*) is the core of Christianity. Of all the virtues that relate to our neighbour, mercy is the greatest (Aquinas, 1272/1990, p. 536).

Wound and cure mesh. *Unde vulneratus fueras, inde curare* (Merton, 1965, pp. 18; 77). Evil is its own punishment. Evil, nevertheless, is reversible. It summons the blessings of forgiveness, and compassion. The "Angelic Doctor" wisely unties the knots in our hearts and clears our conceptual cobwebs. Punishment and vengeance only spur a new cycle of violence and oppression. Two mature capacities must sustain mercy: admitting our flawed fallibility, and experiencing the "sins" of others as if our own. The evil of another "comes so near to us so as to pass to us from him ... then one must grieve or sorrow for another's distress as one's own ... the same may happen to oneself (Aquinas, 1272/1990, p. 534). "Real liberation liberates simultaneously both the oppressor and the oppressed", gracing both with humility (Merton, 1965, p. 14).

Gandhi's Satyagraha

The turn towards compassion requires absurd measures. Non-violence is "a quality of the heart that cannot come by an appeal to the brain" (Gandhi. 1970, p. 276). *Sat*, the Sanskrit word for "truth", is equally absurd. *Satyagraha* literally means "Truth-Force" or "clinging to the truth" (Erikson, 1969, pp. 4; 6; 9; 10; 198). Translating it as "passive resistance" or "non-violent non-cooperation" dilutes it. Even the term "militant non-violence", used by Martin Luther King Jr., fails to highlight the cardinal power of truth—autochthonous with merciful love—as the foundation of Gandhi's non-violent courage.

Satyagraha also includes embodiment. It is meeting the opponent eye-to-eye; putting one's body on the line by linking arms in defensive and advancing phalanxes. "All these confrontations symbolize the conviction that the solidarity of unarmed bodies remains leverage and a measure even against the cold and mechanized gadgetry of the modern state" (Erikson, 1969, p. 198).

Gandhi's *Satyagraha* is not only a logical, political tactic, but he employs the existentially vibrant logic of the hearthead. The law of love rules humankind not violence and hatred, otherwise his arguments would fall to pieces, and our species would have long ago gone extinct (Gandhi, 1970, p. 121). Likewise, truth calls for redress of oppression. Gandhi's most powerful lever is his readiness to die for the truth that approaches on the feet of doves.

Fasting unto death is no strategy either. It bears witness to the power of fragility, mortality, and poverty. It unmasks the spiritual emptiness of colonial exploitation and imperial force. Gandhi (1970) tells us that we are mistaken to believe that democracy rules in the USA and England, and insists that both countries exploit and feed off non-white races.

Desmond Tutu's reconciliation vision of Ubuntu is the counter-foil to the pathetic isolationism and ontology of war stitched within Descartes' "Cogito, ergo sum". Tutu gives the life-affirming, community-building alternative statement: "*I am because we are, and since we are, therefore I am*" (Krog, 1998, p. 110).

At the Muqata

On 12 November, 2004, the Palestinian people offered the world an amazing glimpse of hearts on fire with affection and grief. Bidding farewell at the Muqata, they were living proof: Chaos and ceremony, fury and respect, weave a beautiful seamless tapestry. After a solemn send-off from Paris, and a dignified procession in Cairo, the Palestinian officials flew Arafat's corpse by helicopter to Ramallah with plans for a parade, marching soldiers, and a formal interment. The funeral, however, took on a life of its own. On the ground, the people surged and swarmed in an outpouring of love for their dead leader. Defiantly and definitively, they claimed their Father as their own. Stilted pomp transmuted into wild, raw drama. Viewers around the world held their collective breath. Would the moment decay into defamation?

The bereaved danced with Arafat one last time. While the casket swayed and rotated, tottered, and twisted, the inflamed grievers undraped and re-draped it ... until the spontaneous ritual carried their Father to the stone and marble tomb ... which they hope and pray is only his temporary resting place. On his coffin, they poured dirt from Jerusalem and sprinkled quotations from the Koran and prayers. The frenzied funeral march ended as abruptly as it had begun. At the end of the day, the people themselves had buried Arafat. It was enough to make a body smile and one's heart leap.

We cannot fail to ignore, as we did thirty years ago, Arafat's admonition: 'Don't let the olive branch fall from my hands." Few men receive the grace to enter the Promised Land. Yasser Arafat is still journeying to Jerusalem.

In this vicious cycle of vengeance between Israel and Palestine, the plight of the Jews equally tears my heart. The Holocaust was the most heinous crime of the 20th century. The Hitler virus continues to metastasize like a cancer across Europe and in the USA (Wyden, 2001). The mendacious term "neo-Nazi" hides the guilt over complicity with the Third Reich that Europeans have never liquidated. Since 1945, Nazism has grown unabated in the West. The Christian Churches hold most blame for the spread of this dis-ease. Rome first legitimized Hitler's take over in 1933. Pope Pius XII knew the horror of the "final solution" but condoned the genocide to halt atheistic Russian communism, and to protect the wealth of Christendom.

True power

"Life wants to climb and to overcome itself climbing" (Nietzsche, 1883/1982, p. 101). Acting mercifully presupposes authentic strength. "It is not unthinkable that a society might attain such *consciousness of true power* that it could allow itself the noblest luxury possible ... letting those who harm it go *unpunished*. Mercy remains the privilege of the most powerful man ... What are my parasites to me? May they live and prosper: I am strong enough for that" (Nietzsche, 1887/1969, pp. 72–74, original emphasis).

The Mahatma affirms Nietzsche and gives the formula for peace: "We are drops in the limitless ocean of mercy" (Gandhi, 1970, p. 75).

CHAPTER EIGHTEEN

Regret

Within the economy of human melancholy, the phenomena of sorrow, grief, depression, and regret are kindred. Piggybacking on Freud and Kierkegaard, I have already qualitatively distinguished between normal grief and depression and between depression and sorrow. I also presented excessive and extreme grief reactions and crimes of passion that index temporary insanity. Regret hovers betwixt and between all these phenomena. I could have easily have translated into a regret-episode any of the situations under consideration. The obsessive review, one hallmark of the hyper-investment stage of grief-work, oozes with regret. The god-awful struggle to balance forgetting and remembering hallmarks both that stage and the "moment" of regretful sorrow. The "gone crazy" story of Baba in *Kite Runner* overflows with the emotion.

The next four chapters focus particularly on the place that regret holds within our psychological economy. My insight is that living in regret signifies unresolved grief, but likewise indicates that the sufferer has not lapsed into depression. As a still open wound, regret localizes one's complaint about Life, even as it masks one's dissatisfaction or disappointment with self. Regret keeps at bay the blanket of gloom that depression throws over the sufferer's life-space. Put differently, regret twists my sorrow so that I do not stare straight and unflinchingly at that which causes me pain. Because of this *in-between* status, regret is a central phenomenon in the drama of human loss and lingering hurt. I put it through the ringer, so to speak, trying to squeeze out of it as much meaning as possible. I will be doubling back, re-visiting certain hurts, and hopefully deepening our understanding of sorrow's profiles.

Regret is a dynamic life-orienting posture in the face of some significant melancholic situation. It is a unified gestalt, a "multi-faceted" emotional disposition, not a single, surface reaction to an obvious, observable, specific stimulus (Landman, 1993, p. xxviii). Regret resembles jealousy, humiliation, revenge, and self-pity because it percolates inward and in-depth. It seizes my whole existence, clutches it, refuses to release it, and haunts me. It sucks me into an "existential vortex", dynamically co-determining my actions (Cornelissen, unpublished manuscript).

As a unified gestalt, a constitutive-unit of a cluster of experiences, regret combines heterogeneous contents such as love, hatred, guilt, and loneliness spread out over completely different points of objective time (Scheler, 1994, pp. 38–39). Not surprisingly, it is hard to put a rope around it or put a finger on it.

As a dynamic life-orienting disposition, regret is embedded within a total situation. Jean-Paul Sartre describes a *fundamental choice* in the face of the world. I live with others. I orient myself in respect to them—although never entirely. But my regret always implicates my significant other(s).

Our distinctive bout of regret constitutes a metaphor of self. What each of us, in fact, regrets—if we regret at all—is as individual as our fingerprints. We find out what we are made of by understanding why this slice of life is eating us alive. After all, it seems so insignificant to the disinterested, neutral, third-party observer.

Rain every day during my holidays in the Maldives will most likely trigger sadness, anger, or frustration. If you punch me, I'll get mad. What sparks regret is never so evident or obvious. Regret-triggers are legion. Our most significant "moment" of regret, therefore, is apt to catch us by surprise. None of us sits in anticipation of the feeling. We certainly do not requisition it. It is on nobody's Christmas list. It comes as part and parcel of the run-of-the-mill happenings of life, when the chords of untoward circumstances twist and a knot tightens. We suffer in love; we lose money; we chase a dream; we chase a skirt; we move to another country; we shoot for the moon. At times, I become excitedly caught up and wonderfully swept away in the dance pertaining to some relationship. What happens when the music stops? What do I feel when I look back to the beginning? I may be woefully sorry that I ever took the first step. Or I might kick myself for not taking the decisive step in the instant I turned and walked away from someone smiling and opening his arms to me. We are left wondering: In the moment of meeting our fate, did we allow our destiny to slip away? We are saddled with the price tag of desire, or with paying the cost of the gift ... refused. We kick ourselves for our stupidity or cowardice, even as we struggle to parcel out what was our choice and what was visited upon us. In the living present, as I drive the automobile of life, I am holding on to nothing but the wheel. Finding satisfying answers might take a lifetime.

One hermeneutic of regret

How to access optimally this complex phenomenon?[17] Arguably, it is possible to regret anything. Pangs erupt for having picked the wrong career-path, for allowing parents to control one's life, or for changing our job to settle in an unwelcoming country. One is haunted by burning his bridges behind him, career-wise; another agonizes about a failed investment gamble; still another feels tormented for having humiliated her younger brother; someone else feels sorry that he deliberately hurt a childhood playmate and never sought forgiveness or made reparation. One woman writes: "I regret marrying my husband as a result of a quarrel between us." Another regrets "failing to ask for a divorce ... first, before he dumped me for a younger woman." We regret terminating an unwanted pregnancy; we regret never having begotten a child. Regret is as individual as one's fingerprints.

Regret over love

From the menu, I pick one "dish": the haunting experience of regretting what we did or failed to do "for love". The choice to scrutinize in-depth love-scars is not arbitrary, but both logical and phenomenological. The themes of sorrow in response to death, divorce, or the loss of one's beloved fill this book. Love–Death.

In matters of the heart, we are especially susceptible to finding ourselves swept up in the "dance". Take the "moment" we opened our eyes after an unexpected kiss. We found ourselves in it up to our ears. We had just serendipitously changed each other's lives.

In the aftermath of losing her lover, one Norwegian woman describes "curling up on the couch, dealing with a deep bloody wound in my heart, seeing my reflection in the dark night outside, and feeling like the ugliest most useless creature alive". Such regret is akin to suffering lovesickness, the lovesick blues, *kjærlighetssorg* (the lovely Norwegian word for love-sorrow), and to longing. We will confront this particular ache later. In anticipation, please heed Heidegger (1987), "Longing is the agony of the nearness of what lies far" (p. 217).

The remains of the day

My hermeneutic of Kazuo Ishiguro's (1989) novel, *The remains of the day*, follows. It describes regret over squandered opportunities for love. The tale centres upon the psychological gunfight between a woman and a man that covers more than thirty years.

Ishiguro closes his hauntingly beautiful novel with the chapter, "Day Six—Evening, Weymouth." In fourteen pages, mentioning the word only once, he depicts poignantly a regretful episode. A man and woman, in the evening of their lives, make a last grasp at the love which has eluded them because they had failed to open up to each other.

Mr. Stevens embodies the quintessential archetype of the English butler:

> "Dignity" has to do … with a butler's ability not to abandon the professional being he inhabits. Lesser butlers will abandon their professional being for the private one at the least provocation. For such persons, being a butler is like playing some pantomime role; a small push, a slight stumble, and the façade will drop off to reveal the actor underneath. The great butlers are great by virtue of their ability to inhabit their professional

role and inhabit it to the utmost ... It is ... a matter of "dignity" (Ishiguro, 1989, pp. 42–43).

This dignified, consummate professional never abandons his role, not even when his father is in his death throes and actually dies. It happens precisely on the very night that an event is taking place at Darlington House that will alter the course of European history. Stevens is called to the deathbed. His father, with unprecedented emotional openness, confesses that he had stopped loving his wife. "Love went out of me. I hope I have been a good father to you ..." Stevens, in the act of leaving as soon as he enters, says only, "We'll talk tomorrow." Tomorrow never comes.

This first rate butler does not slacken his professional bearing even in the face of the most intensely personal provocation: the loving overtures of a worthy woman. He lets his chance at love and marriage to Miss Kenton, his chief housekeeper, slip away. The "crucial turning point" in their relationship comes precisely at the moment they are on the verge of intimacy.

Carrying flowers, Miss Kenton enters Mr. Stevens' personal room, his butler's pantry, the parlour resembling a general's headquarters. For a protracted period of time, they had been meeting there regularly, ostensibly to discuss matters of running the Hall, but also to share cocoa and conversation. On this occasion, she cheerfully waltzes in while he is quasi-dozing in dim lighting with a book in his lap. Reaching, she inquires about it. Caught off guard, he stands up, walks behind a desk, and pulls the book to his chest. In point of fact, it is a romance novel. On principle and guarding his privacy, Stevens stubbornly refuses to show it to the woman. Cajoling and teasing that the book might be racy, she moves in close, persistent, impertinent, until she is standing directly before him. In today's jargon, she has entered his personal space, gotten "in his face". Literally, she backs him against the wall. In the shrunken distance, the atmosphere between them changes. It becomes suddenly warm and charged with palpable intensity. Few of us would fail to recognize the "moment", as common as rain in the fjords ... or as sin. Stevens describes it "as though the two of us had been suddenly thrust on to some other plane of being altogether" (Ishiguro, 1989, p. 167).

Lacking attunement to the sensual-sexual undertones-overtones of the moment, Stevens discombobulates. He notices that "everything around us suddenly became very still" (Ishiguro, 1989, p. 167). He also perceives that Miss Kenton's manner changes, becomes both serious and frightened. She's a woman on the verge of reaching across an infinite interval, to claim her man. He is a man trapped in his own insulation, his enclosing reserve. They are at the crossroads. Something must happen. The matter between them has come to a head.

Slowly, she starts to peel his fingers off the volume. Twisting his head to avert her eyes, he suffers her prying fingers, although he does not make it easy for her. She persists. Finally, with book in hand, she announces in astonishment that it is "simply a sentimental love story". Stevens cannot tolerate her gleeful smile of triumph. In the movie version, his face is anguished, with eyes looking so far off they almost vanish. He preserves his dignity with a cock and bull excuse that he reads to gain a better command of the English language, and to continue educating himself. She stares at him, amazed at the rational gobbledygook he is spouting, in recoil that he had just thrown a cold, wet blanket to douse the intimate moment. Before she can protest, he shoos her out of his parlour, sealing the border between them, permanently. In an instant, the atmosphere spoils like the withering flower of a missed chance; then it decays to the point of no return. Immediate reverberations will ensue, as they always do in such boundary situations; but the scene will haunt Stevens for three decades.

Their relationship reverts to formal professionalism. Their pleasant and gratifying meetings in his parlour cease. Reluctantly, Miss Kenton re-orients her daily life. Eventually, she yields to Mr. Benn's wish to court her. When at length she tells Stevens that she has accepted a marriage proposal and serves notice of leave from her post, he takes it in his stride as if were a trifle. She recoils again at the aloof dignity of the detached butler. She verbally taunts him, telling him that he is the butt of jokes between her and Benn because of his peculiarities and odd mannerisms. Stevens feels the sting, flinches, but absorbs it like a boxer taking a punch. When they speak at day's end, he pretends that he can't even remember the nonsense she spoke; it has dripped like water off a duck's back.

In the immediate aftermath of this last exchange, Stevens descends to the wine cellar, busying himself with one more chore before retiring. Uncharacteristically, he drops and breaks a bottle of vintage red wine. In the split second, the look on his face reveals that he doesn't know what he is most distraught about.

Walking past Miss Kenton's room, Stevens hears her crying. He puts his ear to the keyhole and hesitates. He almost walks off. In the movie version, he knocks, enters the room, and finds her bent over prone, weeping with her chest heaving. He looks down at her. As if nothing important and life transforming is happening between them, he officiously mentions a trivial flaw in the running of the House and asks her to rectify the matter. She looks up at him, in total disbelief, his words a kick to her already aching stomach. But she answers in such a way as to maintain her own human, womanly, and professional dignity. Stevens not only lets the "moment" pass, but also hammers the last nail into the coffin.

Miss Kenton marries Benn; they move to the West Country and bear a daughter. The novel opens as Stevens is about to embark upon a six-day motor trip. After thirty years of service at Darlington Hall, he is taking an unprecedented journey through the splendid finest countryside of England, to the West Country. His new American employer, Mr. Farraday (Mr. Lewis in the movie version), insists that Stevens drive his car on a holiday to visit his lady-friend.

Recently, Mrs. Benn had written Stevens an ambiguous letter, the first in seven years. Stevens believes her marriage is finally ending. Nevertheless, he convinces himself that he is en route for a professional reason. Of late, he had made several uncharacteristic errors in discharging his duties. Chalking them up to a "faulty staff plan", the possibility that Mrs. Benn would return to ameliorate the situation buoys and energizes him. He is convinced of her great affection for the house and certain of her exemplary professionalism. In short, he hopes without confessing it that he will get the lady back. He steps on the gas pedal, launching his adventure.

Immediately, the trip becomes a soul-journey. The rhythm of the road and his chance encounters on it co-generate a life-review— already prefigured the moment the drive was conceived. Since Stevens had staked his entire life on serving Lord Darlington, reviewing his existence amounts to an assessment of Darlington's career. By then, Stevens had already forfeited his own interests to it, sacrificed his sexuality, and surrendered his one chance at love. By then, Darlington has been dead three years. The political intrigue, motivated by his love affair with Nazi Germany, had discredited and psycho-spiritually ruined him. Thirsting for meaning, Stevens hopes against hope that his impeccable service to a great gentleman had been his way of serving humanity. The emotional logic of the trip, however, draws him into disturbing thickets with ever thornier realizations. Near his journey's end, the heaviness of his original doubts finally transmute into an acknowledgement of truth:

> How can one possibly be held to blame in any sense because ... the passage of time has shown that Lord Darlington's efforts were misguided, even foolish? Throughout the years I have served him, it was he and he alone who weighed up evidence and judged it best to proceed in the way he did, while I simply confined myself, quite properly, to affairs within my own professional realm ... I carried out my duties to the best of my abilities, indeed to a standard which many may consider "first rate." It is hardly my fault if his lordship's life and work have turned out today to look, at best, a sad waste—and it is quite illogical that I should feel any regret or shame on my own account (Ishiguro, 1989, p. 201).

Stevens is about to lay eyes on Mrs. Benn for the first time since she left Darlington Hall. By admitting that his existence as a dignified butler actually had *colonized* him, his honest motive surfaces of wanting to meet the woman who had never left his thoughts. Just before they meet, however, he smugly tells himself that he feels prepared for disappointment. The statement more truly expresses his hope of rekindling their relationship, picking it up where *he* had dropped it, and building it forward and afresh. Getting a second chance ...

When they meet face to face, he finds that she has aged, albeit gracefully. However, she also seems slower and appears sad, weary, and lacking the spark that once made her volatile and, at times, defiant. He quizzes her in the British manner, graciously apologetic yet insistently reminding her that she wrote to him, "the rest of my life stretches out like emptiness before me" (Ishiguro, 1989, p. 236). She denies writing such words, disowns the feeling, and utters the decisive life-changing truth. Her heart joyfully anticipates becoming a grandmother. Her daughter is pregnant.

In the twinkle of an eye, the upbuilding possibility that Stevens might rectify the wrongs of the past vanishes. He sees the handwriting on the wall. The die is cast. He must re-group. He dons his dignity. He persists with his questioning, now without the vulnerability that started to creep into his speech before she mentioned the grandchild who would tie her to the west coast and to her husband. He asks permission to pose a personal question so that he might clear up his worrisome notions. They concur that their old friendship authorizes such intimate talk. Stevens suggests that the tone of her letters over the years, in particular her last one, gives him the impression that she is unhappy. Likewise, he quizzes why she had temporarily separated from her husband three times during their marriage. His interrogation has a biting edge as if he thinks she had duped him into thinking that a new start was possible between them. The woman goes directly to the heart of the matter: "Mr. Stevens, you're asking whether or not I love my husband" (Ishiguro, 1989, p. 238).

She admits that she did not love him at first, but describes the process of finally coming to love. She also confesses her desolate moments of thinking, "What a terrible mistake I've made with my life … You get to thinking about a different life, a *better* life you might have had … I get to thinking about a life I may have had with you, Mr. Stevens" (Ishiguro, 1989, p. 239). She concludes that her rightful place is with her husband. "After all, there's no turning back the clock now. One can't be forever dwelling on what might have been. One should realize one has it as good as most, perhaps better and be grateful" (Ishiguro, 1989, p. 239, original emphasis).

What now? The woman has spoken her unvarnished truth. She has closed the door, locked it fast, and symbolically thrown away the key. To use the saddest words in the English language, for Stevens truly it is "too late". In one simple, direct, economical paragraph, Ishiguro's masterful prose allows Stevens time to digest her words and feel his sorrow before he hesitantly admits, "At that moment, my heart was breaking" (Ishiguro, 1989, p. 239).

Nevertheless, the first-rate butler is not shaken by external events. He gives her a pep talk or a mini-sermon. He affirms that no foolishness should sabotage the gratitude she has just voiced. Then they take leave. He expresses pleasure in seeing her for what will be the last time. Her eyes fill with tears. She boards a bus and stands at the back, framed there like a portrait, gazing at him getting smaller. They wave a drawn-out goodbye. In the agonizing look between them, shared-regret takes up permanent residence. For this ordinary man and ordinary woman, it has gone past the point of rescue.

Later, left behind and permanently alone now, Stevens sits on a bench as the pier lights come on. A man, a former butler roughly his own age, sits next to him and begins to banter. Stevens, never good at chit-chat, reveals his connection to Darlington Hall and then pours out his heart's regret:

> I gave my best to Lord Darlington ... now ... I find I do not have a great more left to give ... I *trusted* ... in his lordship's wisdom. All those years I served him, I trusted I was doing something worthwhile. I can't even say I made my own mistakes. Really— one has to ask oneself—what dignity is there in that? (Ishiguro, 1989, pp. 242–243)

The question is no question. It is a veiled statement, an admission. Dignity now must take on an entirely different meaning. Stevens radiates perplexity. The trip has revised his past and dashed his hopes for the new future he was yearning for. The stranger, trying to perk him up, insists he has finished his day's work and now he should enjoy the best part, the evening. Stevens agrees. Looking back is futile; blame is wasteful. He resolves to accept his fate. Without *the* woman at his side, his days will be filled only with work, work, and more work ... The devil that one knows! He gives himself one task, at once Herculean and ordinary: expending efforts "to make the best of what remains of my day" (Ishiguro, 1989, p. 244). Resignation! Ishiguro leaves it to you and me to decide if it is authentic.

CHAPTER NINETEEN

Regret themes

It is easy to picture regret as ponderous. At first blush, it seems to be a stagnant emotion that weighs the body down and corrodes the soul. One imagines it as insidiously caustic, part of a process of decay, erosion, or a psycho-spiritual cancer. One pictures the person in regret as a monolithic structure, a big blob infested with termites that are eating away at his vital resources. Regret carries the connotation that something has befallen us and plagues us so that we cannot shake it, or we refuse to. Regret takes its toll. It is purely negative, is it not? It's just a downhill slide.

Such images capture one face of regret, no doubt. But regret is also dynamic, not just passive. Its valence is potentially positive. How so?

Regret provokes a life-review. Reviews lead to revisions. A sense of anticipation is set aflame. Just as the two characters in Chinese that combine to form the word "anxiety" singly mean "opportunity" and "danger", it is the same with regret. Taking stock of myself, I garner power to transform my life. The past opens afresh, and I am able to alter it. Both psychoanalysis and phenomenology give us the gift of demonstrating that the past changes whenever meanings change. Lightly, we say we now possess "20–20 hindsight". But it is

279

more than an eye-opener. The mere accumulation of experience or the passage of time grants nothing. More accurately, either we gain a special insight and undergo a transformation, or the downhill slide turns into a snowball rolling to hell.

No event, object, or relationship is something "in itself". It is what it signifies to some individual. Realism dominates in Western culture as the taken for granted standpoint to explain what transpires in our life. Even more narrowly, nowadays we still believe that there is an "objective" fact that most truly depicts any life-event. Within this ruling rational view, we privilege presence. The pageant of our experience is framed as a picture etched on an unchanging wall and stuck in time, marching independently of us. The revolutions of Albert Einstein and of quantum physics (Max Plank, Werner Heisenberg and Neils Bohr) render hopelessly obsolete this Newtonian view of absolute space, time, substance, and presence. The ideas of a fixed permanent background and pre-ordained objectivity are intellectually bankrupt. If we go to school on the quantum mechanical revolution, existence looks as Heidegger depicts it: dynamic, dialectical, and dialogal. Meaning is co-constituted. Everything filters through my consciousness, with no significance absolutely or by itself. Meaning erupts in the "face-off" between the game of Life and my awareness. Both "players" matter equally. Meaning is not "in" me or "in" the situation, but rather it is "between" us. Spacetime is fluid, continually evolving. No event is fixed.

Concerning regret, we can't take back what has happened. We can't erase a murder, as if it were a smudge on our paper; or delete a sexual tryst like an unwanted email; or shred an abortion as if it were an incriminating file. "Shit happens," as common parlance puts it. Life marks and stains our lives. We must live with those blotches and blemishes. We must live with dirty hands—as I wrote to end Chapter four.

Typically, we express our "curriculum vitae" by listing our accomplishments. Instead, we can catalogue the "moments" in which we lost our innocence in some way, shape, or form. If we have seized the opportunity—by "working through" our bout of regret—we might share with others the "moment" we regained innocence, or more accurately, when we salvaged the capacity to spot any new phosphorescent upsurge of it.

Regret, therefore, is two-faced. It reveals a tear. It triggers ambivalence: two opposing ideas with two opposite emotional valences. As I took pains to express while expounding Freud, the challenge is to convert ambivalence into ambiguity. Bouncing back and forth on the two horns of ambivalence, I remain stigmatized by regret. If only ... if only not. It's a vicious circle. Eventually, my life decays. I cave in. I yield to despair, or lapse into inauthentic resignation.

However, crawling into and coming to terms with my regret—going the "whole nine yards"—I transform ambivalence into ambiguity. The transmutation makes all the difference.

Our battle with regret is a metaphor of self. It drags us to a fork in the road. We are forced to face something serious and to choose. Which path will I take when I come to the crossroads? What will I do when I arrive at the threshold?

In the awesome "moment" when push comes to shove, our pupils dilate, our jaws drop, and our heart skips a beat. We glimpse the exhilarating but terrifying possibility of transgressing a boundary. Using emotional algebra, I say, "These 'moments' we both crave and ... dread."

Some of us will backslide. The devil that we know is easier to cope with than the unknown demon. None of us easily banishes old ghosts; no one simply silences the old tapes sounding with haunting echoes. The higher up the pole the monkey climbs, the more of his backside is showing. Change is hard. Transformation takes courage. Many of us will step backwards and avert the eyes when we picture the possible consequences. But some do take the leap forward. The future approaches me like a snowstorm. I face it. I co-shape it. I become brand-new.

The outcome of regret pivots round the experience of repetition. Freud, sensitive to the fact that we are doomed to repeat what we don't remember or haven't worked through, highlights the compulsion to repeat ... backwards. This compulsion is the arch-conservative constituent of unconsciousness that rivets us to our painful past. Kierkegaard, on the other hand, removes Freud's repetition from the psychological realm of monotonously slavish reiteration of painfully destructive patterns. He re-locates it in the spacetime of existential freedom. He posits the qualitative leap or the leap of faith: "repetition forward". We repeat forward by making a courageous and humble choice. The future, the advancing snowstorm, gives new meaning to the past and vivifies the present.

Retrospective perspective

The *sine qua non* of the experience of regret is looking back. To be regretful is to have assumed a *retrospective perspective*. We re-visit in consciousness our past actions. We see our life as if reading a book and mentally calculate the price of our decisions and comportment. We find the cost exceedingly high. We have a keen sense of what we should have changed. Maybe we did something a second ago. Lickety-split, we flash back to it and immediately we are sorry.

No regrets

Suppose the matter is grave, as in Adrian Lyne's (2002) movie *Unfaithful* when Edward impulsively murders his wife's lover. He discovers that Connie, in her obsessed love for a younger man, gave him as a gift the present that he, Edward, had bought for her several years before. In a "moment" of "gone crazy", he kills the lover. Regret immediately surfaces. Slouching in the dizzying aloneness of panic and confusion, he grinds his face into his blood-stained hands, already apprehending the situation and apprehensive.

At the end of the movie, his wife wants to delete regret, both hers and his, as if they were unnecessary computer files. She prompts him to collude in warding off any repercussions of both their deeds. She concocts an outlandish fantasy-plan for leaving New York City to live for always on a beach in the paradise of La-La Land.

20–20 hindsight

Looking back is necessary. We do not regret something while doing it, or regret decisions while in the midst of trying to realize the value of our choices, or regret a relationship while attempting to build or repair it. The twinge of regret emerges while taking stock of the situation, when it hits you, or you gaze across the clearing provided by distance.

For the most part, however, regret bores in and takes a hold on us whenever we glance back over a long interval, or look again after having looked seemingly a zillion times. After years of living with untoward consequences, I kick myself whenever thinking back. She's gone. I know what I did wrong. It could have been different, if I knew what I know now. But it's too late. It has gone past the point of rescue.

Laughter

Humour is crucial. Humour is imperative both in grief-work and in putting regret into perspective. It is pre-eminently healing to find humour in the situation that agonizes and imprisons us. It is especially beneficial to laugh at ourselves.

Alfonso Lingis writes (2005) "We feel connected to the real world in laughter ..., If we can laugh, we can deal with reality ... Laughter is freedom ... the total opposite of scrupulous self-criticism ... the moment liberated from the future and from the enchainment of moments in time" (pp. 91; 96). "Laughter and tears make us transparent to one another ... Laughter and tears, blessing, and cursing, are the fundamental forms of communication" (Lingis, 2007, p. 68). Ultimately, Lingis comments, we can see whatever we are regretting, as a joke: "We understand that we can laugh in the face of death .... We understand that we can die laughing" (2005, p. 98).

To capture the retrospective dimension of the phenomenon, we use the pleonastic phrase "lingering regret". Regret hinges upon the complex relationship between clock-calendar time and lived-personal time (in the precise distinction the Greek language makes—between *chronos* and *kairos*). In this regard, I wish to liquidate a bias concerning old age, the stereotype that Western civilization considers getting old so horrible because it is the natural time in life to regret. This notion is sheer prejudice, born out of our Western dread of aging that Simone de Beauvoir tells us outstrips even our fear of death.

Are the elderly more prone to regret just because they have logged more miles and counted more calendar years? No. Clock time is not of the essence. Since I have depicted the core issues of *Remains of the Day*, it suits to refer to it to support my argument.

All other things being equal, Stevens could have regretted a slew of the situations between Miss Kenton and himself during her years of employment. Certain encounters between them authentically demand an apology, indeed scream for him to be sorry; they call for him to have done something to show sorrow; later, they should have constituted the burden of having failed to make reparation. Adopting a retrospective perspective is all it would have taken. He could have looked back from the perspective of a year, a week, a day, an hour, or an instant. He didn't. He continued instead to view ongoing events and interactions within the perspective of his exemplary "staff plan". He stays locked in the viewpoint of his *present*. He doesn't look back until he confronts the remains of his day. The happening is contingent, not inevitable. It is not just a function or spin-off of his chronological age.

His regret is co-constituted, a function of his mounting years *plus* his adoption of a retrospective perspective. Certain key events raise Stevens' consciousness: the demise of Lord Darlington; the letters he had received from Mrs. Benn over the years; and the decisive one she sent him after a seven year silence (in which she reports being separated from her husband). Stated differently, it is capricious to predict that the sheer accumulation of years would spur regret in *this* man—given his personality, character, or fused identity between self and role as dignified butler. The weight of measured duration, of time as a cruel and careless thief, cannot be ignored. But it is never the complete or definitive variable.

The classic film, *Alfie* (Gilbert, 1965), shows the point from the opposite slant. In the penultimate scene, Alfie accidentally meets on the street an ex-sex partner whose life he had destroyed many years earlier. He talks to the "bird" in a chipper upbeat tone, as if nothing demeaning and destructive had happened. Time has passed. He's older, and it shows; the years definitely show on her. She is horrified at his display of unreal innocence, and responds as if he were what he indeed is: a psychological axe-murderer. He walks away, perplexed, unable to understand whatever the matter with her is.

The scene depicts the flaw in Alfie's character. Looking back, he still sees only that he should be entitled to what he desires. Whenever push comes to shove, he doesn't get it. He denies the resistance of the world.

Age guarantees nothing. What will be lost or what gained is up for grabs. Getting older is equally a time for harvest as for regret.

A second look at a second chance

This time I blew it. I know it. I want to undo the wrong; I can't. Psychologically, I slit my own throat. I must live on the other side of the decisive "moment", courting depression and despair. Everything hangs in the balance. I'll have to carry to my grave the truth about burned bridges and broken promises.

Before regret festers, we hope for a second chance. Tunes about "the second time around" kept the jukeboxes playing in modernity and nowadays keep the postmodern iPods cranking it out. Let's try again. See what'll happen, if only just for old time's sake. Love is supposed to be better the second time around, right? I'd do anything to prevent you from leaving. Hell, you are the only one who would prompt me to undo or re-do any of my actions. Let's rake through the ashes, find the burning embers, and re-kindle the blaze. Aren't we worth it?

If it turns out that it's too late, that there will be no second chance, then regret sets in. In this instance, we regret the love we threw away.

The common people say it all the time. "If I had it to do over"; "If I could go back"; "Give me another chance ... please." It is one more indication of the bankruptcy of the positivist-quantitative approach to psychological realities that there is no extensive and impressive body of literature on the human wish to have a "second chance".

We common people, in fact, ache for the opportunity to turn back the years. We hope for a new deal, yearn for a chance to live it down, or ache for the blessing of redemption. We want the dealer to re-deal the cards. And we attach optimistic riders to our wish for a second chance: "If I knew then what I know now ... and had the power to change the situation ... then I'd get it right this time." It would be a piece of cake, in the bag. We even imagine dropping to our knees and begging for a fresh start.

Of course, making a new beginning is no led-pipe cinch. The half-cocked belief in the healing power of the second chance parallels the "illusion of closure" in grief-work, the conviction that if only I had finally said I'm sorry, told her I loved her, begged for forgiveness, IT would be—if not perfect—at least as good as it gets.

We are poised on the sharp edge of a double-bladed sword. If "yesterday" should pass again, what would we do? Would we repeat the same mistakes, or make critical changes? Freud is suspicious that we would repeat backwards, go from the frying pan into the fire; Kierkegaard has faith we would repeat forward and create a new, different, more authentic future. Is there an answer? Either-or! You choose.

What is serious, significant, earth-shaking, or grave enough to swallow me up in regret? Something in the shared perceptual field would be judged a spur for regret by any neutral and disinterested third party. Matters include betrayal, hypocrisy, mendacity, broken promises, adultery, abuse, wounded pride, humiliation, or coward-ice. However, the crucial ingredient is how the individual *experiences* what to the outsider looks like a lie or infidelity. If it doesn't "hit home" then no emotion emerges. Recall Alfie, who never grasps the effect on others of his selfish hedonism. Remember that Stevens' blind devotion to Lord Darlington blocks out the horror of rac-ism and political violence unfolding under his eyes. Stevens fails to grasp the impact of his "repressed love". He acts with arrogant condescension toward the gutsy, expressive woman who does recoil at the inhuman terror, who challenges him to wake up and act, but who cares for him even though he prefers myopia and inertia.

A grave matter torments the individual. It does not matter what objective crimes he has committed, or what the preacher at the Church of Christ would call his "sins". In the ultimate moment of standing before the throne in judgement, over and above anything judged "evil" one will regret what he did to ruin his love relation-ship. To capture the essence of the seriousness with no religious overtones, visualize Stephen Spender's (1965) fingers waving:

> They have fingers which accuse
> You of the double way of shame.
> At first you did not love enough
> And afterwards you loved too much
> And you lacked the confidence to choose
> And you have only yourself to blame (pp. 54–55).

We lack the confidence, the courage, and the wisdom to discern the difference. We can't pin it on anyone else, either. Regret, shame, and humiliation are kissing cousins.

Brooding

As I described in the second stage of grieving, thinking readily becomes painfully obsessive. To that degree, reflection is not produc-tive or liberating. It goes around in circles. Repetitive thinking that does not go forward but goes nowhere merges with an ambivalent emotional stance. In regret, the cognitive-emotional disposition is best called brooding.

Brooding means being stuck on the words "I could have ..."/"We should have ..." or indulging in what Alcoholic Anonymous calls "stinkin' thinkin'". Brooding is dark thinking and heavy-feeling, sinister, and menacing. Regret which transmutes into lingering brooding leads to an inherently suicidal disposition.

"Too late": Opportunities abused or missed

Regret dwells upon and obsesses over a remembered situation or a missed chance.

> What a terrible mistake I've made with my life ... You get to thinking about a different life, a *better* life you might have had ... a life I may have had with you, Mr. Stevens .... One can't be forever dwelling on what might have been (Ishiguro, 1989. p. 239).

In regret, I am subjectively convinced it is too late. I've burned my bridges. I broke promises. Poised on the borderline of insane remorse, I'm stuck with an endless ending.

Sense of responsibility

While oozing regret, convoluted feelings of responsibility eat like acid into one's core. I feel irrationally and horribly responsible about that which "back then"—when the "moment" was at hand—my stubborn pride had scoffed at and dismissed as silly or irrelevant. This ironic and acute sense of feeling responsible—sometimes warranted, sometimes warped—is another double-edged sword. Because why? The guilt which our ambivalent brooding holds hostage is potentially liberating.

In our contemporary Western society, we peg guilt as a bogey-man, an evil to be eradicated. Away with it, as quickly as possible! Who needs it? And who can argue with that statement, veiled as a rhetorical question? D.W. Winnicott so argues.

Winnicott (1965a/2005) teaches us that guilt is valuable and necessary because it is on the way to *concern* (pp. 73–82). Consider the cold-blooded murderer who refuses to repent. She shows no warmth, no tenderness, and is well-nigh incapable of blushing over anything whatsoever. Consider one nation that totally destroys the fabric of another nation with a dubious reason and even more dubious intentions. Instead of feeling guilt and regret when the rat-infested twilight sets in, it calls its disguised business venture a military mission of liberation.

Take the situation of a country that got filthy rich on the heinous practice of slavery, the bottom of the barrel of crimes against humanity. Two hundred years later Great Britain cannot make an official act of apology. A decayed ex-imperialistic nation is only sorry ... off the record. No need to multiply examples. Whatever you yourself judge about murders, political blood-letting, military destruction, extraordinary rendition unto torture, or incessant Western racism, the point is clear: with no capacity for guilt, and with no acknowledgement of wrong-doing, nothing changes. Islamic brown peoples will feel the sting of prejudice and xenophobia throughout my lifetime and yours. In matters in which concern and sorrow should abide, instead rule fear, self-righteousness, greed, and hypocrisy.

Guilt is a necessary step on the way to concern. Regret, racism, and humiliation will never cease unless concern, forgiveness and mercy reign. The call to concern addresses both global geopolitical situations and the state of affairs of little ole me. In our regret and our brooding, guilt clicks in its voice, too hard to ignore.

In Freud's vocabulary, guilt means that we have taken inside the eyes of the other; in making a moral choice, and even if standing alone, we hear the voice of the father and the father's father. The superego splits off from the ego. Traditionally, within our Judeo-Christian roots, we call it conscience.

The mind-boggling and gut-wrenching music of guilt leads to concern. Concern leads to forgiveness. Forgiveness and self-tolerance are twinned. With tolerance comes twice blest mercy. Forget about doing your cognitive homework; cultivate mercy; mercy promotes radical cure.

Paying the price: Backing up; backing down

In my regret, I am equally convinced that life levied too high a tax for the deed I did, or for my failure to act. We pay for our stubbornness, false pride, stupidity; we pay for the sins of our youth, for doing what we were too naïve or too innocent to understand fully, or too inexperienced in to be able to readily anticipate the predictable reverberations and likely outcomes; we pay for our rough and rowdy days when we acted impulsively, carelessly, and irresponsibly.

Not backing up or backing down also signifies that acting with integrity, on principle, and with authenticity exacts a high cost. The dialectical possibility of not backing down is caving in, or capitulation. We are mealy mouthed or chicken shit. Our yellow strip shows. We lacked the guts or the balls. We back down. Looking back, we regret our cowardice.

Whichever the meaning, we lost something in the process. Looking back, upon reflection and brooding, we regret the cost. Paying the price and self-pity become synchronized swimmers. The merger exacts a steep, perverse luxury tax: "Whenever something goes wrong in my life, I think I'm being punished for the abortion. I feel like a barren woman, oh, to have had a child! Woe is me."

CHAPTER TWENTY

Excursus into time and memory

Regret's hold is intransigent. What must our hearthead understand about it to pry open its grip? Regret is ineluctably intertwined with and attached to memories. It reverberates over time. More precisely, it wobbles painfully along the shifting axis of remembering–forgetting. To facilitate its release, this chapter probes memory and canvasses its dialectics.

Do I have my memories, or do they have me?

I think back and brood. Repeatedly, I re-experience the triggering situation. It's a multiple whammy. I remember too much, but the memories are distorted, and I am unable to forget. Simultaneously, I have forgotten what it would be to my advantage to remember. Searing questions surface: Are memories all that I "have"? Or the opposite, do my memories "have" me? Being stuffed into the proverbial paper bag from which we cannot punch our way out co-creates regret's peculiar ache. Regretful time lashes across past-present-future, squanders itself confusedly about lost and lingering memories, and meanders in circles—going nowhere.

Seemingly powerless, I can't trust my mind for a minute. It goes childish. If I let it wander, it disobeys me. Memories lure it away. Love-regret haunts a body at random, often it catches me off guard when I least expect it. Even in happy moments, or when I am thoroughly preoccupied with some other matter, suddenly the broken record again plays its sinister tune with the biggest little words: If only. If only not ... Shockwaves then ripple throughout the bone marrow of my soul. Especially in the wee hours of the morning, the very pillow on which I lay my head vibrates a bittersweet song announcing "blues time", and makes impossible the descent of blessed sleep. The next thing you know, dawn breaks and I haven't slept a wink. Can anybody tell me where the Sleep-stealer lives? (Tagore, 1993).

Forgetting to remember to forget ... or to remember

The ambiguity of remembering–forgetting plagues all of sorrow's profiles. "The King" would love this probing of it. It suits to examine the matter through the eyes of seminal and decisive thinkers. In teasing out relevant yet varying views, my intention is not to present fully the philosophical positions of the various thinkers, but rather to expose the shade of emphasis that each contributes to a nuanced understanding of the complex phenomena.

Arthur Schopenhauer: Memory and the will

Understanding regret requires delving into memory at a level beyond mainstream psychology's trivializing it as a brain-trace. Arthur Schopenhauer (1851/1970) underscores that "memory may well become confused by what is put into it, but it cannot really become forfeited ... memory is bottomless" (p. 178).

It's enough to make a body smile! Bottomless is exactly what we think about while drinking the cup of regret. Wrapped up in my memories, confused, without perspective, I put the tea leaves in the espresso maker, or tip over the bottomless cup to see what in the devil keeps this pain flowing even after I have swallowed the last bitter drop of the brew. What does Schopenhauer's vaulted will power have to do with striking a balance? The answer is precious little. Regret signifies that the past refuses to recede to where it belongs: into the past ... as part of my history. Instead, it lingers in the present and wreaks havoc, forcing me to drink from that bottomless cup.

The psychoanalytic achievement is making the past … past. Freud wants to put it back there where it belongs instead of it swallowing up the present. The whole world that each of us encounters, and which becomes part of our lives, exists twice: actually and in memory. Nobody plagued by regret ever doubts—as mainstream psychology does doubt—the validity of Freud's repetition compulsion. Whatever we do not remember, we are doomed to repeat.

Sigmund Freud: Screen memories

Imagine Freud delicately playing on the instrument of the soul and asking himself with each pluck, "Why can't some people, hysterics, remember what is in their best interest to recall? Why can't depressive persons and obsessive individuals forget what painfully and endlessly haunts them?" Like Nietzsche before him and Heidegger afterwards, Freud forces us to rethink our rationalistic Western biases about temporality, especially the view—so ridiculously contrary to everyday experience—that time is linear and successive. There are no straight lines in nature, only in theories. Freud, a contemporary of Einstein and Heidegger, shares the same *zeitgeist* which overthrew the straight-jacket view of absolute spacetime. The contemporary social-medical scientific "decision" to theorize, research, and treat on the basis of the pre-Einstein absolutist viewpoint hamstrings studies of all sorrow's profiles.

Forgetting is a dynamic. It is "work" from the vantage points of Freud, Nietzsche, Heidegger, and Einstein. Time does not heal all wounds. Those healing hands of time never did work. In Chapter two, I mentioned Emily Dickinson's charming dismissal of the notion that remedy comes with the sheer passage of time.

Remember, too, Sartre. Out of sight does not equal out of mind. Absence is a mode of being present. The insentient, absent other can yank me away from the noisy hundred others who sit before me … suddenly silent and unseen.

The screens

Freud's (1899a) discovery of "screen memories" privileges the relationship between retention and its "psychical significance", and also simultaneously destroys the notion that memory is an objectified trace or "connected chain of events" (p. 230).

Around this issue of screen pivot the complex matters of selected memories; false memories (*fausse reconnaissance*); selective amnesia; mediated memories—stories told us so often by family members that we remember the scene ourselves; and constructed memories—those which we concoct in order to save our bacon. Screen memories are of that ilk. Like dreams, symptoms, jokes, and the failed achievements of mistakes, errors, accidents, and slips the screen memories are *compromises*. In the face of psychic conflict, they divert my attention from what is essential: "Instead of the memory which would have been justified by the original event, another memory is produced which has been to some significant degree associatively displaced from the former one" (Freud, 1899a, p. 307). Screen memories reveal the possibility of remembering the "wrong" things precisely to hold at bay the "right" ones, exactly those that hurt most. How convenient!

Freud interprets his patient's screen memory as rooted in a genuine ambivalently experienced situation. In order to cope, the patient "projected the two phantasies on to one another and made a childhood memory of them" (Freud, 1899a, p. 315). It is easy to picture. The patient, lying on the couch and trying to say all that comes to mind, chimes out: "I remember when ..." Freud just smiles in anticipation of an exercise in imagination.

Significantly, Freud finds that the phantasies comprising the so-called childhood memory belong to situations happening much later. Relevant to our theme, the memory is also confabulation of regretful emotions about love. Freud's patient reports that the two memory-making phantasies "sought to improve the past ... *If only* the smash had not occurred. *If only* I had stopped at home and grown in the country ... *If only* I had followed my father's profession and had married her" (Freud, 1899a, p. 313). Through the permeable and porous screen, however, the "forgotten" content seeps, the unconscious "returns". All at once the truth comes rushing back to me ... and my heart aches.

Freud would not have been smiling only in cynicism at the confabulated memory. He appreciates the power of fantasy in our psychological economy. We concoct a story and re-invent history to defend against hurt, salvage our pride, or save face. Looked at in historical perspective, we can see the matter even more clearly than Freud himself articulated it: memory and imagination dance an endless tango. It remains to be seen in each and every expression whether imagination is turning on or off the light necessary for healing.

Fredrick Nietzsche: Active forgetting

Forgetting is a labour. Nietzsche, who links the matter of memory to health and happiness, teaches that we must cultivate the capacity to forget. Remembering–forgetting is not like superficial pragmatic British philosophy-psychology presents it, that is, as a blind chance-riddled hooking together of ideas. Neither does memory resemble Anglo-Saxon's naturalistic, mechanistic "baby" that Nietzsche (1882a/1992) tags "purely passive, automatic, reflexive, molecular and thoroughly stupid" (p. 460). Nietzsche's view anticipates Einstein's.

> Forgetting is no force of inertia; it is rather an active ... positive faculty of repression that is responsible for the fact that what we experience and absorb enters our consciousness little while we are digesting it (one might call the process "impsychation") ... To close the doors and windows of consciousness for a time; to remain undisturbed by the noise and struggle of our underworld ...; a little quietness, a little *tabla rasa* of the consciousness to make room for new things ... that is the purpose of active forgetfulness, which is like a doorkeeper, a preserver of psychic order, repose, and etiquette: so that it will be immediately obvious how there could be no happiness, nor cheerfulness, no hope, no pride, no *present* without forgetfulness (Nietzsche, 1882a/1992, pp. 493–494, original emphasis).

The health of the individual, a people, and a culture depends upon the balance of knowing how to forget and when to remember at the right time. The doorkeeper that distinguishes and deciphers guarantees a bit of psychic respite. Pertinent to the experience of regret, the inability to forget sabotages decision-making, blocks healthy action, and compromises creativity. Engulfed by the past, we sink ever so close to self-pity or despair.

Not surprisingly, since Freud borrowed key ideas from him, Nietzsche paints a similar picture to that of the creator of psychoanalysis. Regretful memories summon a trial by conscience. No God need sit in judgement because I myself wield the gavel. I become judge, jury, and executioner. Brooding endlessly stirs self-confession and penance. Just as if depressed, I suffer "doing my time". The pain of self-punishment comforts me. Since my Will already pays expensive installments of hellish horror, the fantasy of shovelling coal in Hell gives relief. I feed the flames that burn my cargo. Death feels like my sidekick.

Martin Heidegger: The ecstasies of time

Heidegger, who also borrows copiously from Nietzsche, overturns the orthodox Western view of time. *Lived* time is not a straight line sliced and diced into successive segments, or divided neatly into stages and phases. It is a spiral. *Objective* time is successive: the measured duration of the ticks of the clock and the grains of sand slithering down the hourglass. Such succession, however, is abstract. Living time flows as a unity. To explicate the meaning of time as subjectivity, Heidegger utilizes Husserl's phenomenological concept of intentionality.

Husserl (1929/1974) heals Cartesian dualism by demonstrating that consciousness always takes as its object that which is not consciousness itself (pp. 49–51). Consciousness is not stuck thinking its own thoughts; it always in-tends an object, escapes to the things that it feeds on. Heidegger next plucks Husserl's notion from the epistemological level, and plops it on the ontological plane, unifying the self–world relationship. I am being-in-the-world-with-others. Platonic–Cartesian dichotomies are only ideological abstractions with no basis in existence. In a statement of qualitative algebra, dualism is a bad joke waiting for a laugh. The sad side to the joke is that Western civilization can't stop using it to plan, scheme, and ultimately ... to destroy.

In-tention is my relationship to what is present-at-hand. I switch focus by *re-tending*, looking back at what I recollect. Such recalled time or retention is the past, or memory. Whenever I make that past a theme of consciousness, however, it is still with me here-and-now. It makes me weep, evokes my fury, triggers my revenge, and summons regret.

I also anticipate. I wonder about what I foresee either in hope or with dread. That act of *pro-tention* bears the name "future". Time does not pass, but rather Time arises ...

> Temporalizing does not signify that ecstasies come in a "succession." The future is not later than having been, and having been is not earlier than the Present. Temporality temporalizes itself as a future which makes present in the process of having been (Heidegger, 1927/1962, p. 401).

In plain language, don't foolishly tell me that tomorrow I'll forget about yesterday. It is always ... today.

According to Heidegger, we are "thrown" into time; finite subjectivity is death-bound. Meshing time with subjectivity reverses the understanding of forgetting–remembering. "*Remembering* is possible only on the basis of forgetting not the other way around" (Heidegger, 1927/1962, p. 312, original emphasis).

The dialectic of authentic–inauthentic ex-sistence helps clarify the ground of regret. Ex-sistence gets entangled with self (*verfangt*), snarled with the world, estranged from itself, and suffers turbulence (*Wirbel*) (Heidegger, 1927/1962, p. 401). In "moments" we recall who we are and what we have done and thus vulnerably ex-pose ourselves; in other "moments" we withdraw from our relationships of care and close off from ourselves. Within this interweave:

> Forgetting is not nothing ... a failure to remember; it is ... a "positive" ecstatic mode of having-been; a mode with a character of its own. The ecstasy (rapture) of forgetting has the character of backing away from one's ownmost having-been in a way that is closed off from oneself (Heidegger, 1927/1962, p. 388).

In street-talk, forgetting something real powerful takes backing away from it. When you get far enough away, you gotta slam the door and bar it. Then you can talk about what Heidegger (1927/1962) calls "having forgotten [*Vergessenheit*]" (p. 389).

Intertwining of beginning and end

T.S. Eliot also expresses the same seminal vision about time that we find in Einstein, psychoanalysis, and phenomenology. Time is not linear, staged-phased, jerked into a graph, or moulded into a square box. Time cannot be reduced to measured duration. It's a spiral or saddleback. Eliot depicts the Chiasma of time and subjectivity: "a

lifetime burning in every moment ... In my beginning is my end"
(Eliot, 1936b/1963, p. 196).

>Time present and time past
>Are both perhaps present in time future
>And time future contained in time past
>
>The end precedes the beginning,
>And the end and the beginning were always there
>Before the beginning and after the end.
>
>What we call the beginning is often the end
>And to make an end is to make a beginning.
>The end is where we start from.
>
>(Eliot, 1936/1963e, pp. 189; 194, p. 221)

CHAPTER TWENTY ONE

Unmasking regret's lie

In the preceding chapters, I have dragged regret from pillar to post. I delve into it thoroughly, not only because it is incredibly common in everyday life, but also because it is largely neglected in mainstream psychology, psychiatry, and psychoanalysis. More importantly, and as mentioned previously, it holds that middle position of supplanting grief but being qualitatively different from depression.

The labour of grieving eventually culminates. Grief-work is terminable. Freud's unconvincing capitulation to a naturalistic psychic wear-out makes sense on the grounds that the Maestro knows the musical score has to come to an end. Sorrow, I have argued, is the optimal resolution. We forgive, feel forgiven, and hold the dear one close in her absence. Sorrow springs the trap on distorted memories. It brings us genuinely into the calm and serenity of truth. Depression betokens the inability to forgive and eventuates in the untruth of living as split. Consequently, someone or another takes the brunt of our negativity, even as we berate and punish ourselves. Regret is the orienting disposition in-between. The explanation of this is not one sentence long.

The gig's up

Nobody doubts that regret is at rock bottom level a ... ruse. Unmasking the subterfuge takes conceptual and emotional effort. Nobody has clarified any better than T.S. Eliot the futility of merely hankering over an abstract empty possibility: "what might have been".

> All time is unredeemable
> What might have been is an abstraction
> Remaining a perpetual possibility
> Only in a world of speculation.
> What might have been and what has been
> Point to one end, which is always present.
> Footfalls echo in the memory
> Down the passage which we did not take
> Towards the door we never opened
> Into the rose garden. (Eliot, 1936b/1963, p. 189)

These lines articulate the absolute difference between a genuine concrete lifeworld option and the empty possibility of purely abstract, speculative mental gymnastics. I might die tomorrow. Maybe win the lottery. Or eat a peach. However, what occurred or did not take place yesterday is irretrievably gone. In principle and in fact, I cannot have the "moment" back. Thus anything said about "what might have been" is hypothetical or purely imaginative. There is nothing we can do about it now. We can take a perspective upon the past that changes it, even reverses its meaning. But the event itself and the "moment" in which it occurred have slipped away forever.

What purpose does the ruse serve? Kierkegaard unmasks what Eliot describes so well. He pierces this psychological retreat, and also clarifies what is at stake in Freud's screen memories. A twin liar, self-deception/other-deception, lurks behind the misery of regret. What do I mean? What is the "payoff" or the "secondary gain" of crying over spilt milk and of wallowing in regret?

In the algebra of human pain, anxiety is a most horrendous psychological experience. Like a blow to the head, it throws us for a loop. Thus, it generates cognitive confusion and jeopardizes the living heart. In anxiety, we are like squirrels in a cage or a cat in a round house: frantic. Here's the key. Regret binds anxiety and blunts its agonizing pain. Cultivating regret and indulging in forgetting serve the same purpose of promoting obscurity so that we might "play 'lying dead'" about our cowardice or greatest weakness (Kierkegaard, 1849/1974, p. 186). Regret traps me in order to keep anxiety at bay. A Polish adage advises, "When the truth hurts, only a lie can be beautiful." Regretting is one way of forgetting that one cannot forget ... self. Screen memories concoct one vivid picture that blurs another truer self-portrait. Again, how convenient!

The luxury of forgetting painful events and burying them in regret perform the same psychological service. One is blind to the fact that one is blind to the truth of his despairing situation. Kristen Nordentoft expounds Kierkegaard's standpoint when he writes, "Forgetting is not the deliberate exclusion of a particular, traumatic content of consciousness. It is the total suppression of a given, intolerable self-perception with the help of another understanding, which must be defended at all costs" (Nordentoft, 1972/1978, p. 222). At the time of a divorce or a breakup, for example, both parties typically re-invent history.

The wish to have-it-to-do-over, therefore, is the expression of self-deception par excellence. It wants to make the first chance contingent, as if a de-cision is not an irrevocable cut, but weightless. Being granted the second chance, the opportunity to reverse or rectify our commission or omission—is a two-edged sword. Unless we had, authentically, managed our anxiety-perturbed flaw and surpassed ourselves, the chances are that we would repeat the same mistake. A bit of emotional algebra puts it this way: "I wish I'd made that same mistake just one time." Regret is, therefore, a waste of time and tears. Whatever we look back at and wish to re-do, we could have anticipated. With truth, courage, or wisdom then we might have chosen differently.

Stevens, the dignified butler in *Remains of the Day*, presents a vivid example. A nerve of defiance quickens his actions. He lives the existential project of cherishing and protecting an ideal self-image. No weakness shows, only strength. Such is fodder for despair. If truth threatens this preferred picture, better to remain aloof and go off to brood.

Forgiveness or defiance?

If forgiveness like mercy is a twice blest healer and the optimal solution for grief, what blocks it? Why lapse into regret instead of forgiving? *It is easier to defy than to sacrifice.* Within Nietzsche's framework, it empowers me to love my "chosen" destiny so thoroughly I would welcome and cherish it over and again, endlessly. Dag Hammarskjold (1963/1970) elaborates: "we have to be *forgiven*. But we can only believe this is possible if we ourselves can forgive" (p. 156, original emphasis). He gives us the final clue: "[F]orgiveness always entails a sacrifice" that I be willing to forgive "whatever the consequence" (Hammarskjold, 1963/1970, p. 197). Enter from the wings to centre stage, prancing and all puffed up, defiance.

Defiance won't pay the price and won't make the sacrifice. Kierkegaard (1849/1974) uses Shakespeare's Richard III as the exemplar of what he calls "the despair of despairingly willing to be oneself, defiance ... The self despairingly wants to be its own master, or create itself, to make itself into the self it wants to be" (p. 201).

In a nutshell, one senses in self a horrendous flaw, a major weakness, an Achilles heel, the Pauline thorn. It is presumed to be the "real" reason your woman rejected, scorned, abandoned, or dumped you. As such, it gnaws at the very bone marrow of your soul. It gets convoluted. How so?

In defiance, I do not want to be found out. I would rather be a basket case of unfulfilled longing and regret than express vulnerability in letting my genuine weakness become apparent to others. I will moan to you my regrets, berate myself shamelessly, but thou shalt not laugh at my true flaws. No: You must not laugh at me. My true insufficiency and personal flaws evoke humiliation instead of simple, honest humility. Defiance does not want to acknowledge, for example, that the woman in this drama of love and loss abides in truth or is superior in virtue or wisdom. Defiance is too proud to depend upon her. Better to stew in bitter regret than to let others feel pity for me. Even receiving help means humiliation. Richard III exemplifies the defiant person that finds it harder to receive than to give. He condemns himself to demonic hatred. Regret is an alibi. It reeks of hypocrisy.

Anticipation and regret

Regret, therefore, makes everything go haywire. Once upon a time, I had hopes and dreams, prospects, ambitions, and goals. Expectations were high; we shared promises or traded vows. My dreams were wider than the Russian steppes. Then it all came unglued.

The bottom fell out. The centre did not hold. It all added up to ... nothing.

The power of regret and the strength of anticipation are existentially proportionate. No expectations would pre-empt regrets. Both phenomena spin and twirl around the same thin wire. There was a "moment" of vulnerability, at least, and the possibility of surrender. In the blink of an eye, the highest hopes transmute into the deepest regret, even as an ardently desired possibility vanishes. It takes only a look, one word, an unanswered email. The future which yesterday was now has now retreated into ancient history. Dashed hopes, broken promises, lost dreams and acts of betrayal are deep words. To the defiant one, they spell unbearable humiliation.

Nostalgia

For a moment there, you opened yourself to love. Somebody leaves footprints all over your memory. Etched marks and indelible stains remain. Such memories enrich our lives, especially if he had sired my children. Nostalgically, we glance back. The tender recollections of first love, for example, are sad in a beautiful way. Even if these remembrances—old photographs, saved love letters, a CD with the song we fell in love to—eventually melt into bittersweet sentimentality or harden into regret, they are the ore that fills the crucible of our lives.

Subsequent wise choices in loving brighten any lingering dark melancholy with a gentle patina. In the deepest sense, we never totally overcome the regretful situation. If we truly love someone, for example, we always will. This does not mean that we lapse into inauthentic resignation; but we find in our hearts the appropriate place for a lost or faded love. Passionate tenderness or love is the cure for the nihilistic soul. Love waters the wasteland, and studs with a warm heart Eliot's hollow men. It takes a well-timed Kierkegaardian leap, but we can face the truth about self-and-other. Honesty blunts bitterness and transforms regret into the joy of seasoned nostalgia. All it takes is surrender. Regret ceases in an instant.

The saving grace

Is not the great task of living to convert scars into marks? Nietzsche takes this resolution of the agony of regret one step further with his views on *"amor fati"* and "the eternal recurrence of the same": two antidotes to life frozen-in-time and locked-in. He challenges us:

> What if some day or night a demon was to sneak after you into your loneliest loneliness and say to you, "This life as you now live it and have lived it, you will have to live once more and innumerable times more; and there will be nothing new in it, but every pain and every joy and every thought and sigh and everything immeasurably small or great in your life must return to you—all in the same succession and sequence—even this spider and this moonlight between the trees, and even this moment itself. The hourglass of existence is turned over and over, and you with it, speck of dust (Nietzsche, 1882b/1974, p. 101).

What options would we have? Would we curse the Demon for feeding our regret, or laud him as a God? Nietzsche is cocksure that the only prescription for health is this conformation, and that the only triumph over regret and overcoming of self-pity is saying "Yes" to life, never "No".

> My formula for greatness in a human being is *amor fati*: that one wants nothing different, not forward, not backward, not in all eternity ... if I had to do it all over again, I'd choose everything the same and embrace my life in its entirety. "I 'will' to come back eternally—not to a new life, or a better life or a similar life ... but to this same, selfsame life ... Not merely bear what is necessary, still less conceal it—but *love* it" (Nietzsche, 1908/1967, p. 258, original emphasis).

Alfonso Lingis nuances Nietzsche and provides the context for the abiding significance of love-regret. Desire and regret are two sides of the same coin.

> We are never more ... open to being so easily hurt, as when we give ourselves over in love to someone! ... never more vulnerable than when we are in love ... the "glory" of human life resides in our willingness to risk ... There are games in which what one loses, if one loses, is completely disproportionate to what one wins, if one wins. One stands to lose everything (Lingis, 2000, pp. 60; 63; 81).

Lingis ups the ante, insisting that we embrace the opportunity to gamble all.

> Do we not feel a kind of indifference and even disdain for someone who has never ... played the fool by loving someone who was only toying with him or her? Don't we really think that the one thing to regret in life is not to have dared, that the one thing we will never regret is to have made fools of ourselves for love ...? (Lingis, 2000, pp. 60–61; 141).

In a risk-filled free-fall into forgiving–forgiven, I dwell in truth, freedom, dignity, and serenity.

CHAPTER TWENTY TWO

On longing: In Rumi, and Lorca

Who remains a stranger to the agony of longing for a lost beloved? Who has not known the pain of yearning, pining, and aching for the one who is gone? Love takes hostages. It seems pedantic to list longing as one of sorrow's profiles. Call it lovesickness, heartbreak, *kjærlighetssorg*, or the lovesick blues ... whichever fits your experience or your taste. It is extreme loneliness, of living with the loss of one's loss, of an other who may be a live corpse or a haunting ghost.

To repeat, mainstream psychological-psychiatric literature contributes nothing to an understanding of soul-hurt. Susanne Scheibe (2005) mentions lovesickness as an example of *sehnsucht* or longing which she operationally defines as an intense desire for something that is remote, irretrievably lost, or unattainable. Although people commonly experience longing throughout the lifespan, it is rarely investigated. "Surprisingly, the psychological literature on the phenomenon or related concepts such as yearning, nostalgia, homesickness, and wanderlust has been relatively scarce for many years" (Mayser, Scheibe & Riediger, 2008). Such neglect of longing denigrates the phenomenon. *Dum tacit clamat*. Silence shouts. Whatever is missing from a discipline's literature reveals as much as it contains.

307

What does it mean that researchers both in bereavement and in human development ignore longing? Inauthentic silence roars.

Can we imagine any group without its explicit or implicit lists of both buzz words and "dirty words"? Each social organization forbids what it deems four-letter words, those ideas which fly in the face of what it stands for. Natural scientific discourse fails to research longing. Mention of it would only be an indicator of pathology in grief (Klass, Silverman and Nickman, 1996).[18] It would summon forth a way of thinking-valuing less superficial than what the literature's pages hallows.

What happens to an experience that never finds its way into spoken or written discourse? How does the adolescent, for example, process her or his experience of giving or bestowing a hickey? There is nothing written about it in official health, psychology, religious, or educational texts. The glut of popular magazines, concerning dating, sexuality, and love, also ignores it (Alapack, Blichfeldt, and Elden, 2005; Alapack, 2007b). Am I a depraved alien or a leper with this bruise on my neck? Suppose I am in perpetual longing? Shall I not be perturbed that so-called scientists and professional psychologists teach me nothing about it?

Literature, poetry, music, and movies, on the other hand, treat the theme abundantly. From that broad menu, I select a few who capture most poignantly the experience and its meaning. I pick those who treat longing with the dignity it deserves. The leading figures in this chapter are Lorca and Rumi.

Federico Garcia Lorca expresses the phenomenon of lost love with the beautiful fury of deep song, the gypsy siguiriya, and flamenco. Rumi, the Muslim Sufi Mystic—whose massive authorship arguably is the longest "poem" on longing ever written—cries and howls with Divine Madness, moves with the energy and power of chanting and frenzied whirling ... and then he utters the absolutely perfect poetic phrase.

The weight of "nothing"

Western ideas typically explain (away) longing as nothing but an inner state, a self-indulgent act of fantasy. Push the thought ever so slightly, and longing is reduced to one's private illusions. Give one more little shove, and it is disparaged as pathological.

It suits to elaborate. There is no inner life in behavioural psychology. It is a psychology without a soul. Therefore, the god-awful indulgence in longing is a pure waste of time and energy. Longing, a strong persistent yearning or unfulfilled desire, is not conducive to productivity or efficiency. Instead of pining, you should do your cognitive homework; come up with an action plan; make practical choices, and let go of her. Forget this heart-rending, self-indulgent moaning.

Such thinking does not promote health, but bankrupts the human heart. Søren Kierkegaard (1847/1962) insists that a true love relationship always involves three members: the lover, the beloved, and Love (p. 113). From a Christian standpoint, the third party is God. Longing is not a negative emotion. Love endures any human ending. Naturally, we reach for its sustenance. What follows in this chapter—this is an echo—goes against the grain of normal science.

Reaching

Ron Cornelissen's (unpublished manuscript) psychopoetic psychology balances the bland coldness of mainstream positivism: "Longing is the heart's reaching. Reaching and longing are one, united in one single act." The intertwining involves the flesh. Cornelissen's key insight is that the reaching of longing is palpable. Longing describes an arc. The self stretches beyond itself to others (*mitwelt*) and to the surrounding world (*umwelt*). I reach for something that is just beyond my fingertips. I grasp for what had been so precious and near, but now is infinitely far away. In reaching for the beloved with aching fingers, simultaneously I am reaching for the moon and the stars. Nonetheless, my empty hands are not encased in glass, as it were, somehow set apart. They are alive in the universe, gesturing. They wave in the wind; the cold breeze bites them; or the fiery sun blisters them. We must not think of a person in longing as shrivelled up, coiled within self, hiding under a blanket to avoid the world. No. My longing is a gesture. Garcia Lorca best depicts this connectedness between longing and the circumambient universe.

Federico Garcia Lorca: The deep song of longing

> The moon has a halo
> My love has died (Lorca, 1954/1991, p. 31).

The poems of the deep song showcase the *siguiriya* as an unparalleled way of expressing "emotional rightness" and condensing the "mystery ... and highest emotional moments in human life" (Lorca, 1954/1991, p. 30). Vividly and with simple eloquence, Lorca's lines manifest the link between the natural world and Love-Death. Lurking in the depths of the poem is the "terrible question" of longing ... that "has no answer" (Lorca, 1954/1991, p. 31). Even death is not an answer to the pain of longing, but only another question.

What do we do with our Sorrow and Pain? Deep songs reach out by using the extremes of the scream and the sob; shouting "at the stars ... or kiss[ing] the red dust of the road" (Lorca, 1954/1991, p. 32). The poems of the deep song, says Lorca (1954/1991), are "magnificently pantheistic" (p. 34).

> Every morning I go
> to ask the rosemary
> if love's disease can be cured
> for I am dying (Lorca, 1954/1991, p. 34).

Nature is implicated in my longing. I reach out to the elements, to the flowers and herbs; the wind and the rain respond to my pain.

Weeping

The deep song of the Gypsy siguiriya is the perfect poem of tears:

> The breeze wept
> when he saw the deep wounds
> in my heart.
>
> I weep endlessly; you are gone
> But what use is all my longing
> if the wind will not take my sighs
> to your ears ... (Lorca, 1954/1991, pp. 35; 38).

Longing is intense; the pain is deep, blended with blood, with the very seat of life:

> If my heart had
> windowpanes of glass
> you would look in and see it
> cry drops of blood (Lorca, 1954/1991, p. 36).

> Since you stopped listening
> to the echo of my voice,
> my heart has been plunged in pain.
> It sends jets of burning blood
> to my eyes (Lorca, 1954/1991, pp. 35; 38).

> Whenever I look at the place
> where I used to talk to you,
> my poor eyes begin
> crying drops of blood (Lorca, 1954/1991, p. 36).

> To console me, my friends say
> Visit your mistress's tomb.
> Has she a tomb, I answer
> other than in my breast? (Lorca, 1954/1991, p. 37).

What is positive in all of this? This sounds brutal. Valuing such lines does not just reflect a contrast of paradigms. An ontological difference holds between those who hold the heart shallow and those who find it infinitely deep. Lorca's point is that the thread of true love abides. Love, if it is love, lasts a lifetime. If we never long, we have never loved. Pleading and imploring index the depth of love. Lorca invokes Curro Pulla and Omar Khayyam.

> My love will end,
> My grief will end
> My tears will end
> And all will end (Lorca, 1954/1991, p. 39).

Lorca reaffirms what countless poets have insisted—love is stronger than death:

> In the end my bones
> Will turn to dust in the grave
> But the soul will never be able
> To lose such a strong love (Lorca, 1954/1991, p. 39).

Footprints on my memory

Meanwhile, here in the real world and in time—where I am still alive but barely hanging on—my memories are kindling sticks for the wood stove that keeps my longing burning. Memories lie in wait for me. Time ticks away, but memories march in tune and in time, leaving footprints. They hide in the darkness, wait for me, and waylay me. Since they pranced in, uninvited, why can't they just march out of my mind?

Sometimes I forget

Time does not heal all wounds. One does not just automatically forget, in time. Indeed, the healing hands of time are rarely working. Memory, however, is finite.

Here come a few stories.

Sometimes, I forget while waking up in the morning. With eyes still closed, I spontaneously reach across the bed and whisper your name. For a moment: there, you were here again. I forgot …

In the middle of the day, I also forget sometimes. Somehow, I get lost in my routine and everything sees normal. I chat and joke with co-workers as if you're still here. Somehow, I forget.

But that's not the end of my story; it's the beginning. Suddenly, I am alone, sitting at my desk, listening to the roar of silence. And the truth hits me between the eyes and in my heart. You're gone. You ain't coming back. And I must suck it in, summon all my strength just to make it through the rest of the day—hell, no—to survive one more hour on my own.

The truth is hard to live with. It is so human that it feels inhuman. Remember the Polish saying, "If the truth hurts, only a lie can be beautiful." Will I ever strike that balance between what I need to remember and what I must forget? If I could stay in a state of forgetting, I'd feel the way I used to feel before you left me stranded.

Like before you left! Who am I kidding? I guess that's what the saying "it's gone with the wind" means. But sometimes I forget.

Making it on my own

The one who suffers the ending of a love relationship can also behave with incredible vulnerability. She asks her estranged lover for time to get accustomed to being alone. She'll still need to use him … until she can cope on her own. She owns that she might be a pest from time to time, bother him, try to keep in contact, and ask for more than she should. She owns that in "moments" she'll have no pride at all. She knows she'll still need a friend. Why not him, who understands her and has cared? Can't she lean on him, temporarily?

Learning to let go takes time. It takes effort, tears, and telephone calls. The plea is tender. "Let me use you until I get used to losing you, until I get my feet under me and my heart ticking again properly, until I get a handle on this and cope on my own."

Lost love

In *Toward a phenomenology of lost love* Edward Collins Vacek (1989) writes diplomatically that the technical instruments of modern science cannot explain the experience of the death of love. He gently excuses the social sciences for neglecting the theme, and apologizes for using poetry to disclose essential descriptions of pain, anguish, and the restless anomie of lost love (Vacek, 1989).

In fact, his work is the closest in social scientific literature to the theme of longing (although, he does not pursue longing's reach). He clarifies that love is the heart's movement of discovering and affirming the *other* that makes *me a lover* in a self-transcending, mutual way, and creates an emotional fullness of a newborn *us*. Whenever love ends, these categories whither and disappear. Dante's "I in-me-you" vanishes. I cannot be a lover alone; and "Life without loving is blood without a heart" (Vacek, 1989, p. 2). If we are not loved, who are we? If we do not love, what are we? One's value and uniqueness are in peril.

Our shared world collapses and our shared subjectivity goes down the tubes, too. With heart-knowledge, I see clearly that, when I lost you, I lost me and I lost us. That triple whammy is grounds for sorrow. "The deepest dreariest feeling we can experience" (Vacek, 1989, p. 3).

Vancek ends his study with hope. None of the horrific consequences of lost love need happen. He is right. Nevertheless, he preempts too soon the looming sense of regret, revenge, and suicide in favour of lost love "redeemed" (Vacek, 1989, p. 8). In expressing such optimism, he follows the drift of the culture at large which turns a blind eye to our experience of nothingness. Vacek (1989) ends his study by finding for us "higher mountains to climb" (p. 9).

Rumi: Getting to the treasure beneath the foundation

With Rumi, we leave the highest mountains for the zone of shades. Rumi brings us to level ground, to the fragility and vulnerability of the reedbed. Rumi attunes our ear to a thin piece of cane vibrating. We hear the quivering of a reed, and then listen to the silence. Beneath all our utterances, and within each note of the reed flute, lies nostalgia for the reedbed. Language and music are possible only because we are empty, hollow, and separated from the source. All language is a longing for home. This basic image of the reed torn from the reedbed captures the wild agony of longing. The words, "separated from the source", cradle the core meaning of longing.

> Listen to the story told by the reed,
> of being separated.
> Since I was cut from the reedbed,
> I have made this crying sound.
> Anyone apart from someone he loves
> understands what I say.
> Anyone pulled from a source
> Longs to go back (Rumi, 1995, p. 65).

Coleman Barks (1995) comments: "The reed flute makes music because it has already experienced changing mud and rain and light into sugarcane" (p. 47). Love is finite and fragile, yes. We know *separation* only because we have known *union*. We miss such intimate relating because we have tasted it. Yet it all can be taken away in the blink of an eye: finite. My beloved's absence is timelessly present: infinite. Platitudes, pragmatic strategies, and quick-fixes fall far short of giving us relief or remedy:

How does a part of the world leave the world?

> How does a part of the world leave the world?
> How can wetness leave water?
> Don't try to put out a fire
> by throwing on more fire!
> Don't wash a wound with blood! (Rumi, 1995, p. 66)

Barks (1995) expresses the paradox in a slightly different way: "Longing becomes more poignant if in the distance you cannot tell whether your friend is going away or coming back. The pushing away pulls you in" (p. 47). The humanness of this statement is gripping. It is so difficult during life's journey—especially when the issue is the matter of a love relationship breaking apart—to know when we are going uphill or when downhill, whether we are coming or going, or if this is the beginning or the end. Rumi: "You keep me away with your arm, but the keeping away is pulling me in" (Rumi, 1995, p. 53).

Isn't that the way longing goes? You reach from the bottom of your heart; toss and re-toss a rope in the hope that she will seize it … and tug you close again. You cast your line, fishing for the only one who can nourish your soul. Medical science reports on the phantom limb; you feel your whole existence is like that. Your arms are still attached to you, but you know they are amputated. In the hollow of your empty arms, you cradle pain, endlessly. Only an exceptional act of spiritual and cognitive consciousness creates the existential power to stop the reaching. In Damascus, searching for his mystical friend, it hit Rumi like a ton of bricks:

> Why should I seek? I am the same as
> he. His essence speaks through me.
> I have been looking for myself (Rumi, 1995, p. 42).

Praise to all early-waking grievers.

CHAPTER TWENTY THREE

Unconcluding reflections

One last raking through the ashes ... The substance of the book is now complete. But it does not conclude. I cannot even wind down. Because why? It glares with significant absences. Important topics not treated include: the death of a child which is grief writ large; an individual's homesickness, most powerfully expressed by asylum seekers turning into exiles and expatriates, as racism mushrooms across the globe; euthanasia, a grief-riddled phenomenon as shabbily treated by the guardians of the social order as suicide; abortion, that leaves two people vulnerable to grief and regret; torture, shamefully legitimized by academia's finest minds on rational—but not heartfelt—grounds; men and women who are suffering shame at being the Face of the Disease of AIDS ... even as they slowly die; and poverty's unremittingly ugly grief which I merely touch upon by citing *Stuffed and Starved* (Patel, 2008).

In this historical "moment", poverty is indeed the harbinger of the most acute anguish still to come. Two hundred million neighbours are starving even as the price of rice and petrol has risen from high to bizarre and the wide gap between the destitute and the wealthy has become a Grand Canyon. An implicit metaphor in this book is this: while our neighbours are destitute and dying of starvation, the rational community flounders. It is handicapped by fatally flawed rationalistic thinking and therefore incapable of balancing concern with greed. The poor did not create the economic crash of 15 September, 2009, but it has worsened their plight.

What is authentic knowledge?

Did I embody adequately in this book an intellectually challenging and heartfelt approach to the faces of sorrow? Piggybacking on Amedeo Giorgi's (1970; 2009) demonstration that approach, method, and content are dialectically related, I add style-of-communication to his triad and affirm that the question of adequacy addresses at least four interconnected issues: 1) my underlying Vision; 2) my sources of information and insights; 3) my methods for gathering relevant lifeworld data; and 4) the written forms with which I communicate my knowledge. The reader who is not intrigued by a discussion of the philosophy of science might turn to the last section, "Vitality", where my thoughts come full circle.

What constitutes worthwhile knowledge-claims about people and social-communal life? I affirmed in my introduction that there is more than one way for science to be science. There are also many ways outside of natural science of attaining knowledge about psychological realities. And one can truly use a plethora of ways to make knowledge-claims. Nobody needs be hamstrung by the narrow medical model and psychology's 19th-century natural scientific approach.

Kierkegaard affirms that the natural scientific method, when it encroaches upon the sphere of the spirit, is dangerous and pernicious. Let it deal with what it is suited for: for studying plants, animals, the stars, and our melting glaciers; let it explore the surface of Mars; let it take us to Venus. But it should leave my heart and soul alone because it is not adequate to penetrate their mysteries (Kierkegaard, 1846/1968; 1847/1962; 1843/1843a/1974).

Like a relentless refrain, in almost every chapter I have chanted that philosophical rationalism, dualism, and pragmatism, and the scientific positivism/neo-positivism that they underwrite, are inadequate to deal with sorrow's profiles. In as compressed a statement as possible, Christopher Dawson (1952/1960) shows the liabilities and limits of our modern and contemporary love-affair with the "scientifically known and technologically controlled" (p. 230). The dominant thought-frames of Western cultural are so utilitarian, empirical, superficial, and one-dimensional that they are unable to comprehend "unknown factors which lie beyond our horizon of vision [either] below our level of consciousness [or] above the capacity of our reason" (Dawson, 1952/1960, p. 230).

In this book, I have turned to a host of disciplines that delve into the realm of unconsciousness and/or leap into hyper-consciousness. They also treat my bodily drives and spiritual aspirations respectfully, intimately, and individually. They also are open windows and doors to let blow in a far-reaching understanding of the issues that pertain to Death and sorrow.

How should we interpret Einstein's statement that the imagination is more important than knowledge? I take it to mean that discovery is most fundamental and supersedes legitimization. I concur with Kierkegaard that natural scientific reductionism cheats us out of passionate wonder. In specific, the arguments within the philosophy of science about verifying or falsifying knowledge-claims are merely the quibbles and quarrels between true believers within the Club of positivism. Arguably, subsequent generations will mock this historical epoch for having raised a very puny view of science to the status of its religion.

In this book I do not walk the well-beaten path of mainstream rationalistic natural science psychology. But I do not kill positivism's sacred cows either. I did not even slice the "sacred" out of them. Surely, I have confronted them and tried to dialogue with them. But by and large, I just left them to chew contentedly in the barn. For the purpose of expressing relevant knowledge, I even bracket whether our received views about scientific discourse might be compelling at all when it comes to existential, lifeworld concerns. Giorgi (1997), who relentlessly has probed the proper relationship between science and humanism, wonders if psychologists must not begin to honour something "beyond scientific approaches", something he names "metaknowledgeable presences" (Giorgi, 1997, p. 28). To me, it is more straightforward and more radical. We should free knowledge from its straight-jacket, not reduce it to either natural or human scientific criteria. In this book, I make no concessions to scientific psychology. We need a *metanoia*. Since I insist that my heartlines do communicate scientific knowledge, I borrow from this quantum theory viewpoint on science:

> Those who initially formulated [quantum] theory were not realists. They did not believe that human beings were capable of forming a true picture of the world as it exists independent of our actions and observations. They argued instead for a very different vision of science: In their view, *science can be nothing but an extension of the ordinary language we use to describe our actions and observations to one another* (Smolin, 2006, p. 9, my emphasis).

First and foremost, I privilege ordinary language that so-called experts cavalierly dismiss and demean. Suppose that I search sorrow's profiles by driving trucks. I paint each of my many vehicles with identifying labels of music, film, novels, and poetry, as well as philosophy, psychology, psychoanalysis, and psychiatry. Approaching them exclusively with the knowledge in the bank book of the dominant academic and clinical disciplines yields a meager balance: a thin, cold, objectified, superficial product. In instances such as regret or revenge, the bank book is thin. About instances of gone-crazy grief or longing, the bank account is empty. The depth, colour, richness, complexity, and uniqueness of sorrow's profiles are multi-dimensional—what regular folk like you and me live everyday. They require the magnificent touch of the poetry of Alfred, Lord Tennyson, T.S. Eliot, Emily Dickenson, Rumi (who the Persians and Afghanis call Jelaluddin Balkhi), and Federico Garcia Lorca; films by Atom Egoyan and Billy Bob Thornton; the novels of Khaled Hosseini and Kazuo Ishiguro; Peter Marin's care-filled essay concerning our Vietnam veterans; the seminal and decisive thinking of Søren Kierkegaard, Friedrich Nietzsche, Sigmund Freud, Martin Heidegger, Emmanuel Levinas; the autobiographical account of C.S. Lewis; the beauty and elegance of Gustav Mahler, the visual dynamite of Edvard Munch and Vincent van Gogh, and the "shit-kicking" music of George Jones. And that isn't the half of it.

This book honours all nuggets of insights, pans them, and tries to sift out the genuine gold. It does not matter if the source is luminous, sophisticated texts, or homespun expressions of those who would literally recoil at the effrontery of being referred to as "intellectuals". I am not practicing a democracy of knowledge in the way that our political powers practice it: a democracy of Power and Money. I do not bail out banks that then refuse to lend the common man money, all the while moaning that their bonuses might be curtailed. I do not bail out car companies whose executives travel to Washington in private jets to beg for taxpayer "bread". In this book, the common people contribute as much as the Nobel Prize winner, Albert Camus, and the saints: Thomas Aquinas and Mahatma Gandhi. To our stock of knowledge, I slip in the wisdom of popular culture and the "smarts" of the streets. I slot in the thieves, prostitutes, and murderers that I worked with in Pittsburgh and Seward, Alaska—those who help me to frame the composite of Derek, the Avalanche; I include the ordinary citizens of Seward, down-to-earth and rough around the edges—some who ached with greed to grab the malignant currency, and others who, in outrage and disgust, wanted to spit in the face of corporate America. I have in my mind my brother Nick and beloved sister-in-law Barbara—recently deceased—who remind me sincerely and with warm hearts that the USA is a great country, even though it looks to me from the perspective of the European side of the Big Pond that the world since 2003 has either been laughing at Uncle Sam for the pathetically foolish Dog and Pony Show that he is performing in Iraq and all across the Mid-East, or crying because of the grief the prosecution of "war" is creating. It remains to be seen whether the optimism the world is expressing at Obama's victory will sustain and lead to constructive change.

I think of my children, Nicole, Rich, and Boo and my granddaughters Sophie, Olivia, and Natalie Grace who have filled my existence with Light, Life, and Love. I think of my wife, Chili, a constant companion for growing old with, who teaches me that there is nothing in life to regret. My intelligent conversations and heartfelt interactions with them over the years spur me to say what nothing in academic psychology could ever prompt, "If we learn to love, we may learn how to think."

All of the above constitutes a large umbrella, whose various spokes include narratives, parables, stories, a therapeutic dialogue, and presentations of the essential Vision of major thinkers. Likewise, treatment of the spectrum of the sources of sorrow would be paper thin if it failed to acknowledge the ways that the politics of knowledge sullies the production and dissemination of knowledge and destroys the careers—by partisan practices—in terms of hiring and the awarding of tenure.

This book would ape the dualistic myopia of the mainstream if I did not set it against the backdrop of our geopolitical situation. One's particular political stand matters not at all because grief is piling equally high on the right and the left. My personal political stand-point is irrelevant as well. In touching upon the matters of revenge, racism, poverty, so-called delayed traumatic stress disorder, and so forth, I am not giving a political commercial or campaigning. It is not only a particular political administration about which I am in recoil, but the specific issue of playing politics ... with lives. To hope it will cease and desist is, perhaps, vain. It remains an open question whether the new administration will make the changes for which President Obama campaigned. If the first nine months forecast the rest of his tenure, it seems that the cartels that have been running the USA for decades will cling to their Power (Giffin, 1974/2003) aided by the racist nerve that quickens too great a proportion of the nation's populace. Let hope, however, spring eternal. In terms of sorrow's profiles, only you will decide if I have struck a balance between life-filled narratives and thought-rich reflections, including their political ramifications.

We have mucked around in this text in content areas which demand strong and fiery views. I mince few words in showing my true colours and my leopard's spots. I shun the pseudo-democratization of knowledge, especially prevalent in Europe, the idea that all views are equally fine. But my assurance does not demand absolutism; it demands that I share my finding and express my views with genu-ine humility. I acknowledge that I might be one step behind, not one step ahead. A man must go his own way, or he is nothing.

It is condescending to write as if the reader does not know that for any viewpoint held there is a dissenting opinion. The last thing I intend to do is sell you short, or patronize you. It is your intelli-gence, openness, and sincerity as readers that I trust more than the so-called expertise of the Gatekeepers.

Visit your local bar, tavern, or pub, any fitness centre, or beauty salon. Grief, loss, death, and sorrow slide naturally into the chit-chat because the media is following some latest tragedy, or because a lingering horror plagues the global community, the nation, or the local neighbourhood. The common person tries to make sense out of it in terms of what she saw yesterday on Oprah concerning sexually transmitted diseases, or heard when Dr. Phil was pontificating about divorce. One guy is bragging about the way George Clooney's performance in *Syriana* reveals the horror of the politics of oil. A grandmother mentions pictures of Madonna with her adopted 13-month-old Malawian infant, shown in the popular magazine, *People*. She expresses her own ideas about helping underprivileged and orphaned children. A big fan of U2 reminds us that Bono met recently with one more political group to discuss world peace and the eradication of poverty. If you toss into the conversation what Sigmund Freud or Maria Trozzi say about alleviating the pain of loss, the others will listen to you, respectfully. The kibitzing and the back-and-forth jostling of the dialogue include logical arguments, cracking jokes, and telling stories. It's the way of the world. It is how people tick. One woman says, "You have to experience the pain of divorce for yourself." The fellow answers, "I've been there, done that ... had custody and access battles, the whole nine yards." Over a glass of wine or two, a man and a woman who just met, wile away an hour or two talking about heartache and the respective persons they are trying ... to forget. Then negotiating how—or if—to say "good night", one or the other asks, jokingly, "Where are we going, to your place or mine?" It is ordinary life.

When it comes to the variation on the "blues", the common people get their ideas across in various ways. They surely give no more weight to clinical academics than they do to Janis Joplin, Snoop Dog, Faith Hill, 50 Cent, *The Simpsons*, B.B. King, or Gatemouth Brown. And make no bones about it: the weight is equal.

Vitality

This book, like Life, must come to an end. Like Life, its end leaves so much still unfinished. Deliberately and by design, I have been excessively personal throughout the work, offering an alternative to our de-personalized behavioural technology. I desire to present a psychological ... psychology, warm, passionate, and tender. I leave it dangling whether I am like some individuals who, when it has come down to the last breath, do not want it to end or like others who think it is finally ... time.

What matters is the in-between. Have I evoked sufficiently and vividly many, if not all, of sorrow's profiles? Did I provoke you to think about matters that concern us all? I will have succeeded, not because you agree or disagree with me, but because you have been touched by my words, dug deep into your own life experiences and feelings, crawled into your own library, and—in this living "moment"—have chiseled out for yourself conceptual clarity about key issues.

I hope that I have helped you to light a fire. To underscore the essence of my own fire, I leave these ideas glowing: dying is not a crime and sorrowing is not psychopathological. To live through a grief episode authentically, or to research the phenomenon, one must be a rebel who eschews the dominant idea-frames of our times. Death is the first word in the text of this book; the last word is vitality.

ENDNOTES

1. "Moment" differs 180 degrees from any abstract theoretical concept, construct, and model. Living, immediate, concrete and specific, it is woven beautifully with individuality and uniqueness, with decision and choice, with hope and anticipation, with "inwardness", and with the "leap" which creates change, transition, metamorphosis, and personal transformation. It is a "psychological" psychological concept, not a technical, mechanical or behavioural one.

   "One-in-a-row" is an allied key notion. It signifies also uniqueness and an incapability of being replaced. "Once only" is a third phrase of the same ilk. Unlike mainstream psychology, stuck in the 19th century, contemporary physicists thoroughly understand that often they experiment with an event that never will happen again.

2. I have only been privileged listener to one deathbed confession. Although I try to show in this book that sometimes one story is enough to generate relevant, down-to-earth knowledge, the phenomenon of confessing while dying-- like experiences such as the adolescent first kiss, the blush, the caress, the hickey, etc. (Alapack, 2007, pp. 183–187), require many variations. Therefore, I have gathered written descriptive data on the topic from three Christian priests and one Roman Catholic deacon. I used the following item.

"What you think roots a deathbed confession. What is going on? How you understand the need to confess?"

Preliminary results reveal a range of motivational spurs for the revelations and intimate disclosures. 1) The awareness of one's imminent demise, announced by severe illness, pain and suffering; 2) Heightened existential sensitivity about one's death, occasioned by residing in the hospital environment or nursing home and surrounded by other apparently dying people; 3) The wish to reconcile with family members before death; 4) The words of close friends, relatives, caregivers, and ministers, expressing their belief in God's unconditional love, and their deed of willingly sharing the 'final journey' with dying.

Themes of the confession itself are actions, or failure to act, that have provoked guilt or shame. Attuned to death's nearness, individuals break the enclosing reserve of silence and secrecy. In the face of looming death, fear subsides and they open up to guarantee that at least a 'right' or 'special' other will 'really' know them. Nobody wants to die a 'stranger'.

3. In this book, I borrow a slew of ideas from seminal and decisive thinkers, but do not cater to the standard mainstream demand to use current theories, models, or published research in order to cradle my evidence. From my standpoint, the role of theory is merely to orient one's study, inspire thought, and offer something to dialogue with. But in the quest for knowledge, theories are not necessary. They surely are not the sine qua non of meaningful searching. They most surely do not guarantee adequate support for your efforts. Moreover, you never need a theory to back up a knowledge-claim for which you can point to evidence in the lifeworld. Indeed, because theory is typically glued to some ideology, it fits most snugly in a project that is trying to verify some idea, plan, or proposal. It often hinders research aimed at discovering something brand new.

It is similar with method. The culture is obsessed with method. The original Greek meaning of meta-hodos is "in quest of a 'way' or a road." To get somewhere, to travel, to negotiate an intellectual journey, we must take steps. But method should not be reduced to a recipe, to a map, or even to a series of processes and procedures. Each and every time we embark, we can find a new, different and perhaps better 'way'.

Neither do I cater to the pragmatic nerve of mainstream psychology, the incessant presentation of strategies and preoccupation with outcomes and evidence-based solutions. Instead, I present verbal pictures of predicaments, situations, phenomena, and relationships which aim to engage the intelligence and fire the imagination so that the reader might glean solutions appropriate to her/his situation. My work, therefore, is existentially practical, not money-saving pragmatic.

4. The Wild Boy of Averyon, the Indian Wolf Girl, the Bear Boy of Lithuania, the Wild Girl of Champagne, Memmie LeBlanc, and Wild Peter are just a few well-known cases. After having been found in the wild or freed from their confinement, they eventually came into human care. Jean-Marc Gaspard Itard at the end of the 18th century expended Herculean efforts to educate and socialize the wild child. Although during "five years of devoted and ingenious tutelage" "Viktor" learned language, mastered symbolization, showed the capacity for affection, gratitude, and empathy, and even exhibited a sense of justice, he never reached the level of a normal fully functioning human being. In Itard's (1962) report to the French Minister of the Interior, he laments of robbing his young charge of the capacity to ever survive again in the wild, without succeeding in his attempt at enculturation.

Kingsley Davis presents the second body of convincing evidence. He summarizes the educative attempts to bring up two extremely isolated young girls. Anna, the daughter of a mentally impaired woman, was found in 1938 at age five years hidden away in an attic in Pennsylvania. She was in a state of severe sensory and social deprivation, having been fed only enough milk to keep her alive. After four years of intensive quality care, she died, having only learned to walk, speak a few phrases, and care for her basic needs (Davis, 1993).

Isabelle was found also in 1938 in Ohio at the age of six. She was severely retarded physically and intellectually, fearful of strangers, and violently reactive towards men. The outcome of a systematic and skillful training program by doctors and psychologists was astonishingly successful. Isabelle covered in two years the stages of learning that ordinarily requires six. She recaptured the lost years of her early life and reached normal developmental levels by the time she was eight-and-a-half years old. Eventually, she participated in all normal school activities with her peers (Davis, 1949).

What authorized Isabelle's amazing progress? Although secluded, Isabelle experienced ongoing, intimate contact with her mother with whom she communicated through a personal system of gestures. With the advantage of the maternal bond, she was able to negotiate rapidly and remarkably through the intense socialization process which the environmental specialists structured for her.

5. This story I have known and told over the course of decades. I have not found it written anywhere. My research skills with Google and beyond have not unearthed it.

6. Andy Russell, a participant-subject for my doctoral research, told me this story about Bobby Lane.

7. It would be unconscionable to expose Martin Heidegger's thought without discussing his aborted term as Rector in Hitler's Third Reich. The darkness of nihilism truly descended into his life. Swayed by Hitler's hands and voice, he "fell". During 1933–34, he served as Rector of the university of Freiburg-in-Breslau. Later he writes, "The dreadful has already happened," a poetic line supposedly not to be construed as personal. Subsequently, he spent his entire life haunted with ripples of reminders of his fateful choice. Until his 86th year, his pursuit of one star, Being, and his meditation upon the *Seinsfarge* took place under the shadow of the swastika he had worn on his arm. Friends and foes alike begged him to explain the choice to become an important Nazi official, and especially pleaded with him to speak about the horror of the Holocaust. He chose silence. He never did more than offer lame excuses. He said he wanted to checkmate Nazi "politicized science" and thus save the university from the crass Nazi thugs who had destroyed Hitler's revolution. About Auschwitz and Dachau, he said ... nothing. He made three public statements: wrote a mandatory letter in 1945 to the de-Nazification Committee; gave in1966 an interview to the periodical, *Die Spiegel* that he requested remain unpublished until after his death; and did a 1969 TV interview with Richard Wisser. At kindest reading, his utterances are classic examples of parading ambiguity and making it more ambiguous. Less generously addressed, they are riddled with equivocations, half-truths, and lies. He seems to be lying even when telling the truth. In the words of the American philosopher, Richard Rorty, Heidegger was "a coward, a liar, and the greatest philosopher of the 20th century". He shows himself to be sly as a fox, slippery as an eel ... a peasant, a poet, a thinker in destitute times. However, John Sallis is right. We think philosophically now only as echoes after Heidegger—or we blather and babble and don't think philosophically at all. Reiner Schumann is also right. Not Heidegger, the flawed and fragile failed human being, but what concerns us is what we *find* IN Heidegger. The great challenge for us is not just to wonder how this could happen; it is to confront the racist and fascist in self.

8. Can you even imagine it today? The USA has never owned the crimes it committed in Dresden, Hiroshima, Nagasaki, Cambodia,

Vietnam, Nicaragua, and so forth. It resorts instead to high moral ground to justify aggression.

9. Other reasons include the dawning awareness of the ethnic minority warriors that they were shooting the wrong enemy. The Vietnamese freedom fighters were battling the same oppression, subjugation, exploitation, and ravaging to which they—as blacks, Chicanos and native Indians—had been exposed under the USA government (Capps, W. 1991; Neal, J. 2003).

10. This chapter splices together and re-gestalts the attempts I have made over time to express the horror of the Exxon Valdez: Alapack, R.J. (1991). Malignant currency: The psychosocial aftershocks of the Exxon Valdez oil hemorrhage in the lived world of Seward. In C.M. Aanstoos (Ed.), *Studies in Humanistic Psychology* (pp. 134–152). Carrollton, GA: West Georgia Studies in the Social Sciences; Alapack, R.J. (1990). Tore down in Seward: A preliminary report on a phenomenologically-oriented study of Alaska's colossal oil catastrophe. *The 9th International Human Science Research Conference*, Quebec City, Quebec, 9–13 June. Alapack, R.J. (2000). Putting out the dark: The Exxon Valdez oil catastrophe a concrete metaphor of man-made disasters. *The 2nd Conference of Social and Community Psychology*, Norwegian University of Science and Technology, Trondheim, Norway, 16–17 November.

11. Concerning the black death of mammals and birds, a "notice of lodging of summary of effects" was filed at the United States District Court, District of Alaska on April 8, 1991, by the U.S. Department of Justice, Environmental Section. The comprehensive scientific evidence of mortality rates and estimates of future casualities demonstrates the lethality of the Exxon Valdez. Excerpts from this document follow:

> During 1989, a total of 1,011 sea otters' carcasses were recovered in the spill area ... The total number of sea otters estimated to have been killed directly by the spill ranges from 3,500 to 5,500 animals ... Two hundred harbor seals are estimated to have been killed ... One hundred and forty-four (144) dead bald eagles were found following the spill ... More than 2,000 sea duck carcasses were recovered ... including more than 200 harlequin ducks ... It is estimated that between 1,500 and 3,000 pigeon guillemots were killed ... Approximately 36,000 dead birds were recovered after the spill; at least 31,000 of these were attributed to the effects of oil ... No massive die-offs of adult

salmon, for example, were able to migrate to spawning areas after it. However, fish are the most vulnerable to oil contamination during the early stages of their life cycles. During 1991, scientists will begin to be able to assess affects on adult fish ... that would have been exposed to oil as eggs or larvae ... The full extend of the short term injury to pink salmon cannot be assessed until after the 1991 run returns to spawn in the summer ... Whether the adult population (of Pacific herring) has been affected by ... larval injuries will not be determined until the 1989 and 1990 cohorts return to spawn in 1992 and 1993 (Nicoll, 1991, pp. 6ff).

12. It suits to describe this symbiosis: a) between 1969 and 1987 the State of Alaska's oil related income totaled $29 billion, or 80% of its total income; b) in that same period $400 million was distributed to Alaskan residents; c) $800 per year is the average amount given to each resident from a trust established by the oil consortium, the "Permanent Dividend Found" which Alaskans fiercely want politicians to safeguard; d) there is no State income tax or State sales tax; and e) the Exxon Valdez created thousands of jobs in 1989, boosting the employment rate by 6.2 percent, and propelling Alaska out of a three year-old recession.

13. During the optimistic heyday of the 19th century, while the culture believed that the natural scientific method was the magical tool to boundless progress, the gas lamp replaced the candle and revolutionized the social order. Simultaneously, "Gas poisoning soon became a standard method of committing suicide." Wolfgang Schivelbusch, *Disenchanted night: The industrialization of light in the nineteenth century*, trans. Angela Davies (London: The University of California Press, 1995), 39.

14. The self-portrait hanging in the National Art Galley in Oslo, Norway is especially striking, especially since it is not surrounded by a cluster of Vincent's paintings.

15. This chapter draws from my following attempts to replace revenge with mercy: Alapack, R.J. (2005a). Mercy and revenge: Fundamental themes in Dostoevsky, Nietzsche and Gandhi. *Psykologisk Tidsskrift*, 1: 67–70; Alapack, R.J (2002). In: Nietzsche: Revenge, love and mercy. *The 21st International Human Science Research Conference*, Victoria, B.C. Canada, 19–22 June; Alapack, R.J. (2001a). Nietzsche and revenge: The death of psychology in the wake of the terrorist attacks

on the United States. *Psykologisk Tidsskrift*, 4: 24–31; Alapack, R.J. (2004). The Face of Mercy: A hermeneutic of Dostoevsky, Nietzsche and Gandhi. *The Sixth Conference on Social Community Psychology*, NTNU Trondheim, Norway, 8–9 November; Alapack, R.J. (2006a). Hope and mercy: Healing familial and geo-social-political Revenge *The XVth International Family Therapy Association World Congress*, Reykjavik, Iceland, 5 October.

16. The phrase is a Roman proverb from Asinaria of Plautus (dead 184 B.C.). Thomas Hobbes etched it in stone in "De cive, Epistola dedicatoria". Josef de Maistre, an arch counter-revolutionary to the French Revolt of 1789, an authoritarian conservative who wanted to restore the monarchy, not accidentally gives a vivid expression of this belief. De Maisttre gives a simple, solid, and clear preference for the reactionary violence so prominent on today's political landscape, the domination and oppression of the masses by the state's military. One of his statements, propaedeutic to fascism, goes:

Man's destructive hand spares nothing that lives; he kills to feed himself, he kills to clothe himself, he kills to adorn himself, he kills to attack, he kills to defend himself, he kills to instruct himself, he kills to amuse himself, he kills for the sake of killing. Proud and terrible king, he wants everything and nothing resists him ... from the lamb he tears its guts and makes his harp resound ... from the wolf his most deadly tooth to polish his pretty works of art; from the elephant his tusks to make a toy for his child—his table is covered with corpses ... And who [in this general carnage] will exterminate him who exterminates all others? Himself. It is man who is charged with the slaughter of man ... So it is accomplished ... the great law of the violent destruction of living creatures. The whole earth, perpetually steeped in blood, is nothing but a vast altar upon which all that is living must be sacrificed without end, without measure, without pause, until the consummation of things, until evil is extinct, until the death of death.

Thomas Hobbes' *Leviathan*, also totally relevant for our contemporary situation, is concerned with demonstrating the necessity of a strong central authority to short-circuit civil disobedience, discord, civil war, or revolution. He legitimizes any abuses of power by authority as the price of peace. For the common good, the sovereign must control all civil, military, judicial, and ecclesiastical powers. Hobbes never says, of course, that it is only the few elite, not the many commoners, who benefit from the use of total sovereign power.

17. I simply asked subjects to "Please describe your most significant bout of regret."

18. This collection includes twenty chapters that touch upon the matter of the health or pathology of "hanging on" rather than ceasing to sorrow.

REFERENCES

Adams, D. (1989). The Seville Statement on Violence and why it is important. *Journal of Humanistic Psychology*, 29: 333–336.

Alapack, R.J. (1972). The Phenomenology of the Natural Athlete. *Dissertations Abstracts International* (University Microfilms, No. 73–14, 580).

Alapack, R.J. (1986). Death and psychoanalytic praxis: The convergence between Jacques Lacan and depth phenomenology. *The Humanistic Psychologist*, 14: 169–175.

Alapack, R.J. (1988a). No life to spare: A scientific phenomenological study of being on parole. *American Psychological Association*, Division 32, Atlanta, GA, August.

Alapack, R.J. (1988b). Home free: A human scientific study of release from prison. *The Seventh International Human Science Research Conference*, Seattle, WA, June.

Alapack, R.J. (1990). Tore down in Seward: A preliminary report on a phenomenologically-oriented study of Alaska's colossal oil catastrophe. *The 9th International Human Science Research Conference*, Quebec City, Quebec, June.

Alapack, R.J. (1991). Malignant currency: The psychosocial aftershocks of the Exxon Valdez oil hemorrhage in the lived world of Seward.

In C.M. Aanstoos (Ed.), *Studies in Humanistic Psychology* (pp. 134–152). Carrollton, GA: West Georgia Studies in the Social Sciences.

Alapack, R.J. (1997). Technology and the body: Vanishing hickeys and the waning of adolescence. *The Sixteenth International Human Science Research Conference,* Trondheim, Norway, August.

Alapack, R.J. (2000). Putting out the dark: The Exxon Valdez oil catastrophe a concrete metaphor of manmade disasters. *The 2nd Conference of Social and Community Psychology,* Norwegian University of Science and Technology, Trondheim, Norway, 16–17 November.

Alapack, R.J. (2001a). Nietzsche and revenge: The death of psychology in the wake of the terrorist attacks on the United States. *Psykologisk Tidsskrift,* 4: 24–31.

Alapack, R.J. (2001b). When Nana died: An existential narrative of the first talk with your child about death. *Psykologisk Tidsskrift,* 1: 50–54.

Alapack, R.J. (2002). In Nietzsche: Revenge, love and mercy. *The 21st International Human Science Research Conference,* Victoria, B.C. Canada, August.

Alapack, R.J. (2004a). About one's mom: Vigilance for life on a death watch, presented to the *International Congress of Family Psychotherapy,* Istanbul, Turkey.

Alapack, R.J. (2004b). The face of mercy: A hermeneutic of Dostoevsky, Nietzsche and Gandhi. *The Sixth Conference on Social Community Psychology,* NTNU Trondheim, Norway, November.

Alapack, R.J. (2005a). Mercy and revenge: Fundamental themes in Dostoevsky, Nietzsche and Gandhi. *Psykologisk Tidsskrift,* 1: 67–70.

Alapack, R.J. (2005b). The First Talk with Your Child about Death: An Existential Narrative. *The Seventh Conference on Social-Community Psychology,* NTNU Trondheim, Norway, October 11.

Alapack, R.J. (2006a). Hope and mercy: Healing individual, familial and geo-social-political revenge. *The XVth International Family Therapy Association World Congress,* Reykjavik, Iceland, 5 October.

Alapack, R.J. (2006b). Albert Camus on murder: An existential therapeutic dialogue, "Can YOU kill?" *Psykologisk Tidsskrift,* 3: 58–63.

Alapack, R.J. (2007a). *Love's Pivotal Relationships: The Chum, First Love, Outlaw, and the Intimate Partner.* Central Milton Keynes: AuthorHouse.

Alapack, R.J. (2007b). Simulation in cyberspace and touch of the flesh: Kissing, the blush, the hickey, and the caress. *Journal of Psychosocial Research in Cyberspace,* 1: 1–11.

Alapack, R.J. (2007c). Who is my neighbor? Kierkegaard, Nietzsche and Levinas on racism, *Psykologisk Tidsskrift*, 1: 49–53.

Alapack, R.J. (2008). Stranger at the wake: A drama of grief and longing. *Psykologisk Tidsskrift*, 3: 9–14.

Alapack, R.J., Blichfeldt M.F. and Elden Å. (2005). Flirting on the Internet and the hickey: A Hermeneutic. *CyberPsychology and Behavior*, 8: 52–61.

Allen, N. (1975). *Lies my Father Told Me*. Scarborough, Ontario: Signet.

Alley, R. (1973). *Last Tango in Paris*. New York: A Dell Book.

Aquinas, T. (1272). *Summa Theologica, Vol. II*. L. Shapcote (Trans.). Chicago: Chicago University Press, 1990.

Artaud, A. (1956). Van Gogh: The man suicided by society. In: J. Hirschman (Ed.) *Antonin Artaud: Anthology* (pp. 135–163). San Francisco: City Lights Books. 1965. [Copyright Gallimard Editions].

Auden, W.H. (1991). "For the time being: A Christmas oratorio". In Edward Mendelson (Ed.), *W.H. Auden: Collected Poems* (pp. 347–400). New York: Vintage International.

Bachelard, G. (1958). *The Poetics of Space*. M. Jolas (Trans.). [Reprinted Boston: Beacon Press, 1969.]

Barks, C. (1995). Commentary. In: Jelaluddin Balkhi al-din Rumi, *The Essential Rumi*. C. Bark (Trans.). New York: HarperCollins, 65.

BBC News. (14 November 2009). Black Sea faces oil catastrophe. http://news.bbc.co.uk/hi/europe/7092071.stm

Berne, E. (1967). *Games People Play*. New York: Grove Press.

Bettelheim, B. (1983). *Freud and Man's Soul*. New York: Alfred A. Knopf.

Black, R. (19 December, 2003). Exxon Valdez spill still a danger. http://news.bbc.co.uk/2/hi/americas/3333369.stm

Booth, G. (1962). Disease as message. *Journal of Religion and Health*, 1: 309–318.

Braddock, B. and Claude Putman, Jr. "He stopped loving her today" [George Jones]. On *Songs I want to sing* [CD]. CBS Records, Inc, 1990.

Brown, N.O. (1988). *Life against Death: The Psychoanalytical Meaning of History* (2nd ed.) Christopher Lasch (Intro.). Middletown, Connecticut: Wesleyan University Press.

Browning, S. (2003). *Feathers Bush my Heart: True Stories of Mothers Connecting with their Daughters after Death*. New York: WarnerBook.

Camus, A. (1948). *The Plague*. S. Gilbert (Trans.). New York: Vintage International, 1991.

Camus, A. (1954). *The Rebel: An Essay on Man and Revolt*. New York: Vintage Books, 1956.

Camus, A. (1957). *L' Etranger*, Paris: Gallimard.

Capps, W. (1991). Introduction. In: W. Capps (Ed.), *The Vietnam Reader* (pp. 1–12). London: Routledge, Chapman and Hall.

Chessman, C. (2006). *Cell 2455, Death Row: A Condemned Man's Own Story*. New York: Carroll and Graf.

Colaizzi, P. (1978). *Technology and Dwelling: The Secrets of Life and Death*. Library of Congress Card # 78–56749.

Cornelissen, R. Hummingbird. *Unpublished manuscript*. Argosy University, San Bernardino, California.

Davidson, A. (1990). *In the Wake of the Exxon Valdez: The Devastating Impact of the Alaskan Oil Spill*. San Francisco: Sierra Club Books.

Davis, K. (1947). A final note on a case of extreme isolation. *American Journal of Sociology*, 52: 432–447.

Davis, K. (1949). *Human society*. New York Macmillan Co.

Dawson, C. (1952). *Understanding Europe*. New York: Image Books, 1960.

De Beauvoir, S. (1964). *A Very Easy Death*. P. O' Brian (Trans.). [Reprinted New York: Pantheon Books 1965.]

De Chardin, T. (1961). *The Phenomenon of Man*. New York: Harper and Row.

De Leeuw, R. (Ed.) (1997). *The Letters of Vincent van Gogh*. A. Pomerans (Trans.). London: Penguin Books.

Demske, J.M. (1970). *Being, Man & Death: A Key to Heidegger*. Lexington, Kentucky: The University of Kentucky Press.

Derrida J. (1987). *The Post Card: From Socrates to Freud and beyond*, A. Bass (Trans.). Chicago: The University of Chicago Press.

Dickinson, E. (1924). *The Collected Poems of Emily Dickinson*. New York: Barnes & Noble Books, 1993.

Dostoevsky, F. (1864). *Notes from the Underground; The Grand Inquisitor*. R. Matlaw (Intro. and Trans.). [Reprinted New York: E.P. Dutton. 1960.]

Durkheim, E. (1897). *Suicide: A Study in Sociology*. New York: Simon & Schuster, 1979.

Egoyan, A. (Director). (1994). *Exotica* [DVD]. Miramax Films & Alliance Communications Corporation.

Einstein, A. and Freud, S. (1933). Why War? In: S. Gilbert (Trans.) *An International Series of Open Letters. Vol. II*. Paris: International Institute of Intellectual Cooperation.

Eliot, T.S. (1936a). Ash Wednesday. In: *Four Quartets, Collected Poems 1909–1962* (pp. 93–104). London: Faber and Faber, 1963.

Eliot, T.S. (1936b). Burnt Norton. In: *Four Quartets, Collected Poems 1909–1962* (pp. 189–195). [Reprinted London: Faber and Faber, 1963.]

Eliot, T.S. (1936c). Dry Salvages. In: *The Four Quartets, Collected Poems 1909–1962* (pp. 205–213). [Reprinted London: Faber and Faber, 1963.]

Eliot, T.S. (1936d). East Coker. In: *The Four Quartets, Collected Poems 1909–1962* (pp. 196–204). [Reprinted London: Faber and Faber, 1963.]

Eliot, T.S. (1936e). Little Gidding. In: *The Four Quartets, Collected Poems 1909–1962* (pp. 196–204). [Reprinted London: Faber and Faber, 1963.]

Eliot, T.S. (1936f). The love song of J. Alfred Prufrock. In: *The Four Quartets, Collected Poems 1909–1962* (pp. 13–17) [Reprinted London: Faber and Faber, 1963.]

Elkin, H. (1966). Love and violence: A psychoanalytic viewpoint, *Humanitas: Journal of the Institute of man. II*: 168–169.

Elkin, H. (1972). On selfhood and the development of ego structures in infancy. *The Psychoanalytic Review*, 59: 389–416.

Erikson, E. (1959). *Identity and the Life Cycle*. New York: International Universities Press.

Erikson, E. (1969). *Gandhi's Truth: On the Origins of Militant Nonviolence*. New York: W.W. Norton.

Fairbairn, R. (1952). The repression and the return of the bad objects (pp. 59–81). In *Psychoanalytic Studies of the Personality*. London: Tavistock.

Faulkner, W. (1987). *As I Lay Dying*. New York: Vintage Books.

Fitzgerald, F.S. (1934). *Tender is the Night*. [Reprinted New York: Simon & Schuster, 1995.]

Foucault, M. (1973). *Discipline and Punish*. A. Sheridan (Trans.). [Reprinted New York: Vintage Books, 1979.]

Francis, D., Kellaher, L. and Naophytou, G. (2005). *The secret cemetery*. Oxford: Berg Publishers.

Freud, S. (1899a). Screen Memories. S. E., 3: 301{–}322. London: London: Hogarth, 1962 [Reprinted 1978].

Freud, S. (1915b). 'Thoughts for the Times on War and Death'. S. E., 14: 273{–}302. London: Hogarth, 1957, reprinted 1978.

Freud, S. (1917e [1915]). 'Mourning and melancholia'. S. E., 14: 237{–}258. London: Hogarth, 1957 [Reprinted 1978].

Freud, S. (1919h). 'The "Uncanny"'. S. E. 17: 217{–}256. London: London: Hogarth, 1955 [Reprinted 1975].

Freud, S. (1920g). *Beyond the Pleasure Principle*. S. E., 18: 7{–}64. London: Hogarth, 1955 [Reprinted 1975].

Freud, S. (1921c). *Group Psychology and the Analysis of the Ego*. S. E., 18: 67{–}147. London: Hogarth, 1955 [Reprinted 1975].

Freud, A. (1936). *Ego and the Mechanisms of Defense*. New York: International Universities Press.

Freud, S. (1985). *The Complete Letters to Wilhelm Fliess, 1887–1904*. J.M. Masson (Trans.). Cambridge, MA: Harvard University Press.

Frost, R. (1914a). Death of a Hired Hand. In: Edward Connery (Ed.) *The Poetry of Robert Frost: The Collected poems, Complete and Unabridged*. Lathem, [Reprinted New York: Henry Holt, 1979.]

Frost, R. (1914b). Home Burial. In: Edward Connery (Ed.) *The Poetry of Robert Frost: The Collected poems, Complete and Unabridged*. Lathem, New York: [Reprinted Henry Holt, 1979.]

Gandhi, M. (1970). *Non-Violent Resistance: Satyagraha (Clinging to the Truth)*. New York: Chicken Books.

Gilbert, L. (1965). (Dir.) *Alfie*. Paramount Pictures, Sheldrake Films.

Giorgi, A. (1970). *Psychology as a Human Science*. New York: Harper & Row.

Giorgi, A. (1997). Humanistic psychology and the humanism of Karl Jasper, *The Humanistic Psychologist*, 25, 1: 15–29.

Giorgi, A. (2009). *The Descriptive Phenomenological Method in Psychology: A Modified Husserlian Approach*. Pittsburgh: Duquesne University Press.

Gist, R. (1989). Normal responses to an abnormal situation, *Risk Management*, 3: 13–59.

Gordon, D.C. (1972). *Overcoming the Fear of Death*. Baltimore, MD: Penguin Books.

Griffin, G.E. (1974). *A World without Cancer*. [Reprinted Westlake Village, CA: American Media, 2003.]

Grollman, E.A. (1976). *Talking about Death: A Dialogue between Parent and Child*. Boston: Beacon Press.

Gross, D.C. and Gross, E.R. (Eds) (1993). *Jewish Wisdom: A Treasury of Proverbs, Maxims, Aphorisms, Wise Sayings, Memorable Quotations*. New York: Dawcett Crest.

Guardini, R. (1997). *The Essential Guardini*. Heinz R. Kuehn (Intro.). Chicago: Liturgy Training Publications.

Haines, J. (1989). Ice. In: R. Hedin and G. Holthaus (Eds). *Alaska Reflections on Land and Spirit*. Tucson: The University of Arizona Press.

Hammarskjold, D. (1963). *Markings.* Leif Sjoberg and W.H. Auden (Trans.). [Reprinted New York: Alfred A. Knopf, 1970.]

Hedayat, S. (1957). *The Blind Owl.* D.P. Costello (Trans.). [Reprinted Edinburgh, Scotland: Rebel, Inc. 1997.]

Heidegger, M. (1927). *Being and Time.* J. Macquarrie and E. Robinson (Trans.) [Reprinted New York: Harper & Row, 1962.]

Heidegger, M. (1946). What are poets for? In: A. Hofstadter (Trans. and Intro.). *Poetry, Language, Thought* (pp. 91–142). [Reprinted New York: Harper Colophon, 1971c.]

Heidegger, M. (1947). Letters on humanism. In: D.F. Krell (Ed.). *Martin Heidegger: Basic writings* (pp. 217–265). [Reprinted New York: HarperCollins, 1993.]

Heidegger, M. (1950). The origin of the work of art. In: A. Hofstadter (Trans.). *Poetry, language, thought* (pp. 15–88). [Reprinted New York: Harper Colophon, 1971a.]

Heidegger, M. (1952). Building dwelling thinking. In: A. Hofstadter (Trans. and Intro.). *Poetry, Language, Thought* (pp. 143–162). [Reprinted New York: Harper Colophon, 1971b.]

Heidegger, M. (1953). *An Introduction to Metaphysics.* Ralph Manheim (Trans). [Reprinted London: Yale University Press, 1959.]

Heidegger, M. (1954a). *What is Called Thinking?* J. Glenn Gray (Trans.). [Reprinted New York: Harper, Row Publishers, 1968.]

Heidegger, M. (1954b). Who is Nietzsche's Zarathustra? In *Nietzsche Vol. I, Part Two.* (pp. 211–233). [Reprinted San Francisco: HarperSanFrancisco, 1991.]

Heidegger, M. (1961). The concept of "chaos". In: D.F. Krell (Ed.). *Nietzsche Vol. III* (pp. 77–83). [Reprinted San Francisco: HarperSanFrancisco, 1991.]

Heidegger, M. (1962). The turning. K.R. Maly (Trans.). *Research in Phenomenology,* 1: 3–169; 1971c.

Heidegger, M. (1969). The end of philosophy and the task of thinking. In: D.F. Krell (Ed.). *Martin Heidegger: Basic Writings* (pp. 431–449). [Reprinted San Francisco: HarperSanFrancisco, 1993.]

Heegaard, M.E. (1988). *When Someone Very Special Dies: Children Can Learn to Cope with Grief.* Minneapolis, MN: Woodland Press.

Heider, F. (1958). *The Psychology of Interpersonal Relations.* New York: John Wiley & Sons.

Holst-Warhaft, G. (2000). *The Cue for Passion: Grief and its Political Use.* Cambridge, MA: Harvard University Press.

Horwitz, A.V. and Wakefield, J.C. (2007). *The Loss of Sadness: How Psychiatry Transformed Normal Sorrow into Depressive Disorder.* New York: Oxford University Press.

Hosseini, K. (2004). *The Kite Runner.* London: Bloomsbury.

Hurston, Z.N. (1998). *Their Eyes Were Watching God.* New York: Perennial Classics.

Husserl, E. (1929). *The Idea of Phenomenology.* W.P. Alston and G. Hakhnikian (Trans.). [Reprinted The Hague: Martinus Nijhoff, 1974.]

Isaacs, R.H. and Olidzky, K.M. (1991). *A Jewish Mourners Handbook.* Hoboken, NJ: KTAV Publishing House.

Ishiguro, K. (1989). *The Remains of the Day.* New York: Vintage International.

Itard, J.M.G. (1962). *The Wild Boy of Aveyron.* Englewood Cliffs, NJ: Prentice-Hall.

Jackson, E.N. (1983). *Telling a Child about Death.* New York: Hawthorn/Dutton.

Johnson, J. (1999). *Keys to Helping Children Deal with Death and Grief.* New York: Barron's Publishing.

Jung, C.G. (1953) [1966]. Phenomena resulting from the assimilation of the unconscious. In: C.G. Jung, *Two Essays on Analytical Psychology* C.W., 7 (pp. 139–162). R.F.C. Hull (Trans.). London: Routledge & Kegan Paul.

Jung, C.G. (1954). Marriage as a psychological relationship. In: C.G. Jung. [1910–1946]. *The Development of the Personality,* C.W., 17 (pp. 189–201), R.F.C. Hull (Trans.). London: Routledge & Kegan Paul.

Jung, C.G. (1966). *Two Essays on Analytical Psychology* (2nd ed.). R.F.C. Hull (Trans.). [Reprinted Princeton, New Jersey: Princeton University Press.]

Jung, C.G. (1974). Marriage as a psychological relationship. In: J. Campbell (Ed.), *The Portable Jung* (pp. 163–177). New York: The Viking Press.

Kant, I. (1949). *Fundamental Principles of the Metaphysics of Morals,* T.K. Abbott (Trans.). Indianapolis: Bobbs-Merrill.

Kesey, K. (1980). *One Flew over the Cuckoos' Nest.* New York: Penguin Group.

Kevorkian, J. (1993). *Prescription Medicide: The goodness of a planned death.* Amherst, New York: Prometheus.

Kierkegaard, S. (1843a). *Fear and Trembling and* (1849). *Sickness unto Death.* W. Lowrie (Trans.). [Reprinted Princeton, NJ: Princeton University Press, 1974.]

Kierkegaard, S. (1843b). The ancient tragical motif as reflected in the modern. In: *Either/Or, Vol. I.* (pp. 229–277). D.F. Swenson and L.M. Swenson (Trans.). [Reprinted Princeton, NJ; Princeton University Press, 1971.]

Kierkegaard, S. (1846). *Concluding Unscientific Postscript,* D.F. Swenson and W. Lowrie (Trans.). [Reprinted Princeton, NJ: Princeton University Press, 1974.]

Kierkegaard, S. (1847). *Works of Love.* H. Hong and E. Hong (Trans.). [Reprinted New York: Harper Torchbooks, 1962.]

King, H. (Dir.). (1950). *Love is a Many-Splendored Thing.* 20th Century Fox, 2003.

Klass, D., Silverman, P.R. and Nickman, S. (1996). (Eds). *Continuing Bonds: New Understanding of Grief.* New York: Taylor and Francis.

Klein, M. (1975). *Love, Guilt and Reparation and Other Works: 1921–1945.* London: Delacorte Press/Seymour Lawrence.

Knizek, B.L. and Hjelmeland, H. (2007). A theoretical model for interpreting suicidal behaviour as communication, *Theory & Psychology,* 17, 5: 697–720.

Krog, A. (1998). *Country of my Skull.* Johannesburg: Random House.

Kuber-Ross, E. (1970).*On Death and Dying.* New York: Macmillan.

Kugelmann, R. (1985). Stress management: A twentieth century Western disease? *The International Human Science Research Conference,* Edmonton, Canada.

Lacan, J. (1966a). The Freudian thing. In: *Ecrits: A Selection* (pp. 114–145). [Reprinted New York: W.W. Norton, 1977.]

Lacan, J. (1966b). The mirror stage. In: *Ecrits, A Selection* (pp. 1–7) New York: [Reprinted W.W. Norton, 1977.]

Lacan, J. (1966c). The function and field of speech and language in psychoanalysis. In: *Ecrits: A Selection* (pp. 30–113). Alan Sheridan (Trans.). New York: W.W. Norton, 1977.

Laing, R.D. (1959). *The Divided Self: An Existential Study of Sanity and Madness.* [Reprinted London: The Penguin Group, 1990.]

Landman, J. *Regret* (1993). *The Persistence of the Possible.* Oxford: Oxford University Press.

Lawrence, D.H. (1928). *Lady Chatterley's Lover.* [Reprinted Toronto: Bantam Books, 1983.]

Lawrence, T.E. (1926). *Seven Pillars of Wisdom.* [Reprinted New York: Dell Publishing, 1966.]

Lazear, J. (1994). *Remembrance of Mother: Words to Heal the Heart.* New York: Fireside.

Leahy, R. (2003). *Overcoming resistance in cognitive therapy*. New York: Guilford.

Leenaars, A.A. (1986). Brief note on latent content in suicide notes. *Psychological Reports*, 59: 640–642.

Leenaars, A.A. (1987). An empirical investigation of Shneidman's formulations regarding suicide: Age and sex. *Suicide and Life-Threatening Behavior*, 17: 233–250.

Leenaars, A.A. (1991). Suicide notes and their implications for intervention. *Crisis*, 12: 1–20.

Leenaars, A.A. (1992). Suicide notes of the older adult. *Suicide and Life-Threatening Behaviour*, 22, 62–79.

Leenaars, A.A. (1996). Suicide notes at symbolic ages, *Psychological Reports*, 78: 1034.

Leenaars, A.A. (1997). Suicide notes of the elderly and their implications for psychotherapy. *Clinical Gerontologist*, 17: 76–79.

Levinas, E. (1961). *Totality and Infinity*. [Reprinted Pittsburgh: Duquesne University Press, 1969.]

Lewis, C.S. (1961). *A Grief Observed*. [Reprinted Toronto: Bantam Books, 1980.]

Lifton, R.J. (1991). Home from the war. In: W. Capps, (Ed.). *The Vietnam Reader* (pp. 54–67). London: Routledge, Chapman and Hall.

Lingis, A. (1983). *Excesses: Eros and Culture*. Albany, NY: State University of New York Press.

Lingis, A. (1994). *Foreign Bodies*. New York: Routledge.

Lingis, A. (1998). *The Imperative*. Indianapolis, IN: Indiana University Press.

Lingis, A. (2000). *Dangerous Emotions*. Berkeley: University of California Press.

Lingis, A. (2005). *Body Transformation: Evolutions and Atavisms in Culture*. New York: Routledge.

Lingis, A. (2007). *The First Person Singular*. Evanston, IL: Northwestern University Press.

Lopez, B. (1987). *Arctic Dreams: Imagination and Desire in the Northern Landscape*. New York: Bantam.

Lorca, F.G. (1954). *Deep Song and Other Prose*. [Reprinted London: Marion Boyars, 1991.]

Lynch, J. (1960). *Christ and Apollo: The Dimension of the Literary Imagination*. New York: Sheed & Ward.

Lyne, A. (2002). (Dir.) *Unfaithful*. Fox 2000 Pictures and Regency Enterprises.

Malkinson, R. (2007). *Cognitive Grief Therapy*. New York: Norton.

Marin, P. (1991). Living in moral pain. In W. Capps (Ed.). *The Vietnam Reader* (pp. 40–53). New York: Routledge.

Maris, R.W., Berman, A.L. and Silverman, M.M. (2000). *The Comprehensive Textbook of Suicidology*. New York: Guliford Press.

Mayser, S., Scheibe, S. and Riediger, A. (2008). (Un)reachable? An empirical differentiation of goals and life longings, *European Psychologist*, 13: 126–149.

Meganack, W. (1989). Address to the oiled mayors of France and Alaska. In: J. O'Meara (Ed.). *Cries from the heart: Alaskans respond to the Exxon Valdez oil spill*. Homer, Alaska: Wizard Works.

Mellonie, B. and Ingpen, R (2005). *Lifetimes: The Beautiful Way to Explain Death to Children*. New York: Bantam Books.

Merleau-Ponty, M. (1960). Preface to Dr. A. Hesnard's *L'Oeuvre de Freud, et Son Importance pour le Monde Moderne* (pp. 6–7). H. Elkin and T. Doyle (Trans.).

Merleau-Ponty, M. (1964). The child's relations with others. In *The Primacy of Perception and Other Essays* (pp. 96–155). Evanston: IL: Northwestern University Press.

Merton, T. (1965) *Gandhi and the One-Eyed Giant*. In: T. Merton (Ed. and Intro.). *Gandhi: On Non-violence* (pp. 1–20). New York: New Directions.

Michell, R. (2004). (Dir.). *The Mother*. A Sony Pictures Classic Release BBC Film.

Myers, E. (1997). *When Parents Die: A Guide for Adults*. New York: Penguin Books.

Neal, J. (2003). *A People's History of the Vietnam War*. New York: The New Press.

Neimeyer, R.A. (2006). *Lesson of Loss: A Guide to Coping*. New York: Brunner-Routledge.

Nesse, R. (2007). Why we get sick. *The New Science of Darwinian Medicine*, 35: 5.

Nicoll, J.L. Jr. (1991). Summary of effects of the Exxon Valdez oil spill on natural resources and archaeological resources. Notice of Lodging of Summary of Effects: No. A91-082. [Filled at United States District Court, District of Alaska, 8 April.]

Nietzsche, F. (1881). The dawn. In: W. Kaufmann (Ed. and Trans.). *The portable Nietzsche* (pp. 76–92). [Reprinted New York: Penguin Books, 1982.]

Nietzsche, F. (1882a). Seventy-five aphorisms from five volumes. In: W. Kaufmann (Ed. and Trans.). *Basic writings of Nietzsche* (pp. 145–178). [Reprinted New York: The Modern Library, 1992.]

Nietzsche, F. (1882b). The Gay Science. In: W. Kaufmann (Ed. and Trans.). *The portable Nietzsche* (pp. 93–102). [Reprinted New York: Random House, 1974.]

Nietzsche, F. (1883a). *Thus Spoke Zarathustra*, W. Kaufmann (Preface and Trans.). [Reprinted New York: A Viking Compass Book, 1970.]

Nietzsche, F. (1883b). Thus Spoke Zarathustra. In: W. Kaufmann (Ed. and Trans). *The Portable Nietzsche* (pp. 112–439). [Reprinted New York: Penguin Books, 1982.]

Nietzsche, F. (1885). *Beyond Good and Evil.* M. Cowen (Trans. and Intro.). [Reprinted Chicago: Gateway Edition, 1955.]

Nietzsche, F. (1887). *On the Genealogy of Morals.* W. Kaufmann (Ed. and Trans.). [Reprinted New York: Vintage Books, 1969.]

Nietzsche, F. (1889). Twilight of the Idols. In: W. Kaufmann (Ed. and Trans.). *The Portable Nietzsche* (pp. 463–563). [Reprinted New York: Penguin Books, 1982.]

Nietzsche, F. (1908). Human, all-too-human. In: W. Kaufmann (Ed. and Trans.). *On the Genealogy of Morals/Ecce Homo* (pp. 283–289). [Reprinted New York: Vintage Books, 1967.]

Nordentoft, N. (1972). *Kierkegaard's Psychology.* B.H. Kirmmse (Trans.). [Reprinted Pittsburgh: Duquesne University Press, 1978.]

Panger, D. (1979). *Dance of the Wild Mouse.* Glen Ellen, CA: Entwhistle Books.

Parkes, C.M. (1996). *Bereavement: Studies of Grief in Adult Life* (3rd ed.). London: Routeledge.

Pascal, B. (1670). *Pensees,* A.J. Krailsheimer (Intro. and Trans.). [Reprinted New York: Penguin Classics, 1981.]

Patel, R. (2008). *Stuffed and Starved.* Brooklyn, New York: Melville House Publishing.

Paton, A. (1953). *Too late the Phalarope.* [Reprinted New York: Simon and Schuster, 1995.]

Piaget, J. (1952). *The Origins of Intelligence in Children,* M. Cook (Trans.). New York: International Universities Press.

Poggeler, O. (1987). *Martin Heidegger's path of thinking.* Atlantic Highlands, NJ: Humanities Press.

Raucher, H. (1971). *The Summer of '42.* New York: Dell.

Ricoeur, P. (1977). *Freud and philosophy: An essay on interpretation*. Denis Savage (Trans.). New Haven: Yale University Press.

Rosenthal, T. (1973). *How Could I Not Be Among You?* New York: Avon Books.

Rossouw, G. (2007). The limitations of dialectical behaviour therapy and psychodynamic therapies of suicidality from an existential-phenomenological perspective. *The Indo-Pacific Journal of Phenomenology* 7: 1–13.

Rowe, J.O. and Halling, S. (1989). The psychology of forgiving another: A dialogal research approach. In: R.S. Valle and S. Halling (Eds). *Existential-phenomenological perspectives in psychology: Exploring the breath of human experience* (pp. 233–244). New York: Plenum Press.

Rumi, J. al-din (1995). *The Essential Rumi*. C. Bark (Trans.). New York: HarperCollins.

Saint-Exupery, A. (1943). *The Little Prince*. K. Woods (Trans). New York: Harcourt Brace.

Sallis, J. (1990). *Echoes: After Heidegger*. Bloomington, Indiana: Indiana University Press.

Sartre, J.-P. (1943). *No Exit and Three Other Plays*. [Reprinted New York: Vintage Book, 1955.]

Sartre, J.-P. (1956). *Being and Nothingness*. Hazel Barnes (Trans.). New York: Washington Square Press.

Sartre, J.-P. (1957). *Existentialism and Human Emotions*. New York: Citadel Press.

Scheibe, S. (2005). Longing (sehnsucht) as a new lifespan concept: A developmental conceptualization and measurement in adulthood. Retrieved from http://www.diss.fu-berlin.de/2005/159. Doctoral dissertation, Free University, Berlin.

Scheler, M. (1994). *Ressentiment*. Milwaukee, WI: Marquette University Press.

Schivelbusch, W. (1995). *Disenchanted Night: The Industrialization of Light in the Nineteenth Century*, A. Davies (Trans.). London: The University of California Press.

Schopenhauer, A. (1851). *Essays and Aphorisms*, R.J. Hollingdale (Trans. and Intro.). [Reprinted London: Penguin Classics, 1970.]

Schurmann, R. (1982). *Heidegger on Being and Acting: From Principles to Anarchy*, C-M. Gross (Trans.). Bloomington, IN: Indiana University Press, 1987.

Searles, H. (1965). *The Collected Papers on Schizophrenia*. New York: International Universities Press.

Shakespeare, W. (1996). *Macbeth: A Shorter Shakespeare*. New York: Macmillan.' to 'Shakespeare, W. (1937). *The Tragedy of Mcbeth*, G.B. Harrison (Ed.). Montreal: Penguin Books, 1955.

Shakespeare, W. (1997). *The Merchant of Venice*. New York, Penguin.

Shakespeare, W. (2000). *Measure for measure*. Hemel Hempstead, England: Harvester Wheatsheaf.

Shanker, T. (2008 April 6). *New York Times*.

Siirila, A. (1981).*The Voice of Illness: A Study in Therapy and Prophecy*. (2nd ed.). New York: E. Mellin Press.

Smith, E. (1968). *Brief Against Death*. William F. Buckley (Intro.). New York: Knopf.

Smith, H.I. (2003). *Grieving the Death of a Mother*. Minneapolis, MN: Augsburg Book.

Smolin, L. (2006). *The Trouble with Physics: The Rise of String Theory: The Fall of a Science, and What Comes Next*. Boston: Houghton Mifflin Company.

Spencer, P. (1990). *White Silk and Black Tar: A Journal of the Alaskan oil spill*. Minneapolis, MH: Bergamot Books.

Spender, S. (1965). "The Double Shame". In *Selected Poems*. London: Faber & Faber.

Stroebe, M. (2001). Bereavement research and theory: Retrospective and prospective. *American Behavioral Scientist*, 44, 5: 854–865.

Stroebe, M., Schut H. and Stroebe, W. (2005a). Grief work disclosure and counseling: Do they help the bereaved? *Clinical Psychology Review*, 25: 395–414.

Stroebe, M., Stroebe, W. and Abakoumkin, G. (2005b). The broken heart: Suicidal ideation in bereavement. *The American Journal of Psychiatry* 162: 2,178–2,180.

Sullivan, H.S. (1953). *The Interpersonal Theory of Psychiatry*. New York: W.W. Norton.

Sun Honglei (Dir.) (1999). *The Road Home*. Sony Pictures Classic, Culver City, California.

Szasz, T. (1974). *The Myth of Mental Illness: Foundations of a Theory of Personal Conduct*. New York: Perennial Library.

Szasz, T. (1998). *Cruel Compassion: Psychiatric Control of Society's Unwanted*. Syracuse, NY: Syracuse University Press.

Tagore, R. (1993). *Selected Poems: Rabindrath Tagore*. New York: Penguin Group.

Tennyson, A. (1849a). In Memoriam A.H.H. In: *The Poetic Works of Alfred Lord Tennyson*, Collins Clear-Type Press, London and Glasgow.

Tennyson, A. (1849b). The Princess. In: *The Poetic Works of Alfred Lord Tennyson*, Collins Clear-Type Press, London and Glasgow.

The Liber Usualis. (1959). *Exultet* (pp. 1763–1831). In: The Benedictines of Solesmes (Ed.). New York: Desclee Company.

Thomas, D.M. (1982). *The White Hotel*. New York: Pocket Book.

Thornton, B.B. (Dir.). (1996). *Sling Blade*. Miramax Film Corp.

Tick, E. (2005). *War and Soul*. Wheaton: IL: Quest Books.

Toan Anh. (1976). *Phong-tuc Vietnam: Tu Ban than Den Gia Dinh (Customs of Vietnam: From Personal to Family)*. Glendale, CA: Co So Xuat Ban Dai Nam. (pp. 496–532).

Tran Ding Dung. (2004). *The Document Album of Cu Chi: 1960–1975*. Da Nang: Xi Nghiep in Van Hoa Phuong Nam.

Trozzi, M. and Massimini, K. (1999). *Talking with Children about Loss: Words, Strategies & Wisdom to Help Children Cope with Death, Divorce and Other Difficult Times*. New York: Perigee.

Vacek, E.C. (1989). Toward a phenomenology of lost love. *Journal of Phenomenological Psychology, 20*: 1–19.

Van Gennep, A. (1975). *The Rites of Passage*. M.B. Vizedom and G.L. Caffee (Trans.) and S.T. Kimball (Intro.). Chicago: The University of Chicago Press.

Vutlhari bya Vatsonga (Machangana). (1936). *The Wisdom of the Tsonga-Shangana People*. H.P. Junod and A.A. Jacques (Trans.). Braamfontein, South Africa: Sasavona, 1981.

Waley, A. *The Analects of Confucius*. (1989). New York: Vintage Book.

Winnicott, D.W. (1965a).The capacity to be alone. In: D.W. Winnicott, *The Maturational Processes and the Facilitating Environment* (pp. 29–36). [Reprinted London: Karnac, 2005.]

Winnicott, D.W. (1965b). The development of the capacity for concern. In: D.W. Winnicott, *The Maturational Processes and the Facilitating Environment* (pp. 73–82). [Reprinted London: Karnac, 2005.]

Winnicott, D.W. (1965c). The theory of the parent-infant relationship (pp. 37–55). In: D.W. Winnicott, *The Maturational Processes and the Facilitating Environment*. [Reprinted London: Karnac, 2005.]

Wolfersdorf, M., Keller, F. and Kaschka, W.P. (1997). Suicide of psychiatric inpatients 1970–1993 in Baden-Wurttemberg, Germany, *Archives of Suicide Research*, 3: 303–311.

Woodrow, E. (2006). The experience of the loss of a sibling: A phenomenological study. *Unpublished Ph.D. Dissertation.* Department of Psychology, University of Pretoria, Pretoria, South Africa.

Wyden, P. (2001). *The Hitler Virus: The Insidious Legacy of Adolph Hitler.* New York: Arcade Publishing.

INDEX

349